McGraw-Hill Reading

Wonders

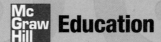

McGraw Hill Education

Bothell, WA • Chicago, IL • Columbus, OH • New York, NY

ETS and the ETS logo are registered trademarks of Educational Testing Service (ETS). TextEvaluator is a trademark of Educational Testing Service.

Cover and Title Pages: **Nathan Love**

www.mheonline.com/readingwonders

C

The McGraw·Hill Companies

Education

Send all inquiries to:
McGraw-Hill Education
Two Penn Plaza
New York, New York 10121

Printed in the United States of America.

8 9 RMN 17 16 15 14

Common Core State Standards© Copyright 2010. National Governors Association Center for Best Practices and Council of Chief State School Officers. All rights reserved.

McGraw-Hill Reading Wonders

CCSS Reading/Language Arts Program

Program Authors

Dr. Diane August
Managing Director,
American Institutes
for Research
Washington, D.C.

Dr. Donald Bear
Iowa State University
Ames, Iowa

Dr. Janice A. Dole
University of Utah
Salt Lake City, Utah

Dr. Jana Echevarria
California State University, Long Beach
Long Beach, California

Dr. Douglas Fisher
San Diego State University
San Diego, California

Dr. David J. Francis
University of Houston
Houston, Texas

Dr. Vicki Gibson
Educational Consultant
Gibson Hasbrouck and Associates
Wellesley, Massachusetts

Dr. Jan Hasbrouck
Educational Consultant
and Researcher
J.H. Consulting
Vancouver, Washington
Gibson Hasbrouck and Associates
Wellesley, Massachusetts

Margaret Kilgo
Educational Consultant
Kilgo Consulting, Inc.
Austin, Texas

Dr. Jay McTighe
Educational Consultant
Jay McTighe and Associates
Columbia, Maryland

Dr. Scott G. Paris
Vice President, Research
Educational Testing Service
Princeton, New Jersey

Dr. Timothy Shanahan
University of Illinois at Chicago
Chicago, Illinois

Dr. Josefina V. Tinajero
University of Texas at El Paso
El Paso, Texas

 **Education**

Bothell, WA • Chicago, IL • Columbus, OH • New York, NY

PROGRAM AUTHORS

Dr. Diane August

American Institutes for Research,
Washington, D.C.

Managing Director focused on literacy
and science for ELLs for the Education,
Human Development and the Workforce
Division

Dr. Donald R. Bear

Iowa State University

Professor, Iowa State University

Author of *Words Their Way, Words Their
Way with English Learners, Vocabulary
Their Way,* and *Words Their Way with
Struggling Readers, 4–12*

Dr. Janice A. Dole

University of Utah

Professor, University of Utah

Director, Utah Center for Reading
and Literacy

Content Facilitator, National Assessment
of Educational Progress (NAEP)

CCSS Consultant to Literacy Coaches,
Salt Lake City School District, Utah

Dr. Jana Echevarria

California State University,
Long Beach

Professor Emerita of Education,
California State University

Author of *Making Content Comprehensible
for English Learners: The SIOP Model*

Dr. Douglas Fisher

San Diego State University

Co-Director, Center for the Advancement
of Reading, California State University

Author of *Language Arts Workshop:
Purposeful Reading and Writing Instruction*
and *Reading for Information in Elementary
School*

Dr. David J. Francis

University of Houston

Director of the Center for Research on
Educational Achievement and Teaching
of English Language Learners (CREATE)

Dr. Vicki Gibson

Educational Consultant
Gibson Hasbrouck and Associates

Author of *Differentiated Instruction:
Grouping for Success, Differentiated
Instruction: Guidelines for Implementation,*
and *Managing Behaviors to Support
Differentiated Instruction*

Dr. Jan Hasbrouck

J.H. Consulting
Gibson Hasbrouck and Associates

Developed Oral Reading Fluency Norms
for Grades 1–8

Author of *The Reading Coach: A How-
to Manual for Success* and *Educators as
Physicians: Using RTI Assessments for
Effective Decision-Making*

Margaret Kilgo

Educational Consultant
Kilgo Consulting, Inc., Austin, TX

Developed Data-Driven Decisions process
for evaluating student performance by
standard

Member of Common Core State Standards
Anchor Standards Committee for Reading
and Writing

Dr. Scott G. Paris

Educational Testing Service, Vice President, Research

Professor, Nanyang Technological University, Singapore, 2008–2011

Professor of Education and Psychology, University of Michigan, 1978–2008

Dr. Timothy Shanahan

University of Illinois at Chicago

Distinguished Professor, Urban Education

Director, UIC Center for Literacy

Chair, Department of Curriculum & Instruction

Member, English Language Arts Work Team and Writer of the Common Core State Standards

President, International Reading Association, 2006

Dr. Josefina V. Tinajero

University of Texas at El Paso

Dean of College of Education

President of TABE

Board of Directors for the American Association of Colleges for Teacher Education (AACTE)

Governing Board of the National Network for Educational Renewal (NNER)

Consulting Authors

Kathy R. Bumgardner

National Literacy Consultant

Strategies Unlimited, Inc. Gastonia, NC

Jay McTighe

Jay McTighe and Associates

Author of *The Understanding by Design Guide to Creating High Quality Units* with G. Wiggins; *Schooling by Design: Mission, Action, Achievement* with G. Wiggins; and *Differentiated Instruction and Understanding By Design* with C. Tomlinson

Dr. Doris Walker-Dalhouse

Marquette University

Associate Professor, Department of Educational Policy & Leadership

Author of articles on multicultural literature, struggling readers, and reading instruction in urban schools

Dinah Zike

Educational Consultant

Dinah-Might Activities, Inc. San Antonio, TX

Program Reviewers

Kelly Aeppli-Campbell
Escambia County School District
Pensacola, FL

Marjorie J. Archer
Broward County Public Schools
Davie, FL

Whitney Augustine
Brevard Public Schools
Melbourne, FL

Antonio C. Campbell
Washington County School District
Saint George, UT

Helen Dunne
Gilbert Public School District
Gilbert, AZ

David P. Frydman
Clark County School District
Las Vegas, NV

Fran Gregory
Metropolitan Nashville Public Schools
Nashville, TN

Veronica Allen Hunt
Clark County School District
Las Vegas, NV

Michele Jacobs
Dee-Mack CUSD #701
Mackinaw, IL

LaVita Johnson Spears
Broward County Public Schools
Pembroke Pines, FL

Randall B. Kincaid
Sevier County Schools
Sevierville, TN

Matt Melamed
Community Consolidated School District 46
Grayslake, IL

Angela L. Reese,
Bay District Schools
Panama City, FL

Eddie Thompson
Fairfield City School District
Fairfield Township, OH

Patricia Vasseur Sosa
Miami-Dade County Public Schools
Miami, FL

Dr. Elizabeth Watson
Hazelwood School District
Hazelwood, MO

TEACHING WITH

McGraw-Hill Reading
Wonders

INTRODUCE

Weekly Concept
Grade Appropriate
Topics, including Science
and Social Studies

- **Videos**
- **Photographs**

Reading/Writing Workshop Big Book

TEACH AND APPLY

**Listening
Comprehension**
Complex Text

**Shared Reading
Minilessons**

Comprehension
Skills and Strategies,
Genre, Phonics,
High-Frequency
Words, Writing,
Grammar

Interactive Read-Aloud Cards

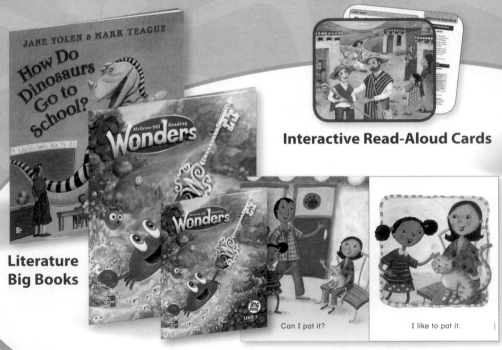

- **Visual Glossary**
- **eBooks**
- **Interactive Texts**
- **Listening Library**
- **English/Spanish
  Summaries**

**Literature
Big Books**

Can I pat it?   I like to pat it.

**Reading/Writing Workshop
Big Book and Little Book**

Master the Common Core State Standards!

- eBooks
- Interactive Texts
- Level Reader Search
- Listening Library
- Interactive Activities

Leveled Readers

DIFFERENTIATE

Leveled Readers
Small Group Instruction
with Differentiated Texts

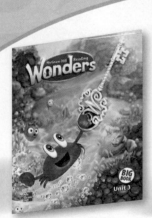

- Online Research
- Interactive Group Projects

Collection of Texts

INTEGRATE

Research and Inquiry
Research Projects

Text Connections
Reading Across Texts

Talk About Reading
Analytical Discussion

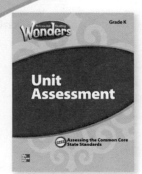

- Online Assessment
- Test Generator
- Reports

**Unit
Assessment**

**Benchmark
Assessment**

ASSESS

Unit Assessment

Benchmark Assessment

PROGRAM COMPONENTS

Big Book and Little Book of Reading/ Writing Workshop

Literature Big Books

Interactive Read-Aloud Cards

Teacher Editions

Teaching Posters

Puppet

Leveled Readers

Your Turn Practice Book

Visual Vocabulary Cards

Leveled Workstation Activity Cards

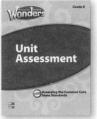

CCSS **Assessing the Common Core State Standards**

Retelling Cards

Photo Cards

High-Frequency Word Cards — the

Sound-Spelling Cards

Response Board

Unit Assessment

Benchmark Assessment

👉 **Go Digital**

For the Teacher

For the Students

Plan
Customizable Lesson Plans

Assess
Online Assessments
Reports and Scoring

Professional Development
Lesson and CCSS Videos

Teach
Classroom Presentation Tools
Instructional Lessons

Collaborate
Online Class Conversations
Interactive Group Projects

Additional Online Resources
ELL Activities
Tier 2 Intervention
Interactive Games and Activities
Word-Building Cards
Sound-Spelling Songs
Sound Pronunciation Audio

Manage and Assign
Student Grouping and Assignments

School to Home
Digital Open House Activities and Messages

My To Do List
Assignments
Assessment

Words to Know
Build Vocabulary

Read
eBooks
Interactive Texts

Play
Interactive Games

Write
Interactive Writing

School to Home
Activities for Home
Messages from the Teacher
Class Wall of Student Work

www.connected.mcgraw-hill.com

UNIT 5 CONTENTS

Unit Planning

Weekly Lessons

Program Information

Nathan Love

UNIT 5 OVERVIEW

Week 1	Week 2
HOW DOES YOUR GARDEN GROW?	**TREES**

READING

Week 1 — HOW DOES YOUR GARDEN GROW?

Oral Language

ESSENTIAL QUESTION
What do living things need to grow?

Build Background

CCSS L.K.5c **Oral Vocabulary Words**
require, plant, crowd, harmful, soak

CCSS L.K.1b Category Words: Size Words

Comprehension
Genre: Fiction

Strategy: Reread

CCSS RL.K.3 **Skill**
Character, Setting, Events

Word Work

CCSS RF.K.2d **Phonemic Awareness**
Phoneme Isolation
Phoneme Blending
Phoneme Categorization

CCSS RF.K.3a **Phonics** /h/h ♪

Handwriting: Hh

CCSS RF.K.3c **High-Frequency Words:** *my*

Fluency
Letter and Word Automaticity
Model Fluency

Week 2 — TREES

Oral Language

ESSENTIAL QUESTION
How do living things change as they grow?

Build Background

CCSS L.K.5c **Oral Vocabulary Words**
amazing, develop, content, enormous, imagine

CCSS L.K.1b Category Words: Tree Parts

Comprehension
Genre: Informational Text

Strategy: Reread

CCSS RI.K.2 **Skill**
Main Topic/Key Details

Word Work

CCSS RF.K.2d **Phonemic Awareness**
Phoneme Isolation
Phoneme Blending
Phoneme Segmentation

CCSS RF.K.3b **Phonics** Short *e* ♪

Handwriting: Ee

CCSS RF.K.3c **High-Frequency Words:** *are*

Fluency
Letter and Word Automaticity
Model Fluency

LANGUAGE ARTS

Week 1

Writing
Trait: Organization
Group Related Ideas

CCSS W.K.8 Shared Writing
Poem

Interactive Writing
Poem

Independent Writing
Poem

CCSS L.1.1d **Grammar**
Pronouns

Week 2

Writing
Trait: Organization
Stick to the Topic

CCSS W.K.1 Shared Writing
Opinion About a Book

Interactive Writing
Opinion About a Book

Independent Writing
Opinion About a Book

CCSS L.1.1d **Grammar**
Pronouns

UNIT 5

FRESH FROM THE FARM

Oral Language
ESSENTIAL QUESTION
What kinds of things grow on a farm?

Build Background

CCSS **Oral Vocabulary Words**
L.K.5c *delicious, fresh, beneath, raise, special*

CCSS Category Words: Food Words
L.K.5a

Comprehension
Genre: Informational Text

Strategy: Reread

CCSS **Skill**
RI.K.2 Main Topic/Key Details

Word Work
CCSS **Phonemic Awareness**
RF.K.2d Phoneme Isolation
Phoneme Blending
Phoneme Addition

CCSS **Phonics** /f/f , /r/r ♪
RF.K.3a **Handwriting:** Ff, Rr

CCSS **High-Frequency Words:**
RF.K.3c *he, with*

Fluency
Letter and Word Automaticity
Model Fluency

> **Unit 5 Assessment**
> **Unit**
> **Assessment Book**
> pages 57–70

Writing
Trait: Organization
Sequence

CCSS Shared Writing
W.K.2 Story Sentences

Interactive Writing
Story Sentences

Independent Writing
Story Sentences

CCSS **Grammar**
L.1.1d Pronouns

Half Day Kindergarten

Use the chart below to help you plan your kindergarten schedule to focus on key instructional objectives for the week. Choose Small Group and Workstation Activities as your time allows during the day.

Oral Language
- **Essential Questions**
- **Build Background**
- **Oral Vocabulary**
- **Category Words**

Word Work
- **Phonemic Awareness**
- **Phonics** /h/h, /e/e, /f/f, /r/r ♪
- **High-Frequency Words:** *my, are, he, with*
- **Letter and Word Automaticity**

Reading/Comprehension
- **Reading/Writing Workshop**
  Hop Can Hop!; Ed and Ned; Ron with Red
- **Big Books:**
  My Garden; A Grand Old Tree; An Orange in January
- **Interactive Read-Aloud Cards**
  "Growing Plants;" "The Pine Tree;" "Farms Around the World"

Language Arts
- **Shared Writing**
- **Interactive Writing**
- **Independent Writing**

Independent Practice
- **Practice Book pages**
- **Workstation Activity Cards**

www.connected.mcgraw-hill.com
Interactive Games and Activities

Reading/Writing Workshop Big Book

READING/WRITING WORKSHOP BIG BOOK, pp. 4–5

The Big Idea *What kinds of things can you find growing in nature?*

Talk About It

Ask children to think of places where they see plants growing. These places may include lawns and landscaping, farms and gardens, and uncultivated, natural areas. They may also include indoor areas—at home, in stores, and in the classroom. Encourage children to notice the wide variety of plants they see, from tiny blades of grass to tall trees. Have children discuss what all the plants have in common, for example what they all need to survive and grow. As children engage in the discussion, encourage them to look at the person speaking and listen to the words they are saying. Help students to respect others by not interrupting them but, as appropriate, to repeat classmates' ideas to check understanding.

♪ Sing the Song

Introduce the unit song: *Before Dinner*. Read the lyrics of the song. Ask children:

→ *Which of the foods that you eat come from plants?*

→ *What do plants need to survive and grow?*

→ *What are some of the ways in which you prepare the fruits, vegetables, and grains that come from plants before you eat them?*

Play the song *Before Dinner*. After listening to the song a few times, ask children to join in. Audio files of the song can be found in the Teacher Resources on www.connected.mcgraw-hill.com.

Research and Inquiry

Weekly Projects Each week children will be asked to find out more about the topic they are reading about. Children will be asked to work in pairs or small groups to complete their work. Children use what they learn from their reading and discussions as well as other sources to find additional information.

Shared Research Board You may wish to set up a Shared Research Board in the classroom. You can post illustrations and other information that children gather as they do their research.

WEEKLY PROJECTS

Students work in pairs or small groups.

Week 1 Plant Poster

Week 2 Tree Life Cycle

Week 3 Fruit Basket

Writing

Write about Reading Throughout the unit children will write in a variety of ways. Each week, writing is focused on a specific writing trait. Scaffolded instruction is provided through Shared Writing and Interactive Writing. Children review a student writing sample together and then write independently, practicing the trait.

WEEKLY WRITING

Week 1 Group Related Ideas

Week 2 Stick to the Topic

Week 3 Sequence

Music Links

www.connected.mcgraw-hill.com Integrate music into your classroom using the downloadable audio files in the Teacher's Resources online. Songs for this unit include:

WEEKLY SONGS

→ My Oak Tree

→ Oats, Peas, Beans, and Barley Grow

→ A Hippo in the House

→ Scrambled Egg, Fried Egg

→ Let's Build a Fire

→ A Rose

HOLIDAY SONGS

→ O Hanukkah; We Wish You a Merry Christmas

→ All Who Born in January; Jolly Old Saint Nicholas

→ The More We Get Together; Turn Me 'Round

→ Bonhomme! Bonhomme!

→ The Year-Naming Race (story)

Celebration Posters

Celebrate Display the Winter Celebrations poster. Use it to remind students of important holidays during the season. Commemorate the holidays by selecting from the activity suggestions provided in the Teacher Resources found at www.connected.mcgraw-hill.com.

Teaching Posters are available for Fall, Winter, Spring, and Summer.

Teaching Posters, pp. 1–4

WEEKLY OVERVIEW

Literature Big Book

Listening Comprehension

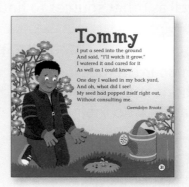

My Garden, 4–29
Genre Fiction

"Poetry," 31–36
Genre Poetry

Interactive Read-Aloud Cards

"Growing Plants"
Genre Informational Text

Oral Vocabulary

crowd	require
harmful	soak
plant	

Minilessons ✓ TESTED SKILLS CCSS

✓ **Comprehension Strategy** .... Reread, T13

✓ **Comprehension Skill** .... Character, Setting, Events, T22

👉 **Go** Digital

www.connected.mcgraw-hill.com

Nathan Love

HOW DOES YOUR GARDEN GROW?

Essential Question
What do living things need to grow?

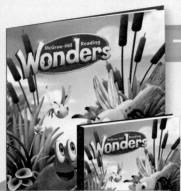

Big Book and Little Book Reading/Writing Workshop

Shared Reading

I am Dot.
I like Hop.

"Hop Can Hop!", 8–15
Genre Fiction

High-Frequency Word my, T17

Minilessons ✔ TESTED SKILLS CCSS

✔ **Phonics** .... /h/h, T15

Writing Traits .... Organization, T18

Grammar .... Pronouns, T19

Differentiated Text

Approaching   **On Level**   **Beyond**   **ELL**

TEACH AND MANAGE

What You Do

INTRODUCE

Weekly Concept

How Does Your
Garden Grow?

**Reading/Writing Workshop
Big Book, 6–7**

**Interactive
Whiteboard**

TEACH AND APPLY

Listening Comprehension

Big Book
My Garden
Genre Fiction
Paired Read Poetry
Genre Poetry

Minilessons
Strategy: Reread
Skill: Character, Setting, Events

**Interactive
Whiteboard**

Shared Reading

Reading/Writing Workshop
"Hop Can Hop!"

Minilessons
/h/ *h*, High-Frequency Word: *my*,
Writing, Grammar

Mobile

Go
Digital

What Your Students Do

WEEKLY CONTRACT

PDF Online

**Online
To-Do List**

Go
Digital

PRACTICE AND ONLINE ACTIVITIES

Your Turn Practice Book, pp. 127–134

**Online
Activities**

Leveled Readers

Mobile

WEEK 1 →

DIFFERENTIATE

Small Group Instruction
Leveled Readers

Mobile

INTEGRATE

Research and Inquiry
Plant Poster, pp. T52–T53

Text Connections
Compare Gardens, p. T54

Talk About Reading
Becoming Readers, p. T55

Online
Research

WORKSTATION CARDS

13

Plant Parts

Plants have roots, stems, and leaves.

SCIENCE

1. Look at a plant closely.   2. Draw the plant.

13

Letter Mapping

Make a word web for the letter *h*.

PHONICS/WORD STUDY

h

hid   hat
had   h   hop

1. Write *h*.   2. Write words.

I can hop!
3. Write a sentence using an h word.

Go Digital! www.connected.mcgraw-hill.com • Interactive Games and Activities • Grade K   13

19

Write a Poem

Some poems can be silly.

WRITING

I am a cat.
I sit on a hat.
How do you like that?

1. Draw a picture of   2. Write a poem.

More
Activities
on back
of cards

3

Character, Setting, Events

Stories tell about people and events.

READING

1. Read a story.   2. Talk about it.

3. Draw something that happens in the story.

Go Digital! www.connected.mcgraw-hill.com • Interactive Games and Activities • Grade K   3

Nathan Love

DEVELOPING READERS AND WRITERS

Write About Reading • Analytical Writing

Write to Sources and Research

Respond to Reading, T13, T61, T69, T75, T79

Connect to Essential Question, T13, T45

Character, Setting, Events, 22

Research and Inquiry, T52

Teacher's Edition

Literature Big Book
My Garden
Paired Read: *"Poetry"*

Interactive Whiteboard

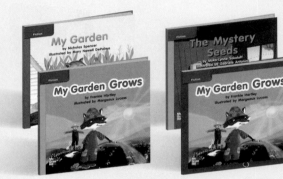

Leveled Readers
Responding to Texts

Writing Process • Independent Writing

Poem
Poetry Writing, T40–T41, T50, T58

Conferencing Routines
Peer Conferences, T50

Interactive Whiteboard

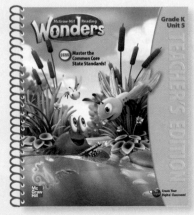

Teacher's Edition

Leveled Workstation Card
Write a Poem, Card 19

Writing Traits • Shared and Interactive Writing

**Writing Trait:
Organization**
Poetry, T18, T32

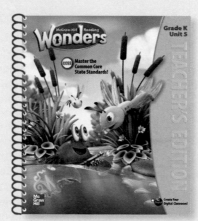

Teacher's Edition

Organization,
p. 18
Pronouns,
p. 19

Reading/Writing Workshop

**Interactive
Whiteboard**

Leveled Workstation Card
Write a Poem, Card 19

Grammar and Spelling/Dictation

Grammar
Pronouns, T19

Spelling/Dictation
Words with Short *a, i, o,* and
h, p, t, T47, T57

**Interactive
Whiteboard**

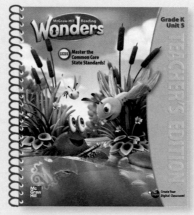

Teacher's Edition

Online Grammar Games

Handwriting

SUGGESTED LESSON PLAN

		DAY 1	DAY 2

 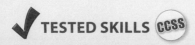
READING

Whole Group

Teach and Model

Literature Big Book

Reading/ Writing Workshop

DAY 1

Build Background How Does Your Garden Grow? T10

Oral Vocabulary Words require, plant, T10

✓ **Listening Comprehension**
• Genre: Fiction
• Strategy: Reread, T13

Big Book My Garden

✓ **Word Work**
Phonemic Awareness:
• Phoneme Isolation, T14

Phonics:
• Introduce /h/h, T15

Handwriting Hh, T16

High-Frequency Word my, T17

Practice Your Turn 127–128

DAY 2

Oral Language How Does Your Garden Grow? T20

✓ **Category Words** Size Words, T21

✓ **Listening Comprehension**
• Genre: Fiction
• Strategy: Reread, T22
• Skill: Character, Setting, Events
• Guided Retelling
• Model Fluency, T27

Big Book My Garden

✓ **Word Work**
Phonemic Awareness:
• Phoneme Blending, T28

Phonics:
• Blend Words with h, T29

High-Frequency Word my, T29

Shared Reading "Hop Can Hop!" T30–T31

Practice Your Turn 129

DIFFERENTIATED INSTRUCTION Choose across the week to meet your student's needs.

Small Group

Approaching Level

DAY 1

Leveled Reader My Garden, T60–T61

Phonological Awareness Count and Blend Syllables, T62 TIER 2

Phonics Sound-Spelling Review, T64 TIER 2

High-Frequency Words Reteach Words, T66 TIER 2

DAY 2

Leveled Reader My Garden, T60–T61

Phonemic Awareness Phoneme Isolation, T62 TIER 2

Phonics Connect h to /h/, T64 TIER 2

High-Frequency Words Cumulative Review, T66

On Level

DAY 1

Leveled Reader My Garden Grows, T68–T69

Phonemic Awareness Phoneme Isolation, T70

DAY 2

Leveled Reader My Garden Grows, T68–T69

Phoneme Awareness Phoneme Blending, T70

Phonics Review Phonics, T71

Picture Sort with h and p, T71

High-Frequency Words Review Words, T73

Beyond Level

DAY 1

Leveled Reader The Mystery Seeds, T74–T75

Phonics Review, T76

DAY 2

Leveled Reader The Mystery Seeds, T74–T75

High-Frequency Words Review, T76

English Language Learners

DAY 1

Leveled Reader My Garden Grows, T78–T79

Phonological Awareness Count and Blend Syllables, T62 TIER 2

Phonics Sound-Spelling Review, T64 TIER 2

Vocabulary Preteach Oral Vocabulary, T80

Writing Shared Writing, T82

DAY 2

Leveled Reader My Garden Grows, T78–T79

Phonemic Awareness Phoneme Isolation, T62 TIER 2

Phonics Connect h to /h/, T64 TIER 2

High-Frequency Words Cumulative Review, T66

Vocabulary Preteach ELL Vocabulary, T80

LANGUAGE ARTS

Whole Group

Writing and Grammar

DAY 1

Shared Writing
Writing Trait: Organization, T18

Write a Poem, T18

Grammar Pronouns, T19

DAY 2

Interactive Writing
Writing Trait: Organization, T32

Write a Poem, T32

Grammar Pronouns, T33

Nathan Love

DAY 3	DAY 4	DAY 5 Review and Assess

READING

Oral Language How Does Your Garden Grow? T34	**Oral Language** How Does Your Garden Grow? T42	**Integrate Ideas**
Oral Vocabulary harmful, soak, crowd, T34	✔ **Category Words** Size Words, T43	• Text Connections, T54
✔ **Listening Comprehension**	✔ **Listening Comprehension**	• Talk About Reading, T55
• Genre: Informational Text	• Genre: Poetry	• Research and Inquiry, T55
• Strategy: Reread, T35	• Strategy: Reread, T44	✔ **Word Work**
• Make Connections, T35	• Literary Element: Rhyme and Repetition, T44	**Phonemic Awareness**
Interactive Read Aloud "Growing Plants," T35	• Make Connections, T45	• Phoneme Categorization, T56
✔ **Word Work**	**Big Book** Paired Read: Poetry, T44	**Phonics**
Phonemic Awareness	✔ **Word Work**	• Read Words with Short *i, o, a* and *h*, T56
• Phoneme Blending, T36	**Phonemic Awareness**	**High-Frequency Word** my, T57
Phonics	• Phoneme Categorization, T46	
• Blend Words with Short *i, o, a* and *h, t, p, m, d*, T37	**Phonics**	
• Picture Sort, T38	• Short *a, i, o* and *h, t, p*, T46	
High-Frequency Word my, T39	**High-Frequency Word** my, T47	
	Shared Reading "Hop Can Hop!" T48–T49	
	Integrate Ideas Research and Inquiry, T52–T53	
Practice *Your Turn* 130–132	**Practice** *Your Turn* 133	**Practice** *Your Turn* 134

DIFFERENTIATED INSTRUCTION

Leveled Reader *My Garden*, T60–T61	**Leveled Reader** *My Garden*, T60–T61	**Leveled Reader** Literacy Activities, T61
Phonemic Awareness Phoneme Blending, T63	**Phonemic Awareness** Phoneme Categorization, T63	**Phonemic Awareness** Phoneme Categorization, T63
Phonics Reteach, T64	**Phonics** Blend Words with /h/h, T65	**Phonics** Reread for Fluency, T65
High-Frequency Words Reteach Words, T66	**Oral Vocabulary** Review Words, T67	Build Fluency with Phonics, T65
		Comprehension Self-Selected Reading, T67

Leveled Reader *My Garden Grows*, T68–T69	**Leveled Reader** *My Garden Grows*, T68–T69	**Leveled Reader** Literacy Activities, T69
Phonemic Awareness Phoneme Categorization, T70	**Phonics** Blend Words with /h/h, T72	**Comprehension** Self-Selected Reading, T73
Phonics Blend Words with /h/h, T72	Reread for Fluency, T72	

Leveled Reader *The Mystery Seeds*, T74–T75	**Leveled Reader** *The Mystery Seeds*, T74-T75	**Leveled Reader** Literacy Activities, T75
Vocabulary Oral Vocabulary: Synonyms, T77	**Phonics** Innovate, T76	**Comprehension** Self-Selected Reading, T77
		⭐ Gifted and Talented

Leveled Reader *My Garden Grows*, T78-–T79	**Leveled Reader** *My Garden Grows*, T78–T79	**Leveled Reader** Literacy Activities, T79
Phonemic Awareness Phoneme Blending, T63	**Phonemic Awareness** Phoneme Categorization, T63	**Phonemic Awareness** Phoneme Categorization, T63
Phonics Reteach, T64	**Phonics** Blend Words with /h/h, T65	**Phonics** Reread for Fluency, T65
High-Frequency Words Review Words, T81	**Vocabulary** Review Category Words, T81	Build Fluency with Phonics, T65
Writing Writing Trait: Organization, T82	**Grammar** Pronouns, T83	

LANGUAGE ARTS

Independent Writing	**Independent Writing**	**Independent Writing**
Writing Trait: Organization, T40	Writing Trait: Organization, T50	Write a Poem
Write a Poem	Write a Poem	Prepare/Present/Evaluate/Publish, T58
Prewrite/Draft, T41	Revise/Final Draft, T50	**Grammar** Pronouns, T59
Grammar Pronouns, T41	**Grammar** Pronouns, T51	

DIFFERENTIATE TO ACCELERATE

 A C T Scaffold to **A**ccess **C**omplex **T**ext

Qualitative / Quantitative
Reader and Task
TEXT COMPLEXITY

IF ➤ the text complexity of a particular **section** is too difficult for children

THEN ➤ see the references noted in the **chart** below for scaffolded instruction to help children Access Complex Text.

	Literature Big Book	**Reading/Writing Workshop**	**Leveled Readers**	

Quantitative	*My Garden* **Lexile** 670 Paired Selection: Poetry **Lexile** NP	"Hop Can Hop!" **Lexile** 110	**Approaching Level** **Lexile** BR **Beyond Level** **Lexile** 240	**On Level** **Lexile** 100 **ELL** **Lexile** BR
Qualitative	What Makes the Text Complex? • **Purpose** Sentence Clues, T22 **A C T** *See Scaffolded Instruction in Teacher's Edition, T22.*	What Makes the Text Complex? **Foundational Skills** • Decoding with *h*, T28–T29 • Identifying high-frequency words, T29	What Makes the Text Complex? **Foundational Skills** • Decoding with *h* • Identifying high-frequency words *my* *See Level Up lessons online for Leveled Readers.*	
Reader and Task	The Introduce the Concept lesson on pages T10–T11 will help determine the reader's knowledge and engagement in the weekly concept. See pages T12–T13, T23–T27, T44–T45 and T52–T55 for questions and tasks for this text.	The Introduce the Concept lesson on pages T10–T11 will help determine the reader's knowledge and engagement in the weekly concept. See pages T30–T31, T48–T49 and T52–T55 for questions and tasks for this text.	The Introduce the Concept lesson on pages T10–T11 will help determine the reader's knowledge and engagement in the weekly concept. See pages T60–T61, T68–T69, T74–T75, T78–T79 and T52–T55 for questions and tasks for this text.	

Nathan Love

BR = Epitome of a beginning reader   NP = Non-Prose   *Go Digital!* www.connected.mcgraw-hill.com

Monitor and *Differentiate*

IF you need to differentiate instruction

THEN use the Quick Checks to assess children's needs and select the appropriate small group instruction focus.

 Quick Check

Comprehension Strategy Reread, T35

Phonemic Awareness/Phonics /h/*h*, T17, T29, T39, T47, T57

High-Frequency Words *my*, T17, T29, T39, T47, T57

If No → | **Approaching** | **Reteach,** pp. T60–T67 |
| **ELL** | **Develop,** pp. T78–T83 |

If Yes → | **On Level** | **Review,** pp. T68–T73 |
| **Beyond Level** | **Extend,** pp. T74–T77 |

Level Up with Leveled Readers

IF children can read their leveled text fluently and answer comprehension questions

THEN work with the next level up to accelerate children's reading with more complex text.

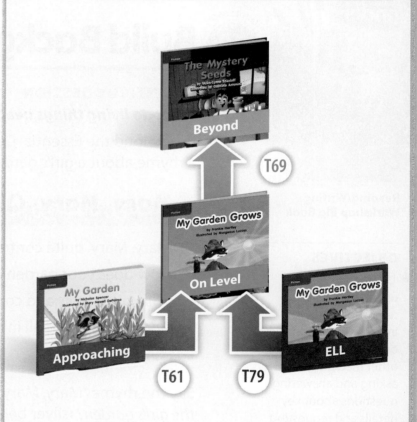

The Mystery Seeds — **Beyond** — T69

My Garden Grows by Frankie Hartley, Illustrated by Margaret Lucass — **On Level**

My Garden by Nicholas Spencer — **Approaching** — T61

My Garden Grows by Frankie Hartley, Illustrated by Margaret Lucass — **ELL** — T79

ENGLISH LANGUAGE LEARNERS SCAFFOLD

IF ELL students need additional support **THEN** scaffold instruction using the small group suggestions.

| Reading-Writing Workshop T11 "Watch It Grow!" Integrate Ideas T53 | Leveled Reader T78–T79 *My Garden Grows* | Phonological Awareness Count and Blend Syllables, T62 Phoneme Isolation, T62 Phoneme Blending, T63 Phoneme Categorization, T63 | Phonics, /h/*h*, T64–T65 | Oral Vocabulary, T80 require, plant, soak, crowd, harmful High-Frequency Word, T81 *my* | Writing Shared Writing, T82 Writing Trait: Organization, T82 | Grammar T83 Pronouns |

Note: Include ELL Students in all small groups based on their needs.

Reading/Writing Workshop Big Book
UNIT 5

Literature Big Book
My Garden

Visual Vocabulary Cards
require
plant

Response Board

Photo Cards
boy   hat
bridge   hippo
comb   hook
doctor   horse
girl   nurse
hair
hammer

Sound-Spelling Cards
hippo

my
High-Frequency Word Cards
my

Think Aloud Cloud

♪ "A Hippo in the House"

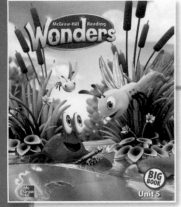

Reading/Writing Workshop Big Book

 OBJECTIVES

CCSS Confirm understanding of a text read aloud or information presented orally or through other media by asking and answering questions about key details and requesting clarification if something is not understood. **SL.K.2**

CCSS Identify real-life connections between words and their use. **L.K.5c**

(→) # Introduce the Concept

MINILESSON
 10 Mins

Build Background

ESSENTIAL QUESTION
What do living things need to grow?

Read aloud the Essential Question. Tell children you are going to read a rhyme about a girl's garden.

Mary, Mary, Quite Contrary

Mary, Mary, quite contrary,

How does your garden grow?

With silver bells and cockle-shells,

And pretty maids all in a row.

Say the rhyme "Mary, Mary, Quite Contrary" with children. *What is in the girl's garden?* (silver bells and cockle-shells) Tell children that those are make-believe plants, but this week they will read to find out what real plants need to grow.

Oral Vocabulary Words

Use the **Define/Example/Ask** routine to introduce the oral vocabulary words **require** and **plant**.

To introduce the theme of "How Does Your Garden Grow?" explain that plants are living things. Plants require things so they can grow. *What is one thing a plant requires before it can grow?* (Possible answers: water, sunlight)

Go Digital

"How Does Your Garden Grow?"

Video

Visual Glossary

Oral Vocabulary Routine

<u>Define:</u> If you **require** something, you need it.

<u>Example:</u> Plants require water to grow.

<u>Ask:</u> What do you require to grow?

<u>Define:</u> A **plant** has roots, stems, and leaves and grows in the ground.

<u>Example:</u> A seed can grow into a plant.

<u>Ask:</u> What is a plant that you can eat?

Visual Vocabulary Cards

Talk About It: How Does Your Garden Grow?

Guide children to name ways to help plants grow. Make a list of their responses. *What kind of plant would you like to grow?* Display pages 6–7 of the **Reading/Writing Workshop Big Book** and have children do the Talk About It activity with a partner.

READING/WRITING WORKSHOP BIG BOOK, pp. 6–7

Collaborative Conversations

Take Turns Talking As children engage in partner, small group, and whole group discussions, encourage them to:

→ Take turns talking.

→ Listen carefully to the speaker.

→ Ask others to share their ideas and opinions.

ENGLISH LANGUAGE LEARNERS SCAFFOLD

Beginning

Use Visuals Explain that the boy and grandmother in the picture are working in a garden together. Point to some plants. Ask: *Are these plants?* Point to the watering can. Ask: *Are the boy and his grandmother giving the plant water?* Allow children ample time to respond.

Intermediate

Describe Ask children to describe what is happening in the picture. Ask them to tell where the boy and his grandmother are. *What are they doing to help the plants grow?* Correct grammar and pronunciation as needed.

Advanced/Advanced High

Discuss Have children elaborate on how the boy and his grandmother are working in the garden. Elicit more details to support children's answers.

→ # Listening Comprehension

Literature Big Book

OBJECTIVES

CCSS With prompting and support, name the author and illustrator of a story and define the role of each in telling the story. **RL.K.6**

CCSS Actively engage in group reading activities with purpose and understanding. **RL.K.10**

- Recognize characteristics of fiction
- Strategy: Reread

ACADEMIC LANGUAGE
capital, period

 MINILESSON **10 Mins**

Read the Literature Big Book

Connect to Concept: How Does Your Garden Grow?

Tell children that you will now read how a make-believe garden grows. *What things have you seen growing in gardens in your neighborhood?*

Concepts of Print

Title Page, Pronoun *I*, and Space Between Words Display the title page of the **Big Book**. *This is the title page. It tells the title of the story and the name of the author.* Identify the title and author. Next, turn to page 14. Point to the word *I* as you explain that this word is always a capital letter. Then point out the spaces between the words on the page. Explain that these spaces make the words easier to read.

Genre: Fiction

Model *My Garden* is a fiction story. Remind children of these characteristics of fiction:

→ The events are made up by the author.

→ Fiction stories often have illustrations that show what is happening.

> **Story Words** Preview these words before reading:
>
> **invisible:** cannot be seen
> **lantern:** a source of light
> **rusty:** covered with a reddish-brown coating

Set a Purpose for Reading

→ Read aloud the title and the name of the author/illustrator. Point out that the same person wrote the words and created the pictures for the story.

→ Ask children to listen as you read aloud the Big Book. They will find out what the girl wants to grow in her garden.

Go Digital

My Garden

Think Aloud Cloud

Strategy: Reread

Model Tell children that, as they read, something might not make sense to them. Then they can reread to help them understand. Explain that the prefix *re-* means *again*. *What do you think* reread *means?*

Think Aloud Read aloud pages 5–6 before sharing this Think Aloud: I just read that the girl's flowers would never die. Flowers do die, so I don't understand. I'll read these pages again so I can figure out what is happening. When I read page 5 again, I see that the girl is talking about a garden that she would like to grow. She must be playing make-believe. She must be talking about what would happen in her make-believe garden.

Apply As you read, use the **Think Aloud Cloud** to model the strategy.

Think Aloud On page 16, when I read that the girl wants to grow a jelly bean bush, I had to reread to understand. When I reread this page and look at the illustration, I understand that the jelly beans would grow like flowers on a bush.

Respond to Reading

After reading, prompt children to describe the things the girl wants to grow in her garden. Discuss the ways that rereading helped children understand the story. Then have children draw a picture of a silly thing that they would like to grow in a garden.

Make Connections

Use pages 4–5 of *My Garden* to discuss some of the things that plants need to grow. (water, no weeds, no rabbits) Revisit the concept behind the Essential Question *What do living things need to grow?* by discussing other things that help plants grow, such as sunshine, warm weather, and soil.

Write About It Have children write about one of the ways the narrator's garden would be different from a real garden. Have them discuss with a partner why this could not happen in a real garden.

ENGLISH LANGUAGE LEARNERS SCAFFOLD

Beginning

Demonstrate Point to pages 4–5. Ask: *Does the girl help to water the plants?* (Yes) *Does she help pull out weeds?* (Yes) *Did I read again to figure out what the girl does?* (Yes) Restate the children's responses in order to develop their oral language. For example: *Yes, the girl waters the plants.*

Intermediate

Discuss Read aloud pages 4–5. Then say: *I don't understand how the girl helps. What can I do?* (Read again to help you understand.) Reread and ask: *How does the girl help?* (She waters. She weeds.) If students give a one-word answer or a nonverbal cue, elaborate on the answer to model fluent speaking and grammatical patterns.

Advanced/Advanced High

Discuss Read aloud page 5. Ask: *How do you know what the girl will talk about next? Listen as I reread the page.* Then ask: *What will the girl talk about next?* (what her garden would be like, if she had one of her own) Clarify children's responses as needed by providing vocabulary. Point out that rereading helps us better understand a story.

(→) # Word Work

Quick Review

Review /d/, /o/: Ask children to tell the initial sounds of the *doctor* and *octopus* Photo Cards.
Build Fluency: Sound-Spellings: Display the following **Word-Building Cards:** *a, c, d, i, m, n, o, p, s, t.* Have children chorally say each sound. Repeat and vary pace.

MINILESSON 5 Mins

Phonemic Awareness

Phoneme Isolation

Photo Card

① **Model** Display the **Photo Card** for *hippo.* *Today we are going to learn a new sound. Listen for the sound at the beginning of* hippo. Hippo *has the /h/ sound at the beginning. Say the sound with me: /h/.* Say *had, hot, heat* and have children repeat. Emphasize /h/.

♪ *Let's play a song. Listen for the words with /h/ at the beginning.* Play "A Hippo in the House," and have children listen for the /h/ sound. *Let's listen to the song again and clap when we hear words that begin with /h/.* Play and/or sing the letter song again, encouraging children to join in. Have children clap when they hear a word that begins with /h/.

② **Guided Practice/Practice** Display and name each Photo Card: *hair, hat, hook. Say each picture name with me. Tell me the sound at the beginning of the word.* Guide practice with the first word.

Photo Cards

OBJECTIVES

CCSS Isolate and pronounce the initial, medial vowel, and final sounds (phonemes) in three-phoneme words. **RF.K.2d**

CCSS Demonstrate basic knowledge of one-to-one letter-sound correspondences by producing the primary or many of the most frequent sounds for each consonant. **RF.K.3a**

ELL

ENGLISH LANGUAGE LEARNERS

Pronunciation
Display and have children name Photo Cards from this lesson to reinforce phonemic awareness and word meanings. Point to the *hand* Photo Card and ask: *What do you see? What is the sound at the beginning of the word* hand? Repeat using *hammer, hair,* and *horse* Photo Cards.

ARTICULATION SUPPORT

Demonstrate the way to say /h/ by opening your mouth. Keep your tongue on the bottom of your mouth. Breathe out a puff of air. Hold your hand in front of your mouth. Can you feel the air? Say *hop, hat, him* and have children repeat.

Go Digital

Phonemic Awareness

Phonics

MINILESSON
10 Mins

Phonics

Hh

hippo

Sound-Spelling Card

Introduce /h/h

1 **Model** Display the *Hippo* **Sound-Spelling Card**. *This is the Hippo card. The sound is /h/. The /h/ sound is spelled with the letter* h. *Say it with me: /h/. This is the sound at the beginning of the word* hippo. *Listen: /h/ /h/ /h/,* hippo. *What is the name of this letter?* (h) *What sound does this letter stand for?* (/h/)

♪ Display the song "A Hippo in the House" (see **Teacher's Resource Book** online). Read or sing the song with children. Reread the title and point out that the word *hippo* begins with the letter *h*. Model placing a self-stick note below the *h* in *hippo*.

2 **Guided Practice/Practice** Read each line of the song. Stop after each line and ask children to place self-stick notes below words that begin with *H* or *h* and say the letter name.

A Hippo in the House

There's a hippo in the house.

There's a hippo in the house.

Not a kitten or a whale, not a hamster or a snail,

but a hippo in the house.

There's a hippo in the house.

There's a hippo in the house.

Not a penguin or a puppy,

not a hedgehog or a guppy,

but a hippo in the house.

Corrective Feedback

Sound Error Say /h/ and have children repeat the sound. *My turn. Hippo, /h/ /h/ /h/. Now it's your turn.* Have children say the words *horse* and *his* and isolate the initial sound.

ENGLISH LANGUAGE LEARNERS

Phoneme Variation in Language
Some children, particularly those whose first language is Spanish, may need extra practice identifying the /h/ sound, as the *h* in Spanish is silent. Emphasize the /h/ sound and demonstrate correct mouth position.

YOUR TURN PRACTICE BOOK pp. 127–128

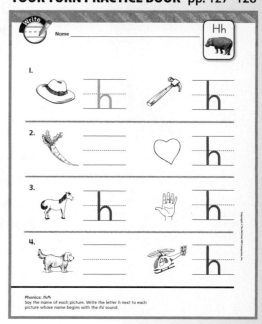

→ # Word Work

OBJECTIVES

CCSS Write a letter or letters for most consonant and short-vowel sounds. **L.K.2c**

CCSS Read common high-frequency words by sight. **RF.K.3c**

ACADEMIC LANGUAGE
uppercase, lowercase

MINILESSON **5 Mins**

Handwriting: Write *Hh*

1 Model Say the handwriting cues below as you write and then identify the **uppercase** and **lowercase** forms of *Hh*. Then trace the letters on the board and in the air as you say /h/.

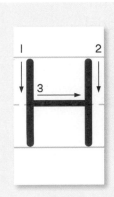
Straight down. Go back to the top. Straight down. Straight across the dotted line.

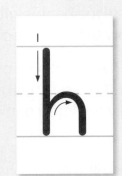
Straight down. Go to the dotted line. Around and down.

2 Guided Practice/Practice

→ Say the cues together as children trace both forms of the letter with their index finger. Have them identify the uppercase and lowercase forms of the letter.

→ Have children write *H* and *h* in the air as they say /h/ multiple times.

→ Distribute **Response Boards** or paper. Observe children's pencil grip and paper position, and correct as necessary. Have children **say** /h/ every time they write the letter *Hh*.

 Daily Handwriting

Throughout the week teach uppercase and lowercase letters *Hh* using the Handwriting models. At the end of the week, have children use the **Your Turn Practice Book** p. 134 to practice handwriting.

Go Digital

Handwriting

High-Frequency Word Routine

High-Frequency Words

5 Mins

my

my

High-Frequency Word Card

❶ **Model** Display the **Big Book** *My Garden.*
Read the title. Point to the high-frequency
word *my*. Use the **Read/Spell/Write** routine
to teach the word.

→ **Read** Point to the word *my* and say the word. *This is the word*
my. Say it with me: my. *My mother has a garden.*

→ **Spell** *The word* my *is spelled m-y. Spell it with me.*

→ **Write** *Let's write the word in the air as we say each letter: m-y.*

→ Point out to children that the letter *m* has the same /m/ sound
as in the word *mad.*

COLLABORATE

→ Have partners create sentences using the word.

❷ **Guided Practice/Practice** Build sentences using the **High-
Frequency Word Cards**, **Photo Cards**, and teacher-made
punctuation cards. Have children point to the high-frequency
word *my*. Use these sentences.

Also online

| I | see | my | | . |

| I | like | my | | . |

High-Frequency Words Practice

Monitor and *Differentiate*

✓ **Quick Check**

Can children isolate /h/ and
match it to the letter *Hh*?

Can children recognize and read
the high-frequency word?

⬇

Small Group Instruction

If No →	Approaching	Reteach pp. T62-67
	ELL	Develop pp. T80-83
If Yes →	On Level	Review pp. T70-73
	Beyond Level	Extend pp. T76-77

→ Language Arts

MINILESSON 10 Mins — Shared Writing

OBJECTIVES

CCSS With guidance and support from adults, recall information from experiences or gather information from provided sources to answer a question. **W.K.8**

CCSS Use personal, possessive, and indefinite pronouns (e.g., *I, me, my; they, them, their; anyone, everything*). **L.1.1d**

- Write poems
- Recognize pronouns

ACADEMIC LANGUAGE

- *organize, pronoun, poem*
- Cognates: *organizar, poema*

Writing Trait: Organization

❶ Model Tell children that writers organize their ideas when they write. Writers put their ideas in an order that makes sense.

→ Write and read aloud: *rose, tulip, blackbird.* Rose *and* tulip *are both flowers; they go together.* Blackbird *names a bird; it is not a flower. It doesn't go with the other two.*

❷ Guided Practice/Practice Write and read aloud: *oranges, apples, lemons, monkeys.* Have children point out which words should be grouped together and which one doesn't belong. *When we organize our ideas, we put things together that belong together.*

Write a Poem

Focus and Plan Tell children that this week they will learn how to write a poem about flowers and trees.

 Brainstorm Have children name some of their favorite flowers and trees. Write their ideas on two separate lists.

Flowers
rose
daisy
tulip

Trees
maple
palm
pine

Write Model writing a poem using a rose as the subject. *I can take one of the things from the list and write a poem about it.*

The Rose
It is red.
She smells the rose.
It smells sweet!

Model writing other poems. Use the other examples on the list. Draw a picture for each poem. Read aloud the poems with children.

Writing

I see a fish.

Grammar

MINILESSON 5 Mins

Grammar

Pronouns

① Model Explain that a pronoun is also a naming word. It takes the place of a noun in a sentence. Nouns used to name people, such as *girl, boy, man,* or *woman,* can be replaced with the pronoun *she* or *he.* A thing can be replaced with the pronoun *it.* Show **Photo Cards** for *girl, boy,* and *bridge.* Read the words aloud.

→ Write and read: *The girl jumps.* Explain that *girl* is a noun that names a person. In a sentence, you can sometimes replace *girl* with the pronoun *she.* Erase *The girl* and write *She* in its place.

→ Write and read: *The boy smiles.* Explain that *boy* is also a noun that names a person. It can sometimes be replaced with the pronoun *he.* Erase *The boy* and write *He* in its place.

→ Write and read: *The bridge is red.* Explain that bridge is a noun that names a thing. It can sometimes be replaced with the pronoun *it.* Erase *The bridge* and write *It* in its place. Chorally read aloud all the sentences.

② Guided Practice/Practice Write and read aloud: *The girl is pretty. Which words can I replace with a pronoun?* (The girl) *What pronoun can I use?* (She) Rewrite the sentence and choral-read it with children: *She is pretty.*

Model how to use the pronouns *he* and *it* in other sentences. For example: *Dan is playing ball. He is playing ball. The bridge is long. It is long.*

Talk About It

COLLABORATE Have partners practice making up sentences, using a pronoun. Encourage children to say two sentences. The first sentence should tell the noun, and the second sentence should use a pronoun to replace the noun.

ELL

ENGLISH LANGUAGE LEARNERS SCAFFOLD

Beginning

Explain Tell children that the pronoun *she* names a woman, the pronoun *he* names a man, and the pronoun *it* names a thing. Display Photo Cards for *doctor, nurse,* and *comb.* Have children tell which pronoun they would use for each. (doctor/she; nurse/he; comb/it) Allow ample time to respond.

Intermediate

Practice Ask children to draw the people in their families. Help children label each drawing with the pronoun, *she* or *he,* that names each person. Correct the meaning of children's responses as needed.

Advanced/Advanced High

Practice Have children choose one friend to write a sentence about. Ask children to tell something their friend likes. For example: *Miguel likes baseball. Jessica likes soccer.* Help children rewrite the sentence, using a pronoun in place of the friend's name. Clarify children's responses as needed by providing vocabulary.

Daily Wrap Up

- Review the Essential Question and encourage children to discuss it, using the new oral vocabulary words. *What did we learn about what living things need to grow?*

- Prompt children to share the skills they learned. How might they use those skills?

Materials

Reading/Writing Workshop Big Book
UNIT 5

Literature Big Book
My Garden

Visual Vocabulary Cards
require
plant

Response Board

Word-Building Cards

Hh
hippo

Sound-Spelling Cards
Hippo

my

High-Frequency Word Cards
my

Retelling Cards

Puppet

→ # Build the Concept

MINILESSON
(10 Mins)

Oral Language

OBJECTIVES

CCSS Use words and phrases acquired through conversations, reading and being read to, and responding to texts. **L.K.6**

CCSS Sort common objects into categories (e.g., shapes, foods) to gain a sense of the concepts the categories represent. **L.K.5a**

CCSS Count, pronounce, blend, and segment syllables in spoken words. **RF.K.2b**

Develop oral vocabulary

ACADEMIC LANGUAGE

• rhyme, sentence, plurals
• Cognates: *rima, plurales*

ESSENTIAL QUESTION

What do living things need to grow?

Remind children that this week they are learning about the things plants need to grow. Point out that plants need certain things to live. Have children share some of those things. (Possible answers: water, sunshine, warm weather, soil, no weeds) Ask children to tell about times when they have helped to take care of a plant.

Recite the rhyme "Mary, Mary, Quite Contrary" with children.

Phonological Awareness

Count and Blend Syllables

We can count the parts of a word. Listen: /gär/ /den/. The word garden *has two parts.* Clap each syllable as you again say: /gär/ /den/. Have children repeat the routine with you. Then say: *We can put the parts of the word together. Listen: /gär/ /den/, /gärden/.* Have children repeat. Repeat routine for *silver.*

Review Oral Vocabulary

Use the **Define/Example/Ask** routine to review the oral vocabulary words **require** and **plant**. Prompt children to use the words in sentences.

Visual Vocabulary Cards

Go Digital

Visual Glossary

Category Words

Category Words: Size Words

❶ Model Use *My Garden* to teach words: *big, small, short,* and *tall.* Explain that size words describe how big, small, short, or tall something or someone is. Display pages 22 and 23 of *My Garden* and reread the text. *The word* big *is a size word. How big is the girl's tomato?* (as big as a beach ball) Point out other illustrations to discuss size words. For example: *On page 4, compare the girl with her mother. Who is short?* (the girl) *Who is tall?* (her mother)

❷ Guided Practice/Practice Identify different objects in the classroom and have children point to them. Use a different-size word in each description. For example: *See the* big *desk. See the* small *block.*

→ Have children work with a partner to use size words in sentences about classroom objects. (Possible answers: I am sitting next to a big table. The small block is blue.)

Vocabulary Strategy: Word Parts/ Plurals -s

❶ Model Explain that words can be broken into parts, including endings. The *-s* ending makes a singular noun into a plural noun. Review that plural nouns end in *-s* and mean more than one. Use *My Garden* to model how to identify plural nouns ending with *-s.*

Think Aloud In *My Garden,* the word *rabbits* is a plural noun that ends with *-s.* The word *rabbit* means "one rabbit." When you add the *-s* ending to the word *rabbit,* you get the plural noun *rabbits,* which means "more than one rabbit."

❷ Guided Practice Point out and discuss other plural nouns in the story that end with *-s.* Discuss what the singular form of each noun is and how it was made plural by adding *-s.*

*There would be no **weeds**, and the **flowers** would keep blooming.*

❸ Practice Use the word plants to discuss and practice plurals. Have children identify the singular form of the word (*plant*) and then practice adding the word part *-s* to form a plural noun. Continue with *seashell/seashells, button/buttons, bean/beans, key/keys.*

LET'S MOVE!

Have children follow simple directions that include size words. Have children pretend they are the object and its size. For example: *Be a big tree! Be a small mouse. Be a tall building. Be a short penguin.*

→ # Listening Comprehension

CLOSE READING

Literature Big Book

OBJECTIVES

CCSS With prompting and support, identify characters, settings, and major events in a story. **RL.K.3**

CCSS With prompting and support, describe the relationship between illustrations and the story in which they appear (e.g. what moment in a story an illustration depicts). **RL.K.7**

• Strategy: Reread
• Skill: Character, Setting, Events

ACADEMIC LANGUAGE

• *fiction*
• Cognates: *ficción*

MINILESSON 15 Mins

Reread Literature Big Book

Genre: Fiction

Display *My Garden*. Guide children in recalling that fiction stories are made-up. The events in fiction stories did not happen in real life. *How do you know that* My Garden *is fiction?* Have children point to evidence in the text and the pictures to show that this story is fiction. (Possible answer: The girl is imagining growing shells and jelly beans and the pictures are illustrations.)

Strategy: Reread

Guide children in recalling that good readers sometimes reread to help them understand the events in a story. *As you read, you can go back to reread and find details that will help you understand what is happening.*

Skill: Character, Setting, Events

Remind children that characters are the people or animals a story is about. The setting is the time and place of the story. Events are the things that happen in the story. *Thinking about characters, setting, and events can help you understand and enjoy a story.* As you read, have children listen for evidence in the text that tells about the characters, setting, and events.

Access Complex Text

Purpose Guide children to understand that the book is mostly about a make-believe garden, so they won't find facts about gardening. This could confuse young readers, as they might initially think they are reading for facts about gardens—as they would in an informational text.

→ Read aloud page 5. Explain that this real garden needs water and weeding. Point out the final phrase: *but if I had a garden . . .* Tell children this phrase helps them understand the girl is thinking of a different kind of garden.

→ Read aloud pages 8 and 10. Explain that these pages show that this story is about a make-believe garden, so children don't need to try to find facts.

Go Digital

My Garden

Retelling Cards

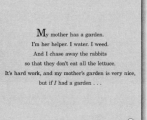

PAGES 4–5

SETTING

Think Aloud I know that *setting* means the place where story events happen. I see many flowers. And I read that the girl's mother has a garden. So I can figure out that the setting is a garden.

pp. 4–5

weed: Weeds are plants we do not want to grow. People weed when they pull out weeds from the ground. Invite children to pantomime pulling weeds with you as they say: *I weed.*

PAGES 6–7

CHARACTER

Who is the character in this story? (the girl) Have a volunteer point to the girl in the illustration.

PAGES 8–9

REREAD

Think Aloud I read that the flowers in the garden change color. I am confused. *Real* flowers don't change colors. I will go back and reread page 5. I understand now. This is a make-believe garden that the girl wants to grow. She's pretending.

pp. 8–9

pattern: Help explain the meaning of *pattern* by contrasting a solid color in children's clothing with clothing that is flowered, checked, striped, dotted, or another pattern. Point out the dotted and plaid sunflowers on page 9.

PAGES 10–11

EVENTS

What is happening on this page? (The girl imagines that she is picking flowers and more flowers are growing back.)

pp. 10–11

in its place: Use two objects, such as a book and an eraser, to help explain this phrase. Put the book on a table or desk. *I put the book here.* Remove the book, and put the eraser in the same spot as you say: *Now the eraser is in the book's place. The eraser is in its place.*

Listening Comprehension

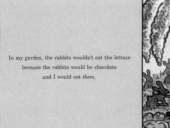 

PAGES 12–13

CHARACTER

What does the girl like to do?
(possible answer: eat chocolate)

PAGES 14–15

REREAD

Think Aloud I see shells from the beach in the picture. I'm confused. Seashells can't grow in gardens. When I reread the page, I see that the girl is talking about planting and growing seashells. I remember that this is a make-believe garden. Now I understand.

pp. 14–15

seashell: Some children might not be familiar with seashells. Use real seashells, illustrations in the **Big Book**, or other illustrations to help explain seashells. Say *seashells* and have children echo you.

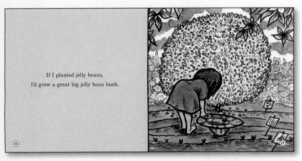

PAGES 16–17

EVENTS

What do you see in this picture? What is the girl doing? (Possible answer: I can see the girl planting jelly beans. The jelly beans are growing like flowers grow on a plant.)

PAGES 18–19

HIGH-FREQUENCY WORDS

Have children identify and read the high-frequency word *my.*

pp. 18–19

pop up: On this page, *pop up* means "to grow quickly." Have children crouch down with you and then jump up, saying: *Pop up!* Guide children to connect your action with plants popping out of the ground.

PAGES 20–21

PHONICS

Reread page 20 and have children identify the words beginning with the /h/ sound. *What letter makes the /h/ sound?* (hundreds, hummingbird, h)

pp. 20–21

humming: Make a humming sound and have children hum with you. Then guide children to understand that the birds' wings were making a humming sound. Point to the wings on page 21 and explain that when wings flap quickly, they can make a humming sound.

PAGES 22–23

REREAD

What does it mean when something is invisible? (You cannot see it.) *Listen while I reread page 22. See if you can figure out why the girl wants the carrots to be invisible.* Reread the page. *What did you learn?* (Possible answer: The girl does not like carrots. That's why she does not want to see them.)

pp. 22–23

as big as: Guide children in understanding that *as big as* means "the same size as."

PAGES 24–25

VISUALIZE

Morning glories are a kind of flower. Have a volunteer point them out on page 25. *Can you make a picture in your mind of flowers shining like stars?*

PAGES 26–27

SETTING

What is the setting on these pages? How do you know? (The girl is still in the garden. Now it is night. I see in the illustration that it is dark out and the words say that it is night.)

pp. 26–27

poke: Show how to poke, such as poking a seed into soil, or poking a pencil into clay. As you do it, say: *poke.* Then have children echo and mimic.

Listening Comprehension

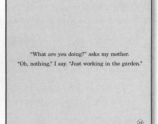

PAGES 28–29

AUTHOR'S PURPOSE

Why do you think the author wrote this story? (Possible answer: He wanted to tell a fun story about things that might grow in a make-believe garden.)

Text Evidence

Explain Remind children that when they answer a question, they need to show where in the story (both words and pictures) they found the answer.

Discuss *The girl wants to grow many unusual things in her garden. What are some things that she wants to grow that could not grow in a real garden? Which pages in the book tell about these things?* (Possible answers: Seashells on pages 14 and 15, jelly beans on pages 16 and 17.)

Guided Retelling

Tell children that now they will use the **Retelling Cards** to retell the story.

→ Display Retelling Card 1. Based on children's needs, use either the Modeled, Guided or ELL retelling prompts. The ELL prompts contain support for English language learners based on levels of language acquisition. Repeat with the rest of the cards, using the prompts as a guide.

→ Choose a place in the book and have children discuss what the girl was growing and how she felt about it. Make certain children add details to their comments.

→ Invite children to choose a favorite part of the story and act it out.

Model Fluency

Turn to page 22. Remind children that we should read aloud words the way a character would say them. Explain: *I can tell that the girl is thinking about how wonderful big tomatoes would be. And I think she would sound happy when she talks about making carrots invisible.* In a happy voice, read aloud: *The tomatoes would be as big as beach balls.* Have children echo. Then have a volunteer repeat after you: *and the carrots would be invisible because I don't like carrots*—the way the girl would say it.

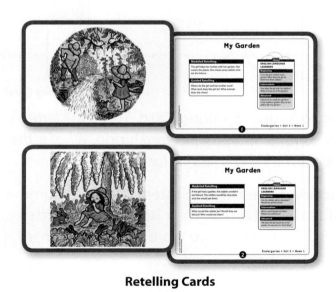

Retelling Cards

YOUR TURN PRACTICE BOOK p. 129

→ # Word Work

Quick Review

Build Fluency: Sound-Spellings
Display the following **Word-Building Cards:** *a, c, d, h, i, m, n, o, p, s, t.* Have children chorally say each sound. Repeat several times.

 MINILESSON **5** Mins

Phonemic Awareness

Puppet

Phoneme Blending

❶ **Model** Use the puppet to demonstrate how to blend phonemes to make words. *The puppet is going to say sounds in a word, /h/ /i/ /p/ /ō/. It can blend those sounds to make a word: /hipō/, hippo. When the puppet blends the sounds together, it makes the word* hippo. *Listen as the puppet blends more sounds to make a word.* Model phoneme blending with the following words.

/h/ /i/ /p/, *hip*   /h/ /ou/, *how*   /h/ /a/ /d/, *had*

❷ **Guided Practice/Practice** Tell children to listen as the puppet says the sounds in words. Have them repeat the sounds, and then blend them to say the word.

/h/ /a/ /t/, *hat*   /h/ /o/ /t/, *hot*   /h/ /e/ /n/, *hen*
/h/ /i/ /m/, *him*   /h/ /e/ /d/, *head*   /h/ /a/ /z/, *has*

 MINILESSON **5** Mins

Phonics

Hh
hippo
Sound-Spelling Card

Review /h/h

❶ **Model** Display the *Hippo* **Sound-Spelling Card**. *This is the letter* h. *The letter* h *stands for the sound /h/ as in the word* hippo. *What is the letter?* (h) *What sound does the letter* h *stands for?* (/h/)

❷ **Guided Practice/Practice** Have children listen as you say some words. Ask them to write the letter *h* on their **Response Boards** if the word begins with /h/. Do the first two words with children.

hand   his   gate   high
jump   into   horse   house

OBJECTIVES

CCSS Isolate and pronounce the initial, medial vowel, and final sounds (phonemes) in three-phoneme words. **RF.K.2d**

CCSS Demonstrate basic knowledge of one-to-one letter-sound correspondences by producing the primary or many of the most frequent sounds for each consonant. **RF.K.3a**

CCSS Read common high-frequency words by sight. **RF.K.3c**

ACADEMIC LANGUAGE
beginning, blend

ENGLISH LANGUAGE LEARNERS

High-Frequency Words: Build Meaning Reinforce use of the word *my* by saying the following sentences and demonstrating them.

• This is *my* book.
• *My* desk is here.
• This is *my* school.
• *My* chair is comfortable.

Go Digital

Phonemic Awareness

c a t
Phonics

| the | is |
| you | do |

High-Frequency Words

A A
a a
Handwriting

Blend Words with *h*

❶ Model Place **Word-Building Cards** *h, i* and *m* in a pocket chart. Point to the *h*. *This is the letter* h. *The letter* h *stands for /h/. Say /h/. This is the letter* i. *The letter* i *stands for /i/. Say /i/. This is the letter* m. *The letter* m *stands for /m/. Say /m/. Listen as I blend the three sounds together: /hiiimmm/. Blend the sounds with me to read the word.*

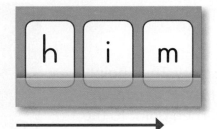

❷ Guided Practice/Practice Change Word-Building Cards to *h, a, t.* Point to the letter *h* and have children say the sound. Point to the letter *a* and have children say the sound. Point to the letter *t* and have children say the sound. Then move your hand from left to right under the word and have children blend and read *hat.* Repeat with *hip* and *hot.*

MINILESSON
5 Mins

High-Frequency Words

my

my

High-Frequency Word Card

❶ Guided Practice Display the **High-Frequency Word Card** *my.* Use the **Read/Spell/Write** routine to teach the word. Ask children to close their eyes, picture the spelling of the word in their minds, and then write it the way they see it. Have children self-correct by checking the High-Frequency Word Card.

❷ Practice Add the word *my* to the cumulative word bank.

→ Have partners create sentences using the word.

→ Have children count the number of letters in the word and then write the word again.

Cumulative Review Review *to, and, go, you, do.*

Repeat the **Read/Spell/Write** routine. Mix the words and have children chorally say each one.

→ # Shared Read

Reading/Writing Workshop Big Book and Reading/Writing Workshop

OBJECTIVES

CCSS Read common high-frequency words by sight. **RF.K.3c**

CCSS Read emergent-reader texts with purpose and understanding. **RF.K.4**

ACADEMIC LANGUAGE

• *predict*

• Cognates: *predecir*

MINILESSON 10 Mins

Read "Hop Can Hop!"

Model Skills and Strategies

Model Concepts About Print Read page 9 of the story. Then point to the spaces between each word. *After each word, there is a space to show where one word ends and the next word begins.* Then point to the period at the end of each sentence. *Each sentence makes a statement, so they both end in a period. The period tells where the sentence ends.* Next, point to the word *I* in each sentence. *Both of these sentences begin with the pronoun* I. *The pronoun* I *is always a capital letter.* Invite volunteers to come up to the **Big Book** and find other examples of the pronoun *I*.

Predict Read the title together and look at the illustration. Ask children to predict who they think the story will be about and where the story will take place.

Read Have children chorally read the story with you. Point to each word as you read it together. Help children sound out the decodable words and say the sight words. If children have difficulty, provide corrective feedback and guide them page by page using the student **Reading/Writing Workshop**.

Ask the following:

→ *Look at pages 8 and 9. What do you see in the picture?* (a girl in a flower garden holding a bunny)

→ *Look at page 10. Why is Dot wearing a hat?* (It is a hot, sunny day, and she is trying to stay cool.)

→ *Look at pages 12 and 13. What can Dot and Hop do?* (They both can hop.)

Go Digital

"Hop Can Hop!"

"Hop Can Hop!"

I am Dot.
I like Hop.

I am hot.
See **my** hat on top!

Hop is hot.
Hop can hop on top.

Hop can hop, hop, hop.

I can hop, hop, hop!

I can sit.
Hop can sit.

Pop and I can sip.
Hop can sip.

READING/WRITING WORKSHOP, pp. 8–15

Rereading

COLLABORATE

Have small groups use the **Reading/Writing Workshop** to reread "Hop Can Hop!" Then review the skills and strategies using the *Phonics* and *Words to Know* pages that come before the selection.

→ Have children describe the characters, setting, and events in the story. Encourage them to reread the story or sections of the story to help them tell about the characters, setting, and events.

→ Have children use page 7 to review the high-frequency word *my*.

→ Have children use page 6 to review that the letter *h* can stand for the sound /h/. Have them identify and name each picture. Guide them to blend the sounds to read the words.

ENGLISH LANGUAGE LEARNERS

Reinforce Vocabulary Display the **High-Frequency Word Cards** *my, do, you, go*. Point to classroom objects and groups of children as you use the high-frequency words in sentences such as the following: *I can see my desk. Can you see my desk?* (Yes, we can see your desk.) *I can see my glasses on the desk. Can you see my glasses on the desk?* (Yes, we can see your glasses on the desk.) *I like to color. Do you like to color?* (Yes, we like to color.) *I go home after school. Do you go home after school?* (Yes, we go home after school.)

→ # Language Arts

 MINILESSON
10 Mins

Interactive Writing

Writing Trait: Organization

Review Remind children that they organize their writing by grouping similar ideas together. *I want to describe a flower. I think of all these ideas: It is yellow, it has a tall green stem, and it smells good. I can organize my ideas. First, I will tell how the flower looks:* It is yellow and it has a tall, green stem. *Then, I will tell how it smells.* It smells sweet.

Write a Poem

Discuss Display the lists of flowers and trees and the sample poem from Day 1. Read aloud each item in the lists. Guide children to choose one item to write about, such as *palm tree*.

Model/Apply Grammar Tell children that you will work together to write a poem about a palm tree. Explain that they don't have to use the words *palm tree* in every line of the poem. They can use the pronoun *it*. Draw a palm tree. Write and say:

Palm Tree
It is _____ .
It has _____ leaves.
It is a _____ tree.

What word can we use to complete the first line of the poem? (tall) *The second line?* (green) *The third line?* (palm) Read the completed poem aloud. Point out that the first and second lines follow each other because they both describe the palm tree. Ask children to name the pronouns.

Write Have children help you write an additional line about the palm tree. Write the sentence frame: *It has a _____ trunk.*

Guide children to complete the sentence frame. (It has a brown trunk.) Write the words. Share the pen with children and have them write the letters they know. Guide children to group this sentence with the other lines that describe the palm tree, not at the end of the poem.

OBJECTIVES

CCSS Use a combination of drawing, dictating, and writing to narrate a single event or several loosely linked events, tell about the events in the order in which they occurred, and provide a reaction to what happened. **W.K.3**

CCSS Use personal, possessive, and indefinite pronouns (e.g., *I, me, my; they, them, their; anyone, everything*). **L.1.1d**

• Write poems
• Use pronouns

ACADEMIC LANGUAGE

• *organize, pronoun*
• Cognates: *organizar*

Grammar

5 Mins MINILESSON

Pronouns

❶ Review Remind children that pronouns are words that can be used in place of a noun. A person's name can be replaced with the pronoun *he* or *she*. A thing can be replaced with the pronoun *it*. *I can use a pronoun to take the place of a person's name so that I don't have to use the name over and over again.* Jim is at home. *What pronoun can I use in place of Jim?* (He) He *is a pronoun that can take the place of a boy's name.* Read aloud: *He is at home.*

Read aloud the following sentence: *Jane is at school.* Have children chorally repeat the sentence. *What pronoun can I use in place of Jane?* (She) Rewrite the sentence and read it aloud: *She is at school.* Have children point to the pronoun in the new sentence.

❷ Guided Practice Write the following words in two columns and read them aloud: (Column 1) *mom, Mike, hat;* (Column 2) *he, she, it.* Ask volunteers to draw a line to match each noun with the pronoun that can replace it. (mom/she; Mike/he; hat/it) *How do you know that* he *can replace* Mike? (He *is a pronoun that is used for boys, and Mike is a boy's name.) What pronoun can take the place of* hat? *Why?* (It; a hat is a thing, and the pronoun *it* takes the place of a thing.)

❸ Practice Have children work with a partner. Ask children to draw pictures of an object and a person that they see in the classroom. Help children use nouns to label each picture. Guide children to write the corresponding pronoun under each label. Have partners share their drawings and read the labels aloud to the class.

Talk About It

Have partners practice making up riddles, using the pronoun *it* to describe a food they like. Encourage partners to guess the food. For example: *It is yellow. It is long. What is it?* (a banana)

ENGLISH LANGUAGE LEARNERS

Describe Display the **Photo Card** for *tree*. Ask children to describe the tree, using complete sentences that include pronouns. For example: "It is tall. It has green leaves." Write the sentences on the board and have children underline the pronoun in each sentence.

Daily Wrap Up

- Discuss the Essential Question and encourage children to use the oral vocabulary words. *What do living things need to grow?*

- Prompt children to review and discuss the skills they used today. How do those skills help them?

Materials

Reading/Writing Workshop Big Book
UNIT 5

Visual Vocabulary Cards
harmful
soak
crowd

Response Board

Word-Building Cards

Puppet

Interactive Read-Aloud Cards

Think Aloud Cloud

 and
High-Frequency Word Cards
and
do
go
my
to
you

Photo Cards
dime   hat
dog   hippo
doll   koala
dolphin
door
hair
hammer
hand

→ Build the Concept

MINILESSON 10 Mins Oral Language

OBJECTIVES

CCSS Actively engage in group reading activities with purpose and understanding. **RI.K.10**

CCSS Identify real-life connections between words and their use. **L.K.5c**

Develop oral vocabulary

ACADEMIC LANGUAGE
• *informational text*
• Cognates: *texto informativo*

ESSENTIAL QUESTION

Remind children that this week they are talking and learning about what living things need to grow. Guide children to discuss the Essential Question using information from the **Big Book** and the weekly rhyme. Remind children about the flowers that grew in "Mary, Mary, Quite Contrary." Say the rhyme and have children join in.

Oral Vocabulary

Review last week's oral vocabulary words, as well as *plant* and *require* from Day 1. Then use the **Define/Example/Ask** routine to introduce *harmful, soak,* and *crowd.*

Oral Vocabulary Routine

Define: Something **harmful** can hurt you.

Example: Pollution is harmful to air and water.

Ask: Why is it important to keep harmful materials out of our oceans?

Define: **Soak** up means "to take in."

Example: You can use a towel to soak up the spilled water.

Ask: What would you use to soak up spilled milk?

Define: When you **crowd** something, you push it into a small space.

Example: I can't crowd another pencil into my pencil box.

Ask: How many coats can we crowd into the closet?

Visual Vocabulary Cards

Go Digital

Visual Glossary

"Growing Plants"

Think Aloud Cloud

Listening Comprehension

Read the Interactive Read Aloud

MINILESSON
10 Mins

Genre: Informational Text

Tell children you will be reading a informational text. Remind them that *informational text* gives true information, or facts, about a topic. Display the **Interactive Read-Aloud Cards**.

Read the title. Point out that all plants need certain things to live and grow.

Interactive Read-Aloud Cards

ENGLISH LANGUAGE LEARNERS

Reinforce Meaning As you read "Growing Plants," make meaning clear by pointing to specific places or objects in the photographs, demonstrating word meanings, paraphrasing text, and asking children questions. For example, on Card 2, point to the root in the photo. Say: *This is a plant root.*

Strategy: Reread

Remind children that good readers reread to help them understand. Something might not make sense to them as they are reading, but reading again can help make the information clear. Remind children to use the **Think Aloud Cloud** as they reread to understand.

Think Aloud I just read that if a plant doesn't get the food and water it needs, it will die. I'm not sure how a plant gets the food and water it needs, so I think I'll reread. Oh, I see. When I reread the paragraph, I see that the text says that a plant's roots soak up food and water from the soil.

Read "Growing Plants," pausing occasionally to model the strategy of rereading.

Make Connections

COLLABORATE

Guide partners to connect "Growing Plants" with *My Garden*. Discuss the ways both selections explain what plants need to grow. *How are the plants in* My Garden *different from the plants in "Growing Plants"?* (Many of them are made up and imagined by the girl.)

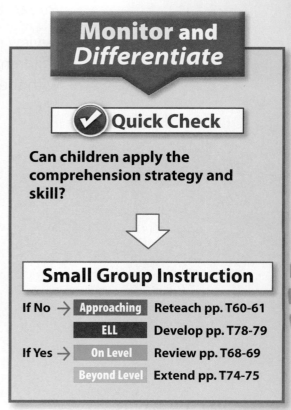

Monitor and *Differentiate*

✓ Quick Check

Can children apply the comprehension strategy and skill?

Small Group Instruction

If No →	Approaching	Reteach pp. T60-61
	ELL	Develop pp. T78-79
If Yes →	On Level	Review pp. T68-69
	Beyond Level	Extend pp. T74-75

→ # Word Work

Quick Review

Build Fluency: Sound-Spellings
Display **Word-Building Cards:** *a, c, d, h, i, m, n, o, p, s, t.* Have children chorally say each sound. Repeat several times.

MINILESSON 10 Mins # Phonemic Awareness

Puppet

Go Digital

OBJECTIVES

CCSS Isolate and pronounce the initial, medial vowel, and final sounds (phonemes) in three-phoneme words. **RF.K.2d**

CCSS Demonstrate basic knowledge of one-to-one letter-sound correspondences by producing the primary or many of the most frequent sounds for each consonant. **RF.K.3a**

Read and blend words with /h/

Phoneme Blending

1 Model Use the puppet to demonstrate how to blend phonemes to make words. *The puppet is going to say sounds in a word /h/ /a/ /z/. It can blend those sounds to make a word: /haaazzz/, has. When the puppet blends the sounds together, it makes the word* has. *Listen as the puppet blends more sounds to make a word.* Model blending with the following:

/h/ /a/ /d/, had   /h/ /o/ /p/, hop   /h/ /i/ /z/, his

2 Guided Practice/Practice *The puppet is going to say the sounds in a different word. Listen as it says each sound: /h/ /o/ /t/. Let's blend these sounds together and then say the word: /hooot/, hot.*

Tell children that the puppet is going to say the sounds in a word. *Listen as it says each sound. You will repeat the sounds, then blend them to say the word.*

/h/ /a/ /d/, had   /h/ /ō/ /p/, hope   /h/ /i/ /m/, him
/h/ /a/ /t/, hat   /h/ /i/ /z/, his   /h/ /o/ /p/, hop

♪ Review initial /h/. Play and sing "A Hippo in the House." Have children clap when they hear initial /h/. Demonstrate as you sing with them.

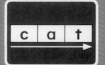
Phonemic Awareness

c a t
Phonics

A A
Handwriting

Phonics

Word-Building Card

Review /h/*h*

❶ Model Display **Word-Building Card** *h. This is the letter* h. *The letter* h *stands for /h/, the sound you hear in the beginning of* hippo. *Say the sound with me: /h/. I will write the letter* h *because* hippo *has /h/ at the beginning.*

❷ Guided Practice/Practice Tell children that you will say some words that begin with /h/ and some words that do not. Have children say /h/ and write the letter *h* on their **Response Boards** when they hear /h/ at the beginning of the word. Guide practice with the first word.

had   him   gym   hat   lot   hold   told   have

Blend Words with Short *i, o, a* and *h, t, p, m, d*

❶ Model Display Word-Building Cards *h, i, t. This is the letter* h. *It stands for /h/. This is the letter* i. *It stands for /i/. This is the letter* t. *It stands for /t/. Let's blend the three sounds together: /hiiit/. The word is* hit. Continue with the following words: *hip, him, hop.*

❷ Guided Practice/Practice Write the following words and sentences. Have children read each word, blending the sounds. Guide practice with the first word.

hop   him   had   hit   hot

Prompt children to read the connected text, sounding out the decodable words: *I like the hat. Dan hid my hat. We like to hop.*

Corrective Feedback

Sound Error Model the sound that children missed, then have them repeat. Tap under the letter *h* in the word *hop* and ask: *What's the sound?* (/h/) Return to the beginning of the word. *Let's start over. Blend the word again.*

Extend the Lesson

Final /z/*s*

Remind children that the letter *s* usually stands for /s/. Have children give examples of words with /s/ spelled *s* such as *sun, same*, and *Sam*. Tell children that sometimes when the letter *s* is at the end of a word, it can sound like /z/. Place the Word-Building Cards *h, i, s* in the pocket chart and model blending and reading the word. Emphasize the /z/ sound at the end. Blend the word *is* with children. Then continue with the words *as* and *has*.

YOUR TURN PRACTICE BOOK p. 130

→ Word Work

Go
Digital

MINILESSON

5 Mins

Phonics

Photo Cards

OBJECTIVES

CCSS Read common high-frequency words by sight. **RF.K.3c**

Sort pictures using initial consonants

ACADEMIC LANGUAGE
sort

Picture Sort

❶ **Model** Remind children that the letter *h* can stand for /h/. Place **Word-Building Card** *h* on the left side of the pocket chart. *What is this letter?* (h) *What sound does this letter stand for?* (/h/)

Hold up the **Photo Card** for *hat*. *Here is the picture for* hat. *Hat begins with /h/. Listen, /h/ /h/,* hat. *I will place* hat *under the letter* h *because the letter* h *stands for /h/.*

Use the same routine for letter *d* and the *dog* Photo Card.

❷ **Guided Practice/Practice** Have children sort the Photo Cards *hand, doll, hippo, door, hair, dime, hammer, dolphin*. Have them say the sound at the beginning of the word and tell which letter the Photo Card should be placed under.

Phonics

the	is
you	do

High-Frequency Word Routine

Photo Cards

High-Frequency Words

MINILESSON 5 Mins

my

❶ Guided Practice Display the **High-Frequency Word Card** *my*. Review the word using the **Read/Spell/Write** routine.

❷ Practice Point to the High-Frequency Word Card *my* and have children read it. Repeat with last week's words *to, and, go, you, do.*

Build Fluency

Word Automaticity Write the following sentences and have children chorally read aloud as you track the print. Repeat several times.

> Do you see *my* hat?
> *My* cat can hop.
> I like *my* top.
> You sat on *my* hat.

Read for Fluency Distribute pages 131–132 of the **Your Turn Practice Book** and help children assemble their Take-Home Books. Chorally read the Take-Home Book with children. Then have children reread the book to review high-frequency words and build fluency.

YOUR TURN PRACTICE BOOK pp. 131–132

Name _____

We do not see my cat.

High Frequency Words: *my*
Read the book aloud to a partner. Reread for fluency.

❹ Unit 5: Wonders of Nature • Week 1

We See It!

Tam and I see my cat.

Monitor and *Differentiate*

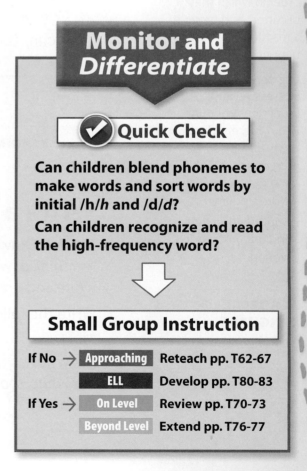

✓ Quick Check

Can children blend phonemes to make words and sort words by initial /h/h and /d/d?

Can children recognize and read the high-frequency word?

⬇

Small Group Instruction

If No →	**Approaching**	Reteach pp. T62-67
	ELL	Develop pp. T80-83
If Yes →	**On Level**	Review pp. T70-73
	Beyond Level	Extend pp. T76-77

→ # Language Arts

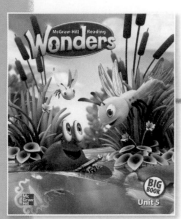

Reading/Writing Workshop Big Book

OBJECTIVES

CCSS Use a combination of drawing, dictating, and writing to narrate a single event or several loosely linked events, tell about the events in the order in which they occurred, and provide a reaction to what happened. **W.K.3**

CCSS Use personal, possessive, and indefinite pronouns (e.g., *I, me, my; they, them, their; anyone, everything*). **L.1.1d**

- Write a poem
- Apply writing trait and grammar to writing

ACADEMIC LANGUAGE
poem, pronoun

MINILESSON 10 Mins

Independent Writing

Writing Trait: Organization

1 Practice Tell children that today they will write a poem about their favorite flower or tree and draw a picture of it.

2 Guided Practice Share the Readers to Writers page in the **Reading/Writing Workshop**. Read the model sentences aloud.

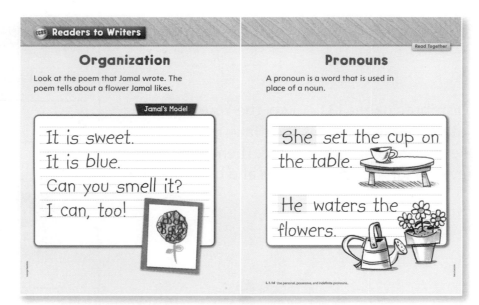

READING/WRITING WORKSHOP BIG BOOK, pp. 18–19

Write a Poem

Model Draw a picture of the tulip. *I will write a poem about the tulip. I will think of words to describe the tulip.* Write and read aloud: *yellow and white* and *pretty.*

Write the following poem. Read each line aloud as you write it.

The Tulip
It is yellow.
It is white, too.
It is pretty.

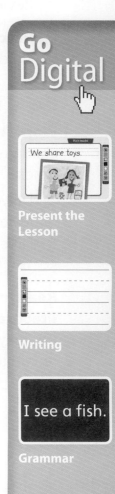

Go Digital

Present the Lesson

Writing

I see a fish.

Grammar

Prewrite

Brainstorm Have children work with a partner. Ask them to think of their favorite flower or tree and to think of words to describe it.

Draft

Ask children to draw a picture of their favorite flower or tree. Give children sentence frames for the poem.

The _____ (This is the title.)

It is _____ .

It is _____ .

It is _____ .

Guide children in writing describing words for their poems.

Apply Writing Trait As children complete their sentence frames, ask them to make sure their ideas are in an order that makes sense.

Apply Grammar Remind children that *it* is a pronoun that can take the place of a thing, such as their favorite flower or tree.

ENGLISH LANGUAGE LEARNERS

Practice Display the Photo Card of the *koala.* Write and read: *The koala is _____. It is _____.* Have children think of describing words about the koala. Fill in the sentences with their responses and read aloud with children. Have children point to the pronoun in the sentence.

MINILESSON
5 Mins

Grammar

Pronouns

❶ **Review** Remind children that a pronoun is a word that can take the place of a noun.

Display the **Big Book** *My Garden*. Show page 7 and point to one sunflower. Write and read aloud: *The sunflower is very large. It is very large. What pronoun did I replace the name with in the second sentence? It is a pronoun because it can take the place of the noun in the sentence.*

❷ **Guided Practice/Practice** Display the **Photo Card** for *koala*. Have children dictate sentences describing the koala, using pronouns. Have children circle the pronouns in the sentences.

Talk About It

Have partners work together to orally generate sentences with pronouns. Have them use pronouns to describe what game they like to play with their friends.

Daily Wrap Up

- Review the Essential Question and encourage children to discuss it, using the oral vocabulary words *require* and *plant. What do living things need to grow?*

- Prompt children to review and discuss the skills they used today. Guide them to give examples of how they used each skill.

Materials

Reading/Writing Workshop Big Book
UNIT 5

Literature Big Book
My Garden

Interactive Read-Aloud Cards

Visual Vocabulary Cards
my

Word-Building Cards

High-Frequency Word Cards
my

Photo Cards

alligator	doctor
ant	farm
book	girl
boy	hammer
camel	hand
cow	jacket
cowboy	
dinosaur	

→ # Extend the Concept

MINILESSON
10 Mins

Oral Language

OBJECTIVES

CCSS Use words and phrases acquired through conversations, reading and being read to, and responding to texts. **L.K.6**

CCSS Count, pronounce, blend, and segment syllables in spoken words. **RF.K.2b**

Develop vocabulary

ESSENTIAL QUESTION
Remind children that this week they have been talking and reading about what plants need to grow. Have them recite "Mary, Mary, Quite Contrary" and think about what plants need. *What does the girl do to help her mother's garden grow at the beginning of* My Garden?

> ### Phonological Awareness
> #### Count and Blend Syllables
> Have children say: *With silver bells and cockle-shells.* Say: *We can count the parts of the word* silver. *Listen:* sil-ver. *The word* silver *has two parts.* Clap each syllable and say: *sil-ver.* Have children repeat. Then say: *We can blend the word parts together. Listen:* silver. Have children repeat. Then invite a volunteer to clap the parts of the word *garden.* (gar-den) Ask: *How many parts does the word* garden *have?* (two) Then have the volunteer blend the word.

Review Oral Vocabulary

Reread the Interactive Read Aloud Use the **Define/Example/Ask** routine to review the oral vocabulary words *plant, require, harmful, soak,* and *crowd.* Then have children listen as you reread "Growing Plants."

→ *What things do all plants require?* (food, water, air, sunlight, space)

→ *What do roots soak up?* (food and water)

Go Digital

Visual Glossary

"Growing Plants"

Category Words

Category Words: Size Words

❶ Explain/Model Read aloud the following story. Ask children to listen for size words, or words that describe how *big, small, short,* or *tall* something or someone is. *When you hear a size word, use your hands to show what size it is.* Demonstrate as you read.

Mom and I went for a hike in the woods. We stopped next to a tall *tree to have a picnic. Mom brought two apples for us to eat. One apple was* big, *and the other was* small. *I wanted the* big *apple because I had a* small *breakfast. Then Mom saw a* small *bird in the* tall *tree. I was too* short *to see it, so Mom lifted me up on her shoulders. I felt so* tall!

❷ Guided Practice Display the **Photo Cards** for *alligator, ant,* and *dinosaur.* Read the following sentences as you display each Photo Card. Ask children to name the size words in each sentence.

The big *alligator ate a* small *fish.*
The tall *dinosaur chased the* short *dinosaur.*

→ Work with children to identify other size words to describe the animals. (Possible answers: tiny, little, huge, giant, great)

Vocabulary Strategy: Word Parts/ Plurals -*s*

❶ Model Remind children that the word ending -*s* can make a singular noun into a plural noun. Review that plural nouns ending with -*s* mean "more than one."

Think Aloud In *My Garden,* I can read this phrase: *In my garden, there would be birds.* I see two nouns: *garden* and *birds. Garden* does not end with -*s.* The word *garden* means "one garden." *Birds* ends with -*s.* The word *birds* means "more than one bird."

❷ Guided Practice/Practice Work with children to create plural nouns. Point to singular items in the classroom, such as a desk, a pen, and a book. Have children say the name of each item and then add -*s* to the end of each word to create a plural noun.

LET'S MOVE!

Play a game of Simon Says. Have children move around the room as you give them directions. *Simon says, move to the big table. Simon says, find a small crayon. Simon says, stand by the tall flag. Move to the short stool.*

ENGLISH LANGUAGE LEARNERS

Describe Display Photo Cards of objects that can easily be described using size words. Name the object on the card and describe its size. For example: *A big gorilla.* Then ask: *What size is the gorilla?* Repeat, using different Photo Cards and size words.

YOUR TURN PRACTICE BOOK p. 133

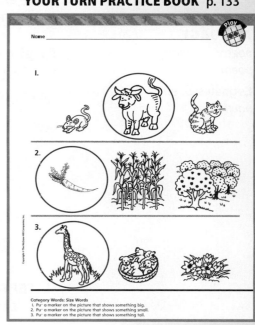

→ # Listening Comprehension

CLOSE READING

MY GARDEN
KEVIN HENKES

Literature Big Book

OBJECTIVES

CCSS Recognize common types of texts (e.g., storybooks, poems). **RL.K.5**

• Understand the characteristics of poetry

• Use the literary elements rhyme and repetition

• Apply the comprehension strategy: Reread

• Make connections across texts

ACADEMIC LANGUAGE

• *poetry, rhyming, poem*

• Cognates: *poesía, poema*

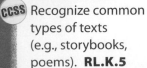
MINILESSON
10 Mins

Read Poetry

Genre: Poetry

Display pages 31–36 of the **Big Book**. Ask children what kinds of texts are in these pages. (poems) Read aloud the title of the first poem. Remind children that poetry is creative writing that often includes rhyming words.

Set a Purpose for Reading

Read aloud the title "Tommy" on page 31. Tell children to listen for rhyming words as you read aloud the other poems.

Strategy: Reread

Remind children that good readers reread parts of a text if there is something they do not understand. Reread the second line in the first stanza on page 31. *What does the word* it *refer to? If I reread the first sentence, I know that* it *refers to the seed.*

Literary Element: Rhyme and Repetition

Explain Tell children that many poems use rhyme or repetition. Read aloud "Maytime Magic" on pages 32–33. *Words that rhyme have the same ending sounds. Two words that rhyme in this poem are* sow *and* grow. *This poem also repeats the words* "A little."

Apply Have children listen for rhyming words as you read aloud the first stanza of "The Seed" on page 34. *Which words rhyme?* (know, grow; seed, weed)

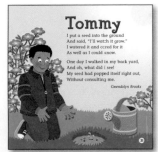

Tommy

I put a seed into the ground
And said, "I'll watch it grow."
I watered it and cared for it
As well as I could know.

One day I walked in my back yard,
And oh, what did I see!
My seed had popped itself right out,
Without consulting me.

Gwendolyn Brooks

LITERATURE BIG BOOK PAGE 31

LITERARY ELEMENT

Reread the second stanza. Have children identify the rhyming words *see* and *me*.

Go Digital

MY GARDEN
KEVIN HENKES

"My Garden"

LITERATURE BIG BOOK   PAGES 32–33

REREAD

Reread the last stanza of the poem aloud. *What does the flower need to grow?* (a little sun, a little shower) *What does a little shower mean?* (a little rain)

LITERATURE BIG BOOK   PAGES 34–35

ASK AND ANSWER QUESTIONS

How are the plants in the poems alike? (Possible responses: They all grow from a seed; they need water and sun.) *How are they different?* (Possible responses: different shapes and colors.)

LITERATURE BIG BOOK PAGE 36

REREAD

Reread the last two lines. *What does the word* they *refer to?* (the carnations)

VOCABULARY

Point to the word *replanting* in line 6 and explain that the prefix *re-* means *again*. *What does* replanting *mean?*

ENGLISH LANGUAGE LEARNERS

Reinforce Meaning As you read aloud the text, make the meaning clear by pointing to details in the illustrations. Ask children questions and elicit language.

Retell and Respond

Have children discuss the selection by asking the following questions:

→ *How are all of the poems alike?* (They rhyme and are about gardens.)

→ *What might the seed in "The Seed" grow into?* (flower, weed, vine, shoot, tree)

Make Connections

Have children recall the selections they read this week.

→ *What special thing did the girl plant in her garden?* (a seashell)

Write About It Write about two things all plants need to grow that are shown in "Growing Plants."

CONNECT TO CONTENT

How Flowers Are Alike and Different Discuss the illustration on pages 32 to 33. Ask children to describe what the picture shows (the way flowers grow). Have children point to the things in the picture that help a flower to grow (sun, rain, soil). Explain to children that most flowers are alike because they need soil, sunlight, and water to grow. Have children discuss how flowers are different (size, color, shape).

STEM

 **Word Work**

 MINILESSON **5** Mins

Phonemic Awareness

Phoneme Categorization

Photo Cards

OBJECTIVES

CCSS Distinguish between similarly spelled words by identifying the sounds of the letters that differ. **RF.K.3d**

CCSS Read common high-frequency words by sight. **RF.K.3c**

Categorize words by initial phoneme.

1 Model Display the **Photo Cards** for *hand, hammer,* and *jacket. Which picture names begin with the same sound?* Say the picture names. Hand *and* hammer *both begin with /h/.* Jacket *does not begin with /h/.* Jacket *does not belong.*

2 Guided Practice/Practice Show children sets of Photo Cards. Name the pictures with children and have them identify the picture in each set that does not begin with the same sound. Guide children with the first set.

hair, hat, night   sing, soup, helicopter   hippo, hook, nut

horse, light, house   seal, hair, hammer   door, dog, hay

 MINILESSON **5** Mins

Phonics

Blend Words with Short *a, i, o* and *h, t, p*

1 Guided Practice Display **Word-Building Cards** *h, i, p.* Point to the letter h. *This is the letter* h. *The letter* h *stands for /h/. Say /h/. This is* i. *The letter* i *stands for /i/. Listen as I blend the two sounds, /hiii/. This is the letter* p. *The letter* p *stands for /p/. Listen as I blend the sounds: /hiiip/,* hip. *Now you say it. Let's change the* i *to* o. *Repeat with* hop.

2 Practice Write *hat, hot* and *hit.* Have children blend the sounds to read the words. *Which letters are the same in all three words?* (h, t) *Which letters are different?* (a, o, i) Have children identify the sounds of the letters that are different. Point to *a* in *hat. What sound does the letter* a *stand for?* (/a/) *Let's read the word.* (hat) Point to *hot. What sound does the letter* o *stand for?* (/o/) *Let's read the word.* (hot) Continue with *hit.* Discuss the sound each letter stands for and how it changes the word.

Go Digital

Phonemic Awareness

Phonics

Handwriting

Visual Glossary

High-Frequency Word Routine

Dictation

Review Dictate these sounds for children to spell. Have them repeat the sound and then write the appropriate letter. Repeat several times.

/h/   /i/   /n/   /k/   /o/   /d/   /a/   /t/   /p/

Dictate the following words for children to spell: *hit, hat, hot, hop, hip.* Model for children how to segment each word to scaffold the spelling. Say: *When I say the word* hit *I hear three sounds: /h/ /i/ /t/. I know the letter* h *stands for /h/, the letter* i *stands for /i/, and the letter* t *stands for /t/. I will write the letters* h, i, t *to spell the word* hit.

When children finish, write the letters and words for them to self-correct.

Extend the Lesson

Extend with final /z/s
Write the word *his*. Underline *s*. Point out that when *s* appears at the end of a word, it sometimes stands for /z/. Blend *his* with children, emphasizing the /z/ sound at the end. Write *is, as, has*. Blend each word with children.

MINILESSON
5 Mins

High-Frequency Words

Practice Say the word *my* and have children write it. Then display the **Visual Vocabulary Card** *my*. Follow the Teacher Talk routine on the back.

Visual Vocabulary Card

Build Fluency Build sentences in the pocket chart using the **High-Frequency Word Cards**, **Photo Cards** and teacher-made punctuation cards. Have children chorally read the sentences as you track the print. Then have them identify the word *my*.

I like my kitten.
We can go to my house.
Do you see my bike?

Also online

| I | see | my | | . |

High-Frequency Words Practice

Have partners create sentences using the word *my*.
COLLABORATE

Monitor and *Differentiate*

✓ **Quick Check**

Can children categorize words with the same initial phoneme and blend words with /h/ and match it to the letter *Hh*?

Can children read and recognize high-frequency words?

⬇

Small Group Instruction

If No →	Approaching	Reteach pp. T62-67
	ELL	Develop pp. T80-83
If Yes →	On Level	Review pp. T70-73
	Beyond Level	Extend pp. T76-77

→ # Shared Read

Reading/Writing Workshop Big Book and Reading/Writing Workshop

---

OBJECTIVES

CCSS Read common high-frequency words by sight. **RF.K.3c**

CCSS Read emergent-reader texts with purpose and understanding. **RF.K.4**

MINILESSON
10 Mins

Read "Hop Can Hop!"

Model Skills and Strategies

Model Concepts About Print Read the sentences on page 10. Ask a volunteer to point to a single word on the page. Then have the volunteer point to the spaces that separate the words. Next, point out the period at the end of the first sentence and the exclamation mark at the end of the second sentence. Remind children that a period and an exclamation point end a sentence. Then point to the pronoun *I* in the first sentence. *This sentence begins with the pronoun* I. *The pronoun* I *is always capitalized.* I *refers to the little girl, Dot. She is telling the story.*

Reread Have children chorally read the story. Children should sound out the decodable words and say the sight words. Offer support as needed using the student **Reading/Writing Workshop**.

Ask the following:

→ *Look at page 9. Who is Hop?* (Hop is a bunny.)

→ *Look at page 11. How did Hop solve a problem?* (Possible answer: Hop jumped on top of the potted plant to get cooler.)

→ *Look at page 14. What can both Dot and Hop do?* (They can both sit.)

Go Digital

"Hop Can Hop!"

"Hop Can Hop!"

READING/WRITING WORKSHOP, pp. 8–15

Fluency: Pace and Volume

1 Explain Tell children that as you read the story, you will be reading with confidence without stopping. You will only pause when you come to the end of a sentence or to emphasize a word or a phrase. Tell children that you will be keeping your voice loud enough so that it can be heard.

2 Model Model reading the story "Hop Can Hop!" Read the text accurately and fluently. Pause in appropriate spots and read in a loud, clear voice with expression and feeling.

3 Guided Practice Invite children to chorally read the story using a steady pace and appropriate volume.

→ Language Arts

Independent Writing

Write a Poem

Revise

Distribute the children's draft poems with drawings from Day 3.

Apply Writing Trait: Organization Explain that as writers revise, they make sure their writing is well organized. On individual index cards, write the words: *green; red; bushy.* Read each aloud. Guide children in taping the index cards in an order to form an organized poem. Write and read aloud this poem:

The Apple Tree
It is green.
It is red.
It is bushy.

Then have children reread the poems they wrote on Day 4 and check for the following:

→ Did I write about my favorite flower or tree?

→ Did I organize the poem in a way that makes sense?

→ Does my poem tell about the picture I drew?

Apply Grammar Review that pronouns can be used in place of nouns. *Where did you use pronouns in your poems?*

Peer Edit Have children work in pairs to do a peer edit, in which they read their partner's draft. Ask partners to check that their poems describe the pictures drawn. Have children check that the poem is organized. Provide time for children to make revisions to their poems.

Final Draft

After children have edited their own papers and finished their peer edits, have them write their final draft. Explain that they should try to write letters carefully and leave spaces between words so that readers can read their writing. Remind children that each sentence in their poems should be on a new line on the paper. As children work, conference with them to provide guidance.

OBJECTIVES

CCSS With guidance and support from adults, respond to questions and suggestions from peers and add details to strengthen writing as needed. **W.K.5**

CCSS Use personal, possessive, and indefinite pronouns (e.g., *I, me, my; they, them, their; anyone, everything*). **L.1.1d**

- Revise a poem
- Use pronouns in sentences

ACADEMIC LANGUAGE

- *revise, poem*
- Cognates: *revisar, poema*

Go Digital

Writing

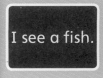

I see a fish.

Grammar

Grammar

MINILESSON
5 Mins

Pronouns

❶ **Review** Explain to children that different pronouns are used to replace different kinds of nouns. Write and read aloud these sentences: *Dad is funny. He tells jokes.* Ask: *Which word is a pronoun?* (He) *What noun does it replace?* (Dad)

❷ **Guided Practice** Display the following **Photo Cards**: *camel, cow, boy, farm, girl*. Read the label on each card aloud as you track the print.

Write the following pronouns on separate index cards: *it, it, it, he, she*. Read each word aloud.

Say: *We can match each noun in the picture with a pronoun that can replace it in a sentence.* Have children help you tape a pronoun index card next to each Photo Card. (camel–it; cow–it; boy–he; farm–it; girl–she)

❸ **Practice** Display the same Photo Cards again. Read the label on each card aloud as you track the print.

Write this sentence frame and read it aloud: _____ *is a girl.* Have children work with a partner to choose the correct pronoun to complete the sentence. (She) Have children work together to complete the sentence frame with the correct word.

Talk About It

Have partners work together to orally generate sentences with pronouns. Have them use pronouns to describe how they work with a partner to do a class activity.

ENGLISH LANGUAGE LEARNERS

Photo Cards and Sentences
Provide sentences that go with images on the Photo Cards, replacing nouns with pronouns. For example, hold up the Photo Card for *book* and say, *The book is on the table.* Then say, *It is on the table.* Repeat with the Photo Cards for *doctor* (she) and *cowboy* (he).

Daily Wrap Up

● Review the Essential Question and encourage children to discuss it, using the oral vocabulary words.

● Prompt children to discuss the skills they practiced and learned today. Guide them to share examples of each skill.

 Go Digital

www.connected.mcgraw-hill.com
RESOURCES
Research and Inquiry

→ **Wrap Up the Week**
Integrate Ideas

RESEARCH AND INQUIRY

How Does Your Garden Grow?

OBJECTIVES

 Participate in shared research and writing projects (e.g., explore a number of books by a favorite author and express opinions about them). **W.K.7**

 With guidance and support from adults, recall information from experiences or gather information from provided sources to answer a question. **W.K.8**

ACADEMIC LANGUAGE
research

Make a Poster

 Tell children that today they will do a research project with a partner to make a poster of what a plant needs to grow. Review the steps in the research process below.

STEP 1 Choose a Topic

Show children pictures of plants and point out their names. Guide partners to decide which one they want to research.

STEP 2 Find Resources

Talk about locating and using resources. Direct children to use this week's selections, books on plants, and web sites as resources. If possible plant seeds with children and have them observe and draw pictures of the seeds growing. Have children use the Research Process Checklist online.

STEP 3 Keep Track of Ideas

Have children list their plant ideas by cutting photographs from magazines, drawing pictures, and writing words. Children should also note at least one thing that the plant needs to grow.

Collaborative Conversations

Ask and Answer Questions As children engage in partner, small-group, and whole-class discussions, encourage them to:

→ ask questions to clarify ideas they do not understand.

→ ask for help in getting information.

→ give others a chance to think before they respond.

→ answer questions with complete ideas, not one-word answers.

STEM

This is a cactus. It needs sun.

STEP 4 **Create the Project: Plant Poster**

Explain the characteristics of the poster:

→ **Information** A poster can give information. This poster will give information about a plant and what it needs to grow.

→ **Text** Explain that each poster will have sentences that tell what the plant is and what it needs to grow. Provide these sentence frames:

This is a _____. It needs _____.

→ **Illustration** The drawing of the plant will show what it needs.

Explain that each pair will create a poster with a picture of the plant and what it needs. They will also write sentences about the plant.

→ Encourage children who can generate more writing to do so.

→ Prompt children to include details in their illustrations that reflect their investigations into what their plant needs to grow.

ELL ENGLISH LANGUAGE LEARNERS SCAFFOLD

Beginning	Intermediate	Advanced/Advanced High
Use Sentence Frames Pair children with more fluent speakers. Provide sentence frames to help children describe their plant and what it needs to grow. For example: *Our picture shows a ____. It needs ____ to grow.* Have partners practice these presentation sentences before they share their work with other students.	**Elicit Details** Direct partners to talk about the parts of the plant they are showing in their picture. When they share their work with the class, prompt them to point to and identify the stem, leaves, buds, flowers, and so on.	**Demonstrate Understanding** Prompt children to think about what happens if a plant does not get what it needs to grow. When partners present their work, have them answer this question: *What happens if the plant doesn't get enough [light/water/air]?*

Materials

Reading/Writing Workshop Big Book
UNIT 5

Literature Big Book
My Garden

Interactive Read-Aloud Cards

Word-Building Cards

Photo Cards
hippo
hook
kitten

Response Board

"A Hippo in the House"

High-Frequency Word Cards
can
go
I
my
to
you

Visual Vocabulary Cards
my

→ Integrate Ideas

TEXT CONNECTIONS

Connect to Essential Question

OBJECTIVES

CCSS Recognize common types of texts (e.g., storybooks, poems). **RL.K.5**

CCSS Participate in collaborative conversations with diverse partners about *kindergarten topics and texts* with peers and adults in small and larger groups. **SL.K.1**

- Make connections among texts
- Make connections to the world

Text to Text

Remind children that all week they have been reading different kinds of selections about how plants grow. *What is a fiction story that we read? What is one poem that we read?* Tell them that now they will connect the texts, or think about how the selections are alike. Model comparing *My Garden* with another selection from the week.

Think Aloud In *My Garden,* the little girl helps her mother tend the garden. They grow a lot of different flowers and crops. In the poem "Garden," I learn that the speaker's mother likes to plant carnations. In both poems, the mothers enjoy gardening and do a lot of work to take care of the plants.

Have children compare *My Garden* and the poem "May Time Magic." Guide them to focus on what the characters do to care for the plants in their gardens. Have children compare other selections from the week.

Text to Self

Have children tell about a time when they cared for a plant or helped someone work in a garden. Guide children to focus on the growth of the plants or on specific things they did to care for the plants.

Text to World

Talk about parks or other areas in the community where there are growing things. *Why are parks important? Why is it important to take care of the plants that grow there?*

TALK ABOUT READING

OBJECTIVES

 Confirm understanding of a text read aloud or information presented orally or through other media by asking and answering questions about key details and requesting clarification if something is not understood. **SL.K.2**

Becoming Readers

Talk with children about the genres, strategy, and skill they have learned about this week. Prompt them to discuss how this knowledge helps them to read and understand selections.

→ Remind children that one genre they learned about is fiction. Recall with them some of the characteristics of fiction.

→ Discuss with children the strategy of rereading. *How did rereading a page help you to understand the way plants grew in the different stories and selections from this week?*

→ Talk about how children learned to use the words and illustrations to learn information about character, setting, and events. *What did you learn about the character in* My Garden *by looking at the illustrations? What did you learn about the setting? What did you learn about events?*

RESEARCH AND INQUIRY

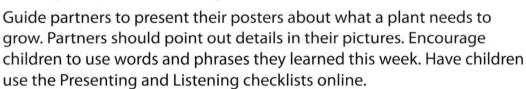
How Does Your Garden Grow?

OBJECTIVES

 Participate in shared research and writing projects (e.g. explore a number of books by a favorite author and express opinions about them). **W.K.7**

Wrap Up the Project

Guide partners to present their posters about what a plant needs to grow. Partners should point out details in their pictures. Encourage children to use words and phrases they learned this week. Have children use the Presenting and Listening checklists online.

→ # Word Work

Quick Review
Build Fluency: Sound-Spellings: Show the following **Word-Building Cards:** *a, c, d, h, i, m, n, o, p, s, t*. Have children chorally say the sounds. Repeat and vary the pace.

MINILESSON
5 Mins

Phonemic Awareness

Phoneme Categorization

❶ Model Display the **Photo Cards** for *hook, hippo,* and *kitten. Listen for which picture names begin with the same sound.* Say the picture names. Hook *and* hippo *both begin with /h/.* Kitten *does not begin with /h/.* Kitten *does not belong.*

❷ Guided Practice/Practice Show children sets of Photo Cards. Name the pictures with children and have them identify the picture in each set that does not begin with the same sound.

inch, house, hat	horse, insect, hay	dog, hay, helicopter
hand, house, jump	egg, hair, hat	hook, cowboy, comb

OBJECTIVES

CCSS Demonstrate basic knowledge of one-to-one letter-sound correspondences by producing the primary sound for each consonant. **RF.K.3a**

CCSS Spell simple words phonetically, drawing on knowledge of sound-letter relationships. **L.K.2d**

CCSS Read common high-frequency words by sight. **RF.K.3c**

Categorize words by initial phonemes

MINILESSON
5 Mins

Phonics

Read Words with Short *i, o, a* and *h*

❶ Guided Practice Remind children that the letter *h* can stand for the sound /h/. Display **Word-Building Cards** *a, t.* Point to the letter *a. The letter* a *stands for the sound /a/. Say /aaa/. The letter* t *stands for /t/. Say /t/. Let's blend the sounds to make the word: /aaat/* at. *Now let's add* h *to the beginning.* Blend and read *hat* with children.

❷ Practice Write these words and sentences for children to read:

hop   hit   hot   ham

I like ham.   Pam can hop.
Pam and Pat like the hat.   Tim can hit.

Remove words from view before dictation.

♪ Review initial /h/*h*. Have children write the letter *h* on their **Response Boards**. Play and sing "A Hippo in the House." Have children hold up and show the letter *h* on their boards when they hear initial /h/. Demonstrate as you sing with children.

Go Digital

Phonemic Awareness

Phonics

Handwriting

High-Frequency Word Cards

Dictation

Review Dictate the following sounds for children to spell. As you say each sound, have children repeat it and then write the letter on their **Response Boards** that stands for the sound.

/h/   /i/   /n/   /k/   /o/   /d/

Dictate the following words for children to spell. Model for children how to segment words to scaffold the spelling. *I will say a word. You will repeat the word, then think about how many sounds are in the word. Use your sound boxes to count the sounds. Then write one letter for each sound you hear.*

hip   nip   hat   hop   pin   hot   hit   ham

Then write the letters and word for children to self-correct.

High-Frequency Words

MINILESSON
5 Mins

my

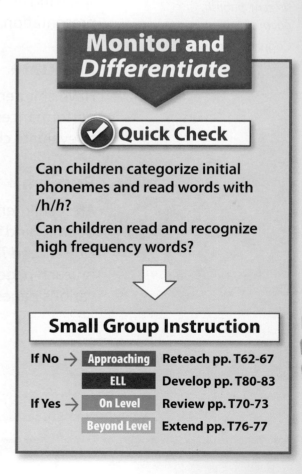
Visual Vocabulary Card

Review Display **Visual Vocabulary Card** *my*. Have children **Read/Spell/Write** the word. Then choose a Partner Talk activity.

Distribute the following **High-Frequency Word Cards** to children: *I, can, go, to, my, you.* Tell children that you will say some sentences. *When you hear the word that is on your card, stand and hold up the word card.*

I can go to my house.
Sam *can* ride *my* horse.
My garden is beautiful.
Nat will *go* in *my* car.
Would *you* like *to* share *my* lunch?
I like *to go* fishing in *my* boat.

Build Fluency: Word Automaticity Display High-Frequency Word Cards *to, and, go, you, do, my.* Point to each card, at random, and have children read the word as quickly as they can.

Monitor and *Differentiate*

✓ Quick Check

Can children categorize initial phonemes and read words with /h/*h*?

Can children read and recognize high frequency words?

⬇

Small Group Instruction

If No →	**Approaching**	Reteach pp. T62-67
	ELL	Develop pp. T80-83
If Yes →	**On Level**	Review pp. T70-73
	Beyond Level	Extend pp. T76-77

→ Language Arts

 Independent Writing
10 Mins

Write a Poem

Prepare

Tell children that they will present their finished poems and drawings from Day 3 to the class. Hold up an example from Day 3 and read it aloud, tracking the print. Use words to describe the drawing clearly. Say: *I read my poem clearly so that everyone could understand what I was saying. I talked about my drawing clearly so that everyone could understand what I was saying.*

Present

Have children take turns standing up and reading their poems aloud and talking about their drawings. Remind children to speak clearly. Encourage the rest of the class to listen carefully to the person speaking and to speak clearly when asking questions about the presentation.

Evaluate

Have children discuss their own presentations and evaluate their performances, using the presentation rubric. Use the teacher's rubric to evaluate children's writing.

Publish

After children have finished presenting, collect the drawings and poems. Bind the pages together into a class book with the title *Our Flowers and Trees.* Read the class book aloud, tracking the words on each page with a finger. Ask children to point out pronouns on various pages.

Go Digital

Writing

I see a fish.

Grammar

Grammar

Pronouns

1 Review Write and read aloud this sentence: *Mandy went skating. Which word is a noun?* (Mandy) *What pronoun can be used to replace the noun?* (She) Rewrite the sentence with the correct pronoun and read it aloud.

2 Review Practice Write these sentences:

The car is fast.
Joe likes to drive.
Sandy likes to drive.

Read each sentence aloud as you track the print. Write these sentence frames on the board:

_____ *is fast.*
_____ *likes to drive.*
_____ *likes to drive.*

Have children work with a partner to choose the correct pronoun to replace the noun in each sentence. (it, he, she) Then have partners copy the sentence frames and complete each, using the correct pronoun. (It is fast. He likes to drive. She likes to drive.) Help children complete the sentences as needed.

Have children circle the pronouns in their sentences. Gather the sentences and store them in a folder for a center or review activity.

Wrap Up the Week

- Review blending words with initial /h/h. Remind children that a pronoun is a word that can take the place of a noun in a sentence.

- Use the **High-Frequency Word Cards** to review the Words to Know.

- Remind children that when they write, they should organize their ideas in a way that makes sense.

→ Approaching Level

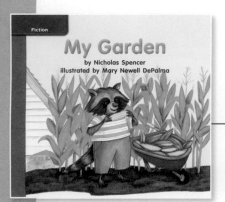

Leveled Reader

OBJECTIVES

CCSS With prompting and support, ask and answer questions about key details in a text. **RL.K.1**

CCSS With prompting and support, identify characters, settings, and major events in a story. **RL.K.3**

CCSS Demonstrate understanding of the organization and basic features of print. **RF.K.1**

CCSS Read emergent-reader texts with purpose and understanding. **RF.K.4**

Leveled Reader:
My Garden

Leveled Reader

Before Reading

Preview and Predict

Read aloud the title and the names of the author and the illustrator. Turn to the title page and read it aloud. Ask children what is happening in the picture. Preview the rest of the illustrations and identify the rebus pictures. Ask: *Who is this story about? Where does this story take place? What do you think will happen?*

Review Genre: Fantasy

Remind children that fantasy is a kind of fiction. Fantasy stories have made-up characters and events. Explain that what happens in a fantasy story could never happen in real life. Ask: *What tells you that this is a fantasy story?* (Raccoon acts like a person.)

Model Concepts of Print

Demonstrate concepts of print. Open the book to page 3 and point to the spaces between words. Say: *In a sentence there is a space between each word. At the end of the sentence is a period.*

Review High-Frequency Words

Point out the word *my* on page 2, and read it with children. Have them find the word *my* on pages 3, 4 and 5.

Essential Question

Set a purpose for reading: *What things does a plant need to grow? Let's read the book to find out how Raccoon helps his plants grow.*

During Reading

Guided Comprehension

As children read *My Garden,* monitor and provide guidance by correcting blending and modeling the strategy and skill.

Strategy: Reread

Remind children that if they come to a part of a story that is confusing, they can reread the text to make sure they understand it.

Skill: Character, Setting, Events

Tell children that they can learn a lot about the characters, the setting, and the events in a story by looking at the pictures. After reading, ask: *Who is this story about? Where does this story take place?*

Think Aloud The words on page 4 tell me that Raccoon likes his gloves. I can see in the picture that his wheelbarrow is full of other things he uses in his garden. I can see a garden tool—a hoe—and a hose. And I can see his garden in the background, too.

Guide children to identify the character and the setting in the illustrations on the rest of the pages. Ask them to tell what is happening on pages 6 and 7.

After Reading

Respond to Reading

→ *Where does the story take place?* (garden) *How can you tell?* (Raccoon's garden is shown in the illustrations.)

→ *Whose garden is this? How do you know?* (illustrations show Raccoon)

→ *What happens at the end of the story?* (Raccoon has grown corn.)

→ *In this story, what do plants need to grow?* (seeds, water, sun)

Retell

Have children take turns retelling the story by acting it out. Help them make a personal connection. Ask: *What would you grow in a garden?*

Model Fluency

Reread the story aloud, pausing after each page to have children chorally repeat.

Apply Have children practice reading with partners.

LITERACY ACTIVITIES

Have children complete the activities on the inside back cover of the reader.

Level Up

Level-up lessons available online.

IF Children read *My Garden* **Approaching Level** with fluency and correctly answer the Respond to Reading questions,

THEN Tell children that they will read another story about a garden.

• Have children page through *My Garden Grows* **On Level** as you introduce the story and characters. Preview the illustration on page 7.

• Have children read the story, monitoring their comprehension and providing assistance as necessary.

Approaching Level

Phonological Awareness

COUNT AND BLEND SYLLABLES

OBJECTIVES

CCSS Count, pronounce, blend, and segment syllables in spoken words. **RF.K.2b**

 I Do *Let's count the parts of the word,* contrary. *Listen: /kon/ /tre/ /rē/. The word* contrary *has three parts.* Clap each syllable as you say the word. Then blend the syllables to say the word: /kon/ /tre/ /rē/, contrary.

 We Do *Listen to this word:* pretty. *Clap with me as we say the parts together:* /prit/ /ē/. *Say the word parts, then say the word with me:* /prit/ /ē/, pretty. Repeat with *Mary. How many word parts do you hear?*

 You Do Say *pretty* and *garden.* Have children say the words, clapping on each syllable. *How many word parts do you hear?* Then have children blend the syllables to say the words.

Phonemic Awareness

PHONEME ISOLATION

OBJECTIVES

 CCSS Isolate and pronounce the initial, medial vowel, and final sounds (phonemes) in three-phoneme words. **RF.K.2d**

 I Do Display the *Hat* **Photo Card**. *This is a* hat. *The first sound in* hat *is /h/.* Have children repeat the word with you, emphasizing the initial sound. Then have children say the first sound with you: /h/.

 We Do Display the *Hand* Photo Card. Name the photo and have children say the name. *What is the first sound in* hand? (/h/) Say the sound together. Repeat with the *Horse* Photo Card.

 You Do Show the *House* Photo Card. Have children name it and say the initial sound of the picture name. Repeat with the *Hippo* and *Hook* Photo Cards.

You may wish to review Phonological Awareness and Phonemic Awareness with **ELL** using this section.

PHONEME BLENDING

OBJECTIVES

Isolate and pronounce the initial, medial vowel, and final sounds (phonemes) in three-phoneme words. **RF.K.2d**

 The puppet is going to say the sounds in a word: /h/ /ō/ /m/. *The puppet can blend these sounds together:* /hōōōmmm/, home. *Repeat with* hit.

 Now the puppet is going to say the sounds in another word. Say the sounds with the puppet: /h/ /o/ /t/. *Let's blend the sounds together:* /hooot/, hot. *Repeat with* hip *and* ham.

 Have children blend sounds to form words. Practice together: /h/ /o/ /p/, /hooop/, hop. Then have children blend the following sounds to say the words: /h/ /a/ /d/ had; /h/ /o/ /g/ hog; /h/ /i/ /l/ hill; /h/ /e/ /m/ hem

PHONEME CATEGORIZATION

OBJECTIVES

Isolate and pronounce the initial, medial vowel, and final sounds (phonemes) in three-phoneme words. **RF.K.2d**

 Display the *Hammer, Hippo,* and *Dinosaur* **Photo Cards**. Say each picture name, emphasizing the initial sound. Hammer *and* hippo *begin with* /h/. Dinosaur *does not begin with* /h/. Dinosaur *does not belong.*

We Do Display the *Corn, Hand,* and *Cow* Photo Cards. Have children name each picture with you, emphasizing the initial sound. *Which word does not have the same beginning sound?* Repeat the routine with the *Rake, Horse,* and *Rock* Photo Cards.

You Do Display and name the *Mouse, Moon,* and *House* Photo Cards. Have children name each picture and tell which picture does not have the same initial sound. Repeat the routine with these sets of Photo Cards: *Helicopter, Hat, Net; Pizza, Pumpkin, House.*

ELL ENGLISH LANGUAGE LEARNERS

For the **ELLs** who need **phonics, decoding,** and **fluency** practice, use scaffolding methods as necessary to ensure children understand the meaning of the words. Refer to the Language Transfer Handbook for phonics elements that may not transfer in children's native languages.

→ Approaching Level

Phonics

SOUND-SPELLING REVIEW

TIER 2

OBJECTIVES

CCSS Demonstrate basic knowledge of one-to-one letter-sound correspondences by producing the primary sound for each consonant. **RF.K.3a**

 I Do Display **Word-Building Card** *n*. Say the letter name and the sound it stands for: *n*, /n/. Repeat for *c, o, d,* and *i*.

 We Do Display Word-Building Cards one at a time and together say the letter name and the sound that each letter stands for.

You Do Display Word-Building Cards one at a time and have children say the letter name and the sound that each letter stands for.

CONNECT *h* TO /h/

TIER 2

OBJECTIVES

CCSS Demonstrate basic knowledge of one-to-one letter-sound correspondences by producing the primary or many of the most frequent sounds for each consonant. **RF.K.3a**

 I Do Display *Hippo* **Sound-Spelling Card**. *The letter* h *stands for* /h/, *the sound at the beginning of* hippo. *What is this letter? What sound does it stand for? I will write* h *when I hear* /h/ *in these words.* Say: *happy, cow, heart, heat, open.*

 We Do *The word* head *begins with* /h/. *Let's write* h. Guide children to write *h* when they hear a word that begins with /h/. Say: *hope, sink, candle, horse, hide.*

 You Do Say the following words and have children write the letter *h* if the word begins with /h/: *ink, high, core, happy, deep, hello, hop.*

RETEACH

OBJECTIVES

CCSS Know and apply grade-level phonics and word analysis skills in decoding words. **RF.K.3**

 I Do Display **Reading/Writing Workshop**, p. 6. *The letter* h *stands for the* /h/ *sound you hear at the beginning of* hippo. Say *hippo,* emphasizing the /h/.

 We Do Have children name each picture in row 1. Repeat the names, emphasizing /h/. Repeat for row 2.

 You Do Guide children in reading the words in row 3. Then have them read the words in row 4, offering assistance as needed.

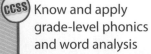

BLEND WORDS WITH /h/h

OBJECTIVES

Isolate and pronounce the initial, medial vowel, and final sounds (phonemes) in three-phoneme words. **RF.K.2d**

 Display **Word-Building Cards** *h, a,* and *t. This is the letter* h. *It stands for* /h/. *This is the letter* a. *It stands for* /a/. *This is the letter* t. *It stands for* /t/. *Listen as I blend all three sounds:* /haaat/, hat. *The word is* hat. Repeat for *has.*

 Now let's blend more sounds to make words. Display the word *ham. Let's blend:* /haaammm/, ham. Have children blend to read the word. Repeat with the word *him. Let's blend:* /hiiimmm/, him.

 Distribute Word-Building Cards with *h, a, i, t,* and *m.* Write: *hit, hat, ham, him.* Have children form the words and then blend and read the words.

REREAD FOR FLUENCY

OBJECTIVES

Read emergent-reader texts with purpose and understanding. **RF.K.4**

 Turn to p. 8 of **Reading/Writing Workshop** and read aloud the title. *Let's read the title together.* Page through the book. Ask children what they see in each picture. Ask children to find the word *my* on p. 10.

 Then have children open their books and chorally read the story. Have children point to each word as they read. Provide corrective feedback as needed. After reading, ask children to recall what kind of animal the characters meet in the story.

 Have children reread "Hop Can Hop!" with a partner for fluency.

BUILD FLUENCY WITH PHONICS

Sound/Spelling Fluency

Display the following Word-Building Cards: *i, n, c, o, d,* and *h.* Have children chorally say each sound. Repeat and vary the pace.

Fluency in Connected Text

Write the following sentences. *You and I like to hop! Do you see him in the hat?* Have children read the sentences and identify the words with /h/h.

Approaching Level

High-Frequency Words

RETEACH WORDS

 OBJECTIVES
Read common high-frequency words by sight. **RF.K.3c**

I Do Display **High-Frequency Word Card** *my* and use the **Read/Spell/Write** routine to reteach the word.

We Do Have children turn to p. 7 of **Reading/Writing Workshop** and discuss the first photo. Then read aloud the first sentence. Reread the sentence with children. Then distribute index cards with the word *my* written on them. Have children match their word cards with the word *my* in the sentence. Use the same routine for the other sentence on the page.

You Do Write the sentence frame *I can see my* _____ . Have children copy the sentence frame on their **Response Boards**. Then have partners work together to read and orally complete the frame by talking about what they can see in or on their desk.

CUMULATIVE REVIEW

 OBJECTIVES
Read common high-frequency words by sight. **RF.K.3c**

I Do Display the **High-Frequency Word Cards** *I, can, the, we, see, a, like, to, and, go, you, do,* and *my.* Use the **Read/Spell/Write** routine to review words. Use the High-Frequency Word Cards and **Word-Building Cards** to create sentences, such as *I can go to see him. Do you like to go?*

We Do Use the High-Frequency Word Cards and Word-Building Cards to create sentences, such as *I can go to the house. You and I like my cats.* Have children identify the high-frequency words that are used in each sentence.

You Do Have partners use the High-Frequency Word Cards and Word-Building Cards to create short sentences.

Oral Vocabulary

REVIEW WORDS

OBJECTIVES

Identify real-life connections between words and their use. **L.K.5c**

Develop oral vocabulary: *plant, require, harmful, soak, crowd*

 Use the **Define/Example/Ask** routine to review words. Use the following definitions and provide examples:

plant   A **plant** has roots, stems, and leaves and grows in the ground.

require   If you **require** something, you need it.

harmful   Something **harmful** can hurt you.

soak   To **soak** up something is to take it in.

crowd   When you **crowd** something, you push it into a small space.

 Ask questions to build understanding. *What kind of plant could we grow in our classroom? What do you require to draw a picture? What is something that is harmful to us? What can you use to soak up water? Why might it be hard to crowd a lot of toys into a shoe box?*

You Do Have children complete these sentence frames: *One thing a plant needs to grow is _____. Children require a coat and mittens when _____. Running down the stairs can be harmful because _____. The dirty clothes soak in water before _____. People sometimes have to crowd into _____.*

Comprehension

SELF-SELECTED READING

OBJECTIVES

With prompting and support, ask and answer questions about key details in a text. **RL.K.1**

Apply the strategy and skill to reread the text.

Read Independently

Help children select an illustrated story for sustained silent reading. Remind them that they can use the pictures to help them understand what is happening with the place and the characters in a story. Encourage children to reread the text if something doesn't make sense in the story.

Read Purposefully

Before reading, help children choose an illustration of a character or a place they would like to find out more about. Remind them to use the picture and to reread if they do not understand something. After reading, guide children to explain how the illustration they identified earlier helped them understand. *How did rereading help you better understand the story?*

→ On Level

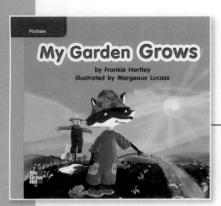

Leveled Reader

OBJECTIVES

(CCSS) With prompting and support, ask and answer questions about key details in a text. **RL.K.1**

(CCSS) With prompting and support, identify characters, settings, and major events in a story. **RL.K.3**

(CCSS) With prompting and support, describe the relationship between illustrations and the story in which they appear (e.g., what moment in a story an illustration depicts). **RL.K.7**

(CCSS) Read emergent-reader texts with purpose and understanding. **RF.K.4**

Leveled Reader:
My Garden Grows

Before Reading

Preview and Predict

Read the title and the names of the author and illustrator. Ask children to identify the animal on the cover. Preview the illustrations and identify the rebus pictures. Explain that the fox is the main character in the story. Ask: *What is the fox doing?* (working in her garden) *What do you think this book is about?*

Leveled Reader

Review Genre: Fantasy

Remind children that fantasy is a kind of fiction. Fantasy stories are made-up about characters and events that are not real, and could never happen in real life. Ask: *How do you know this story is fantasy?* (Foxes don't wear clothes in real life.) Have children point to evidence in the pictures to support their answers.

Model Concepts of Print

Have children open their books to page 2 and point to the sentence. Say: *I read each sentence from left to right. The sentence begins with a capital letter and ends with a period.*

Review High-Frequency Words

Point out the word *my* on page 2, and read it with children. Have them look through the book and find the word *my* on pages 6 and 7.

Essential Question

Set a purpose for reading: *What things does a plant need to grow? Let's read the book to find out how Fox fixes problems so her plants can grow.*

During Reading

Guided Comprehension

As children whisper-read, monitor and provide guidance by correcting blending and modeling the strategy and skill.

Strategy: Reread

Remind children that if they are confused about what is happening in the story, they can reread the text to better understand it.

Skill: Character, Setting, Events

Help children understand that they can learn about the character, setting, and events by reading the words and looking at the pictures.

Think Aloud On page 6, the words and pictures tell me about a problem Fox has. I read that the garden has rabbits. The picture shows me that they are eating the lettuce in the garden. On page 7, I see that Fox has built a fence to keep the rabbits out. The pictures give me details about the events in the story.

Guide children to use the words and pictures on pages 3, 4, and 5 to find details about Fox and what happens in her garden. Have children point to evidence in the text or pictures to support their statements.

After Reading

Respond to Reading

→ *What do the birds do to Fox's garden?* (They eat the seeds.)

→ *How does Fox solve this problem?* (She puts up a scarecrow.)

→ *What does Fox grow in her garden?* (berries) *How do you know?* (from the words and pictures)

Retell

Have children make a paper bag puppet of Fox to help them retell the story. Help them make personal connections. Ask: *Do you think Fox did a good job solving problems in her garden? Tell why or why not.*

Model Fluency

Read the book aloud with expression. Point out that using expression while reading can increase enjoyment and add meaning to the story.

Apply Have children take turns reading a page at a time with expression. Then read the entire book aloud together.

LITERACY ACTIVITIES

Have children complete the activities on the inside back cover of the reader.

Level Up

IF Children read *My Garden Grows* On Level with fluency and correctly answer the Respond to Reading questions,

THEN Tell children that they will read another story about someone who has a garden.

- Have children page through *The Mystery Seeds* Beyond Level. Point out the dialogue in the story, and remind children that words characters say to each other are in quotation marks.

- Have children read the story, monitoring their comprehension and providing assistance as necessary.

On Level

Phonemic Awareness

PHONEME ISOLATION

OBJECTIVES
Isolate and pronounce the initial, medial vowel, and final sounds (phonemes) in three-phoneme words. **RF.K.2d**

I Do Display the *Hair* **Photo Card**. *This is* hair. *The first sound is* /h/. *Say it with me. Say* hope. *The first sound in* hope *is* /h/. *Say the sound with me.*

We Do Say *hike* and have children repeat it. *What is the first sound in* hike? Say the sound together. Repeat with *hat, net,* and *can*.

You Do Say *had, mud, pin, hip,* and *new* and have children tell the initial sound.

PHONEME BLENDING

OBJECTIVES
Isolate and pronounce the initial, medial vowel, and final sounds (phonemes) in three-phoneme words. **RF.K.2d**

I Do Place the *Hair, Hand, Hat, Hay,* and *Hook* **Photo Cards** facedown. Choose a card. Do not show the card. *The sounds in the word are:* /h/ /a/ /t/. *I'll blend the sounds:* /haaat/, hat. *The word is* hat. Show the picture.

We Do Choose another picture and say the sounds in the word. Together say and blend the sounds to say the word. Then show the picture.

You Do Continue choosing Photo Cards. Say the sounds and have children blend the sounds and say the words.

PHONEME CATEGORIZATION

OBJECTIVES
Isolate and pronounce the initial, medial vowel, and final sounds (phonemes) in three-phoneme words. **RF.K.2d**

I Do Display the *Hook, House,* and *Sock* **Photo Cards**. Say each picture name. Hook *and* house *begin with* /h/. Sock *does not.* Sock *does not belong.*

We Do Display the *Pea, Pig,* and *Hand* Photo Cards. Have children name each picture with you. *Which word does not have the same beginning sound?*

You Do Display and name the *Hat, Moon,* and *Hair* Photo Cards. Have children name each picture and tell which picture does not have the same initial sound. Repeat with *table, hair, tie; dog, fish, dolphin*.

Phonics

REVIEW PHONICS

OBJECTIVES

Demonstrate basic knowledge of one-to-one letter-sound correspondences by producing the primary or many of the most frequent sounds for each consonant. **RF.K.3a**

I Do

Display **Reading/Writing Workshop**, p. 6. Point to the *Hippo* **Sound-Spelling Card**. *What letter stands for the* /h/ *sound you hear at the beginning of* hippo? *The letter is* h.

We Do

Have children say the name of each picture in rows 1 and 2. Then ask them to identify the initial sound and which letter stands for that sound. (/h/, *h*)

You Do

Have children read each word in rows 3 and 4. Repeat, asking them to tug their ears if they hear /h/ at the beginning of the word.

PICTURE SORT WITH /h/*h*, /p/*p*

OBJECTIVES

Isolate and pronounce the initial, medial vowel, and final sounds (phonemes) in three-phoneme words. **RF.K.2d**

I Do

Display **Word-Building Cards** *h* and *p* in a pocket chart. Then show the *House* **Photo Card**. Say *house*. Tell children that the sound at the beginning is /h/. *The letter* h *stands for* /h/. *I will put the house under the letter* h. Show the *Pie* Photo Card. Say *pie*. Tell children that the sound at the beginning is /p/. *The letter* p *stands for* /p/. *I will put the* Pie *Photo Card under the letter* p.

We Do

Show the *Hook* Photo Card and say *hook*. Have children repeat. Then have them tell the sound they hear at the beginning of *hook*. Ask them if they should place the photo under the *h* or the *p*.

You Do

Continue the activity using the *Hammer, Helicopter, Hippo, House, Hat, Horse, Paint, Penguin, Penny, Piano,* and *Pitcher* Photo Cards. Have children say the picture name and the initial sound. Then have them place the card under the letter *h* or *p*.

On Level

Phonics

BLEND WORDS WITH /h/h

OBJECTIVES

 Isolate and pronounce the initial, medial vowel, and final sounds (phonemes) in three-phoneme words. **RF.K.2d**

 I Do Use **Word-Building Cards** or write *h, o, p*. *This is the letter* h. *It stands for* /h/. *Say it with me:* /h/. *This is the letter* o. *It stands for* /o/. *Say it with me:* /ooo/. *This is the letter* p. *It stands for* /p/. *Say it with me:* /p/. *I'll blend the sounds together to read the word*: /hooop/, hop.

 We Do Use the words *hen* and *him*. Guide children to blend the words sound by sound to read each word.

 You Do Use the following words and have children blend the words sound by sound to read each word.

hip   hat   hem   hot   hid

REREAD FOR FLUENCY

OBJECTIVES

 Read emergent-reader texts with purpose and understanding. **RF.K.4**

 I Do Point to the title "Hop Can Hop!" on p. 8 of **Reading/Writing Workshop** and tell children that when they see an exclamation point, like the one in the title, they should make their voices sound excited. Work with children to read for accuracy and expression. Model reading page 10: *When I read, "See my hat on top!" I read all the way to the end of the sentence before pausing. This makes my reading sound natural, as if I were talking.*

 We Do Reread p. 10. Then have children chorally read the page with you. Continue choral reading the remainder of the pages.

You Do Have children read "Hop Can Hop!" Provide time to listen as children read the pages. Comment on their accuracy and expression and provide corrective feedback by modeling proper fluency.

High-Frequency Words

REVIEW WORDS

OBJECTIVES

Read common high-frequency words by sight. **RF.K.3c**

I Do Use the **High-Frequency Word Card** *my* with the **Read/Spell/Write** routine to review the word.

We Do Have children turn to p. 7 of **Reading/Writing Workshop**. Discuss the photographs and read aloud the sentences. Point to the word *my* and have children read it. Then chorally read the sentences. Have children frame the word *my* in the sentences and read the word.

You Do Say the word *my*. Ask children to close their eyes, picture the word, and write it as they see it. Have children self-correct.

Reteach previously introduced high-frequency words using the **Read/Spell/Write** routine.

Fluency Point to the High-Frequency Word Cards *I, can, the, we, see, a, like, to, and, go, you, do,* and *my* in random order. Have children chorally read. Repeat at a faster pace.

Comprehension

SELF-SELECTED READING

OBJECTIVES

With prompting and support, ask and answer questions about key details in a text. **RL.K.1**

Apply the strategy and skill to reread the text.

Read Independently

Have children select an illustrated story for sustained silent reading. Remind them that illustrations can help them understand details about character, setting, and events as they read. Explain that when they don't understand a story detail, they should read again to help them better understand.

Read Purposefully

Before reading, ask children to choose an illustration of a character or setting they think looks interesting. Tell them that as they read, they should find out more about the character or setting they have chosen. Ask them to focus on ways the illustration can help them better understand the story. Remind them to reread when something is unclear. After reading, ask children to explain how rereading helped them better understand parts of the story.

Beyond Level

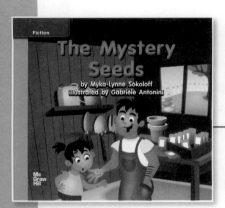

Leveled Reader

OBJECTIVES

With prompting and support, retell familiar stories, including key details. **RL.K.2**

With prompting and support, identify characters, settings, and major events in a story. **RL.K.3**

With prompting and support, name the author and illustrator of a story and define the role of each in telling the story. **RL.K.6**

With prompting and support, describe the relationship between illustrations and the story in which they appear (e.g., what moment in a story an illustration depicts). **RL.K.7**

Leveled Reader:
The Mystery Seeds

Before Reading

Preview and Predict

Ask children to point to the title on their books while you read it aloud. Read the author and illustrator's names aloud. Ask children to explain what the author does and what the illustrator does. Have children describe the picture on the front cover. Ask: *What do you think this story will be about? What do you think the "mystery seeds" are?* Have children page through the book and look at the illustrations. Ask: *Do you have any more ideas about what this story is about?*

Review Genre: Fiction

Remind children that a fiction story has made-up characters and events. Say: *The events in this story, about a girl growing a garden, could happen in real life. So why is it fiction?* (The girl is not a real girl, but a character the author made up.)

Essential Question

Ask: *What do plants need to grow?* Have children set a purpose for reading by asking: *How does this girl take care of her garden to help her plants grow?*

During Reading

Guided Comprehension

As children whisper-read *The Mystery Seeds,* monitor and provide guidance by correcting blending and modeling the strategy and skill. Remind them that the dialogue, or the words the characters say, is placed in quotation marks.

Strategy: Reread

Remind children that they can reread text to help them better understand the story.

Go
Digital

Leveled Reader

Skill: Character, Setting, Events

Review with children that fiction stories have characters, events, and settings. Point out that this story mostly takes place in Uncle Hank's garden.

Think Aloud After reading page 2, I learned that the two characters are the girl and her Uncle Hank. On page 3, I see that the girl and her uncle are in his shed. I see lots of tools for gardening. The girl's uncle is giving her some seeds. I'll keep reading and looking at the pictures to find out what happens next.

Guide children to read the rest of the story. Have them use the text and the details in the illustrations to explain what is happening on each page.

After Reading

Respond to Reading

→ *Who are the main characters in this story?* (Uncle Hank and the little girl) *What is the setting?* (Uncle Hank's garden)

→ *What happens after the girl tells her uncle she wants a garden?* (He gives her some seeds.)

→ *What does the girl do to help her seeds grow?* (plants them, waters them, picks weeds)

→ *How can you tell the girl enjoys working in the garden?* (Possible answer: She looks happy in the pictures.)

Retell

Have partners take turns retelling the story to another set of partners. To retell, have children take turns playing the parts of Uncle Hank and the little girl.

Gifted and Talented

EVALUATING Have children recall how the little girl and Uncle Hank helped their gardens grow. Challenge children to talk about what plants need to grow big and strong.

HAVE children draw a picture of their favorite fruit or vegetable. Ask them to write on the stem, the leaves, the fruit, and/or the vegetable all the things a plant needs to grow. For example, sun, water, and room to grow.

LITERACY ACTIVITIES

Have children complete the activities on the inside back cover of the reader.

→ Beyond Level

Phonics

OBJECTIVES

CCSS Know and apply grade-level phonics and word analysis skills in decoding words. **RF.K.3**

 I Do Display **Reading/Writing Workshop**, p. 6. Point to the *Hippo* **Sound-Spelling Card**. *What is the sound at the beginning of* hippo? *What letter can stand for* /h/? *The letter is* h.

 We Do Have children say the name of each picture in rows 1 and 2. Then ask children to share other words they know that begin with /h/.

 You Do Have partners read each word in rows 3 and 4. Ask them to write the words on their **Response Boards**, and underline the letter in each word that stands for /h/.

Fluency Have children reread the story "Hop Can Hop!" for fluency.

Innovate Have children create a new page for "Hop Can Hop!" using the sentence frame *Dot can see a* _____. Have children suggest other things that Dot sees near the garden.

High-Frequency Words

OBJECTIVES

 CCSS Read common high-frequency words by sight. **RF.K.3c**

 I Do Create **High-Frequency Word Cards** for *around* and *school*. Introduce the words using the **Read/Spell/Write** routine.

 We Do Display the High-Frequency Word Cards for *we, can, go, the, I*, and *to*. Have children help you complete the following sentence frames using the High-Frequency Word Cards: *We can go around the* _____. *I go to school to* _____.

 You Do Have partners write sentences using the High-Frequency Words *around* and *school* on their Response Boards. Have them read their sentences.

Vocabulary

ORAL VOCABULARY: SYNONYMS

OBJECTIVES

 With guidance and support from adults, explore word relationships and nuances in word meaning. **L.K.5**

Develop oral vocabulary: Synonyms

 I Do Review the meanings of the oral vocabulary words *require* and *soak*. Explain that a synonym is a word that means almost the same thing as another word. *A synonym for* require *is* need. *When you need something, you have to have it.* I need paper to write a letter. *A synonym for* soak *is* wet. *To wet something is to pour a liquid all over it.* I know the heavy rain will wet the grass.

 We Do Work with children to think of a few sentences together using the new words *need* and *wet*.

 You Do Have partners think of two or three sentences to give directions for planting and caring for a garden. Tell them to use the words *need* and *wet* in their directions. Ask them to share their directions with the class.

 Extend Have partners act out different jobs two people can do together that need lots of water (e.g., washing a dog, washing a car, watering flowers). Encourage group members to use the words *need* and *wet* in their dialogue.

Comprehension

SELF-SELECTED READING

OBJECTIVES

 With prompting and support, ask and answer questions about key details in a text. **RL.K.1**

Apply the strategy and skill to reread the text

Read Independently

Have children choose an illustrated story for sustained silent reading. Tell them that rereading can help them better understand characters, setting, and events in a story. Remind them that illustrations often provide support for the text they are rereading.

Read Purposefully

Before reading, ask children to choose an illustration of a character or setting they think will be important to the story. After reading, ask children to explain how the illustration they chose was important to the plot. Ask them to tell how rereading helped them understand the story better.

 Independent Study Have children choose two illustrations showing two separate events from the week's reading selections. Challenge them to compare and contrast the pictures and then write a few sentences describing both events.

English Language Learners

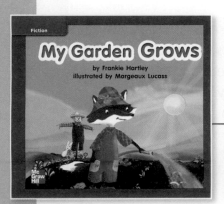

Leveled Reader

OBJECTIVES

With prompting and support, ask and answer questions about key details in a text. **RL.K.1**

Actively engage in group reading activities with purpose and understanding. **RL.K.10**

Read emergent-reader texts with purpose and understanding. **RF.K.4**

Shared Read:
My Garden Grows

 **Go Digital**

Leveled Reader

Before Reading

Preview and Predict

Show children the cover of the book. Read the title and have children repeat the name of the story with you. Point to the cover and say: *I see a fox. She is in a garden. The fox's garden has many things. What else can you see in the garden?* Have children describe what they see in the picture. Walk children through the book and identify the rebus pictures and labels for *seeds, birds, sun, water, rabbits, weeds,* and *berries.* Use simple language to describe each picture. Immediately follow up with questions, such as *What is this? What is the fox doing?*

Essential Question

Set a purpose for reading: *What things does a plant need to grow? Let's read the book to find out how Fox helps her garden grow.* Encourage children to seek clarification when they encounter a word or phrase that doesn't make sense. Model asking for clarification: *I'm not sure what Fox has done to the garden. Can you show me?* Remind children to look at the rebuses, illustrations, and labels as they read.

During Reading

Interactive Question Response

Pages 2–3 Point to the illustration on page 2 and say: *I see Fox. Where is she?* (in her garden) *What is she doing?* (planting seeds) *Let's read the sentence that tells us what Fox's garden has.* Point to the illustration on page 3. *I see birds. What are they doing?* (eating the seeds) *Let's read the sentence.*

Pages 4–5 Point to the illustration on page 4 and discuss what a scarecrow does. Point to the rebus label on page 4. *The garden has what?* (sun) *Let's reread the sentence that tells what Fox's garden has.* Point to the picture on page 5. *What is Fox doing?* (watering her garden) *What else do you see in the picture?* (rabbits) *Let's read to find out what Fox's garden has. Read the words with me.*

Pages 6–7 Point to the illustration and label on page 6. *The garden has what?* (rabbits) *What are the rabbits doing?* (eating lettuce from the garden) *Let's read the sentence.* Point to the illustration on page 7. *Where are the rabbits?* (other side of a fence) *How did Fox solve her problem?* (put up a fence) *What is Fox doing?* (pulling weeds) *Let's read about that.*

Page 8 Point to the illustration on page 8. *What is Fox doing?* (eating berries) *What else do you see in the picture?* (healthy plants, lettuce, corn, tomatoes) *How did Fox grow all those plants?* (She took care of them. She solved problems, like the birds and the rabbits.) *Read the sentence on this page.*

After Reading

Respond to Reading

→ *What is the first thing Fox's garden has?* (seeds) *What is the next thing?* (birds)

→ *What does Fox do to keep the birds from eating the seeds?* (puts a scarecrow in the garden)

→ *What does Fox have at the end of the story?* (berries)

Retell

Let's retell the story together. Fox says, "My garden has seeds." My garden has _____. Allow children to say the missing word. Repeat with the rest of the book.

Model Fluency

Read the sentences one at a time as you track the print. Point out that when you say *my*, Fox is talking about her garden.

Apply Have children read the story with partners.

LITERACY ACTIVITIES

Have children complete the activities on the inside back cover of the reader.

Level Up

Level-up lessons available online.

IF Children read *My Garden Grows* **ELL Level** with fluency and correctly answer the Respond to Reading questions,

THEN Tell children that they will read a more detailed version of the story.

• Have children page through *My Garden Grows* **On Level** and conduct a picture walk to describe each picture in simple language.

• Have children read the story, monitoring their comprehension and providing assistance as necessary.

→ English Language Learners
Vocabulary

PRETEACH ORAL VOCABULARY

OBJECTIVES

CCSS Speak audibly and express thoughts, feelings, and ideas clearly. **SL.K.6**

LANGUAGE OBJECTIVE

Preview vocabulary

I Do Display the images from the **Visual Vocabulary Cards** one at a time to preteach the oral vocabulary words *require* and *plant*.

We Do Display each image again and explain how it illustrates or demonstrates the word. Model using sentences to describe the image.

You Do Display the word *plant* again and have children talk to a partner about how the picture demonstrates the word. Encourage children to talk about or pantomime giving a plant the water it needs.

Beginning	Intermediate	Advanced/High
Use the word *plant* in a sentence and ask children to repeat it and say the vocabulary word.	Have children tell what *plants* they would grow if they had a garden of their own.	Ask children to use each of the words in a sentence of their own.

PRETEACH ELL VOCABULARY

OBJECTIVES

CCSS Speak audibly and express thoughts, feelings, and ideas clearly. **SL.K.6**

LANGUAGE OBJECTIVE

Preview ELL vocabulary

I Do Display the images from the **Visual Vocabulary Cards** one at a time to preteach the ELL vocabulary words *gardener* and *pests*. Follow the routine. Say each word and have children repeat it. Define the word in English.

We Do Display each image again and incorporate the words in a short discussion about the images. Model using sentences to describe the image.

You Do Display the word *gardener*. Have children say the word and use it in a sentence by using a sentence frame: *I see the gardener_____.*

Beginning	Intermediate	Advanced/High
Use each word in an oral sentence and have children raise their hand when they hear you use the word *gardener* or *pests*.	Ask pairs of children to work together to find the cards that illustrate the words *gardener* and *pests*.	Ask children to give additional examples of ways to complete the sentence frame *I see the gardener ____.*

High-Frequency Words

REVIEW WORDS

OBJECTIVES
Read common high-frequency words by sight (e.g., *the, of, to, you, she, my, is, are, do, does*). **RF.K.3c**

LANGUAGE OBJECTIVE
Review high-frequency words

 I Do Display the **High-Frequency Word Card** for *my*. Read the word. Use the **Read/Spell/Write** routine to teach the word. Have children write the word on their **Response Boards**.

 We Do Write a sentence frame that uses the week's high-frequency word along with words from other weeks: *I like my _____.* Explain the difference between *my* and *me*. Say: *The word* my *shows what belongs to* me.

 You Do Display a sentence that uses the high-frequency word *my*. Ask children to point to the word *my* and say it aloud. Then work with children to read and say the entire sentence aloud.

Beginning	Intermediate	Advanced/High
Help children locate the word *my* in additional sentences. Read each sentence and have children repeat.	Ask partners to complete the sentence frame: *I like my _____.*	Ask children to write the word *my* and use it in a sentence.

REVIEW CATEGORY WORDS

 OBJECTIVES
Identify real-life connections between words and their use (e.g., note places at school that are colorful). **L.K.5c**

LANGUAGE OBJECTIVE
Use category words

 I Do Say *big, small, short,* and *tall* and have children repeat each word after you. Define the words in English and then in Spanish, if appropriate, identifying any cognates.

 We Do Tell children that these words have to do with size. Illustrate each word by showing pictures or using concrete objects of things that are big, small, short, or tall.

 You Do Provide children with photos or classroom objects that appear big, small, short, or tall. Have children identify each photo or object by using the appropriate category word. For example: *The pen is small.*

Beginning	Intermediate	Advanced/High
Point to each photo or object and ask children questions about size.	Have partners find their own examples of pictures that demonstrate the category words.	Have children use the category words in sentences.

→ English Language Learners
Writing

SHARED WRITING

OBJECTIVES

CCSS Use a combination of drawing, dictating, and writing to narrate a single event or several loosely linked events, tell about the events in the order in which they occurred, and provide a reaction to what happened. **W.K.3**

LANGUAGE OBJECTIVE

Contribute to a shared writing project

 I Do Review the names of flowers and trees from the chart in the Whole Group Shared Writing project. Then model using some of the words to write the start of a poem: *I like roses, I like maple trees.*

 We Do With children, choose a flower or tree they would like to write about. Write two lines of the poem together, for example, *I see a red rose. Its petals are soft, its thorns are sharp.*

 You Do Help partners choose a flower or tree and write a short poem about it. Provide them with sentence frames to use for their poem, for example, *I see a _____. Its _____ are _____.*

Beginning	**Intermediate**	**Advanced/High**
Ask children to draw a picture of a flower or tree. Help them write a sentence about the plant.	Help children write different lines of their poem. Have them compose some lines by themselves.	Ask children to write the poem on their own, assuring them that it can be short and does not need to rhyme.

WRITING TRAIT: ORGANIZATION

OBJECTIVES

CCSS Use a combination of drawing, dictating, and writing to narrate a single event or several loosely linked events, tell about the events in the order in which they occurred, and provide a reaction to what happened. **W.K.3**

LANGUAGE OBJECTIVE

Organize ideas for writing

 I Do Explain that writers organize their ideas before they write. They think about and write down ideas before they write. Then they write.

 We Do Point to the **Big Book** *My Garden.* Talk about how the writer may have organized ideas before writing. *The author thought about what would grow in the garden. What else did the writer think about?*

 You Do Have children think about a garden they would like to grow. Have them look at the Big Book for ideas. Ask them to list their ideas.

Beginning	**Intermediate**	**Advanced/High**
Using the illustrations, work with children to help them come up with ideas as you list them.	Ask partners to come up with a list of ideas. Have them dictate the list as you write them down.	Ask children to make their list on their own, dictating the ideas to you as necessary.

Grammar

PRONOUNS

OBJECTIVES

 Produce and expand complete sentences in shared language activities. **L.K.1f**

LANGUAGE OBJECTIVE

Learn to use pronouns

Language Transfers Handbook

In Spanish, nouns have feminine or masculine gender, so children may carry over gender labeling into English with neutral nouns. Children may say: *The day is sunny. She is beautiful.* Guide children to use appropriate pronouns for neutral nouns.

 I Do Review with children that a pronoun is a naming word. It takes the place of the name of a person, an animal, or a thing. Say this sentence: *The boy plants a flower. He gives it water.* Explain that *he* is a pronoun that takes the place of the word *boy*.

 We Do Say the following sentence pairs. Guide children to identify the pronoun in the second sentence. Have them tell who or what the pronoun replaces.

Jane likes to garden. She *grows flowers.*

Tomas helped at the community garden. He *planted trees.*

The ball bounced into the vegetable garden. It *rolled over the pumpkin vine.*

You Do Use the following sentence frames.

Ms. Gardener likes to plant flowers. _____ pulls weeds each day.

Pair children and have them orally complete the sentence frame. Then have partners create a pair of sentences. The second sentence should use a pronoun to replace the person or thing in the first sentence. Circulate, listen in, and take note of each child's language use and proficiency.

Beginning	Intermediate	Advanced/High
Ask: *Who likes to plant flowers? Who pulls weeds each day?*	Have partners write another sentence about Ms. Gardener using a pronoun.	Ask children to create another sentence using pronouns.

PROGRESS MONITORING

Weekly Assessment

Use your Quick Check observations and the assessment opportunities identified below to evaluate children's progress in key skill areas.

✔ TESTED SKILLS (CCSS)	Quick Check Observations	Pencil and Paper Assessment
PHONEMIC AWARENESS/ PHONICS **h** /h/ (initial) **RF.K.3a**	Can children isolate /h/ and match it to the letter *Hh*?	Practice Book, pp. 127–128, 130
HIGH-FREQUENCY WORDS *my* **RF.K.3c** **my**	Can children recognize and read the high-frequency word?	Practice Book, pp. 131–132
COMPREHENSION Character, Setting, Events **RL.K.3**	As you read *My Garden* with children, can they use the text and illustrations to identify and discuss character, setting, and events?	Practice Book, p. 129

Quick Check Rubric

Skills	1	2	3
PHONEMIC AWARENESS/ PHONICS	Does not connect the sound /h/ with the letters *Hh*.	Usually connects the sound /h/ with the letters *Hh*.	Consistently connects the sound /h/ with the letters *Hh*.
HIGH-FREQUENCY WORDS	Does not identify the high-frequency word.	Usually recognizes the high-frequency word with accuracy, but not speed.	Consistently recognizes the high-frequency word with speed and accuracy.
COMPREHENSION	Does not use the texts and illustrations to identify and discuss character, setting, and events.	Usually uses the text and illustrations to identify and discuss character, setting, and events.	Consistently uses the text and illustrations to identify and discuss character, setting, and events.

Go Digital! www.connected.mcgraw-hill.com

Using Assessment Results

TESTED SKILLS	If ...	Then ...
PHONEMIC AWARENESS/ PHONICS	**Quick Check Rubric:** Children consistently score 1 or **Pencil and Paper Assessment:** Children get 0–2 items correct	... reteach tested Phonemic Awareness and Phonics skills using Lessons 16–17 in the *Tier 2 Phonemic Awareness Intervention Online PDFs* and Lesson 21 in the *Tier 2 Phonics/ Word Study Intervention Online PDFs.*
HIGH-FREQUENCY WORDS	**Quick Check Rubric:** Children consistently score 1	... reteach tested skills by using the High-Frequency Word Cards and asking children to read and spell the word. Point out any irregularities in sound-spellings.
COMPREHENSION	**Quick Check Rubric:** Children consistently score 1 or **Pencil and Paper Assessment:** Children get 0–1 items correct	... reteach tested skill using Lessons 22–30 in the *Tier 2 Comprehension Intervention Online PDFs.*

Response to Intervention

Use the children's assessment results to assist you in identifying children who will benefit from focused intervention.

Use the appropriate sections of the *Placement and Diagnostic Assessment* to designate children requiring:

TIER 2 **Tier 2 Intervention Online PDFs**

TIER 3 **WonderWorks Intervention Program**

→ Phonemic Awareness

→ Phonics

→ Vocabulary

→ Comprehension

→ Fluency

WEEKLY OVERVIEW

Listening Comprehension

O*nce there was a grand old tree.*

A Grand Old Tree, 4–32
Genre Informational Text

"From a Seed to a Tree," 33–36
Genre Informational Text

Interactive Read-Aloud Cards

"The Pine Tree"
Genre Fairy Tale

Oral Vocabulary

amazing	enormous
content	imagine
develop	

Minilessons ✓ TESTED SKILLS CCSS

✓ **Comprehension Strategy** .... Reread, T95

✓ **Comprehension Skill** .... Main Topic and Key Details, T104

👉 **Go Digital**

www.connected.mcgraw-hill.com

TREES

Essential Question
How do living things change as they grow?

WEEK 2

**Big Book and Little Book
Reading/Writing Workshop**

Shared Reading

Ed and Ned

Ed is not a pet.
Ned is not a pet.

"Ed and Ned," 22–29
Genre Nonfiction

High-Frequency Word   are, T99

Minilessons   ✓ TESTED SKILLS CCSS

✓ **Phonics** .... Short *e*, T97
Writing Traits .... Organization, T100
Grammar .... Pronouns, T101

Differentiated Text

Approaching

On Level

Our Apple Tree

Beyond

ELL

TEACH AND MANAGE

What You Do

INTRODUCE

Weekly Concept

Trees

**Reading/Writing Workshop
Big Book, 20–21**

TEACH AND APPLY

Listening Comprehension

Big Book
A Grand Old Tree
Genre Informational Text
Paired Read "From a Seed to a Tree"
Genre Informational Text

Minilessons
Strategy: Reread
Skill: Main Topic and Key Details

Shared Reading

Reading/Writing Workshop
"Ed and Ned"

Minilessons
Short *e*, High-Frequency Word:
are, Writing, Grammar

 Go Digital

 Interactive Whiteboard

 Interactive Whiteboard

Mobile

What Your Students Do

WEEKLY CONTRACT

PDF Online

PRACTICE AND ONLINE ACTIVITIES

Your Turn Practice Book, pp. 135–142

Leveled Readers

Go Digital

 Online To-Do List

Online Activities

 Mobile

Go Digital! www.connected.mcgraw-hill.com

WEEK 2 →

DIFFERENTIATE

Small Group Instruction
Leveled Readers

INTEGRATE

Research and Inquiry
Tree Life Cycle Display, pp. T134–T135

Text Connections
Compare Trees, p. T136

Talk About Reading
Becoming Readers, p. T137

Mobile

Online Research

WORKSTATION CARDS

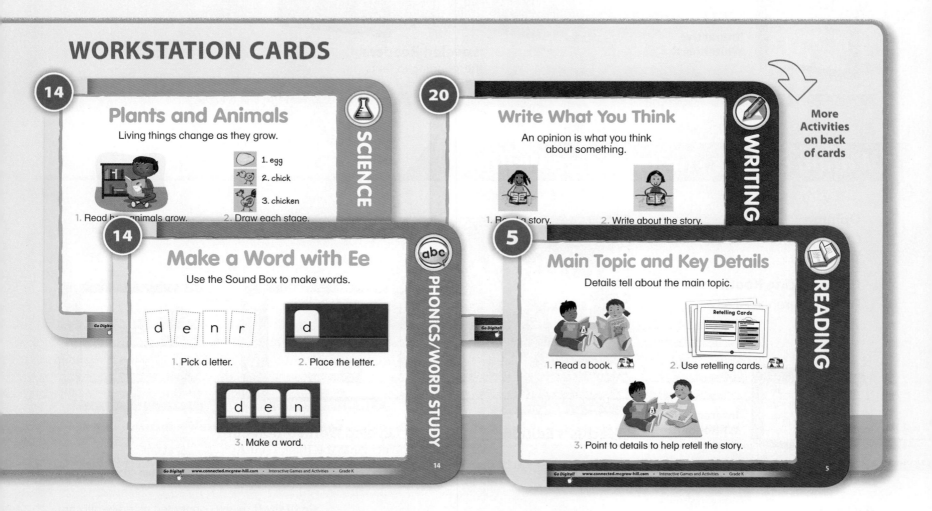

14

Plants and Animals
Living things change as they grow.

1. egg
2. chick
3. chicken

1. Read how animals grow.   2. Draw each stage.

SCIENCE

20

Write What You Think
An opinion is what you think about something.

1. Read a story.   2. Write about the story.

WRITING

More Activities on back of cards

14

Make a Word with Ee
Use the Sound Box to make words.

d e n r   d

1. Pick a letter.   2. Place the letter.

d e n

3. Make a word.

PHONICS/WORD STUDY

5

Main Topic and Key Details
Details tell about the main topic.

Retelling Cards

1. Read a book.   2. Use retelling cards.

3. Point to details to help retell the story.

READING

DEVELOPING READERS AND WRITERS

Write to Sources and Research

Respond to Reading, T95, T143, T151, T157, T161

Connect to Essential Question, T95, T127

Main Topic and Key Details, 104

Research and Inquiry, T134

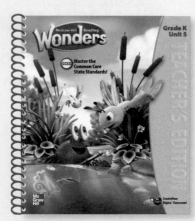

Teacher's Edition

Literature Big Book
A Grand Old Tree
Paired Read: *"From a Seed to a Tree"*

Interactive Whiteboard

Leveled Readers
Responding to Texts

Opinion
Opinion Writing, T122–T123, T132, T140

Conferencing Routines
Peer Conferences, T132

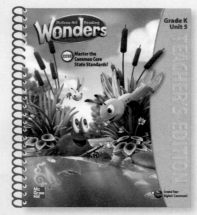

Interactive Whiteboard

Teacher's Edition

Leveled Workstation Card
Write What You Think, Card 20

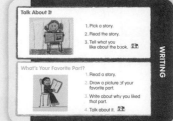

WEEK 2 →

Writing Traits • Shared and Interactive Writing

Writing Trait:
Organization
Opinion Writing, T100, T114

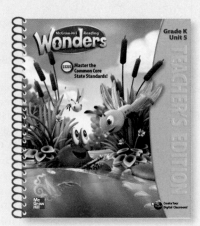

Teacher's Edition

Organization,
p. 32

Pronouns,
p. 33

Reading/Writing Workshop

20

Write What You Think

An opinion is what you think about something.

1. Read a story.　2. Write about the story.

I liked the part about the bear.

3. Share your thoughts.

WRITING

Talk About It

1. Pick a story.
2. Read the story.
3. Tell what you like about the book.

What's Your Favorite Part?

1. Read a story.
2. Draw a picture of your favorite part.
3. Write about why you liked that part.
4. Talk about it.

WRITING

Go Digital

Interactive
Whiteboard

Leveled Workstation Card
Write What You Think, Card 20

Grammar and Spelling/Dictation

Grammar
Pronouns, T101

Spelling/Dictation
Words with Short *e, a, i, o,*
and *n, s, t,* T129, T139

Go Digital

Interactive
Whiteboard

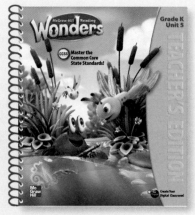

Teacher's Edition

Go Digital

make

Online Grammar Games

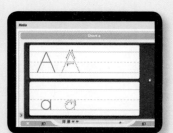

Short a

A A

a

Handwriting

SUGGESTED LESSON PLAN

✔ TESTED SKILLS CCSS	DAY 1	DAY 2

READING

Whole Group

Teach and Model

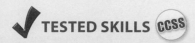

Literature Big Book

Reading/ Writing Workshop

DAY 1

Build Background Trees, T92
Oral Vocabulary Words develop, amazing, T92
✔**Listening Comprehension**
• Genre: Informational Text
• Strategy: Reread, T95
Big Book *A Grand Old Tree*
✔**Word Work**
Phonemic Awareness:
• Phoneme Isolation, T96
Phonics:
• Introduce /e/e, T97
Handwriting Ee, T98
High-Frequency Word are, T99

Practice *Your Turn* 135–136

DAY 2

Oral Language Trees, T102
✔**Category Words** Tree Parts, T103
✔**Listening Comprehension**
• Genre: Informational Text
• Strategy: Reread, T104
• Skill: Main Topic and Key Details
• Guided Retelling
• Model Fluency, T109
Big Book *A Grand Old Tree*
✔**Word Work**
Phonemic Awareness
• Phoneme Blending, T110
Phonics
• Blend Words with Short *e*, T111
High-Frequency Word are, T111
Shared Reading "Ed and Ned," T112–T113

Practice *Your Turn* 137

DIFFERENTIATED INSTRUCTION Choose across the week to meet your student's needs.

Small Group

Approaching Level

Leveled Reader *The Tree*, T142–T143
Phonological Awareness
Onset/Rime Blending, T144 (TIER 2)
Phonics Sound-Spelling Review, T146 (TIER 2)
High-Frequency Words
Reteach Words, T148 (TIER 2)

Leveled Reader *The Tree*, T142–T143
Phonemic Awareness
Phoneme Isolation, T144 (TIER 2)
Phonics Connect *e* to /e/, T146 (TIER 2)
High-Frequency Words Cumulative Review, T148

On Level

Leveled Reader *Many Trees*, T150–T151
Phonemic Awareness
Phoneme Isolation, T152

Leveled Reader *Many Trees*, T150–T151
Phonemic Awareness Phoneme Blending, T152
Phonics Review Phonics, T153
Picture Sort with Medial /e/e, /o/o, T153
High-Frequency Words Review Words, T155

Beyond Level

Leveled Reader *Our Apple Tree*, T156–T157
Phonics Review, T158

Leveled Reader *Our Apple Tree*, T156–T157
High-Frequency Words Review, T158

English Language Learners

Leveled Reader *Many Trees*, T160–T161
Phonological Awareness
Onset/Rime Blending, T144 (TIER 2)
Phonics Sound-Spelling Review, T146 (TIER 2)
Vocabulary Preteach Oral Vocabulary, T162
Writing Shared Writing, T164

Leveled Reader *Many Trees*, T160–T161
Phonemic Awareness
Phoneme Isolation, T144 (TIER 2)
Phonics Connect *e* to /e/, T146 (TIER 2)
High-Frequency Words Cumulative Review, T148
Vocabulary Preteach ELL Vocabulary, T162

LANGUAGE ARTS

Whole Group

Writing and Grammar

Shared Writing
Writing Trait: Organization, T100
Write an Opinion About a Book, T100
Grammar Pronouns, T101

Interactive Writing
Writing Trait: Organization, T114
Write an Opinion About a Book, T114
Grammar Pronouns, T115

Nathan Love

DAY 3	DAY 4	DAY 5 Review and Assess

READING

Oral Language Trees, T116 **Oral Vocabulary** content, enormous, imagine, T116 ✓**Listening Comprehension** • Genre: Fairy Tale • Strategy: Reread, T117 • Make Connections, T117 **Interactive Read Aloud** "The Pine Tree," T117 ✓**Word Work** **Phonemic Awareness** • Phoneme Blending, T118 **Phonics** • Blend Words with Short *e* and *m, t, h, n, h, s, p*, T119 • Picture Sort, T120 **High-Frequency Words** are, T121	**Oral Language** Trees, T124 ✓**Category Words** Tree Parts, T125 ✓**Listening Comprehension** • Genre: Informational Text • Strategy: Reread, T126 • Text Feature: Diagram • Make Connections, T127 **Big Book** Paired Read: "From a Seed to a Tree," T126 ✓**Word Work** **Phonemic Awareness** • Phoneme Segmentation, T128 **Phonics** • Blend Words with Short *e, a, i, o* and *t, n*, T128 **High-Frequency Words** are, T129 **Shared Reading** "Ed and Ned,"T130–T131 **Integrate Ideas** Research and Inquiry, T134–T135	**Integrate Ideas** • Text Connections, T136 • Talk About Reading, T137 • Research and Inquiry, T137 ✓**Word Work** **Phonemic Awareness** Phoneme Segmentation, T138 **Phonics** • Read Words with Short *e* and *n, t, s, n, d*, T138 **High-Frequency Word** are, T139 
Practice *Your Turn* 138–140	**Practice** *Your Turn* 141	**Practice** *Your Turn* 142

DIFFERENTIATED INSTRUCTION

Leveled Reader *The Tree,* T142–T143 **Phonemic Awareness** Phoneme Blending, T145 **Phonics** Reteach, T146 **High-Frequency Words** Reteach Words, T148	**Leveled Reader** *The Tree,* T142–T143 **Phonemic Awareness** Phoneme Segmentation, T145 **Phonics** Blend Words with Short *e,* T147 **Oral Vocabulary** Review Words, T149	**Leveled Reader** Literacy Activities, T143 **Phonemic Awareness** Phoneme Segmentation, T145 **Phonics** Reread for Fluency, T147 Build Fluency with Phonics, T147 **Comprehension** Self-Selected Reading, T149
Leveled Reader *Many Trees,* T150–T151 **Phonemic Awareness** Phoneme Segmentation, T152 **Phonics** Blend Words with Short *e,* T154	**Leveled Reader** *Many Trees,* T150–T151 **Phonics** Blend Words with Short *e,* T154 Reread for Fluency, T154	**Leveled Reader** Literacy Activities, T151 **Comprehension** Self-Selected Reading, T155
Leveled Reader *Our Apple Tree,* T156–T157 **Vocabulary** Oral Vocabulary: Synonyms, T159 	**Leveled Reader** *Our Apple Tree,* T156–T157 **Phonics** Innovate, T158	**Leveled Reader** Literacy Activities, T157 **Comprehension** Self-Selected Reading, T159
Leveled Reader *Many Trees,* T160–T161 **Phonemic Awareness** Phoneme Blending, T145 **Phonics** Reteach, T146 **High-Frequency Words** Review Words, T163 **Writing** Writing Trait: Organization, T164	**Leveled Reader** *Many Trees,* T160–T161 **Phonemic Awareness** Phoneme Segmentation, T145 **Phonics** Blend Words with Short *e,* T147 **Vocabulary** Review Category Words, T163 **Grammar** Pronouns, T165	**Leveled Reader** Literacy Activities, T161 **Phonemic Awareness** Phoneme Segmentation, T145 **Phonics** Reread for Fluency, T147 Build Fluency with Phonics, T147

LANGUAGE ARTS

Independent Writing Writing Trait: Organization, T122 Write an Opinion About a Book Prewrite/Draft, T123 **Grammar** Pronouns, T123	**Independent Writing** Writing Trait: Organization, T132 Write an Opinion About a Book Revise/Final Draft, T132 **Grammar** Pronouns, T133	**Independent Writing** Write an Opinion About a Book Prepare/Present/Evaluate/Publish, T140 **Grammar** Pronouns, T141

DIFFERENTIATE TO ACCELERATE

IF ➤ the text complexity of a particular **section** is too difficult for children

THEN ➤ see the references noted in the chart below for scaffolded instruction to help children Access Complex Text.

Qualitative / Quantitative
Reader and Task
TEXT COMPLEXITY

Literature Big Book	**Reading/Writing Workshop**	**Leveled Readers**	

Quantitative			
A Grand Old Tree **Lexile** 470	"Ed and Ned" **Lexile** 230	**Approaching Level** **Lexile** BR	**On Level** **Lexile** 70
Paired Selection: "From a Seed to a Tree" **Lexile** 400		**Beyond Level** **Lexile** 250	**ELL** **Lexile** BR
Qualitative			
What Makes the Text Complex? • **Organization** Sequence of Events, T104 **A C T** *See Scaffolded Instruction in Teacher's Edition, T104.*	What Makes the Text Complex? **Foundational Skills** • Decoding with short *e*, T110–T111 • Identifying high-frequency words, T111	What Makes the Text Complex? **Foundational Skills** • Decoding with short *e* • Identifying high-frequency words *are* *See Level Up lessons online for Leveled Readers.*	
Reader and Task			
The Introduce the Concept lesson on pages T92–T93 will help determine the reader's knowledge and engagement in the weekly concept. See pages T94–T95, T105–T109, T126–T127 and T134–T137 for questions and tasks for this text.	The Introduce the Concept lesson on pages T92–T93 will help determine the reader's knowledge and engagement in the weekly concept. See pages T112–T113, T130–T131 and T134–T137 for questions and tasks for this text.	The Introduce the Concept lesson on pages T92–T93 will help determine the reader's knowledge and engagement in the weekly concept. See pages T142–T143, T150–T151, T156–T157, T160–T161 and T134–T137 for questions and tasks for this text.	

Nathan Lowe

Monitor and *Differentiate*

IF you need to differentiate instruction

THEN use the Quick Checks to assess children's needs and select the appropriate small group instruction focus.

 Quick Check

Comprehension Strategy Reread, T117

Phonemic Awareness/Phonics Short *e*, T99, T111, T121, T129, T139

High-Frequency Words *are*, T99, T111, T121, T129, T139

If No → | **Approaching** **Reteach,** pp. T142–T149
| **ELL** **Develop,** pp. T160–T165

If Yes → | **On Level** **Review,** pp. T150–T155
| **Beyond Level** **Extend,** pp. T156–T159

Level Up with Leveled Readers

IF children can read their leveled text fluently and answer comprehension questions

THEN work with the next level up to accelerate children's reading with more complex text.

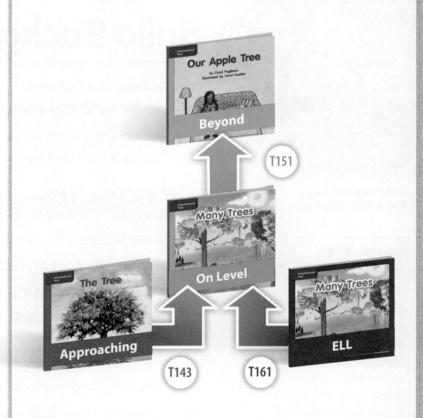

Our Apple Tree
by Carol Pugliano
Illustrated by Carol Koeller
Beyond
T151

Many Trees
On Level

The Tree
Approaching
T143

Many Trees
ELL
T161

ENGLISH LANGUAGE LEARNERS
SCAFFOLD

IF ELL students need additional support **THEN** scaffold instruction using the small group suggestions.

| **Reading-Writing Workshop** T93 "Growing Tall" **Integrate Ideas** T135 | **Leveled Reader** T160–T161 *Many Trees* | **Phonological Awareness** Onset/Rime Blending, T144 Phoneme Isolation, T144 Phoneme Blending, T145 Phoneme Segmentation, T145 | **Phonics,** Short *e*, T146–T147 | **Oral Vocabulary,** T162 develop, amazing, enormous, imagine, content **High-Frequency Word,** T163 *are* | **Writing** Shared Writing, T164 Writing Trait: Organization, T164 | **Grammar** T165 Pronouns |

Note: Include ELL Students in all small groups based on their needs.

Materials

Reading/Writing Workshop Big Book
UNIT 5

Literature Big Book
A Grand Old Tree
BY MARY NEWELL DEPALMA

Visual Vocabulary Cards
develop
amazing

Response Board

Photo Cards
egg
elbow
elevator
envelope
exit

Ee
egg

Sound-Spelling Cards
egg

are

High-Frequency Word Cards
are

When I read _____, I had to reread...

Think Aloud Cloud

♪ "My Oak Tree"
"Scrambled Egg, Fried Egg"

Reading/Writing Workshop Big Book

OBJECTIVES

CCSS Confirm understanding of a text read aloud or information presented orally or through other media by asking and answering questions about key details and requesting clarification if something is not understood. **SL.K.2**

CCSS Identify real-life connections between words and their use. **L.K.5c**

→ # Introduce the Concept

MINILESSON
10 Mins

Build Background

ESSENTIAL QUESTION
How do living things change as they grow?

Read aloud the Essential Question. Tell children you are going to read about how a tree changes as it grows.

My Oak Tree

> I saw a little acorn, lying on the ground.
>
> I put it in my pocket, told Daddy what I found.
>
> He helped me plant it in the earth; up came a little tree!
>
> Just see what we have grown, my daddy and me! An oak tree!

Sing "My Oak Tree" with children.

What does the child find? (an acorn) *What happens when the child plants the acorn in the ground?* (It grows into an oak tree.) Tell children that this week, they will read to find out about how a tree changes as it grows.

Oral Vocabulary Words

Use the **Define/Example/Ask** routine to introduce the oral vocabulary words **develop** and **amazing**.

To introduce the theme of "Trees," explain that trees develop in amazing ways as they grow. *What is one amazing way a tree develops as it grows?* (Possible answer: It starts very small and gets very big.)

Go Digital

"Trees"

Video

Visual Glossary

Photos

Visual Vocabulary Cards

Oral Vocabulary Routine

Define: To **develop** is to grow.

Example: Trees develop into big plants.

Ask: What is one way a person develops?

Define: To be **amazing** is to be surprising and wonderful.

Example: The fruit that grows on trees is amazing.

Ask: What is an amazing animal you have seen?

Talk About It: Trees

Guide children to describe amazing leaves they have seen. Make a list of their responses. *What amazing trees and leaves have you seen?* Display pages 20–21 of the **Reading/Writing Workshop Big Book** and have children do the **Talk About It** activity with a partner.

READING/WRITING WORKSHOP BIG BOOK, pp. 20–21

Collaborative Conversations

Take Turns Talking As children engage in partner, small group, or whole group discussions, encourage them to:

→ Look at the person who is speaking.

→ Listen to the words they are saying.

→ Respect others by not interrupting them.

→ Repeat classmates' ideas to check understanding.

ELL

ENGLISH LANGUAGE LEARNERS SCAFFOLD

Beginning

Use Visuals Explain that the picture shows many trees. The older trees are taller; the younger one is smaller. *Is this tree older? Is this tree going to grow to be a big tree?* Allow children ample time to respond.

Intermediate

Describe Ask children to describe the trees in the picture. Ask which of the trees is the smallest. *Which tree do you think is the youngest?* Correct grammar and pronunciation as needed.

Advanced/Advanced High

Discuss Have children elaborate on how the trees in the picture are the same and how they are different. Elicit more details to support children's answers.

→ # Listening Comprehension

A Grand Old Tree
BY MARY NEWELL DEPALMA

Literature Big Book

OBJECTIVES

CCSS Name the author and illustrator of a text and define the role of each in presenting the ideas or information in a text. **RI.K.6**

CCSS Actively engage in group reading activities with purpose and understanding. **RI.K.10**

• Recognize characteristics of informational text
• Strategy: Reread

ACADEMIC LANGUAGE

• *informational text, fact*
• Cognates: *texto informativo*

 MINILESSON 10 Mins

Read the Literature Big Book

Connect to Concept: Trees

Tell children that you will now read about the ways one amazing tree develops as the years pass. *What kinds of changes have you seen in trees in your neighborhood?*

Concepts of Print

Title Page, Directionality, and Space Between Words Display the title page of the **Big Book**. *The title page tells the title of the story,* A Grand Old Tree, *and the name of the author/illustrator, Mary Newell DePalma.* Track the print from left to right as you read. Point out the space between each of the words.

Genre: Informational Text

Model *A Grand Old Tree* is an informational text. Share these characteristics of informational text with children:

→ Informational text give facts, or information, about things that happen in real life.

> **Story Words** Preview these words before reading:
>
> **grand:** big and wonderful
> **bore:** made or grew
> **sowed:** spread
> **shed:** lost or had something fall off

Set a Purpose for Reading

→ Identify and read aloud the title and the name of the author/illustrator. Point out that the same person wrote the words and created the pictures for the story.

→ Ask children to listen as you read aloud the Big Book to find out how a tree changes as it grows.

Go Digital

A Grand Old Tree

When I read ____, I had to reread...

Think Aloud Cloud

Strategy: Reread

Explain Tell children that something might not make sense to them as they read. Rereading, or reading again, can help them understand the text.

Think Aloud Read aloud pages 8–9: I just read that the tree was a home. But people don't live in trees. I don't understand. When I reread I find out that the tree is a home for animals, not people.

Model As you read, use the **Think Aloud Cloud** to model the strategy.

Think Aloud On page 21, I read that the branches no longer swayed and danced. I wonder why? Then I reread: *At last the grand old tree was very, very old.* I see. The branches stopped dancing because the tree got older.

Respond to Reading

After reading, prompt children to describe one way the tree changed in the story. Discuss the ways that rereading helped children understand the story. Then have children draw a picture of one part of a tree's life that they learned about from the selection.

Make Connections

Use pages 18–19 of *A Grand Old Tree* to describe how the tree changed as it grew. Revisit the concept behind the Essential Question *How do living things change as they grow?*.

Write About It Have children write about the ways the tree in the story changed as it grew.

ENGLISH LANGUAGE LEARNERS SCAFFOLD

Beginning

Demonstrate Point to page 22. Read aloud: *Finally she fell, and snow gently covered her.* Say: *Who is she? Listen as I reread.* Read aloud page 21. Ask: *Does the word* she *mean the tree?* (Yes) *Did the tree fall?* (Yes) *Was the tree covered with snow?* (Yes) Repeat children's correct answers, adding details for clarity. For example: *Yes,* she *means the tree.*

Intermediate

Discuss Point to page 22 and read aloud. Read aloud: *Finally she fell, and snow gently covered her.* Then say: *Wait, I don't know whom the author is writing about with the words* she *and* her. *What should I do?* (Read again to help you understand.) Reread aloud page 21. Ask: *What is the author writing about with the words* she *and* her? (the tree) Restate children's responses, adding details in order to develop their oral language proficiency.

Advanced/Advanced High

Discuss Point to page 22. Read aloud: *Finally she fell, and snow gently covered her.* Then say: *The author writes the words* she *and* her. Turn to page 21. *Ask: How can rereading page 21 help me figure out who* she *and* her *is?* (The writer names the tree on this page and then uses the pronouns *she* and *her*.) Elicit more details to support children's answers.

→ # Word Work

MINILESSON 5 Mins — Phonemic Awareness

Photo Card

OBJECTIVES

CCSS Isolate and pronounce the initial, medial vowel, and final sounds (phonemes) in three-phoneme words. **RF.K.2d**

CCSS Associate the long and short sounds with the common spellings (graphemes) for the five major vowels. **RF.K.3b**

Phoneme Isolation

1 Model Display the **Photo Card** for *egg. Listen for the sound at the beginning of* egg. Egg *has the /e/ sound at the beginning. Say the sound with me: /e/.* Say *end, Ed, enter* and have children repeat. Emphasize /e/.

♪ *Let's play a song. Listen for the words with /e/ at the beginning.* Play "Scrambled Egg, Fried Egg," and have children listen for the /e/ sound. *Let's listen to the song again and signal thumbs' up when we hear words that begin with /e/.* Play and/or sing the letter song again, encouraging children to join in. Have children signal thumbs up when they hear a word that begins with /e/.

2 Guided Practice/Practice Display and name each Photo Card: *elevator, elbow, envelope, exit. Say each picture name with me. Tell me the sound at the beginning of the word.* Guide practice with the first word.

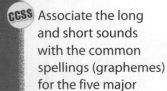

Photo Cards

ENGLISH LANGUAGE LEARNERS

Minimal Contrasts Focus on articulation. Make the /e/ sound and point out your mouth position. Have children repeat. Repeat for the /i/ sound. Have children say both sounds, noticing the differences.

ARTICULATION SUPPORT

Demonstrate the way to say /e/. Open your mouth a little. Start with your tongue in the middle of your mouth. Now, use your voice and just let your jaw move down a bit as you say /e/. Say *egg, enter, elbow* and have children repeat. Stretch initial /e/.

Phonics

10 Mins

Sound-Spelling Card

Introduce /e/e

① **Model** Display the *Egg* **Sound-Spelling Card**. *This is the* Egg *card. The sound is /e/. The /e/ sound is spelled with the letter* e. *Say it with me: /e/. This is the sound at the beginning of the word* egg. *Listen: /eeeg/,* egg. *What is the name of this letter?* (e) *What sound does this letter stand for?* (/e/)

♪ Display the song "Scrambled Egg, Fried Egg" (see **Teacher's Resource Book** online). Read or sing the song with children. Reread the title and point out that the word *egg* begins with the letter *e*, which can stand for /e/. Model placing a self-stick note below the *e* in *egg*.

② **Guided Practice/Practice** Read each line of the song. Stop after each line and ask children to place self-stick notes below words that begin with *E* or *e* and say the letter name.

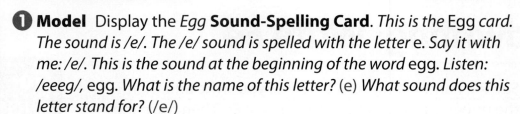

Scrambled Egg, Fried Egg

Scrambled egg, fried egg, egg on a plate,

boiled egg, egg on toast, hurry, don't be late!

Eggs are good for breakfast or in a salad, too.

No matter how you cook them, they are good for you.

Scrambled egg, fried egg, egg on a plate,

boiled egg, egg on toast, hurry, don't be late!

But no matter where you go, and no matter what you do, never, ever put an egg in your shoe!

YOUR TURN PRACTICE BOOK pp. 135–136

Corrective Feedback

Sound Error Say /e/, then have children repeat the sound. *My turn. Egg, /e/ /e/ /e/. Now it's your turn.* Have children say the words *egg* and *exit* and isolate the initial sound.

→ # Word Work

MINILESSON 5 Mins

Handwriting: Write *Ee*

OBJECTIVES

CCSS Write a letter or letters for most consonant and short-vowel sounds (phonemes). **L.K.2c**

CCSS Read common high-frequency words by sight. **RF.K.3c**

ACADEMIC LANGUAGE

uppercase, lowercase

1 Model Say the handwriting cues below as you write and then identify the uppercase and lowercase forms of *Ee*. Then trace the letters on the board and in the air as you say /e/.

Straight down. Straight across. Straight across. Straight across.

Straight across. Circle back and around, then stop.

2 Guided Practice/Practice

→ Say the cues together as children trace both forms of the letter with their index finger. Have children identify the uppercase and lowercase forms of the letter.

→ Have children write *E* and *e* in the air as they say /e/ multiple times.

→ Distribute **Response Boards** or paper. Observe children's pencil grip and paper position, and correct as necessary. Have children say /e/ every time they write the letter *Ee*.

 Daily Handwriting

Throughout the week teach uppercase and lowercase letters *Ee* using the Handwriting models. At the end of the week, have children use the **Your Turn Practice Book** page 142 to practice handwriting.

Go Digital

Handwriting

the	is
you	do

High-Frequency Word Routine

MINILESSON

5 Mins

High-Frequency Words

are

are

High-Frequency Word Card

❶ Model Display pages 31–32 of the **Big Book** *A Grand Old Tree*. Read the sentence "They are home to many creatures, just like the grand old tree." Point to the high-frequency word *are*. Use the **Read/Spell/Write** routine to teach the word.

→ **Read** Point to the word *are* and say the word. *This is the word* are. *Say it with me:* are. *The branches are home to many creatures.*

→ **Spell** *The word* are *is spelled a-r-e. Spell it with me.*

→ **Write** *Let's write the word in the air as we say each letter: a-r-e.*

→ Point out to children that the letter *a* followed by *r* has a different sound from the /a/ sound in *am*.

COLLABORATE

→ Have partners create sentences using the word.

❷ Guided Practice/Practice Build sentences using the **High-Frequency Word Cards**, **Photo Cards**, and teacher-made punctuation cards. Have children point to the high-frequency word *are*. Use these sentences.

> We *are* at my house.
> You *are* like a kitten.

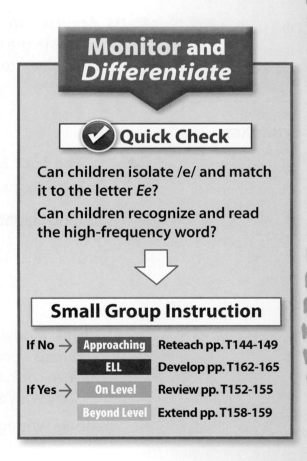

Monitor and *Differentiate*

✔ Quick Check

Can children isolate /e/ and match it to the letter *Ee*?

Can children recognize and read the high-frequency word?

⬇

Small Group Instruction

If No →	**Approaching**	Reteach pp. T144-149
	ELL	Develop pp. T162-165
If Yes →	**On Level**	Review pp. T152-155
	Beyond Level	Extend pp. T158-159

→ Language Arts

MINILESSON 10 Mins Shared Writing

Writing Trait: Organization

1 **Model** Tell children that when they write, they should make sure all of their sentences are about the same thing.

→ Write and read aloud: *I like apples. I play soccer. Apples taste sweet. One of my sentences is not about apples. I need to erase the sentence about soccer because it is not about apples.*

2 **Guided Practice/Practice** Write and read aloud: *Jeff goes to the zoo. He sees apes. He goes to school. Jeff sees dolphins.* Help children determine the sentence that doesn't belong. (He goes to school.)

Write an Opinion About a Book

Focus and Plan Tell children that this week they will learn how to write a few sentences about a favorite book they have read.

 Brainstorm Have children name some books they have read at home, in the classroom, and in the library. Create a three-column chart to write some of their ideas.

Books at Home	Books in the Classroom	Books in the Library
The Foot Book	Cloudy With a Chance of Meatballs	First Day Jitters
Lost and Found	My Garden	All About Friends
Goodnight Moon	The Handiest Things in the World	When You Go to Kindergarten

Write Model writing an opinion about a book from the chart. Write and read: *Food falls from the sky. Juice falls instead of rain. People never have to cook. I think this story is funny. All of my sentences tell about* Cloudy With a Chance of Meatballs. *I also give my opinion of the story.*

Model writing an opinion about another book from the list.

Go Digital

Writing

I see a fish.

Grammar

Grammar

MINILESSON
5 Mins

Pronouns

❶ Model Write and read aloud: *Sarah likes apples. She likes apples.* Tell children that the pronoun *she* replaced the girl's name. Review *he, she,* and *it,* using sentences.

→ Then introduce the pronouns *you, I,* and *we* as you point to yourself and to the children. *I like cookies. You like cookies. We all like cookies. I, you,* and *we are pronouns. We can use them in place of our names.*

→ Write: *I like cookies. You like cookies. We like cookies.* Point to the pronoun in each sentence as you read the sentences aloud. Remind children that every sentence begins with a capital letter.

→ Write: *Can I have a cookie?* Point to the word *I* and say: *We always use a capital letter to spell the word I.*

❷ Guided Practice/Practice Write and read aloud the following sentence pairs, substituting your name and the names of children in your classroom and pointing as appropriate:

(Mrs. Johnson) wakes up early.
I wake up early.

(Donald) is wearing a blue shirt.
You are wearing a blue shirt.

(Amy, Devon, and I) go to the library.
We go to the library.

After each sentence pair, ask children to identify the naming word or words in the first sentence and the pronoun that replaced the word or words in the second sentence.

Talk About It

Pair children, and have partners make up sentences about themselves, using *I, you,* and *we.* As children share their sentences, ask them to identify the pronoun and the name or names it replaces.

ENGLISH LANGUAGE LEARNERS SCAFFOLD

Beginning

Explain *The pronoun I refers to the person who is speaking.* Have children take turns saying the sentence: *I am _____,* using their names. Explain that the pronoun *you* refers to the person whom the speaker is talking to. *You are (name of a child).* Have children take turns saying the sentence: *You are _____,* using the name of a classmate. Allow children ample time to respond.

Intermediate

Practice Write: *_____ like reading. Will _____ play with me? _____ go shopping.* Help children complete each sentence frame with a pronoun that makes sense. Help children read each sentence aloud. Model correct pronunciation as needed.

Advanced/Advanced High

Practice Write: *I, you, we.* Have children write a sentence about something they do in class, using each pronoun. Correct the meaning of children's responses as needed.

Daily Wrap Up

- Review the Essential Question and encourage children to discuss it, using the new oral vocabulary words. *What do you know about how living things grow?*

- Prompt children to share the skills they learned. How might they use those skills?

Materials

Reading/Writing Workshop Big Book
UNIT 5

Literature Big Book *A Grand Old Tree*
BY MARY NEWELL DEPALMA

Visual Vocabulary Cards
develop
amazing

♪ "My Oak Tree"

Retelling Cards

Puppet

Sound-Spelling Cards
Egg

Response Board

Word-Building Cards

High-Frequency Word Cards
are

⭢ # Build the Concept

MINILESSON
10 Mins

Oral Language

OBJECTIVES

CCSS Use words and phrases acquired through conversations. **L.K.6**

CCSS Blend onsets and rimes of single-syllable spoken words. **RF.K.2c**

CCSS Use frequently occurring nouns and verbs. **L.K.1b**

Develop oral vocabulary

ACADEMIC LANGUAGE

• *rhyme, sentence*
• Cognates: *rima*

ESSENTIAL QUESTION
How do living things change as they grow?

Remind children that this week they are learning how a tree changes as it grows. Point out that trees begin as very small plants. Ask children to tell about times they have seen a tree change.

Sing the song "My Oak Tree" with children.

Phonological Awareness
Onset/Rime Blending
Say the word *ground*. Repeat the word, segmenting and blending the onset and rime: /gr/ /ound/. Have children repeat. Then segment and blend *little* and *plant*. (/l/ /itəl/; /pl/ /ant/) Have children repeat. Then have children blend other words from the song, such as: /tr/ /ē/, *tree*; /h/ /elpt/, *helped*.

Review Oral Vocabulary

Use the **Define/Example/Ask** routine to review the oral vocabulary words **develop** and **amazing**. Prompt children to use the words in sentences.

Visual Vocabulary Cards

Go Digital

Visual Glossary

Category Words

Category Words: Tree Parts

❶ Model Use *A Grand Old Tree* to introduce words that name tree parts: *roots,* page 6; *branches,* page 8; *leaves,* page 9; *trunk,* page 27; and *bark,* page 27. Point out each tree part in the illustrations. Then display different pages of the book and ask questions about each tree part. For example, on page 6: *What sank deep into the earth?* (the tree's roots) Then, on page 7: *Where is the little blue bird?* (on a branch)

❷ Guided Practice/Practice Display an illustration of the tree from the Big Book. Ask children to describe the picture and point to the different tree parts. Ask children to identify each part. *Which tree part is this?*

→ Have children discuss what they know about trees. Encourage them to use words that describe tree parts in their answers. (Possible answer: We rake leaves every fall.)

Vocabulary Strategy: Word Parts/ Inflectional Ending *-ed*

❶ Model Explain to children that adding the word part *-ed* to the end of a present-tense verb (a verb that is happening now) changes the verb into a past-tense verb (a verb that happened earlier). Use *A Grand Old Tree* to show how the *-ed* ending can change word meanings.

Think Aloud In *A Grand Old Tree,* I can read this sentence: *Caterpillars and ladybugs crawled about.* I see the *-ed* ending at the end of the word *crawl,* which tells me that the action happened in the past. I can also read this sentence on page 29: *Their arms reach high into the sky.* I don't see the *-ed* ending on the word *reach.* This tells me that the action is happening now.

❷ Guided Practice Point out and discuss other verbs in the **Big Book** that end with *-ed.* Cover the *-ed* ending and read the present tense form of the verb. Then reveal the *-ed* ending and read the past-tense form.

*The grand old tree **flowered**, bore fruit, and **sowed** seeds.*

❸ Practice Talk about the verb *develop* and use it in context to help children understand its meaning. Have children add the ending *-ed* to *develop* to form a past-tense verb. Point out that sometimes *-ed* stands for /t/. Continue with the verbs *sway, nest,* and *crawl.*

ENGLISH LANGUAGE LEARNERS

Identify Help children identify tree parts by pointing to a tree in the schoolyard or in an illustration from a book or magazine. As you point to each tree part, use the word in a sentence. For example: *This is a tree branch. This is the tree's bark.* Have children repeat the tree-part words with you.

LET'S MOVE!

Tell children to stand up tall and straight like a big tree. Call out different tree parts *(trunk, branches, leaves, roots)* and have children move the body part that represents that tree part *(waist, arms, fingers, feet).*

Listening Comprehension

A Grand Old Tree
BY MARY NEWELL DEPALMA

Literature Big Book

OBJECTIVES

CCSS With prompting and support, ask and answer questions about key details in a text. **RI.K.1**

CCSS With prompting and support, identify the main topic and retell key details of a text. **RI.K.2**

• Strategy: Reread
• Skill: Main Topic and Key Details

ACADEMIC LANGUAGE

• *informational text*
• Cognates: *texto informativo*

MINILESSON 15 Mins

Reread Literature Big Book

Genre: Informational Text

Display *A Grand Old Tree*. Guide children in recalling that informational text gives facts about real things or events. *How do you know that A Grand Old Tree is an informational text?* Have children point to evidence in the **text** and the pictures to show that this is informational text. (Possible answer: Trees are planted and grow and die in real life.)

Strategy: Reread

Remind children that good readers sometimes reread to help them understand what they have read. *You can reread to find details that will help you understand what you read.*

Skill: Main Topic and Key Details

Tell children that the main topic is what a selection is mostly about. Key details in the text and illustrations all tell about the main topic. Explain that knowing what the main topic of a selection is can help you understand it better. *What do you think the main topic of this selection will be?* As you read, have children listen for evidence in the text to figure out the main topic.

Access Complex Text

Organization This book is set up cyclically. To guide children in recognizing these sequential events, draw a large circle on the board. Starting at the top of the circle, draw an image that illustrates the part of the cycle you are discussing. Move clockwise around the circle until you end back at the top. 1) The book starts with the tree growing leaves. 2) The tree grows fruit with seeds. 3) The seeds land on the ground. 4) The seeds start to grow into new trees. 5) The tree dies and becomes part of the earth. 6) The new trees grow fruit. Explain that this cycle, or circle of life, repeats again and again.

Go Digital

A Grand Old Tree

Retelling Cards

PAGES 4–5

MAIN TOPIC

Think Aloud This page tells me about a grand old tree. That was also the title of the book. I think that the main topic will be something about the tree.

PAGES 6–7

REREAD

Think Aloud I can reread the page to find out what the pictures are showing. I see now. The pictures are showing the roots of the tree and the branches of the tree.

pp. 6–7

arms reached high into the sky: Show children how you can reach high into the sky. Explain that the tree's branches are like our arms.

PAGES 8–9

MAIN TOPIC AND KEY DETAILS

What is the main thing these pages tell about? (The tree was home to many creatures.) *What key details tell about the big idea?* (Birds nested. Squirrels scurried. Caterpillars and ladybugs crawled.)

pp. 8–9

scurried: Point to the squirrels scurrying. Say: *The squirrels are scurrying. Scurrying is when animals or people move quickly from place to place.* Say *scurried* and have children echo.

PAGES 10–11

ASK AND ANSWER QUESTIONS

Think Aloud I know the tree had many leaves before it flowered. I wonder what will happen *after* it flowers. I will continue reading to find out.

pp. 10–11

flowered: Children might be confused by the use of *flower(ed)* as a verb. Point to the tree on page 11 as you say: *Flowers grew. The tree flowered.* Have children repeat as they point to the tree.

Listening Comprehension

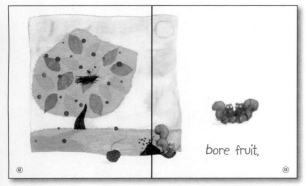

bore fruit,

PAGES 12–13

KEY DETAILS

What is growing on the tree now? (fruit)

pp. 12–13

bore fruit: Make sure children understand that this phrase means that fruit grew on the tree. Have them mimic you as you point to the fruit and say: *The tree bore fruit. Fruit grew on the tree.*

and sowed seeds. ...   She had many children.

PAGES 14–15

REREAD

Listen as I reread these pages. Who are the tree's children? (Little trees. The text tells us that the tree "sowed seeds" and we know that seeds grow into trees.)

pp. 14–15

sowed seeds: Children might hear the word *sowed* and think of sewing. To clarify, explain that a tree sows seeds when the seeds begin to spread out over the ground.

They changed the landscape for miles around,

perhaps even   farther than the old tree knew.

PAGES 16–17

KEY DETAILS

Look at this illustration. Where does the bird take the seed? (All the way to the ocean.)

pp. 16–17

landscape: With your hand, sweep the landscape in the illustration as you have children repeat: *landscape.* Then provide additional illustrations of landscapes from classroom books and repeat the routine.

The grand old tree lived a long, long time. She basked in the sun, bathed in the rain, swayed in the breeze, and danced in the wind.

She grew and shed...

PAGES 18–19

MAIN TOPIC AND KEY DETAILS

What different kinds of weather does the tree live in? How does the tree change in the pictures? (Possible answer: Rain, sun, snow, wind. It gets bigger, has more leaves, bears fruit.)

pp. 18–19

shed: Shed means to get rid of. Put on a sweater, cap, or other piece of outerwear. Take it off as you say: *I shed my (name of item).* Have children echo and mimic.

PAGES 20–21

VOCABULARY

Point to the word *swayed*. *I wonder what* swayed *means. The text says the branches no longer* swayed *and danced in the wind. I think* swayed *means "moved back and forth".* Ask children what *snapped* means.

PAGES 22–23

VISUALIZE

Can you picture in your mind the grand old tree falling down? Try to imagine the noise it would make. In the illustration we can see that all of the animals came to look.

PAGES 24–25

MAIN TOPIC AND KEY DETAILS

What is the main topic on these pages? (The old tree died.) *What details tell about the main topic?* (The tree no longer flowered. It no longer bore fruit or sowed seeds.)

ELL

pp. 24–25

no longer: Guide children in understanding that *no longer* means that something is not happening anymore. Put a pencil on the table and say: *The pencil is on the table.* Pick up the pencil and say: *The pencil is no longer on the table.*

PAGES 26–27

REREAD

Listen as I reread to find out what lives in the grand old tree now. (Raccoons, centipedes, lichen.) *What other animal do you see in the picture?* (mice)

pp. 26–27

raccoons, centipedes, lichen: Point to the living things in the illustration—*raccoons, centipedes, lichen*—as you name them.

Listening Comprehension

PAGES 28–29

PAGES 30–31

just like the grand old tree.

PAGE 32

KEY DETAILS

Point out that the word *sink* sometimes means the place where we wash our hands. *What do you think the word sink means on this page?* (go down) *What sinks deep into the earth?* (roots)

HIGH-FREQUENCY WORD

Have children identify and read the high-frequency word *are* on page 31.

AUTHOR'S PURPOSE

Why do you think the author wrote this story? (Possible answer: She wanted to give information about the life of a tree in time order.)

pp. 28–29

crumbled: Explain that when something crumbles it breaks in to lots of little pieces. Use a cookie or another item to demonstrate crumbling. After you crumble the item, say: *crumbled.* Have children mimic and echo.

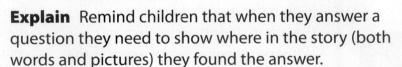

Text Evidence

Explain Remind children that when they answer a question they need to show where in the story (both words and pictures) they found the answer.

Discuss *What is the main topic of this selection? What are some details?* (The life of a grand old tree; p. 4. It grows roots and flowers; pp. 6, 10. Then leaves fall and it dies; pp. 20–21.)

Guided Retelling

Tell children that now they will use the **Retelling Cards** to retell the story.

→ Display Retelling Card 1. Based on children's needs, use either the Modeled, Guided or ELL retelling prompts. The ELL prompts contain support for English language learners based on levels of language acquisition. Repeat with the rest of the cards, using the prompts as a guide.

→ Choose a scene in the book and ask children why the event(s) on that page are a necessary part of a tree's life. Encourage children to offer details to defend their comments. Offer support when necessary.

→ Invite children to choose a favorite part of the story and act it out.

Model Fluency

Turn to pages 6–7. Tell children that the words in a story should be read in a way that shows the feelings the author wants to show. *I think the author wanted to show a happy feeling on these pages.* Then read page 6 aloud, using a positive, upbeat voice: *Her roots sank deep into the earth.* Have children echo.

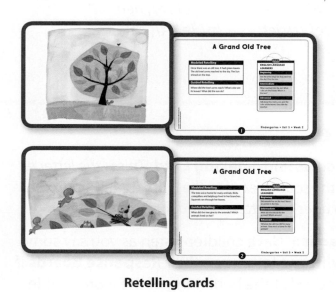

Retelling Cards

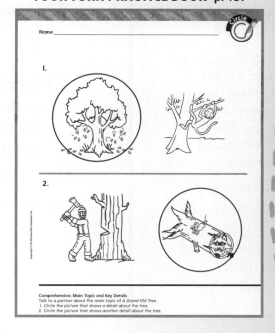

YOUR TURN PRACTICE BOOK p. 137

Word Work

Quick Review

Build Fluency: Sound-Spellings
Display the following **Word-Building Cards:** *a, c, d, e, h, i, m, n, o, p, s, t.* Have children chorally say each sound. Repeat and vary the pace.

 MINILESSON 5 Mins

Phonemic Awareness

Puppet

Phoneme Blending

❶ **Model** Use the puppet to demonstrate how to blend phonemes to make words. *Let's listen for /e/ in the middle of a word:* pet. *The puppet is going to say the sounds in* pet: /p/ /e/ /t/. *The puppet can blend those sounds to make the word:* /peeet/, pet. *Listen as the puppet says the sounds and blends them to make words.* Tell children to listen for /e/ in the middle of the word. Model phoneme blending with the following.

/s/ /e/ /t/, set   /m/ /e/ /t/, met   /m/ /e/ /n/, men

❷ **Guided Practice/Practice** *Listen to the puppet as it says the sounds in words. You will repeat the sounds and then blend them to say the word.*

/b/ /e/ /g/, beg   /t/ /e/ /n/, ten   /h/ /e/ /n/, hen
/d/ /e/ /n/, den   /j/ /e/ /t/, jet   /p/ /e/ /t/, pet

 MINILESSON 5 Mins

Phonics

Review Short *e*

❶ **Model** Display the *Egg* **Sound-Spelling Card**. *This is the letter* e. *The letter* e *stands for the sound /e/ as in the word* egg. *What is the letter?* (e) *What sound does the letter* e *stand for?* (/e/)

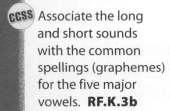
❷ **Guided Practice/Practice** Have children listen as you say some words. Ask them to write the letter *e* on their **Response Boards** if the word has the sound /e/ at the beginning of the word. Guide children with the first word.

echo   Ed   have   end   elf

Have children listen for /e/ in the the middle of the word.

door   ten   five   get   pen

Blend Words with Short *e*

❶ Model Place **Word-Building Cards** *m, e,* and *t* in a pocket chart. Point to the *m. This is the letter* m. *The letter* m *stands for /m/. Say /m/. This is the letter* e. *The letter* e *stands for /e/. Say /e/. This is the letter* t. *The letter* t *stands for /t/. Say /t/. Listen as I blend the three sounds together: /mmmeeet/.* Met. *Now blend the sounds with me to read the word.*

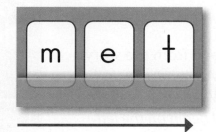

❷ Guided Practice/Practice Change Word-Building Cards to *n, e, t.* Point to the letter *n* and have children say /n/. Point to the letter *e* and have children say /e/. Point to the letter *t* and have children say /t/. Move your hand from left to right under the word and have children blend and read *net*. Repeat with *ten, hen, men.*

MINILESSON
10 Mins

High-Frequency Words

are

are

High-Frequency Word Card

❶ Guided Practice Display the **High-Frequency Word Card** *are*. Use the **Read/Spell/Write** routine to teach the word. Ask children to close their eyes, picture the spelling of the word in their minds, and then write it the way they see it. Have children self-correct by checking the High-Frequency Word Card.

❷ Practice Add the word *are* to the cumulative word bank.

COLLABORATE

→ Have partners create sentences using the word.

→ Have children count the number of letters in the word and then write *are* again.

Cumulative Review Review *my, do, you, go.*

Repeat the **Read/Spell/Write** routine. Mix the words and have children chorally say each one.

Monitor and *Differentiate*

✓ **Quick Check**

Can the children identify initial and medial /e/ and match /e/ to the letter *Ee*?

Can children recognize and read the high-frequency word?

⬇

Small Group Instruction

If No →	**Approaching**	Reteach pp. T144-149
	ELL	Develop pp. T162-165
If Yes →	**On Level**	Review pp. T152-155
	Beyond Level	Extend pp. T158-159

→ # Shared Read

Reading/Writing
Workshop Big Book
and Reading/Writing
Workshop

OBJECTIVES

CCSS Read common high-
frequency words by
sight. **RF.K.3c**

CCSS Read emergent-reader
texts with purpose
and understanding.
RF.K.4

**ACADEMIC
LANGUAGE**
• predict
• Cognates: predecir

MINILESSON

10 Mins

Read "Ed and Ned"

Model Skills and Strategies

Model Concepts About Print Model reading a page from the story
as you track the print with your finger or a pointer. *As I read, I begin
with the first word on the left and move to the right. When I'm done with
the first sentence, I read the sentence below it. Again, I begin on the left
and move to the right.* Invite volunteers to take turns coming up to the
Big Book and pointing to the words in order as you read them.

Predict Read the title together. Encourage children to describe the
photo. Invite them to tell what is happening in the photo and predict
what the story will be about.

Read Have children chorally read the story with you. Point to each
word as you read it together. Help children sound out the decodable
words and say the sight words. If children have difficulty, provide
corrective feedback and guide them page by page using the student
Reading/Writing Workshop.

Ask the following:

→ *Look at page 23. What baby animals do you see?* (bear cubs)

→ *Look at page 26. What are the cubs doing now?* (They are sipping
water from the river.)

→ *Look at page 28. What is Ed doing?* (He is hopping.)

Go Digital

"Ed and Ned"

"Ed and Ned"

Ed is not a pet.
Ned is not a pet.

Ned is up, up, up.
See Ned! See Ned!

Ed met Ned.
Ned met Ed.

Ed can sip, sip, sip.
Ned can sip, sip, sip.

Are Ed and Ned hot?
Are Ed and Ned wet?

Ed can hop, hop, hop.

Ned can nap, nap, nap.

READING/WRITING WORKSHOP, pp. 22–29

Rereading

Have small groups use the **Reading/Writing Workshop** to reread "Ed and Ned." Then review the skills and strategies using the *Phonics* and *Words to Know* pages that come before the selection.

→ As they reread, have children discuss the main topic and key details that support the selection. If children are not sure about the main topic or a key detail, have them reread the entire story or a section of the selection.

→ Have children use page 21 to review the high-frequency word *are*.

→ Have children use page 20 to review that the letter *e* can stand for the sound /e/. Encourage them to identify and name each picture that includes the sound /e/ in the initial or medial position. Guide them to blend the sounds to read the words.

ENGLISH LANGUAGE LEARNERS

Reinforce Vocabulary Display the **High-Frequency Word Cards** *are, my, to, and*. Point to classroom objects and groups of children as you use the high-frequency word in sentences such as the following: *Are we going to have a snack today?* (Yes, we are going to have a snack today.) *My shirt is red. Are my shoes red?* (No, your shoes are not red.) *I can count to ten. Can you count to ten?* (Yes, we can count to ten.) *I can jump and spin. Can you jump and spin?* (Yes, we can jump and spin.)

→ # Language Arts

Interactive Writing

Writing Trait: Organization

Review Remind children that they should make sure all the sentences they write are about the same topic.

Write and read aloud: *I like that movie. The people in it were funny. The movie had a happy ending. I can write to tell people how I feel about a movie. I can make sure all of my sentences are about the same thing.*

Write an Opinion About a Book

Discuss Display the list of books from Day 1. Read the book titles aloud. Talk about why children like those books. Guide children to choose one book to write about, such as *My Garden.*

Model/Apply Grammar Tell children that you will work together to write an opinion about *My Garden.* Remind children that all of the sentences should be about the book.

Write and read the sentence frame: *I _____ My Garden. What word can I add to finish the sentence and give my opinion of the book?* (like) Finish the sentence and read it aloud: *I like My Garden.* Have children read the sentence chorally with you.

Have children help you write more sentences about *My Garden,* using pronouns in place of nouns. *What else can we say about the book?* Have children help you write more sentences about the story. For example: *It is about a girl who wants to grow a garden. She wants to grow chocolate rabbits.* Read the completed sentences aloud. Point out the pronouns in each sentence.

Write Have children help you write about another book from the chart that they like.

Guide children to dictate sentences about the book. Write the words. Share the pen with children and have them write the letters they know.

OBJECTIVES

 CCSS Use a combination of drawing, dictating, and writing to compose opinion pieces in which they tell a reader the topic or the name of the book they are writing about and state an opinion or preference about the topic or book (e.g., *My favorite book is . . .*). **W.K.1**

CCSS Capitalize the first word in a sentence and the pronoun *I.* **L.K.2a**

• Use pronouns *I, we, you*
• Organize writing

ACADEMIC LANGUAGE
topic, pronoun

Go Digital

Writing

I see a fish.

Grammar

Grammar

Pronouns

1 Review Remind children that pronouns are words that can take the place of a noun. *I go to school. Which word is a pronoun?* (I) *The word* I *is a pronoun. It takes the place of my name in the sentence. It tells who goes to school.*

Write and read the sentence: *We go to school.*

Have children chorally repeat the sentence and clap once whenever they hear a pronoun. (we) *What does the pronoun* we *take the place of?* (the names of everyone in the class)

Write and read aloud: *When do I go to school?* Ask which word is the pronoun. (I) Point out that the word *I* is always a capital letter.

2 Guided Practice Write and read aloud the sentence frame: _____ *go to school.* Ask children to think of a pronoun to complete the sentence besides *I* or *we.* (You) *How do you know that* you *is a pronoun?* (*You* takes the place of a person's name in a sentence.)

3 Practice Have children work with a partner. Give each pair a **Photo Card**. Have partners think of sentences about the item on the Photo Card that can begin with the pronoun *I, you,* or *we.* For example, for the Photo Card for *bus,* they might say: *I ride the bus. You ride the bus. We ride the bus.* Have partners share their sentences with the class.

Talk About It

Pair children, and have partners make up sentence about something they do at school, using *I, you,* and *we.* As children share their sentences, ask them to identify the pronoun and the name or names it replaces.

ELL

ENGLISH LANGUAGE LEARNERS

Use Visuals Display the Photo Card for *jump.* As you point to yourself and jump, say *I jump.* As you point to one child, say *You jump.* Have the child jump. As you point to a group of children or to yourself and a child, say *We jump.*

Daily Wrap Up

- Discuss the Essential Question and encourage children to use the oral vocabulary words. *How do plants change as they grow?*

- Prompt children to review and discuss the skills they used today. How do those skills help them?

Materials

**Reading/Writing
Workshop Big Book**
UNIT 5

**Visual
Vocabulary
Cards**

enormous
imagine
content

Word-Building Cards

Puppet

**Interactive Read-Aloud
Cards**

Photo Cards

egg	hippo
elbow	jet
elevator	net
envelope	pen
exit	web
gem	

Think Aloud Cloud

**High-Frequency
Word Cards**

are
my

→ Build the Concept

 MINILESSON 10 Mins

Oral Language

ESSENTIAL QUESTION

 COLLABORATE

Remind children that this week they are talking and learning about how living things change as they grow. Guide children to discuss the Essential Question using information from the **Big Book** and the weekly song.

Remind children about the tree that grew from the acorn in "My Oak Tree." Sing the song and have children join in.

Oral Vocabulary

Review last week's oral vocabulary words, as well as *develop* and *amazing*. Then use the **Define/Example/Ask** routine to introduce *enormous, imagine,* and *content.*

Oral Vocabulary Routine

Define: Something that is **enormous** is very large.

Example: The mall is an enormous building with many shops.

Ask: An elephant is enormous. What other animal is enormous?

Define: When you **imagine** something, you see it in your mind.

Example: I can imagine what happens at a carnival.

Ask: What do you imagine it would be like to fly an airplane?

Define: When you are **content**, you feel happy and satisfied.

Example: I am content when I spend time with my family.

Ask: What does a content person look like?

Vocabulary
Define
Example
Ask:

Visual Vocabulary Cards

Go Digital

Visual Glossary

"The Pine Tree"

When I read _____,
I had to reread...

**Think Aloud
Cloud**

→ Listening Comprehension

Read the Interactive Read Aloud

MINILESSON
10 Mins

Genre: Fairy Tale

Tell children that you will be reading a fairy tale. A *fairy tale* is a story with made-up characters and places. Fairy tales are often stories from long ago. Display the **Interactive Read-Aloud Cards**.

Read the title. Point to the illustration as you explain that a pine tree has thin, narrow leaves called needles.

Interactive Read-Aloud Cards

Strategy: Reread

Remind children if they do not understand something while they read, it can be helpful to read a section again. Model using the **Think Aloud Cloud** to demonstrate the strategy.

Think Aloud I just read that the pine tree asked the sparrows to follow the big trees, but I'm not sure why. I'll reread. I think that will help me understand. When I read the paragraph again, I figured out that the pine tree sent the sparrows to follow the trees that were cut down because those trees were his friends. He wants to know where they are going.

Read the story. Pause occasionally to model the strategy of rereading.

Make Connections

Guide partners to connect "The Pine Tree" with *A Grand Old Tree*. Discuss the ways both stories show how trees change as they grow. *What kind of animal lived in both trees?* (Answers may vary: birds)

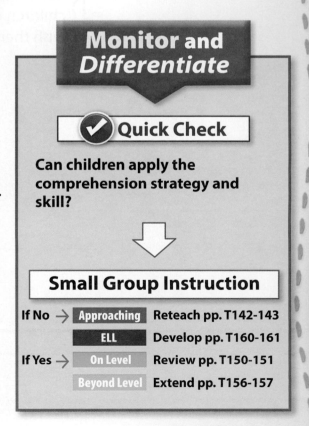

ELL

ENGLISH LANGUAGE LEARNERS

Reinforce Meaning As you read "The Pine Tree," make meaning clear by pointing to specific characters, places, or objects in the illustrations, demonstrating word meanings, paraphrasing text, and asking children questions. For example, on Card 2, point to the sailboat in the illustration. Say: *This is a sailboat.*

Monitor and *Differentiate*

✓ Quick Check

Can children apply the comprehension strategy and skill?

↓

Small Group Instruction

If No →	**Approaching**	Reteach pp. T142–143
	ELL	Develop pp. T160–161
If Yes →	**On Level**	Review pp. T150–151
	Beyond Level	Extend pp. T156–157

→ # Word Work

MINILESSON 10 Mins

Phonemic Awareness

Puppet

Phoneme Blending

OBJECTIVES

CCSS Demonstrate basic knowledge of one-to-one letter-sound correspondences by producing the primary or many of the most frequent sounds for each consonant. **RF.K.3a**

CCSS Associate the long and short sounds with common spellings (graphemes) for the five major vowels. **RF.K.3b**

Blend words with short *e*

❶ **Model** Use the puppet to demonstrate how to blend phonemes to make words. *The puppet is going to say sounds in a word: /s/ /e/ /t/. It can blend those sounds to make a word: /seeet/ set. When the puppet blends the sounds together, it makes the word set. Listen as the puppet blends more sounds to make a word.* Model phoneme blending with the following:

/n/ /e/ /t/ *net*   /l/ /e/ /d/ *led*   /r/ /e/ /d/ *red*

❷ **Guided Practice/Practice** Have children blend sounds to form words. *The puppet is going to say the sounds in a word. Listen as it says each sound. You will repeat the sounds, and then blend them to say the word.* Guide practice with the first word.

/e/ /d/ *Ed*   /t/ /e/ /n/ *ten*   /e/ /g/ *egg*
/e/ /d/ /j/ *edge*   /b/ /e/ /d/ *bed*   /g/ /e/ /t/ *get*

♪ Review initial /e/. Play and sing "Scrambled Egg, Fried Egg." Have children clap when they hear initial /e/. Demonstrate as you sing with them.

Go Digital

Phonemic Awareness

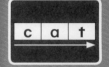

Phonics

Handwriting

MINILESSON
5
Mins

Phonics

e

Word-Building Card

Review Short *e*

① **Model** Display **Word-Building Card** *e*. *This is the letter* e. *The letter* e *can stand for /e/, the sound you hear at the beginning of* egg. *Say the sound with me: /e/. I will write the letter* e *because* egg *has /e/ at the beginning.* Repeat the routine using the word *bed*.

② **Guided Practice/Practice** Tell children that you will say some words that have the /e/ sound in the middle of the word and some words that do not have /e/. Have children say /e/ and write the letter *e* on their **Response Boards** when they hear /e/ in the middle of the word. Guide practice with the first word.

jet	ride	man	set	could
wet	bed	two	hot	pen

Blend Words with Short *e* and *m, t, h, n, h, s, p*

① **Model** Display Word-Building Cards *s, e, t*. *This is the letter* s. *It stands for /s/. This is the letter* e. *It stands for /e/. This is the letter* t. *It stands for /t/. Let's blend the three sounds together: /ssseeet/, /set/. The word is* set. Continue with *ten, Ted, men*.

② **Guided Practice/Practice** Write the following words and sentences. Have children read each word, blending the sounds. Then have them read the sentences.

met   Ed   den   hen   net   set   pet

Prompt children to read the connected text, sounding out the decodable words: *We are in the den. I like the hen. Ed can see the net.*

YOUR TURN PRACTICE BOOK p. 138

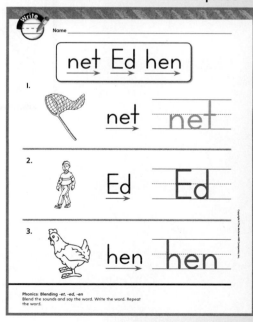

Corrective Feedback

Sound Error Model the sound that children missed, then have them repeat. Tap under the letter *e* in the word *met* and ask: *What's the sound?* (/e/) Return to the beginning of the word. *Let's start over.* Blend the sounds in the word again.

→ # Word Work

MINILESSON 5 Mins

Phonics

Photo Cards

Picture Sort

OBJECTIVES

CCSS Read common high-frequency words by sight. **RF.K.3c**

Sort names of objects by initial and medial /e/

ACADEMIC LANGUAGE
sort

1 Model Remind children that the letter *e* can stand for /e/. Place **Word-Building Card** *e* at the top center of the pocket chart. *What is this letter?* (e) *What sound does this letter stand for?* (/e/) Hold up the **Photo Card** for *egg. Here is the picture for* egg. Egg *has the /e/ sound at the beginning. Listen, /eeeg/.* Place the *egg* Photo Card on one side of the pocket chart.

Use the same routine for medial /e/ and the Photo Card for *jet.* Place *jet* on the other side of the pocket chart.

Hold up Photo Card for *elevator.* Elevator *begins with /e/. I will place it under the egg because they both begin with /e/.*

2 Guided Practice/Practice Have children sort the Photo Cards *elbow, envelope, exit, gem, net, pen, web.* Have them identify if /e/ is at the beginning or in the middle of the word. Then have them tell which Photo Card each should be placed under: *egg* or *jet.* Guide children with the first Photo Card.

Photo Cards

Go Digital

Phonics

High-Frequency Word Routine

MINILESSON
5 Mins

High-Frequency Words

are

❶ Guided Practice Display the **High-Frequency Word Card** *are*. Review the word using the **Read/Spell/Write** routine.

❷ Practice Point to the High-Frequency Word Card *are* and have children read it. Repeat with last week's word *my*.

Build Fluency

Word Automaticity Write the following sentences and have children chorally read aloud as you track the print. Repeat several times.

> We *are* in the den.
> Ted and Sam *are* like you.
> Pam and Tim *are* in.
> You *are* in the pen.

Read for Fluency Distribute pages 139–140 of the **Your Turn Practice Book** and help children assemble their Take-Home Books. Chorally read the Take-Home Book with children. Then have children reread the book to review high-frequency words and build fluency.

YOUR TURN PRACTICE BOOK pp. 139–140

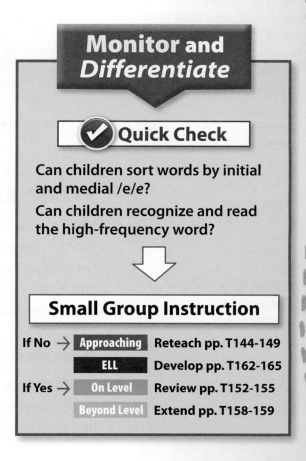

Monitor and Differentiate

✓ Quick Check

Can children sort words by initial and medial /e/*e*?

Can children recognize and read the high-frequency word?

⬇

Small Group Instruction

If No →	**Approaching**	Reteach pp. T144-149
	ELL	Develop pp. T162-165
If Yes →	**On Level**	Review pp. T152-155
	Beyond Level	Extend pp. T158-159

→ # Language Arts

Reading/Writing Workshop Big Book

MINILESSON 10 Mins

Independent Writing

Writing Trait: Organization

1 Practice Tell children that today they will write to tell their opinion of a book they have read.

2 Guided Practice Share the Readers to Writers page in the **Reading/Writing Workshop Big Book**. Read the model sentences aloud.

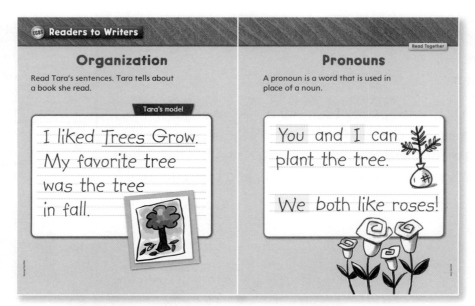

READING/WRITING WORKSHOP BIG BOOK, pp. 32–33

Write an Opinion About a Book

Model Say: *This week we read a book about an old tree. We can write our opinion about this book.* Write the title: *The Grand Old Tree.* Below the book title, write **opinion** sentences about it, such as: *I liked* The Grand Old Tree. *It was good. You will learn how trees change. You will like it, too.* Read the sentences aloud, tracking the print.

Prewrite

Brainstorm Have children work with a partner to think about a book they would like to write about. Ask them to discuss why they like the book.

Go Digital

Present the Lesson

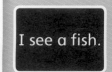

Writing

I see a fish.

Grammar

Draft

Ask children to complete these sentence frames about the book they chose: *I liked [book title]. It was _____. You will learn about _____. You will _____ it, too.* Guide children in writing the sentence frames and help children complete them.

Apply Writing Trait As children complete their sentence frames, ask them to tell the class what topic their sentences are all about.

Apply Grammar Remind children that a pronoun takes the place of a noun in a sentence. *The words* he, she, it, you, *and* we *are all pronouns.*

ENGLISH LANGUAGE LEARNERS

Oral Language Support children as they use pronouns to talk about things they see. Have children point to an object they see in the classroom. Help them name the object. Then help children use the name of the object to dictate a sentence about it. For example: *I see a desk.*

MINILESSON 5 Mins

Grammar

Pronouns

❶ **Review** Display the **Photo Card** for *hippo*. Write and read aloud the sentence: *I see a hippo. What is the pronoun in the sentence?* (I) I *is a pronoun because it takes the place of a noun. It takes the place of my name in the sentence.* Circle the pronoun in the sentence.

❷ **Guided Practice/Practice** Ask children to choose a Photo Card and look at the picture. Have children copy the sentence frame *I see _____.* Help children complete the sentence frame. Share some of their completed sentences with the class.

Talk About It

COLLABORATE

Pair children, and have partners look outside the window and choose something they see. Encourage children to talk about what they see with prompts such as these: *What does it look like? Is it a living thing?*

Daily Wrap Up

- Review the Essential Question and encourage children to discuss it, using the oral vocabulary words *develop* and *amazing. How do living things change as they grow?*

- Prompt children to review and discuss the skills they used today. Guide them to give examples of how they used each skill.

Materials

Reading/Writing Workshop Big Book
UNIT 5

Literature Big Book
A Grand Old Tree

Interactive Read-Aloud Cards

Word-Building Cards

High-Frequency Word Cards
are

Photo Cards
egg
gem
tree

Response Board

Visual Vocabulary Cards
are

→ # Extend the Concept

Oral Language

OBJECTIVES

CCSS Use words and phrases acquired through conversations, reading and being read to, and responding to texts. **L.K.6**

CCSS Blend and segment onsets and rimes of single-syllable spoken words. **RF.K.2c**

Develop vocabulary

ESSENTIAL QUESTION

Remind children that this week they have been talking and reading about how living things change as they grow. Have them sing "My Oak Tree." Then ask how the tree changes in *A Grand Old Tree*. Prompt children as necessary. Ask: *What happened first? What happened next?* (Its roots sank into the ground. It grew tall. It grew flowers. It shed its leaves. It fell.)

Phonological Awareness
Onset/Rime Blending
Have children sing "My Oak Tree" with you. Say the word *found*. Have children repeat. Repeat the word, segmenting and blending the onset and rime: /f/ /ound/. Have children repeat. Say: *We can blend these sounds to make the word* found. Repeat the routine with *Daddy*, *pocket*, and *grown*.

Review Oral Vocabulary

Reread the Interactive Read Aloud Use the **Define/Example/Ask** routine to review the oral vocabulary words *develop, amazing, enormous, imagine,* and *content*. Have children listen as you reread "The Pine Tree." Then ask:

→ *Why was the pine tree content at the end of the story?* (He was happy in the forest.)

→ *Why did the pine tree say, "I imagine that lying in a pile in a lumberyard wouldn't be very fun"?* (He thought it would be lonely and boring.)

Go Digital

Visual Glossary

"The Pine Tree"

Category Words

Category Words: Tree Parts

❶ Explain/Model Divide children into groups. Assign each group a tree part: *roots, trunk, branches, leaves,* and *bark*. Have children draw their tree part. Then read the following passage. Have them hold up their pictures whenever they hear the tree part they drew.

A tree begins as a tiny seed. The seed breaks open, and roots *begin to grow. Soon a stem pops out of the ground. This is the beginning of the tree's* trunk. *Over time, the tree grows bigger. Soon it has* branches, *which look like arms.* Leaves *grow from the* branches. *The* trunk *and the* branches *are covered with* bark. *The* bark *protects the tree.*

❷ Guided Practice Display the **Photo Card** for *tree*. Help children identify each tree part. Read the following sentences and have children point to each tree part on the Photo Card.

A squirrel climbs up the trunk. A bird builds a nest on a branch. Roots soak up water from the ground. Tree bark is brown and rough. Leaves change color and fall to the ground.

→ Have children draw and label a picture to go with one of the sentences.

Vocabulary Strategy: Word Parts/ Inflectional Ending *-ed*

❶ Model Remind children that the *-ed* ending can be added to many present-tense verbs to make past-tense verbs. Review that past-tense verbs tell what happened before now.

Think Aloud Most of the text in *A Grand Old Tree* tells us about what happened to the tree long ago. Most of the verbs end with *-ed* because we are reading about the past. We can look for the *-ed* ending to tell when the action happened in a story.

❷ Guided Practice/Practice Say a present-tense verb aloud. Have children repeat the verb back to you. Then ask volunteers to change the verb to a past-tense verb by adding the *-ed* ending, and have them say the new verb aloud. Invite volunteers to make up sentences with verbs that end with *-ed*.

YOUR TURN PRACTICE BOOK p. 141

Category Words: Tree Parts
Look at each picture. Tell about it. Put a marker on each picture that shows a tree part. Say the name of each tree part.

→ # Listening Comprehension

CLOSE READING

A Grand Old Tree
BY MARY NEWELL DEPALMA

Literature Big Book

Go Digital

"From a Seed to a Tree"

OBJECTIVES

CCSS With prompting and support, identify the main topic and retell key details of a text. **RI.K.2**

- Understand the characteristics of informational text
- Use the text feature diagram to understand information
- Apply the comprehension strategy: Reread
- Make connections across texts

ACADEMIC LANGUAGE
- *diagram*
- Cognates: *diagrama*

MINILESSON

10 Mins

Read "From a Seed to a Tree"

Genre: Informational Text

Display "From a Seed to a Tree" on pages 33–36 of the **Big Book** and read aloud the title. Explain to children that this informational text gives real information about how an apple tree grows.

Set a Purpose for Reading

Read aloud page 33. Tell children to listen as you continue reading to learn how seeds grow into trees.

Strategy: Reread

Remind children that good readers reread part of a text if there is something they do not understand. Point to page 33. *I can reread one line or the whole page if I need to. This will help me better understand the text.*

Text Feature: Diagram

Explain Point out the diagram on page 34 and read aloud the labels. *This diagram shows pictures and text. It shows the different stages in how a seed grows into a sapling, or young tree.* Explain to children that they can learn more about plants by observing how they grow.

Apply Have volunteers point to the part of the diagram that shows when the seed begins to grow leaves, or sprouts.

LITERATURE BIG BOOK PAGE 33

REREAD

Reread page 33 aloud. Have children look up the word *seed* in the Review the New Words You Learned on page 36.

LITERATURE BIG BOOK   PAGES 34–35

TEXT FEATURE

Look at the pictures in the diagram. Which picture shows the plant with the most leaves? (a sapling) Explain to children that we can learn about how plants grow by observing them closely.

LITERATURE BIG BOOK PAGE 36

MAIN TOPIC/KEY DETAILS

What is the main topic? (how an apple tree grows) Tell a detail about what a tree needs to grow. (water and sunlight)

ENGLISH LANGUAGE LEARNERS

Reinforce Meaning As you read aloud the text, make the meaning clear by pointing to details in the photographs and diagram. Ask children questions and elicit language.

Retell and Respond

Have children discuss the selection by asking the following questions:

→ *What does a seedling grow into?* (a sapling)

→ *Where do new apple seeds come from?* (inside the apples)

Make Connections

Have children recall the selections they read this week.

→ *What happened after the grand old tree flowered?* (It bore fruit.)

Write About It Write about how the pine tree changed as it grew.

 CONNECT TO CONTENT

Observe How a Tree Grows
Review with children the different life stages of an apple tree (seed, seedling, sapling). Have partners discuss the trees they have seen growing in their neighborhood. Ask them to describe the size, color, and shape of the changes in the trees.

STEM

 → # Word Work

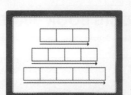

Quick Review

Build Fluency: Sound Spellings:
Display **Word-Building Cards:** *a, c, d, e, h, i, m, n, o, p, s, t.* Have children chorally say each sound. Repeat several times.

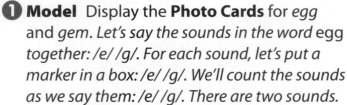

Phonemic Awareness

MINILESSON
5 Mins

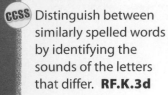

OBJECTIVES

CCSS Distinguish between similarly spelled words by identifying the sounds of the letters that differ. **RF.K.3d**

CCSS Read common high-frequency words by sight. **RF.K.3c**

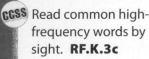

Segment words into phonemes

Phoneme Segmentation

1 Model Display the **Photo Cards** for *egg* and *gem. Let's say the sounds in the word* egg *together: /e/ /g/. For each sound, let's put a marker in a box: /e/ /g/. We'll count the sounds as we say them: /e/ /g/. There are two sounds.* Place markers in sound boxes for each sound. *Say the sounds in* egg: */e/ /g/. Now say the word:* egg. Repeat the routine for *gem.*

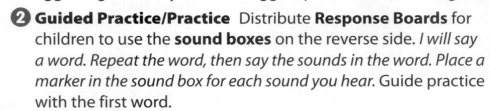

Sound Box

2 Guided Practice/Practice Distribute **Response Boards** for children to use the **sound boxes** on the reverse side. *I will say a word. Repeat the word, then say the sounds in the word. Place a marker in the sound box for each sound you hear.* Guide practice with the first word.

den (/d/ /e/ /n/)	*bed* (/b/ /e/ /d/)	*echo* (/e/ /k/ /ō/)
edge (/e/ /d/ /j/)	*led* (/l/ /e/ /d/)	*fed* (/f/ /e/ /d/)
bell (/b/ /e/ /l/)	*else* (/e/ /l/ /s/)	

MINILESSON
5 Mins

Phonics

Blend Words with Short *e, a, i, o* and *t, n*

1 Guided Practice Display **Word-Building Cards** *t, e, n.* Point to the letter *t. This is the letter* t. *The letter* t *stands for /t/. Say /t/. This is the letter* e. *The letter* e *stands for /e/. Listen as I blend the two sounds together: /teee/. This is the letter* n. *The letter* n *stands for /n/. Listen as I blend the three sounds: /teeennn/,* ten. *Now you say it. Let's change the* e *to* i. Use the same routine to blend the word *tin.*

2 Practice Write *pet, pit, pat, pot.* Have children blend and read the words. *Which letters are the same?* (p, t) *Which letters are different?* (e, i, a, o) Discuss the sound each letter stands for and how it changes the word.

Go Digital

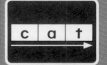
Phonemic Awareness

c a t
Phonics

A A
a
Handwriting

Visual Glossary

| the | is |
| you | do |
High-Frequency Word Routine

Dictation

Review Dictate these sounds for children to spell. Have them repeat the sound and then write the appropriate letter. Repeat several times.

/h/   /n/   /e/   /d/   /t/   /p/

Dictate the following words for children to spell: *ten, men, hen, pen, pet, set*. Model for children how to segment each word to scaffold the spelling. *When I say the word* ten, *I hear three sounds /t/ /e/ /n/. I know the letter* t *stands for /t/, the letter* e *stands for /e/, and the letter* n *stands for /n/. I will write the letters* t, e, n *to spell the word* ten.

When children finish, write the letters and words for them to self-correct.

High-Frequency Words

Practice Say the word *are* and have children write it. Then display the **Visual Vocabulary Card** for *are* and follow the Teacher Talk routine on the back.

Visual Vocabulary Card

Build Fluency Build sentences in the pocket chart using the **High-Frequency Word Cards** and **Photo Cards**. Use an index card to create a punctuation card for a period. Have children chorally read the sentences as you track the print. Then have them identify the word *are*.

Have partners create sentences using the word *are*.

 You and I **are** upside down.

 You **are** a girl.

 You **are** a boy.

 Are you a doctor?

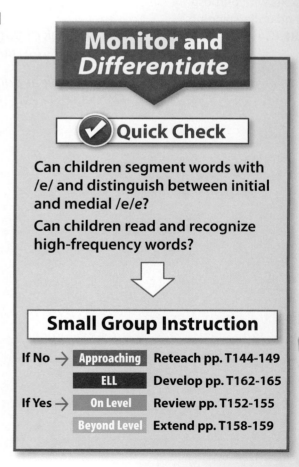

Monitor and *Differentiate*

✔ Quick Check

Can children segment words with /e/ and distinguish between initial and medial /e/e?

Can children read and recognize high-frequency words?

Small Group Instruction

If No →	**Approaching**	Reteach pp. T144–149
	ELL	Develop pp. T162–165
If Yes →	**On Level**	Review pp. T152–155
	Beyond Level	Extend pp. T158–159

→ # Shared Read

Reading/Writing Workshop Big Book and Reading/Writing Workshop

---

OBJECTIVES

CCSS Read common high-frequency words by sight. **RF.K.3c**

CCSS Read emergent-reader texts with purpose and understanding. **RF.K.4**

MINILESSON **10** Mins

Read "Ed and Ned"

Model Skills and Strategies

Model Concepts About Print Begin reading the story. Model reading from left to right and top to bottom (return sweep) using a finger or a pointer. *When I read, I start on the left side of the page and move to the right. I begin at the top of the page and move to the bottom.* Then invite a volunteer to come up to the **Big Book** and model reading from left to right and top to bottom, tracking the print with his or her finger, and doing a return sweep in between lines.

Reread Have children chorally read the story. Children should sound out the decodable words and say the sight words. Offer support as needed using the student **Reading/Writing Workshop**.

Ask the following:

→ *Look at page 24. What is the cub doing?* (The cub is climbing up a tree.)

→ *Look at page 27. Are Ed and Ned wet? How do you know?* (Ed and Ned are wet. I know this because their fur is dripping water.)

→ *Look at page 29. What is Ned doing now? Why?* (Ned is napping. He is tired.)

Go Digital

"Ed and Ned"

"Ed and Ned"

READING/WRITING WORKSHOP, pp. 22–29

Fluency: Intonation

1 Explain Tell children that as you read the selection, you will change the tone of your voice when reading sentences that end with a period, a question mark, or an exclamation point. Point out different kinds of punctuation in the story.

2 Model Model reading page 24 of "Ed and Ned." Read each sentence with the proper intonation and expression. Then point to the punctuation mark at the end of each sentence. *When I read each sentence, the tone of my voice sounds different. When there is a period at the end of the sentence, I am making a statement. When there is an exclamation point at the end of the sentence, I read it with more emotion, like this.* Then point out differences in intonation by reading other sentences in the story that end with a period, an exclamation point, or a question mark.

3 Guided Practice Read each sentence in the story and have children echo you. Encourage children to repeat each sentence using proper intonation. Then invite the class to choral read the story as you listen for proper intonation.

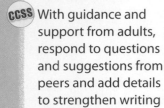 **Language Arts**

 MINILESSON 10 Mins

Independent Writing

Write an Opinion About a Book

Revise

Distribute the children's draft sentences from Day 3.

Apply Writing Trait Organization Explain that as writers revise, they make sure their writing is well organized. Each sentence should be about the topic they chose to write about. Write and read: *I like swimming. It is fun on a hot day. My dad is playing golf. My opinion is that I like swimming. All of my sentences should be about swimming. Let's work together to find the sentence that is not about swimming. My dad is playing golf is not about swimming.* Erase the sentence that doesn't belong and do a choral-read of the sentences. Then have children reread the sentences they wrote on Day 3 and check for the following:

→ Did I write about a book I have read?

→ Did I give my opinion of the book?

→ Do all of my sentences tell about the book?

Apply Grammar Explain that writers use pronouns so they don't have to use the same noun over and over again. Write and read: *The book is funny. The book has many pictures.* Have children identify a pronoun to replace *The book* in the second sentence.

 Peer Edit Have children work in pairs to do a peer edit in which they read their partner's draft. Ask partners to check that all the sentences are about the same book. Have children check that an opinion is given about the book. Provide time for children to make revisions to their sentences.

Final Draft

After children have edited their own papers and finished their peer edits, have them write their final draft. Explain that they should try to write letters carefully. Suggest that children use a finger as they write to keep the words evenly spaced. Conference with children to provide guidance as they work.

OBJECTIVES

CCSS With guidance and support from adults, respond to questions and suggestions from peers and add details to strengthen writing as needed. **W.K.5**

CCSS Use personal, possessive, and indefinite pronouns (e.g., *I, me, my; they, them, their; anyone, everything*). **L.1.1d**

Write an opinion

ACADEMIC LANGUAGE

• *revise, opinion, topic*
• Cognates: *revisar, opinión*

Go Digital

Writing

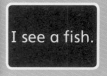

I see a fish.

Grammar

Grammar

5 Mins

Pronouns

1 Review Write and read aloud this sentence: *The fish swims fast.* Ask: *Which word is a naming word?* (fish) *What pronoun can we use instead of* The fish? (It)

2 Guided Practice Have one child stand in front of the class. Ask that child to tell something that he or she likes to do. For example, she might say that she likes to jump rope.

Write the sentence frame: _____ *likes to jump rope.* Have children help you complete the sentence frame by telling you what pronoun completes the sentence. (He; She) Ask if other children like to jump rope. Write: _____ *like to jump rope.* Have a child fill in the pronoun to complete the sentence. (I; We)

3 Practice Have all the children in the class clap their hands for a few seconds. Write this sentence frame and read it aloud: _____ *clap our hands.* Have children work with a partner to choose the pronoun that best completes the sentence. (We) Have children choral-read the completed sentence using the pronoun.

Talk About It

Pair children, and have partners give an opinion about the games they like to play. Encourage children to talk about what they like about each game.

ENGLISH LANGUAGE LEARNERS

Picture Cards and Sentences Provide sentences that go with images on the **Photo Cards**. As you read a sentence aloud, hold up a Photo Card as you say the pronoun and use it in a sentence, such as *It is a horse.*

Daily Wrap Up

- Review the Essential Question and encourage children to discuss it, using the oral vocabulary words.
- Prompt children to discuss the skills they practiced and learned today. Guide them to share examples of each skill.

Go Digital

www.connected.mcgraw-hill.com
RESOURCES
Research and Inquiry

→ ## Wrap Up the Week
Integrate Ideas

RESEARCH AND INQUIRY

Trees

OBJECTIVES

CCSS Participate in shared research and writing projects (e.g., explore a number of books by a favorite author and express opinions about them). **W.K.7**

CCSS With guidance and support from adults, explore a variety of digital tools to produce and publish writing, including in collaboration with peers. **W.K.6**

ACADEMIC LANGUAGE

• *research, Internet*
• Cognates: *internet*

Make a Tree Life Cycle Display

 Tell children that today, as part of a small group, they will do a research project to make an apple tree life cycle display. Review the steps in the research process below.

STEP 1 Choose a Topic

Prompt children to talk about the different stages of an apple tree's life cycle: seed, sprout, seedling, and sapling. Prompt groups to discuss further stages of the tree. Tell groups that they will draw a picture of just one part of the apple tree's life cycle.

STEP 2 Find Resources

Discuss locating and using resources with children. Direct them to use the selections from the week. Children may also find more details about the parts of an apple tree's life in books in the library or on the Internet. Use a child-friendly search engine. Have children use the Research Process Checklist online.

STEP 3 Keep Track of Ideas

Have children note their ideas by drawing pictures and writing words in a two-column list. Provide help with content words such as *seedling*.

Collaborative Conversations

Take Turns Talking As children engage in partner, small-group, and whole-class discussions, encourage them to:

→ take turns talking.

→ speak clearly and loudly enough so others can hear.

→ ask others to share their ideas and opinions.

STEM

**STEP 4 Create the Project:
Tree Life Cycle**

Assign each group one stage of the apple tree's life cycle. Explain the characteristics of the project:

→ **Information** This display will give information about the life cycle of an apple tree.

→ **Text** The display will describe the different stages of the life cycle. Provide this sentence frame:

This is a _____ .

→ **Illustration** Each picture will show one part of the tree's life cycle.

Explain that each group will illustrate one part of the tree's life cycle and write a sentence about it. The pictures will be put together to make a life cycle display.

→ Guide children to use the research from the Internet sources and digital tools to produce and publish their writing.

→ Guide children to write a complete sentence that begins with a capital letter and ends with a period.

→ Encourage children who can write more about their topic to do so.

→ Encourage children to include details in their illustration.

This is a full-grown apple tree.

 **ENGLISH LANGUAGE LEARNERS
SCAFFOLD**

Beginning	Intermediate	Advanced/Advanced High
Use Sentence Frames Pair children with more fluent speakers. Provide sentence frames to help children talk about their life cycle stage. For example: *This is a _____. It has _____.*	**Demonstrate Understanding** Encourage children to tell as much about their picture as they can. Prompt them with questions such as these: *What does the seed do?* Have children point to parts of their illustrations as they answer. *What part of a tree's life do you show?*	**Expand** Encourage children to express opinions. Provide this sentence frame: *We like this part of a tree's life because _____.* As children talk about their pictures, elicit fuller responses by asking additional questions. Restate students' responses in complete sentences, if necessary.

Materials

Reading/Writing Workshop Big Book
UNIT 5

Literature Big Book
A Grand Old Tree

Interactive Read-Aloud Cards

Word-Building Cards

a b c

Photo Cards
jet
net

Response Board

Visual Vocabulary Cards
are

High-Frequency Word Cards
and
are
I
my
the
to
you

→ Integrate Ideas

TEXT CONNECTIONS

Connect to Essential Question

OBJECTIVES

 CCSS With prompting and support, identify basic similarities in and differences between two texts on the same topic (e.g., in illustrations, descriptions, or procedures). **RI.K.9**

CCSS Participate in collaborative conversations with diverse partners about *kindergarten topics and texts* with peers and adults in small and larger groups. **SL.K.1**

• Make connections among texts
• Make connections to the world

Text to Text

Remind children that all week they have been reading selections about how trees grow. Tell them that now they will connect the texts, or think about how the selections are alike. Model comparing *A Grand Old Tree* with another selection from the week.

 Think Aloud In *A Grand Old Tree,* the illustrations showed me how a tree grew. In "From a Seed to a Tree," the photos and illustrations showed me how an apple tree grows. In both books, I saw how trees change as they grow.

Guide children to compare the changes shown in "The Pine Tree" with the changes shown in "An Apple Tree Grows." Remind children that "The Pine Tree" is a kind of fiction.

Text to Self

Have children tell about trees they have seen at different stages, from young sprouts to huge, mature trees. Prompt children to include details about seasonal changes as well.

Text to World

Ask children to talk about what trees are for. Lead them to the conclusion that trees are used for making things but they are also for beauty, and that it is important to plant trees and care for them.

TALK ABOUT READING

OBJECTIVES

CCSS Confirm understanding of a text read aloud or information presented orally or through other media by asking and answering questions about key details and requesting clarification if something is not understood. **SL.K.2**

Becoming Readers

Talk with children about the genres, strategy, and skill they have learned about this week. Prompt them to discuss how this knowledge helps them to read and understand selections.

→ Remind children that one genre they learned about is informational text. Recall with them some characteristics of informational text.

→ Talk with children about the strategy of rereading. *How did rereading a page in* A Grand Old Tree *help you to understand the text?*

→ Discuss with children how identifying the main topic and key details in "From a Seed to a Tree" helped them to understand the text.

RESEARCH AND INQUIRY

OBJECTIVES

CCSS Participate in shared research and writing projects (e.g., explore a number of books by a favorite author and express opinions about them). **W.K.7**

Wrap Up the Project

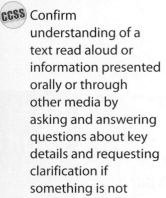

Guide groups to share information about their part of the tree life cycle display and to point out details in their pictures. Encourage children to use words and phrases they learned this week. Have children use the Presenting and Listening checklists online.

→ # Word Work

 MINILESSON **5 Mins**

Phonemic Awareness

OBJECTIVES

CCSS Isolate and pronounce the initial, medial vowel, and final sounds in three-phoneme words. **RF.K.2d**

Spell simple words phonetically, drawing on knowledge of sound-letter relationships. **L.K.2d**

CCSS Read common high-frequency words by sight. **RF.K.3c**

Segment words into phonemes

Phoneme Segmentation

1 Model Display the **Photo Card** for *net*. *This is a net. Let's say the sounds in the word* net *together. /n/ /e/ /t/. For each sound, let's put a marker in a box: /n/ /e/ /t/. We'll count the sounds as we say them: /n/ /e/ /t/. There are three sounds. Say the sounds in* net: */n/ /e/ /t/. Now say the word:* net. *Repeat the routine for* jet.

2 Guided Practice/Practice Distribute **Response Boards**. Have children put a marker in a box for each sound and say the word. *I will say a word. Say each sound in the word. Place a marker in the* **Sound Box** *for each sound.* Guide practice with the first word.

pen (/p/ /e/ /n/)	led (/l/ /e/ /d/)	ten (/t/ /e/ /n/)	Ed (/e/ /d/)
den (/d/ /e/ /n/)	men (/m/ /e/ /n/)	bet (/b/ /e/ /t/)	egg (/e/ /g/)

 MINILESSON **5 Mins**

Phonics

Read Words with Short *e* and *n, t, s, n, d*

1 Guided Practice Remind children that the letter *e* can stand for the sound /e/. Display **Word-Building Cards** *n, e, t*. Point to the letter *n. The letter* n *stands for /n/. The letter* e *stands for /e/. Say /eee/. The letter* t *stands for /t/. Say /t/. Let's blend the sounds: /nnneeet/* net. *Let's change the* n *to an* s. *Repeat routine with* set.

2 Practice Write these words and sentences for children to read:

ten   den   pen   pet   met

I like my pet.   Sam met Pam in the den.
We are in the den.   Ted has a pen.

Remove words from view before dictation.

♪ Review initial /e/e. Have children write the letter *e* on their **Response Boards**. Play and sing "Scrambled Egg, Fried Egg." Have children hold up and show the letter *e* on their boards when they hear initial /e/. Demonstrate as you sing with children.

Dictation

Review Dictate the following sounds for children to spell. As you say each sound, have children repeat it and then write the letter on their **Response Boards** that stands for the sound.

/h/   /i/   /n/   /k/   /o/   /d/   /e/

Dictate the following words for children to spell. Use the first word to model how to segment words to scaffold the spelling. *I will say a word. You will repeat the word, then think about how many sounds are in the word. Use your* **sound boxes** *to count the sounds. Then write one letter for each sound you hear.*

net   pen   set   met   pit   pat   pin   pet

Then write the letters and words for children to self-correct.

High-Frequency Words

are

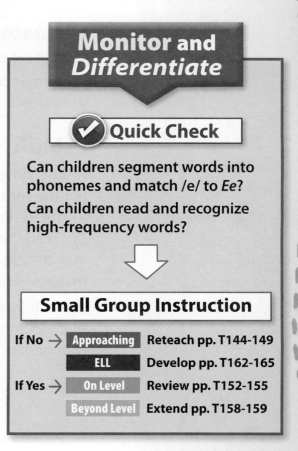
Visual Vocabulary Card

❶ **Review** Display **Visual Vocabulary Card** *are*. Have children **Read/Spell/Write** the word. Then choose a Partner Talk activity.

Distribute the following **High-Frequency Word Cards** to children: *and, my, are, the, to, you, I.* Tell children that you will say some sentences. *When you hear the word that is on your card, stand and hold up the word card.*

Emily **and** *Pat like* **my** *tree house.*
They **are** *at* **my** *school.*
The *peaches* **are** *amazing.*
Fruits **and** *vegetables* **are** *good things* **to** *eat.*
Are you *planting flower seeds?*
I *think* **you are** *nice.*

❷ **Build Fluency: Word Automaticity** Display High-Frequency Word Cards *and, my, are, the, to, you, I.* Point to each card, at random, and have children read the word as quickly as they can.

Monitor and *Differentiate*

✓ Quick Check

Can children segment words into phonemes and match /e/ to *Ee*?

Can children read and recognize high-frequency words?

Small Group Instruction

If No →	**Approaching**	Reteach pp. T144-149
	ELL	Develop pp. T162-165
If Yes →	**On Level**	Review pp. T152-155
	Beyond Level	Extend pp. T158-159

→ # Language Arts

MINILESSON 10 Mins Independent Writing

OBJECTIVES

 CCSS Speak audibly and express thoughts, feelings, and ideas clearly. **SL.K.6**

 CCSS Capitalize the first word in a sentence and the pronoun *I*. **L.K.2a**

Give a presentation

ACADEMIC LANGUAGE
• *present, publish*
• Cognates: *presente*

Write an Opinion About a Book

Prepare

Tell children that they will present their finished sentences from Day 4 to the class. Hold up an example from Day 4 and read it aloud, tracking the print. Read clearly, but not too slowly. *I read my sentences loudly so that everyone could hear me. I spoke loudly but did not yell. I read my sentences clearly so that everyone could understand my opinions about the book.*

Present

Have children take turns standing up and reading their sentences aloud. Remind children to speak clearly. Encourage the rest of the class to listen carefully to the person speaking and to be respectful by looking at the speaker while he or she is talking.

Evaluate

Have children discuss their own presentations and evaluate their performances, using the presentation rubric. Use the teacher's rubric to evaluate children's writing.

Publish

After children have finished presenting, collect the opinion sentences. Put the sentences in a three-ring binder in the reading corner. Explain to children that when they are looking for a new book to read, they can read their classmates' opinions about books they like. Then they may decide that they want to read one of those books. Tell children that you will help them read the sentences if needed.

Have children add their writing to their Writer's Portfolio. Then have them look back at their previous writing and discuss how they have changed as writers throughout the year.

Go Digital

Writing

I see a fish.

Grammar

Grammar

Pronouns

1 Review Remind children that a pronoun is a word that takes the place of a noun in a sentence. Write and read aloud this sentence: *Tim, Anne, and I will plant a tree. Which pronoun can we use to replace* Tim, Anne, *and* I? (We)

2 Review Practice Write and read aloud: *We will go to the playground.* Have children work with a partner to copy the sentence. Have children circle the pronoun in the sentence. (We) Write and read aloud: *You will go on the swings. I will push you on the swings. It will be fun.* Have children work with their partners to circle all of the pronouns in the sentences. (You, I, you, It) Have children share what they circled with the class.

Gather the sentences and store them in a folder for a center or review activity.

Wrap Up the Week

- Review blending words with initial and medial /e/e. Remind children that a pronoun is a word that can take the place of a noun.

- Use the **High-Frequency Word Cards** to review the Words to Know.

- Remind children that they can write to give an opinion about a book.

Approaching Level

Leveled Reader

OBJECTIVES

CCSS With prompting and support, identify the main topic and key details of a text. **RI.K.2**

CCSS With prompting and support, ask and answer questions about unknown words in a text. **RI.K.4**

CCSS Demonstrate understanding of the organization and basic features of print. **RF.K.1**

CCSS Read emergent-reader texts with purpose and understanding. **RF.K.4**

Leveled Reader:
The Tree

Leveled Reader

Before Reading

Preview and Predict

Read the title and the names of the author and illustrator as children follow along in their books. Ask children to describe what they see on the cover. Turn to the title page, point to the title and say: *Let's read the title together.* Preview the illustrations and identify the rebus pictures. Ask: *What do you think this book is about?*

Review Genre: Informational Text

Remind children that informational text gives facts and information about a topic. Ask: *What information might we learn in this story?* (How a tree grows through the seasons.) Have children point to evidence in the pictures to support their answers.

Model Concepts of Print

Hold up your copy of the book and demonstrate how you read it. Say: *I begin reading on page 2. I read the words from left to right. I read page 3. When I am finished, I turn the page. I keep reading from left to right.*

Review High-Frequency Words

Point to the word *are* on page 2, and read it with children. Have them look through the book and find the word on pages 4 and 5.

Essential Question

Set a purpose for reading: *Let's read the book to find out how a tree changes as it grows.* Remind children to use the rebuses.

During Reading

Guided Comprehension

As children whisper-read *The Tree*, monitor and provide guidance by correcting blending and modeling the strategy and skill.

Strategy: Reread

Remind children that they can reread text to help them better understand the story.

Skill: Main Topic and Key Details

Review with children that reading the words and looking at the pictures will help them learn about the main topic and key details in this selection about a tree.

Think Aloud The words on page 4 tell me "the branches are big." I can see snow, so it must be winter. The words on page 5 tell me "the buds are big." It looks warmer outside. It must be spring. These details in the words and the pictures tell me about the main topic—how a tree grows and changes through the year.

Guide children to identify key details about the tree in the words and pictures on pages 6 and 7 and have them explain how it supports the main topic.

After Reading

Respond to Reading

→ *What do you learn about the roots of the tree?* (The roots are big.)

→ *When does the tree grow leaves?* (in summer)

→ *What is the main topic of this book?* (How a tree grows and changes.)

→ *What happens at the end of the story?* (The tree has cherries and a boy and girl eat the cherries.)

Retell

Have children take turns retelling the story to a partner. Help them make a personal connection by asking: *What do you like about trees?*

Model Fluency

Read the story aloud, pausing after each page to have children chorally repeat.

Apply Have children practice reading individually or with partners.

LITERACY ACTIVITIES

Have children complete the activities on the inside back cover of the reader.

Level Up

IF Children read *The Tree* **Approaching Level** with fluency and correctly answer the Respond to Reading questions,

THEN Tell children that they will read another story about trees and how they change through the seasons.

• Have children page through *Many Trees* **On Level** as you talk about how trees change and grow through the seasons.

• Have children read the story, monitoring their comprehension and providing assistance as necessary.

Approaching Level
Phonological Awareness

ONSET/RIME BLENDING

 OBJECTIVES

CCSS Blend and segment onsets and rimes of single-syllable spoken words. **RF.K.2c**

 I Do   Say *found* from the song "My Oak Tree." Repeat the word, segmenting and then blending the onset and rime, /f/ /ound/, found.

 We Do   Segment and blend the onset and rime in *found*. Have children repeat after you. Together segment and blend *saw*: /s/ /aw/, saw; and *just* /j/ /ust/, just.

 You Do   Ask children to segment and blend onsets and rimes in other words from the song, such as *ground, told,* and *tree.*

PHONEME ISOLATION

OBJECTIVES

CCSS Isolate and pronounce the initial, medial vowel, and final sounds (phonemes) in three-phoneme words. **RF.K.2d**

 I Do   Display the *Egg* **Photo Card**. *This is an* egg. *The first sound in* egg *is* /e/. Have children repeat the word with you, emphasizing the initial sound. Then have children say the first sound with you: /e/.

 We Do   Display the *Exit* Photo Card. Name the photo and have children say the name. *What is the first sound in* exit? (/e/) Say the sound together. Repeat with the *Elbow* Photo Card.

 You Do   Show the *Egg* Photo Card. Have children name it and say the initial sound of the picture name. Repeat with the *Envelope* Photo Card.

You may wish to review Phonological Awareness and Phonemic Awareness with **ELL** using this section.

PHONEME BLENDING

CCSS
OBJECTIVES
Isolate and pronounce the initial, medial vowel, and final sounds (phonemes) in three-phoneme words. **RF.K.2d**

 The puppet is going to say the sounds in a word. Listen: /mmm/ /eee/ /t/. The puppet can blend these sounds together: /mmmeeet/, met. *Repeat with* pet.

 Now the puppet is going to say the sounds in the word, web. *Say the sounds with the puppet: /w/ /eee/ /b/. Let's blend the sounds together: /weeeb/,* web. *Repeat with* let *and* ten.

 Have children blend sounds to form words. Practice together: /sss/ /eee/ /t/, *set.* Then have children practice blending the following sounds to say the words.

/t/ /e/ /d/ Ted   /p/ /e/ /t/ pet   /d/ /e/ /n/ den   /r/ /e/ /d/ red

PHONEME SEGMENTATION

OBJECTIVES
Isolate and pronounce the initial, medial vowel, and final sounds (phonemes) in three-phoneme words. **RF.K.2d**

 Use **Sound Boxes** and markers. *Listen as I say a word:* let. *There are three sounds in the word* let: /l/ /e/ /t/. *I'll place a marker in one box for each sound.* Repeat with the word *well.*

 Distribute Sound Boxes and markers. *Let's listen for the number of sounds in more words. Listen as I say a word:* web. *Say the word with me:* web. *Say the sounds with me: /w/ /e/ /b/. Let's place a marker in one box for each sound. There are three sounds in* web. *Repeat with* exit.

 Say the following words. Have children repeat the word, segment the word into sounds and place a marker in a box for each sound.

net /n/ /e/ /t/   hen /h/ /e/ /n/   egg /e/ /g/   end /e/ /n/ /d/

ENGLISH LANGUAGE LEARNERS

For the **ELLs** who need **phonics, decoding,** and **fluency** practice, use scaffolding methods as necessary to ensure children understand the meaning of the words. Refer to the Language Transfer Handbook for phonics elements that may not transfer in children's native languages.

→ Approaching Level

Phonics

TIER 2

SOUND-SPELLING REVIEW

OBJECTIVES

CCSS Demonstrate basic knowledge of one-to-one letter-sound correspondences by producing the primary sound for each consonant. **RF.K.3a**

 Display **Word-Building Card** *h*. Say the letter name and the sound it stands for: *h*, /h/. Repeat for *d, o, c, n, i*.

 Display Word-Building Cards one at a time and together say the letter name and the sound that each letter stands for.

 Display Word-Building Cards one at a time and have children say the letter name and the sound that each letter stands for.

CONNECT *e* TO /e/

TIER 2

OBJECTIVES

CCSS Associate the long and short sounds with common spellings (graphemes) for the five major vowels. **RF.K.3b**

 Display the *Egg* **Sound-Spelling Card**. *The letter* e *can stand for* /e/, *the sound at the beginning of* egg. *What is this letter? What sound does it stand for? I will write* e *when I hear* /e/ *in these words:* empty, horse, end, ever, pin.

 The word elephant *begins with* /e/. *Let's write* e. Guide children to write *e* when they hear a word that begins with /e/. Say: *every, find, elf, elk, camp.*

 Say the following words and have children write the letter *e* if a word begins with /e/: *match, extra, part, egg, end, actor, enjoy.*

RETEACH

OBJECTIVES

CCSS Know and apply grade-level phonics and word analysis skills in decoding words. **RF.K.3**

 Display **Reading/Writing Workshop 5**, p. 20. The letter *e* stands for the /e/ sound you hear at the beginning of *egg*. Say *egg*, emphasizing the /e/.

 Have children name each picture in row 1. Repeat the name, emphasizing initial /e/. Repeat for row 2, emphasizing the medial /e/ sound.

 Guide children in reading the words in row 3. Then have them read the words in row 4, offering assistance as needed.

BLEND WORDS WITH SHORT *e*

OBJECTIVES

Isolate and pronounce the initial, medial vowel, and final sounds (phonemes) in three-phoneme words. **RF.K.2d**

 I Do Display **Word-Building Cards** *p, e,* and *t*. *This is the letter* p. *It stands for* /p/. *This is the letter* e. *It stands for* /e/. *This is the letter* t. *It stands for* /t/. *Listen as I blend all three sounds:* /peeet/, pet. *The word is* pet. Repeat for *set*.

 We Do *Now let's blend more sounds to make words.* Display the word *hen*. *Let's blend:* /heeennn/, hen. Have children blend to read the word. Repeat with the word *met*. *Let's blend:* /mmmeeet/, met.

 You Do Distribute Word-Building Cards with *s, e, t, p, n,* and *m*. Write: *set, pet, ten, pen*. Have children form the words and then blend and read the words.

REREAD FOR FLUENCY

OBJECTIVES

Read emergent-reader texts with purpose and understanding. **RF.K.4**

 I Do Turn to p. 22 of **Reading/Writing Workshop** and read aloud the title. *Let's read the title together.* Page through the book. Ask children what they see in each picture. Ask children to find the word *are* on p. 27.

 We Do Then have children open their books and chorally read the story. Have children point to each word as they read. Provide corrective feedback as needed. After reading, ask children to recall what the characters were sipping.

 You Do Have children reread "Ed and Ned" with a partner for fluency.

BUILD FLUENCY WITH PHONICS

Sound/Spelling Fluency

Display the following Word-Building Cards: *i, n, c, o, d, h,* and *e*. Have children chorally say each sound. Repeat and vary the pace.

Fluency in Connected Text

Write the following sentences. *My pet cat sat in the den. I see the hen. Can you see the net?* Have children read the sentences and identify the words with /e/e.

→ Approaching Level

High-Frequency Words

 TIER 2

RETEACH WORDS

OBJECTIVES

 CCSS Read common high-frequency words by sight. **RF.K.3c**

I Do Display the **High-Frequency Word Card** *are* and use the **Read/Spell/Write** routine to reteach the word.

We Do Have children turn to p. 21 of **Reading/Writing Workshop** and discuss the first photo. Then read aloud the first sentence. Reread the sentence with children. Then distribute index cards with the word *are* written on them. Have children match their word cards with the word *are* in the sentence. Use the same routine for the other sentence on the page.

You Do Write the sentence frame *We are _____.* Have children copy the sentence frame on their **Response Boards**. Then have partners work together to read and orally complete the frame by talking about how they are feeling today.

CUMULATIVE REVIEW

OBJECTIVES

 CCSS Read common high-frequency words by sight. **RF.K.3c**

I Do Display the **High-Frequency Word Cards** *I, can, the, we, see, a, like, to, and, go, you, do, my,* and *are.* Use the **Read/Spell/Write** routine to review words. Use the High-Frequency Word Cards and **Word-Building Cards** to create sentences, such as *You are in the car.*

We Do Use the High-Frequency Word Cards and Word-Building Cards to create sentences, such as *Do you like my map? We are in the cab.* Have children identify the high-frequency words that are used in each sentence.

You Do Have partners use the High-Frequency Word Cards and Word-Building Cards to create short sentences.

Oral Vocabulary

REVIEW WORDS

OBJECTIVES

Identify real-life connections between words and their use. **L.K.5c**

Develop oral vocabulary: *develop, amazing, enormous, imagine, content*

 I Do Use the **Define/Example/Ask** routine to review words. Use the following definitions and provide examples:

develop	To **develop** means to grow.
amazing	Something that is **amazing** is surprising and wonderful.
enormous	Something that is **enormous** is very large.
imagine	When you **imagine** something, you see it in your mind.
content	When you are **content**, you feel happy and satisfied.

We Do Ask questions to build understanding. *How can you help a pet develop good behavior? What is the most amazing book you have ever read? Tell about an enormous place you have seen. How does it help you understand a story when you imagine it? How do you show that you are content?*

You Do Have children complete these sentence frames: *I know that people develop over time because _____. Dinosaurs are amazing because _____. A lion needs an enormous living space to _____. When I think of a cold, snowy day, I imagine _____. I feel content when I am _____.*

Comprehension

SELF-SELECTED READING

OBJECTIVES

With prompting and support, ask and answer questions about key details in a text. **RL.K.1**

Apply the strategy and skill to reread the text.

Read Independently

Help children select an informational story for sustained silent reading. Remind them that figuring out what the story is mainly about can help them understand the story. Tell them that they might not always figure out what the story is about when they read it the first time, but that reading again can help them understand the information in a story.

Read Purposefully

Before reading, guide children to take a picture walk through the book. Remind them to reread to help them figure out the big idea. After reading, ask children to tell what they thought the big idea was before they read. Then have them tell what they found out about the big idea as they read.

On Level

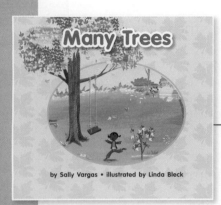

Many Trees

by Sally Vargas • illustrated by Linda Bleck

Leveled Reader

___

OBJECTIVES

CCSS With prompting and support, ask and answer questions about key details in a text. **RI.K.1**

CCSS With prompting and support, identify the main topic and retell key details of a text. **RI.K.2**

CCSS Demonstrate understanding of the organization and basic feature of print. **RF.K.1**

CCSS Read emergent-reader texts with purpose and understanding. **RF.K.4**

Leveled Reader:
Many Trees

Before Reading

Preview and Predict

After reading the title, ask: *What do you see on the cover?* Then read the author and illustrator's names aloud. Preview the illustrations, pointing out how the trees change. Ask: *What do you think the book will be about?*

Review Genre: Informational Text

Remind children that informational text gives details about a topic. Ask: *What information might we learn in this selection?* (That there are many kinds of trees.)

Model Concepts of Print

Ask children to follow along in their own books as you track the print on pages 2 and 3. Say: *I start reading on page 2. I read from left to right.*

Review High-Frequency Words

Point out the high-frequency word *are* on page 3, and read it with children. Have them find *the* on page 5. Ask them to use the word in an oral sentence.

Essential Question

Set a purpose for reading: *Let's read the book to find out how trees change as they grow through the seasons of the year.* Remind children to use the illustrations to help them as they read.

During Reading

Guided Comprehension

As children whisper-read *Many Trees*, monitor and provide guidance by correcting blending and modeling the strategy and skill.

Go Digital

Leveled Reader

Strategy: Reread

Remind children that they can reread text to help them better understand the selection.

Skill: Main Topic and Key Details

Tell children that both words and pictures give key details about a selection and its main topic. Explain that identifying the key details will help children to figure out the main topic of the selection.

Think Aloud On page 4, I read, "There are wet trees." In the picture on page 4, I see that it's raining. The tree leaves are dripping with rain. Reading the words *and* looking at the pictures helps me understand key details—such as why the trees are wet. It also gives me information about the main topic—that trees grow and change.

Guide children to read the words and use the pictures on pages 5 and 6 to find key details about the selection and its main topic.

After Reading

Respond to Reading

→ *What is the first thing you read about trees?* (There are small trees.)

→ *Why are there red trees?* (It is fall. The leaves have turned red.)

→ *What is the main topic of this book?* (Trees grow and change with the seasons.)

→ *What kind of changes do trees go through during the year?* (Possible answers: They grow. They get wet. Their leaves change color.)

Retell

Have children retell the story to a partner. Help them make personal connections. Ask: *What do you know about how trees change?*

Model Fluency

Model moving your finger along a line of text as you read. Have children do the same with their books.

Apply Have children practice reading with a small group. Children may take turns leading, while the rest of the group echo-reads.

LITERACY ACTIVITIES

Have children complete the activities on the inside back cover of the reader.

Level Up

IF Children read *Many Trees* On Level with fluency and correctly answer the Respond to Reading questions,

THEN Tell children that they will read another story about trees and how they grow and change.

• Have children page through *Our Apple Tree* Beyond Level as you talk about how a tree grows from a seed.

• Have children read the story, monitoring their comprehension and providing assistance as necessary.

On Level

Phonemic Awareness

PHONEME ISOLATION

OBJECTIVES

 Isolate and pronounce the initial, medial vowel, and final sounds (phonemes) in three-phoneme words. **RF.K.2d**

 I Do Display the *Elbow* **Photo Card**. *This is an* elbow. *The first sound is* /e/. *Say it with me. Say* end. *The first sound in* end *is* /e/. *Say the sound with me.*

 We Do Say *exit* and have children repeat it. *What is the first sound in* exit? *Say the sound together.* Repeat with *ever, egg, edge.*

You Do Say *egg, empty, dot, tip, enter,* and *ox* and have children tell the initial sound.

PHONEME BLENDING

OBJECTIVES

 Isolate and pronounce the initial, medial vowel, and final sounds (phonemes) in three-phoneme words. **RF.K.2d**

 I Do Place the *Jet, Nest, Net, Vest,* and *Web* Photo Cards facedown. Choose a card. Do not show card. *These are the sounds in the word:* /n/ /e/ /t/. *I will blend the sounds:* /nnneeet/, net. *The word is* net. Show the picture.

 We Do Choose another picture and say the sounds in the word. Together say and blend the sounds to say the word. Then show the picture.

 You Do Continue choosing Photo Cards. Say the sounds and have children blend the sounds and say the words.

PHONEME SEGMENTATION

OBJECTIVES

 Demonstrate understanding of spoken words, syllables, and sounds (phonemes). **RF.K.2**

 I Do Distribute **Sound Boxes** and markers. *How many sounds in this word:* set. *There are three sounds:* /s/ /e/ /t/. *I'll place a marker in one box for each sound.*

 We Do *Let's listen for the number of sounds in more words. Listen:* ten. *Let's place a marker in one box for each sound. There are three sounds in* ten.

 You Do Repeat with the following words: test /t/ /e/ /s/ /t/; pet /p/ /e/ /t/; egg /e/ /g/; hat /h/ /a/ /t/; cap /k/ /a/ /p/; so /s/ /ō/.

Phonics

REVIEW PHONICS

 OBJECTIVES

Associate the long and short sounds with the common spellings (graphemes) for the five major vowels. **RF.K.3b**

 I Do Display **Reading/Writing Workshop**, p. 20. Point to the *Egg* **Sound-Spelling Card**. *What letter stands for the /e/ sound you hear at the beginning of* egg? *The letter is* e.

 We Do Have children say the name of each picture in rows 1 and 2. Then ask them to identify the words with initial /e/ and the words with medial /e/.

 You Do Have children read each word in rows 3 and 4. Repeat, asking them to raise their hands if they hear /e/ in the middle of the word and keeping their hands lowered if they hear /e/ in the beginning of the word.

PICTURE SORT WITH MEDIAL /e/*e*, /o/*o*

 OBJECTIVES

Isolate and pronounce the initial, medial vowel, and final sounds (phonemes) in three-phoneme words. **RF.K.2d**

 I Do Display **Word-Building Cards** *e* and *o* in a pocket chart. Then show the *Pen* **Photo Card**. Say *pen*. Tell children that the sound in the middle is /e/. *The letter* e *stands for* /e/. *I will put the* pen *under the letter* e. Show the *Mop* Photo Card. Say *mop*. Tell children that the sound in the middle is /o/. *The letter* o *stands for* /o/. *I will put the* mop *Photo Card under the* o.

 We Do Display and name the *Lock* Photo Card. Have children repeat and say the sound in the middle of *lock*. Ask if the photo should be placed under the *e* or the *o*.

 You Do Continue the activity using the *Jet, Net, Vest, Web, Rock, Doll,* and *Top* Photo Cards. Have children say the picture name and the sounds in the name. Then have them place the card under the *e* or *o*.

→ On Level

Phonics

BLEND WORDS WITH SHORT *e*

OBJECTIVES

(CCSS) Isolate and pronounce the initial, medial vowel, and final sounds (phonemes) in three-phoneme words. **RF.K.2d**

 I Do Use **Word-Building Cards** or write the letters *n, e, t. This is the letter* n. *It stands for* /n/. *Say it with me:* /nnn/. *This is the letter* e. *It stands for* /e/. *Say it with me:* /eee/. *This is the letter* t. *It stands for* /t/. *Say it with me:* /t/. *I'll blend the sounds together to read the word*: /nnneeet/, net.

 We Do Use the words *ten* and *tin*. Guide children to blend the words sound by sound to read each word.

 You Do Use the following words and have children blend them sound by sound to read each word and to contrast /e/ and /i/.

set   sit   Ed   pen   pin   pet   pit   hen   met

REREAD FOR FLUENCY

OBJECTIVES

(CCSS) Read emergent-reader texts with purpose and understanding. **RF.K.4**

 I Do Point to the title "Ed and Ned" on p. 22 of **Reading/Writing Workshop**. Work with children to read for accuracy and expression. Model reading page 26: *When I read, "Ed can sip, sip, sip." I read all the way to the end of the sentence before pausing. This makes my reading sound natural, as if I were talking.*

 We Do Read p. 23. Then have children chorally read the page with you. Continue choral reading the remainder of the pages.

 You Do Have children read "Ed and Ned." Provide time to listen as children read the pages. Comment on their accuracy and expression and provide corrective feedback by modeling proper fluency.

High-Frequency Words

OBJECTIVES

 Read common high-frequency words by sight. **RF.K.3c**

I Do Use the **High-Frequency Word Card** *are* with the **Read/Spell/Write** routine to review the word.

We Do Have children turn to p. 21 of **Reading/Writing Workshop**. Discuss the photographs and read aloud the sentences. Point to the word *are* and have children read it. Then chorally read the sentences. Have children frame the word *are* in the sentences and read the word.

You Do Say the word *are*. Ask children to close their eyes, picture the word, and write it as they see it. Have children self-correct.

Reteach previously introduced high-frequency words using the **Read/Spell/Write** routine.

Fluency Point to the High-Frequency Word Cards *I, can the, we, see, a, like, to, and, go, you, do, my,* and *are* in random order. Have children chorally read. Repeat at a faster pace.

Comprehension

OBJECTIVES

 With prompting and support, ask and answer questions about key details in a text. **RL.K.1**

Apply the strategy and skill to reread the text.

Read Independently

Have children select an illustrated informational story for sustained silent reading. Explain that figuring out what a story is mainly about and identifying key details will help them better understand and enjoy a story. Remind children that if they have difficulty determining the main idea, they can reread parts of the story to help them understand.

Read Purposefully

Before reading, ask children to take a picture walk through the book and then write a sentence telling what they think the book is mainly about. Explain that they should reread parts of the story when something is unclear. After reading, ask children to tell what they thought the story would be about, and then what they discovered the story was actually about as they read.

→ Beyond Level

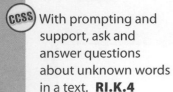

Leveled Reader

Leveled Reader: *Our Apple Tree*

Go Digital

Leveled Reader

Before Reading

Preview and Predict

Have children point to and read the title, then read to them the names of the author and illustrator. Ask children to describe the pictures on the front and back covers. Ask: *What do you think this book is about?* Have children page through the book and look at the illustrations.

Review Genre: Informational Text

Remind children that informational text gives details and information about a topic. Ask: *What information might we learn in this selection?* (How an apple tree grows.)

Essential Question

Remind children about the Essential Question: *How do living things change as they grow?* Have children set a purpose for reading. Say: *Find out how an apple tree changes as it grows.*

During Reading

Guided Comprehension

As children whisper-read *Our Apple Tree,* monitor and provide guidance by correcting blending and modeling the strategy and skill. As children read, stop periodically to ask questions, such as, *How has the apple tree changed?* Build on children's responses to help them develop a deeper understanding of the text.

Strategy: Reread

Remind children that whenever they are uncertain about what they are reading, they can reread to clarify what is happening in the selection.

OBJECTIVES

CCSS With prompting and support, ask and answer questions about key details in a text. **RI.K.1**

CCSS With prompting and support, identify the main topic and retell key details of a text. **RI.K.2**

CCSS With prompting and support, ask and answer questions about unknown words in a text. **RI.K.4**

CCSS Read emergent-reader texts with purpose and understanding. **RF.K.4**

Skill: Main Topic and Key Details

Review with children that reading the words and looking at the illustrations will help them learn about the main topic and key details in a selection. After reading ask: *What is this selection mainly about?*

Think Aloud On page 4, I learn from the text and the illustration that roots grow from an apple seed and that the roots grow down into the soil. These key details give me information about the main topic—how an apple tree grows from a seed into a tree that bears apples.

Guide children to read the words and use the pictures on pages 5 and 6 to find key details about the selection and its main topic. Have children point to evidence in the text and pictures to support their answers.

After Reading

Respond to Reading

→ How does the apple tree change during the story *Our Apple Tree?* (begins as a seed, grows roots, stem, leaves, flowers and, finally, apples)

→ How did the apple tree change in the spring? (It grew flowers.)

→ How does the little girl change during the story? (She is little when they plant the seed and grows up alongside the tree.)

Retell

Have children draw a series of pictures showing an apple tree growing from a seed into a tree. Have them use the pictures as they take turns retelling the story. Help them make a personal connection by asking: *What kind of tree would you like to plant? Explain your choice.*

Gifted and Talented

EVALUATING Ask children to recall how the tree in *Our Apple Tree* changed as it grew. Challenge children to compare how trees grow and change to how children grow and change.

HAVE children make a scrapbook about themselves with real photographs or self-created drawings to show how they've grown and changed through the years.

LITERACY ACTIVITIES

Have children complete the activities on the inside back cover of the reader.

→ Beyond Level

Phonics

REVIEW

OBJECTIVES

CCSS Know and apply grade-level phonics and word analysis skills in decoding words. **RF.K.3**

 I Do Display **Reading/Writing Workshop**, p. 20. Point to the *Egg* **Sound-Spelling Card**. *What is the sound at the beginning of* egg? *What letter can stand for* /e/? *The letter is* e.

 We Do Have children say the name of each picture in rows 1 and 2. Then ask children to share other words they know with /e/.

 You Do Have partners read each word in rows 3 and 4. Ask them to write the words on their **Response Boards** and underline the letter in each word that stands for /e/.

Fluency Have children reread the story "Ed and Ned" for fluency.

Innovate Have children create a new page for "Ed and Ned" using the sentence frame: *Ed and Ned* _____ .

High-Frequency Words

REVIEW

OBJECTIVES

 CCSS Read common high-frequency words by sight. **RF.K.3c**

 I Do Create **High-Frequency Word Cards** for *fun* and *carry*. Introduce the words using the **Read/Spell/Write** routine.

 We Do Display the High-Frequency Word Cards for *are, to, see, do,* and *you*. Have children help you complete the following sentence frames using the High-Frequency Word Cards: _____ *are fun to see. Do you carry a* _____?

 You Do Have partners write sentences using the High-Frequency Words *fun* and *carry* on their **Response Boards**. Have them read their sentences.

Vocabulary

OBJECTIVES

With guidance and support from adults, explore word relationships and nuances in word meaning. **L.K.5**

Develop oral vocabulary: Synonyms

 I Do Review the meanings of the oral vocabulary words *develop* and *amazing*. Explain that a synonym is a word that means almost the same thing as another word. *A synonym for* develop *is* grow. *When something grows, it changes.* I will grow taller as I get older. *A synonym for* amazing *is* fantastic. *Something that is fantastic is very good or excellent.* My lunch was fantastic.

We Do Create sentences together using the new words *grow* and *fantastic*. Read the sentences aloud.

You Do Have partners draw a picture and think of two or three sentences to describe a place that would be fun to visit. Tell them to use *grow* and *fantastic*. Ask them to share their pictures and descriptions with the class.

 Extend Challenge children to work with a partner to generate more synonyms for *grow* and *fantastic*. Then have partners tell a story about a trip using some of the synonyms they generated.

Comprehension

OBJECTIVES

With prompting and support, ask and answer questions about key details in a text. **RL.K.1**

Apply the strategy and skill to reread the text.

Read Independently

Have children select an informational text for sustained silent reading. Tell them to take a picture walk through the book and identify the main topic and two supporting details. Remind them to reread as needed.

Read Purposefully

Before reading, have children predict what they think the main topic of the text is. Remind them to reread as needed. After reading, ask children to state the main idea and compare that with their prediction. If their prediction was correct, ask them how the picture walk helped them figure it out. *What else helped you predict the main topic of the text?*

 Independent Study Ask children to choose an informational text they haven't read this week. Challenge them to use the title and photographs to write a prediction about the main topic of the book. Then have them read the book to confirm their predictions.

English Language Learners

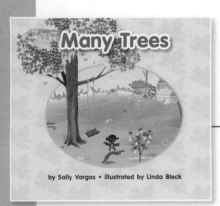

Many Trees

by Sally Vargas • illustrated by Linda Bleck

Leveled Reader

 OBJECTIVES
With prompting and support, ask and answer questions about key details in a text. **RI.K.1**

 Actively engage in group reading activities with purpose and understanding. **RI.K.10**

Read emergent-reader texts with purpose and understanding. **RF.K.4**

Shared Read:
Many Trees

Go Digital

Before Reading

Preview and Predict

Read the title *Many Trees* aloud. Then have children read it with you. Repeat with the author and illustrator's name. Point to the cover and say: *I see many trees in this picture.* Have children describe what they see. Then walk children through the book, using simple language to describe each picture. Identify the labels and rebus pictures. Follow up with questions, such as *What is this?* Encourage children to respond in full sentences.

Essential Question

Set a purpose for reading: *How do living things change as they grow? Let's read the book to find out how trees grow and change.* Encourage children to ask questions when they encounter a word or phrase that is unfamiliar.

During Reading

Interactive Question Response

Pages 2–3 Point to the illustration and labels on page 2. Say: *I see a small girl. What are these?* (small trees) *Let's read the sentence that tells us about the trees.* Point to the illustration and labels on page 3. Say: *I see the same small girl. What are these?* (big trees) *Let's find the sentence that tells about these trees.* Underline the sentence with your finger and then read it with children.

Pages 4–5 Point to the illustration on page 4. Say: *I see rain. What kind of trees are these?* (wet trees) *Let's read the sentence that tells us about these trees.* Point to the text on page 5. Say: *Let's read to find out about these trees. How do you know these are dry trees?* (the picture shows dry trees)

Leveled Reader

Pages 6–7 Point to the illustration and label on page 6. Say: *What does the label say?* (leaf) *What color are these trees?* (green) *Let's find and read the text that tells us that.* Point to the illustration on page 7. Say: *What color are these trees?* (red) Point to the sentence that tells us about these trees. *Let's read it together.*

Page 8 Ask: *Now what do you see?* (many trees) *Let's read the sentence.* Point to the exclamation mark at the end of the sentence. Say: *When we see an exclamation mark, it means the speaker is excited. We say the sentence with expression. Let's read it again together.*

After Reading

Respond to Reading

→ *What kind of trees do you read about first?* (small trees)

→ *What kind of trees do you read about next?* (big trees)

→ *What different colors of trees did you read about?* (green and red trees)

→ *What happens at the end of the book?* (We see many trees.)

Retell

Model retelling the story using hand motions and/or props (a red card and a green card, for example). Then have children join you and retell the story again.

Model Fluency

Read the sentences one at a time as you track the print. Have children chorally repeat. Point out that your voice gets a little louder with excitement when you read the last sentence, which has an exclamation point.

Apply Have children read the story with partners. Encourage children to use the pictures for clues if they have trouble with unfamiliar words.

LITERACY ACTIVITIES

Have children complete the activities on the inside back cover of the reader.

Level Up

IF Children read *Many Trees* ELL Level with fluency and correctly answer the Respond to Reading questions,

THEN Tell children that they will read a more detailed version of the story.

- Have children page through *Many Trees* On Level and guide them to describe each picture in simple language.

- Have children read the story, monitoring their comprehension and providing assistance as necessary.

→ English Language Learners
Vocabulary

PRETEACH ORAL VOCABULARY

OBJECTIVES

CCSS Speak audibly and express thoughts, feelings, and ideas clearly. **SL.K.6**

LANGUAGE OBJECTIVE

Preview vocabulary

 I Do Display images from the **Visual Vocabulary Cards** and use the routine to preteach the oral vocabulary words.

 We Do Explain how each image illustrates or demonstrates the word. Model using sentences to describe the image.

 You Do Explain that the word *develop* can mean the same as *grow*. Ask children how a plant can *develop*. Help children understand that a plant develops by getting bigger and growing flowers or fruit.

Beginning	Intermediate	Advanced/High
Prompt children to talk about how they have developed.	Ask children to draw pictures of a plant at different stages to illustrate the meaning of *develop*.	Have children use *develop* in a complete sentence.

PRETEACH ELL VOCABULARY

OBJECTIVES

CCSS Speak audibly and express thoughts, feelings, and ideas clearly. **SL.K.6**

LANGUAGE OBJECTIVE

Preview ELL vocabulary

 I Do Display images from the **Visual Vocabulary Cards** one at a time to preteach the ELL vocabulary words *forest* and *canopy*. Follow the routine. Say each word and have children repeat it. Define each word in English.

 We Do Develop a short discussion about the images. Model using sentences to describe the image.

 You Do Display *forest* again. Have partners name things that live in a forest. Remind them that a forest is a place with many trees. List their ideas.

Beginning	Intermediate	Advanced/High
Display pictures of a forest and ask children what they see.	Ask children to work in pairs to talk about what they know about forests.	Ask children to work in pairs to tell a story that takes place in a forest.

High-Frequency Words

REVIEW WORDS

OBJECTIVES

(CCSS) Read common high-frequency words by sight (e.g., *the, of, to, you, she, my, is, are, do, does*). **RF.K.3c**

LANGUAGE OBJECTIVE

Review high-frequency words

 I Do Display the **High-Frequency Word Card** for *are*. Read the word. Use the **Read/Spell/Write** routine to teach the word. Have children write the word on their **Response Boards**.

 We Do Write a sentence frame that uses the week's high-frequency word along with words from other weeks: *We are _____ .* Track the print as children read and complete the sentence. Explain to children that the word *are* is used when talking about more than one person.

 You Do Write *Ted and Pam* are *hot.* Ask children to point to the word *are* and say it aloud. Then work with children to read the entire sentence aloud.

Beginning	Intermediate	Advanced/High
Say several simple sentences with the word *are*. Have children repeat.	Ask partners to say sentences with *are*.	Ask children to name more things to complete the sentence starter *We are _____.*

REVIEW CATEGORY WORDS

OBJECTIVES

(CCSS) Identify real-life connections between words and their use (e.g., note places at school that are colorful) **L.K.5c**

LANGUAGE OBJECTIVE

Use category words

I Do Write the words *roots, branches, leaves,* and *trunk* and say the words aloud. Ask children to repeat each word after you. Tell children that these words name parts of a tree. Define the words in English and then in Spanish, if appropriate, identifying any cognates.

We Do Ask children to draw a tree and then work together to identify the different parts.

You Do Have children work with partners. Have one child say a category word and have the partner draw it.

Beginning	Intermediate	Advanced/High
Point to a drawing of a tree and prompt children to identify the parts.	Guide partners to work together to draw a tree and label its parts with the category words.	Have children use at least two of the category words together in a sentence.

→ English Language Learners
Writing

SHARED WRITING

OBJECTIVES

Use a combination of drawing, dictating, and writing to narrate a single event or several loosely linked events, tell about the events in the order in which they occurred, and provide a reaction to what happened. **W.K.3**

LANGUAGE OBJECTIVE

Contribute to a shared writing project

 Review the names of books in the chart in the Whole Group Shared Writing project as possible ideas of books children have seen. Then model using one of the books to write a sentence about it: *I like* Goodnight Moon *because it makes me feel cozy.*

 With children, choose a book to write a shared sentence about. Encourage children to give an opinion about it, for example, *We like* My Garden *because the pictures are nice.*

 Help partners choose a book to write about. Provide them with sentence frames to start their sentences: *I like* _____ *because* _____.

Beginning	Intermediate	Advanced/High
Discuss with children what they want to say about their book.	Have partners talk about the books they like.	Ask children to write more than one sentence. Have them read their sentences aloud when they are done.

WRITING TRAIT: ORGANIZATION

OBJECTIVES

With guidance and support from adults, respond to questions and suggestions from peers and add details to strengthen writing as needed. **W.K.5**

LANGUAGE OBJECTIVE

Organize ideas for writing

 Explain that good writers first think about what they will write and then organize their ideas. They write down ideas to use as they work.

We Do Show the **Big Book** *A Grand Old Tree.* Say: *The author thought about which parts of the tree's life to write about. Which part of a plant's life do you want to write about?* Point out ideas from the story to give children ideas.

You Do Have children write a sentence that describes a plant. Provide them with sentence frames, such as: *This tree is* _____. *It has* _____.

Beginning	Intermediate	Advanced/High
Before helping children complete the sentence frame, talk with children about what the plant is like.	Ask children to talk about their ideas with a partner before writing a sentence.	Challenge children to write two more sentences that describe the plant.

Grammar

PRONOUNS

OBJECTIVES

 Capitalize the first word in a sentence and the pronoun *I*. **L.K.2a**

LANGUAGE OBJECTIVE

Recognize and use pronouns correctly

Language Transfers Handbook

Korean and Spanish speakers often drop the subject pronoun in English because in their native language the verb ending gives information about the number and/or gender. You may find children say *Mom isn't home. Is at work.* Remind children that the pronoun is needed because every sentence needs a subject.

I Do Review that a pronoun is a word that takes the place of a person, an animal, or a thing. Give the following example: *I planted a sunflower.* Say: I *is a pronoun. It replaces my name in the sentence.*

Say the following sentences. Guide children to identify the pronoun.

You *can see the leaves fall from the trees.*

She *rakes the leaves.*

He *waits for winter.*

You Do Use the following sentence frame:

I think plants _____.

Pair children and have them complete the sentence frame by providing details from this week's readings. Circulate, listen in, and take note of each child's language use and proficiency.

Beginning	Intermediate	Advanced/High
Before completing the sentence frame, guide children to identify the pronoun.	Have partners use the selections to get ideas about plants. Remind them that *I* means they will give their own ideas.	Ask children to use a different pronoun to write another sentence.

PROGRESS MONITORING

Weekly Assessment

Use your Quick Check observations and the assessment opportunities identified below to evaluate children's progress in key skill areas.

✔ TESTED SKILLS CCSS	Quick Check Observations	Pencil and Paper Assessment
PHONEMIC AWARENESS/ PHONICS /e/ (initial/medial) **RF.K.3b** **e**	Can children isolate /e/ and match it to the letter *Ee*?	Practice Book, pp. 135–136, 138
HIGH-FREQUENCY WORDS *are* **RF.K.3c** **are**	Can children recognize and read the high-frequency word?	Practice Book, pp. 139–140
COMPREHENSION Main Topic and Key Details **RI.K.2**	As you read *A Grand Old Tree* with children, can they identify and discuss the main topic and key details from the text?	Practice Book, p. 137

Quick Check Rubric

Skills	1	2	3
PHONEMIC AWARENESS/ PHONICS	Does not connect the sound /e/ with the letters *Ee*.	Usually connects the sound /e/ with the letters *Ee*.	Consistently connects the sound /e/ with the letters *Ee*.
HIGH-FREQUENCY WORDS	Does not identify the high-frequency word.	Usually recognizes the high-frequency word with accuracy, but not speed.	Consistently recognizes the high-frequency word with speed and accuracy.
COMPREHENSION	Does not identify the main topic and key details from the text.	Usually identifies the main topic and key details from the text.	Consistently identifies the main topic and key details from the text.

Go Digital! www.connected.mcgraw-hill.com

Using Assessment Results

✓ TESTED SKILLS	If ...	Then ...
PHONEMIC AWARENESS/ PHONICS	**Quick Check Rubric:** Children consistently score 1 or **Pencil and Paper Assessment:** Children get 0–2 items correct	… reteach tested Phonemic Awareness and Phonics skills using Lessons 16–17 in the *Tier 2 Phonemic Awareness Intervention Online PDFs* and Lesson 23 in the *Tier 2 Phonics/ Word Study Intervention Online PDFs.*
HIGH- FREQUENCY WORDS	**Quick Check Rubric:** Children consistently score 1	… reteach tested skills by using the High-Frequency Word Cards and asking children to read and spell the word. Point out any irregularities in sound-spellings.
COMPREHENSION	**Quick Check Rubric:** Children consistently score 1 or **Pencil and Paper Assessment:** Children get 0–1 items correct	… reteach tested skill using Lessons 85–87 in the *Tier 2 Comprehension Intervention Online PDFs.*

Response to Intervention

Use the children's assessment results to assist you in identifying children who will benefit from focused intervention.

Use the appropriate sections of the **Placement and Diagnostic Assessment** to designate children requiring:

TIER 2 Tier 2 Intervention Online PDFs

TIER 3 WonderWorks Intervention Program

→ Phonemic Awareness

→ Phonics

→ Vocabulary

→ Comprehension

→ Fluency

WEEKLY OVERVIEW

Literature Big Book

Listening Comprehension

An Orange in January, 4–33
Genre Informational Text

"Farmers' Market," 34–40
Genre Informational Text

Interactive Read-Aloud Cards

"Farms Around the World"
Genre Informational Text

Oral Vocabulary

beneath   raise

delicious   special

fresh

Minilessons   ✓ TESTED SKILLS CCSS

✓ **Comprehension Strategy** .... Reread, T177

✓ **Comprehension Skill** .... Main Topic and Key
Details, T186

 **Go Digital**

www.connected.mcgraw-hill.com

Nathan Love

FRESH FROM THE FARM

Essential Question
What kinds of things grow on a farm?

WEEK 3 →

Big Book and Little Book
Reading/Writing Workshop

Shared Reading

Ron is **with** Red.
Red is a pet.

"Ron with Red," 36–43

Genre Fiction

High-Frequency Words with, he, T181

Minilessons   ✓ TESTED SKILLS CCSS

✓ **Phonics** . . . . /f/f and /r/r, T179

Writing Traits . . . . Organization, T182

Grammar . . . . Pronouns, T183

Differentiated Text

Approaching

On Level

Beyond

ELL

TEACH AND MANAGE

What You Do

INTRODUCE

Weekly Concept

Fresh from the Farm

Reading/Writing Workshop Big Book, 34–35

TEACH AND APPLY

Listening Comprehension

Big Book
An Orange in January
Genre Informational Text
Paired Read "Farmers' Market"
Genre Informational Text

Shared Reading

Reading/Writing Workshop
"Ron with Red"

Minilessons
Strategy: Reread

Skill: Main Topic and Key Details

/f/f and/r/r, High-Frequency Words: *with*, *he*, Writing, Grammar

 Go Digital

 Interactive Whiteboard

 Interactive Whiteboard

 **Mobile**

What Your Students Do

WEEKLY CONTRACT

PDF Online

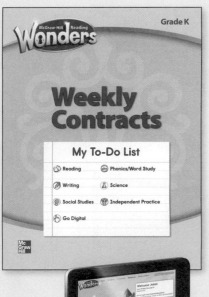

Go Digital **Online To-Do List**

PRACTICE AND ONLINE ACTIVITIES

Your Turn Practice Book, pp. 143–152

Leveled Readers

 **Online Activities**

 **Mobile**

Go Digital! www.connected.mcgraw-hill.com

WEEK 3 →

DIFFERENTIATE

Small Group Instruction
Leveled Readers

 Mobile

INTEGRATE

Research and Inquiry
Fruit Basket, pp. T216–T217

Text Connections
Compare Crops, p. T218

Talk About Reading
Becoming Readers, p. T219

 Online Research

WORKSTATION CARDS

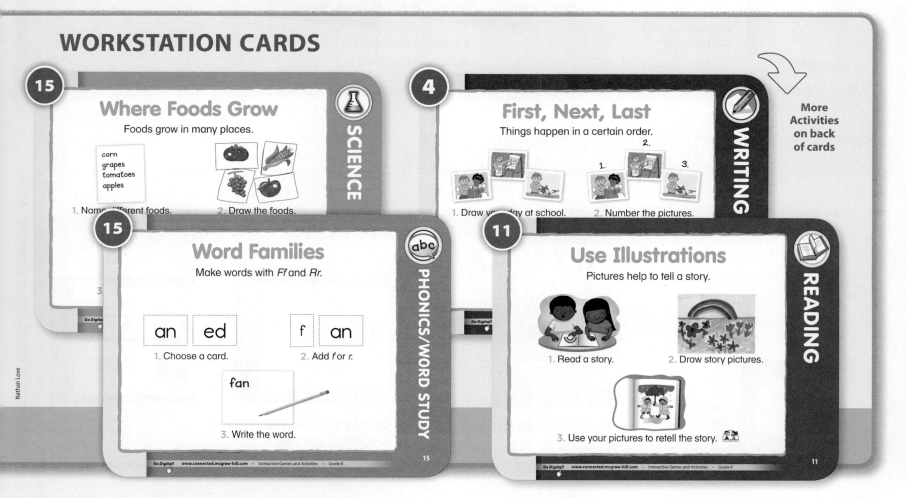

15

Where Foods Grow
Foods grow in many places.

SCIENCE

corn
grapes
tomatoes
apples

1. Name different foods.   2. Draw the foods.

15

Word Families
Make words with *Ff* and *Rr*.

PHONICS/WORD STUDY

| an | ed | | f | an |

1. Choose a card.   2. Add *f* or *r*.

| fan |

3. Write the word.

4

First, Next, Last
Things happen in a certain order.

WRITING

2.
1.   3.

1. Draw your day at school.   2. Number the pictures.

More Activities on back of cards

11

Use Illustrations
Pictures help to tell a story.

READING

1. Read a story.   2. Draw story pictures.

3. Use your pictures to retell the story.

Go Digital! www.connected.mcgraw-hill.com • Interactive Games and Activities • Grade K   15

Go Digital! www.connected.mcgraw-hill.com • Interactive Games and Activities • Grade K   11

Nathan Love

DEVELOPING READERS AND WRITERS

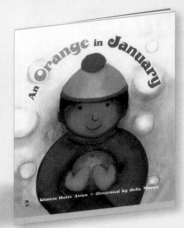

Write to Sources and Research

Respond to Reading, T177, T225, T233, T239, T243

Connect to Essential Question, T177, T209

Main Topic and Key Details, 186

Research and Inquiry, T216

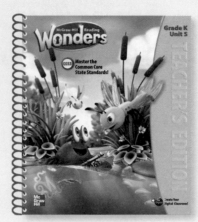

Teacher's Edition

Literature Big Book
An Orange in January
Paired Read: *"Farmers' Market"*

Interactive Whiteboard

Leveled Readers
Responding to Texts

Informational Text
Story Sentences, T204–T205, T214, T222

Conferencing Routines
Peer Conferences, T214

Interactive Whiteboard

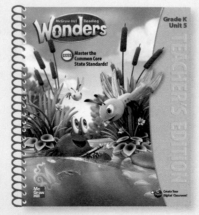

Teacher's Edition

Leveled Workstation Card
First, Next, Last, Card 4

Writing Traits • Shared and Interactive Writing

Writing Trait:
Organization
Story Sentences, T182, T196

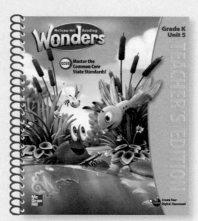

Teacher's Edition

Organization,
p. 46

Pronouns,
p. 47

Reading/Writing Workshop

First, Next, Last
Things happen in a certain order.

1. Draw your day at school.
2. Number the pictures.
3. Tell what you do in order.

Act Out the Order

1. Think of the things you do when you wake up.
2. Act out the things in order.
3. Have a friend guess what you do.

List the Order

1. Write a list of what you will do today.
2. Put the list in order.
3. Read your partner's list.

Interactive Whiteboard

Leveled Workstation Card
First, Next, Last, Card 4

Grammar and Spelling/Dictation

Grammar
Pronouns, T183

Spelling/Dictation
Words with Short *a, e, i, o,*
and *f, r, n, d, p, t,* T211, T221

Interactive Whiteboard

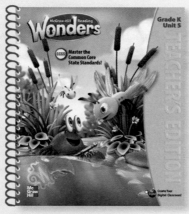

Teacher's Edition

Online Grammar Games

Handwriting

SUGGESTED LESSON PLAN

✓ TESTED SKILLS CCSS	DAY 1	DAY 2

READING

Whole Group

Teach and Model

Literature Big Book

Reading/ Writing Workshop

DAY 1

Build Background Fresh from the Farm, T174
Oral Vocabulary Words fresh, delicious, T174
✓ **Listening Comprehension**
• Genre: Informational Text
• Strategy: Reread, T177
Big Book *An Orange in January*
✓ **Word Work**
Phonemic Awareness
• Phoneme Isolation, T178
Phonics
• Introduce /f/f, /r/r, T179
Handwriting *Ff* and *Rr*, T180
High-Frequency Words with, he, T181

Practice *Your Turn* 143–146

DAY 2

Oral Language Fresh from the Farm, T184
✓ **Category Words** Food Words, T185
✓ **Listening Comprehension**
• Genre: Informational Text
• Strategy: Reread, T186
• Skill: Main Topic and Key Details
• Guided Retelling
• Model Fluency, T191
Big Book *An Orange in January*
✓ **Word Work**
Phonemic Awareness
• Phoneme Blending, T192
Phonics
• Blend Words with *f* and *r*, T193
High-Frequency Words with, he, T193
Shared Reading "Ron With Red," T194–T195

Practice *Your Turn* 147

DIFFERENTIATED INSTRUCTION Choose across the week to meet your student's needs.

Small Group

Approaching Level

Leveled Reader *The Farmer*, T224–T225
Phonological Awareness
Recognize Rhyme, T226 **TIER 2**
Phonics Sound-Spelling Review, T228 **TIER 2**
High-Frequency Words Reteach Words, T230 **TIER 2**

Leveled Reader *The Farmer*, T224–T225
Phonemic Awareness
Phoneme Isolation, T226 **TIER 2**
Phonics Connect *f* to /f/ and *r* to /r/, T228 **TIER 2**
High-Frequency Words Cumulative Review, T230

On Level

Leveled Reader *Let's Make a Salad!* T232–T233
Phonemic Awareness
Phoneme Isolation, T234

Leveled Reader *Let's Make a Salad!* T232–T233
Phoneme Awareness Phoneme Blending, T234
Phonics Review Phonics, T235
Picture Sort, T235
High-Frequency Words Review Words, T237

Beyond Level

Leveled Reader *Farm Fresh Finn*, T238–T239
Phonics Review, T240

Leveled Reader *Farm Fresh Finn*, T238–T239
High-Frequency Words Review, T240

English Language Learners

Leveled Reader *Let's Make a Salad!* T242–T243
Phonological Awareness
Recognize Rhyme, T226 **TIER 2**
Phonics Sound-Spelling Review, T228 **TIER 2**
Vocabulary Preteach Oral Vocabulary, T244
Writing Shared Writing, T246

Leveled Reader *Let's Make a Salad!* T242–T243
Phonemic Awareness
Phoneme Isolation, T226 **TIER 2**
Phonics Connect *f* to /f/ and *r* to /r/, T228 **TIER 2**
High-Frequency Words Cumulative Review, T230
Vocabulary Preteach ELL Vocabulary, T244

LANGUAGE ARTS

Whole Group

Writing and Grammar

Shared Writing
Writing Trait: Organization, T182
Write Story Sentences, T182
Grammar Pronouns, T183

Interactive Writing
Writing Trait: Organization, T196
Write Story Sentences, T196
Grammar Pronouns, T197

Nathan Love

DAY 3	**DAY 4**	**DAY 5** Review and Assess

READING

DAY 3	DAY 4	DAY 5
Oral Language Fresh from the Farm, T198 **Oral Vocabulary** beneath, raise, special, T198 ✓**Listening Comprehension** • Genre: Informational Text • Strategy: Reread, T199 • Make Connections, T199 **Interactive Read Aloud** "Farms Around the World," T199 ✓**Word Work** **Phonemic Awareness** • Phoneme Blending, T200 **Phonics** • Blend Words with Short *i, a, e* and *f, r, t, n, d, p*, T201 • Picture Sort, T202 **High-Frequency Words** with, he, T203	**Oral Language** Fresh from the Farm, T206 ✓**Category Words** Food Words, T207 ✓**Listening Comprehension** • Genre: Informational Text • Strategy: Reread, T208 • Text Feature: Lists • Make Connections, T209 **Big Book** Paired Read: "Farmers' Market," T208 ✓**Word Work** **Phonemic Awareness** • Phoneme Addition, T210 **Phonics** • Blend Words with Short *e, i, a* and *f, r, d, p, n*, T210 **High-Frequency Words** with, he, T211 **Shared Reading** "Ron With Red," T212–T213 **Integrate Ideas** Research and Inquiry, T216–T217	**Integrate Ideas** • Text Connections, T218 • Talk About Reading, T219 • Research and Inquiry, T219 ✓**Word Work** **Phonemic Awareness** • Phoneme Addition, T220 **Phonics** • Read Words with Short *a, e, i, o* and *f, r, n, d, t, p*, T220 **High-Frequency Words** with, he, T221 
Practice *Your Turn* 148–150	**Practice** *Your Turn* 151	**Practice** *Your Turn* 152

DIFFERENTIATED INSTRUCTION

DAY 3	DAY 4	DAY 5
Leveled Reader *The Farmer*, T224–T225 **Phonemic Awareness** Phoneme Blending, T227 **Phonics** Reteach, T228 **High-Frequency Words** Reteach Words, T230	**Leveled Reader** *The Farmer*, T224–T225 **Phonemic Awareness** Phoneme Addition, T227 **Phonics** Blend Words with /f/f and /r/r, T229 **Oral Vocabulary** Review Words, T231	**Leveled Reader** Literacy Activities, T225 **Phonemic Awareness** Phoneme Addition, T227 **Phonics** Reread for Fluency, T229 Build Fluency with Phonics, T229 **Comprehension** Self-Selected Reading, T231
Leveled Reader *Let's Make a Salad!* T232–T233 **Phonemic Awareness** Phoneme Addition, T234 **Phonics** Picture Sort, T235	**Leveled Reader** *Let's Make a Salad!* T232–T233 **Phonics** Blend Words with *f* and *r*, T236 Reread for Fluency, T236	**Leveled Reader** Literacy Activities, T233 **Comprehension** Self-Selected Reading, T237
Leveled Reader *Farm Fresh Finn*, T238–T239 **Vocabulary** Oral Vocabulary: Synonyms, T241 	**Leveled Reader** *Farm Fresh Finn*, T238–T239 **Phonics** Innovate, T240	**Leveled Reader** Literacy Activities, T239 **Comprehension** Self-Selected Reading, T241
Leveled Reader *Let's Make a Salad!* T242–T243 **Phonemic Awareness** Phoneme Blending, T227 **Phonics** Reteach, T228 **High-Frequency Words** Review Words, T245 **Writing** Writing Trait: Organization, T246	**Leveled Reader** *Let's Make a Salad!* T242–T243 **Phonemic Awareness** Phoneme Addition, T227 **Phonics** Blend Words with /f/f and /r/r, T229 **Vocabulary** Review Category Words, T245 **Grammar** Pronouns, T247	**Leveled Reader** Literacy Activities, T243 **Phonemic Awareness** Phoneme Addition, T227 **Phonics** Reread for Fluency, T229 Build Fluency with Phonics, T229

LANGUAGE ARTS

DAY 3	DAY 4	DAY 5
Independent Writing Writing Trait: Organization, T204 Write Story Sentences Prewrite/Draft, T205 **Grammar** Pronouns, T205	**Independent Writing** Writing Trait: Organization, T214 Write Story Sentences Revise/Final Draft, T214 **Grammar** Pronouns, T215	**Independent Writing** Write Story Sentences Prepare/Present/Evaluate/Publish, T222 **Grammar** Pronouns, T223

DIFFERENTIATE TO ACCELERATE

IF ▶ the text complexity of a particular section is too difficult for children

THEN ▶ see the references noted in the chart below for scaffolded instruction to help children Access Complex Text.

Qualitative | Quantitative
Reader and Task
TEXT COMPLEXITY

Literature Big Book	Reading/Writing Workshop	Leveled Readers	

Quantitative			
An Orange in January **Lexile** 780	"Ron with Red" **Lexile** 170	**Approaching Level** **Lexile** BR	**On Level** **Lexile** BR
Paired Selection: Farmers' Market **Lexile** 340		**Beyond Level** **Lexile** 260	**ELL** **Lexile** BR
Qualitative			
What Makes the Text Complex? • **Sentence Structure** Ellipses, T186 **A C T** *See Scaffolded Instruction in Teacher's Edition, T186.*	**What Makes the Text Complex?** **Foundational Skills** • Decoding with *f, r*, T192–T193 • Identifying high-frequency words, T193	**What Makes the Text Complex?** **Foundational Skills** • Decoding with *f, r* • Identifying high-frequency words with, *he* *See Level Up lessons online for Leveled Readers.*	
Reader and Task			
The Introduce the Concept lesson on pages T174–T175 will help determine the reader's knowledge and engagement in the weekly concept. See pages T176–T177, T187–T191, T208–T209 and T216–T219 for questions and tasks for this text.	The Introduce the Concept lesson on pages T174–T175 will help determine the reader's knowledge and engagement in the weekly concept. See pages T194–T195, T212–T213 and T216–T219 for questions and tasks for this text.	The Introduce the Concept lesson on pages T174–T175 will help determine the reader's knowledge and engagement in the weekly concept. See pages T224–T225, T232–T233, T238–T239, T242–T243 and T216–T219 for questions and tasks for this text.	

Nathan Love

Monitor and *Differentiate*

IF you need to differentiate instruction

THEN use the Quick Checks to assess children's needs and select the appropriate small group instruction focus.

✔ Quick Check

Comprehension Strategy Reread, T199

Phonemic Awareness/Phonics /f/f and /r/r, T181, T193, T203, T211, T221

High-Frequency Words *with*, *he*, T181, T193, T203, T211, T221

If No → | **Approaching** | **Reteach,** pp. T224–T231 |
| **ELL** | **Develop,** pp. T242–T247 |
If Yes → | **On Level** | **Review,** pp. T232–T237 |
| **Beyond Level** | **Extend,** pp. T238–T241 |

Level Up with Leveled Readers

IF children can read their leveled text fluently and answer comprehension questions

THEN work with the next level up to accelerate children's reading with more complex text.

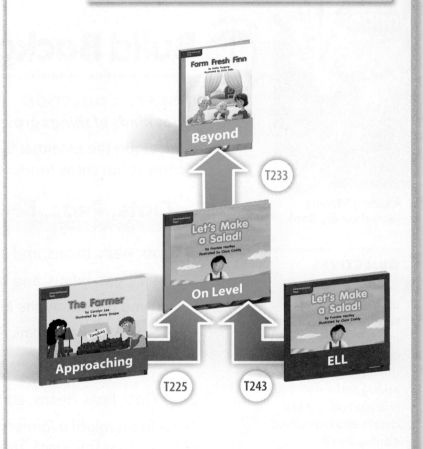

ELL ENGLISH LANGUAGE LEARNERS SCAFFOLD

IF ELL students need additional support **THEN** scaffold instruction using the small group suggestions.

| Reading-Writing Workshop T175 "Farm Fresh"

Integrate Ideas T217 | Leveled Reader T242–T243 *Let's Make a Salad!* | Phonological Awareness Recognize Rhyme, T226 Phoneme Isolation, T226 Phoneme Blending, T227 Phoneme Addition, T227 | Phonics, /f/f, /r/r, T228–T229 | Oral Vocabulary, T244 fresh, delicious, beneath, raise, special

High-Frequency Words, T245 *he, with* | Writing Shared Writing, T246

Writing Trait: Organization, T246 | Grammar T247 Pronouns |

Note: Include ELL Students in all small groups based on their needs.

Materials

Reading/Writing Workshop Big Book
UNIT 5

Literature Big Book
An Orange in January

Visual Vocabulary Cards
fresh
delicious

Response Board

Photo Cards
apple   pumpkin
fire   strawberry
rabbit
rock
rope
rose
peach
pear

Sound-Spelling Cards
Fire
Rose

High-Frequency Word Cards
he
with

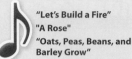
Think Aloud Cloud

♪ "Let's Build a Fire"
"A Rose"
"Oats, Peas, Beans, and Barley Grow"

Reading/Writing Workshop Big Book

OBJECTIVES

CCSS Confirm understanding of a text read aloud or information presented orally or through other media by asking and answering questions about key details and requesting clarification if something is not understood. **SL.K.2**

CCSS Identify real-life connections between words and their use. **L.K.5c**

→ # Introduce the Concept

MINILESSON
10 Mins

Build Background

ESSENTIAL QUESTION
What kinds of things grow on a farm?

Read aloud the Essential Question. Tell children you are going to sing a song about some foods that are grown on farms.

Oats, Peas, Beans, and Barley Grow

Oats, peas, beans, and barley grow;

Oats, peas, beans, and barley grow.

Do you or I or anyone know

How oats, peas, beans, and barley grow?

Sing "Oats, Peas, Beans, and Barley Grow" with children.

What foods might a farmer grow? (oats, peas, beans, and barley) Tell children that this week, they will read to find out about the kinds of foods that people grow.

Oral Vocabulary Words

Use the **Define/Example/Ask** routine to introduce the oral vocabulary words **fresh** and **delicious**.

To introduce the theme of "Fresh from the Farm," explain that foods grown on farms are fresh and delicious. Many other foods besides the ones in the song are grown on farms. *What other kinds of food grows on a farm?* (Possible answers: corn, potatoes, tomatoes)

Go Digital

"Fresh from the Farm"

Video

Photos

Visual Glossary

Oral Vocabulary Routine

<u>**Define:**</u> Food that is **fresh** has just been grown or made.

<u>**Example:**</u> We picked the apple from the tree and ate the fresh fruit.

<u>**Ask:**</u> What fresh food you have eaten?

<u>**Define:**</u> Something that is **delicious** tastes very good.

<u>**Example:**</u> The juicy strawberry was delicious.

<u>**Ask:**</u> What delicious food have you eaten?

Visual Vocabulary Cards

Talk About It: Fresh from the Farm

COLLABORATE

Guide children to describe a delicious food they have eaten for a snack. Make a list of their responses. *What is your favorite kind of food?* Display pages 34–35 of the **Reading/Writing Workshop Big Book** and have children do the **Talk About It** activity with a partner.

READING/WRITING WORKSHOP BIG BOOK, pp. 34–35

Collaborative Conversations

Add New Ideas As children engage in partner, small group, and whole group discussions, encourage them to:

→ Stay on topic.

→ Connect their own ideas to the ideas of others.

→ Connect their personal experiences to the conversation.

ENGLISH LANGUAGE LEARNERS SCAFFOLD

Beginning

Use Visuals Explain that the picture shows a girl picking carrots on a farm. *Is this girl picking carrots? Can we eat carrots?* Allow children ample time to respond.

Intermediate

Describe Ask children to tell what the girl is doing. Help them identify the different vegetables in the picture. *Have you eaten carrots and broccoli before?* Correct grammar and pronunciation as needed.

Advanced/Advanced High

Discuss Have children elaborate on what the girl is doing. *What is she picking? Which are your favorite vegetables to eat?* Elicit more details to support children's answers.

→ Listening Comprehension

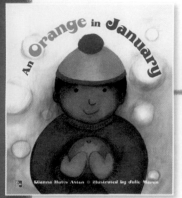

Literature Big Book

OBJECTIVES

 CCSS Name the author and illustrator of a text and define the role of each in presenting the ideas or information in the text. **RI.K.6**

CCSS Actively engage in group reading activities with purpose and understanding. **RI.K.10**

- Recognize characteristics of informational text
- Strategy: Reread

ACADEMIC LANGUAGE
- *informational text, period*
- Cognates: *texto informativo*

MINILESSON **10 Mins**

Read the Literature Big Book

Connect to Concept: Fresh from the Farm

Tell children that you will now read about a fruit that grows on a tree. *What foods have you eaten that come from a farm?*

Concepts of Print

Directionality, Print-Speech Match, Word Length Display page 4 of the **Big Book**. Track the print from left to right with your finger as you read aloud the sentence. Point to the word *In* and read it aloud. Then point to *blossomed* and read the word aloud. *Some words are longer than others. Which word is longer,* In *or* blossomed*?* (blossomed)

Genre: Informational Text

Model *An Orange in January* is an informational text. Share these characteristics of informational text with children:

→ Informational text gives facts, or real information, about people, places, or events.

> **Story Words** Preview these words before reading:
>
> **nectar:** something sweet and wet in flowers
> **drenched:** covered in something
> **skyway:** part of a road that seems to go up to the sky
> **segments:** pieces

Set a Purpose for Reading

→ Identify and read aloud the title and the names of the author and illustrator. *Which person wrote the words in this book?* (the author) *Which one drew the pictures?* (the illustrator)

→ Ask children to listen as you read aloud the Big Book to find out what happens to an orange after it is picked from the tree.

Go Digital

An Orange in January

When I read _____, I had to reread...

Think Aloud Cloud

Strategy: Reread

Model Remind children that something might not make sense to them as they read, but rereading can help them understand. Recall with children that the prefix *re-* means *again*. *What does the word* reread *mean?*

Think Aloud Read aloud page 4 before sharing this Think Aloud: *I wonder when this story begins. I will reread the page to find out.* In a land that glowed with spring light, an orange blossomed. *Oh, the words* spring light *tell me that it must be springtime. That makes sense. A lot of flowers and trees grow in the springtime.*

Apply As you read, use the **Think Aloud Cloud** to model the strategy.

Think Aloud *On page 13, I read that the orange grew plump and bright, but I'm not sure why. I'll reread the page to figure out why.* Soaked with rain and drenched in sunshine, the orange grew plump and bright . . . *That makes sense. The sunshine and rain helped the orange grow.*

Respond to Reading

After reading, prompt children to tell one way the orange traveled from place to place in the book. Discuss the ways rereading helped children understand the story. Have children draw a picture of their favorite farm food being transported.

Make Connections

Use pages 22–23 of *An Orange in January* to discuss foods that grow. Revisit the concept behind the Essential Question *What kinds of things grow on farms?* by having children name foods besides oranges that grow on trees and on farms.

Write About It Have children write about one of the steps on the orange's long journey.

ENGLISH LANGUAGE LEARNERS SCAFFOLD

Beginning

Demonstrate Read aloud pages 16–18: *From bag to basket, truck to truck . . .* Say: *Wait, I don't understand. What happened to the orange? Listen as I reread.* Read aloud the pages again. Ask: *Is the orange taken out of a bag and put in a basket?* (Yes) *Is the orange taken out of one truck and put in another?* (Yes) Clarify children's responses as needed by providing vocabulary. For example: *Yes, the orange goes from a bag to a basket.*

Intermediate

Discuss Read aloud pages 16–18: *From bag to basket, truck to truck . . .* Then say: *Wait, I'm not sure what* bag to basket *means. What could help me understand?* (reading those pages again) Reread aloud the pages. Ask: *What happens first to the orange on these pages?* (It is taken out of a bag and put in a basket.) *Then what happens to the orange?* (It is taken out of one truck and put in a smaller truck.) Restate children's responses, adding details in order to develop their oral language proficiency.

Advanced/Advanced High

Discuss Read aloud pages 16–18: *From bag to basket, truck to truck . . .* Ask: *How can rereading this page help me understand what is happening to the orange?* (The pages tell how the orange is traveling.) Model correct pronunciation as needed.

→ # Word Work

MINILESSON 5 Mins Phonemic Awareness

Phoneme Isolation

1 Model Display the **Photo Card** for *fire*. *Listen for the sound at the beginning of* fire. Fire *has the /f/ sound at the beginning. Say the sound with me: /f/.* Say these words and have children repeat: *fast, fish.* Emphasize the phoneme /f/.

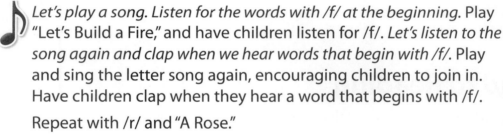

Photo Cards

Repeat with /r/ using the *rose* Photo Card and the words *red, right*.

♪ *Let's play a song. Listen for the words with /f/ at the beginning.* Play "Let's Build a Fire," and have children listen for /f/. *Let's listen to the song again and clap when we hear words that begin with /f/.* Play and sing the letter song again, encouraging children to join in. Have children clap when they hear a word that begins with /f/.

Repeat with /r/ and "A Rose."

2 Guided Practice/Practice Display and name the following Photo Cards: *feet, five, fan. Say each picture name with me. Tell me the sound at the beginning of the word.* Guide practice with the first word.

Repeat with /r/ and the *rock, rabbit,* and *rope* Photo Cards.

ARTICULATION SUPPORT

Demonstrate the way to say /f/. Put your top front teeth on your lower lip. Don't use your voice. Push air through your teeth. Hold your hand in front of your mouth as you practice. Can you feel the air? Say *fish, fan, fed* and have children repeat. Stretch /f/.

Demonstrate the way to say /r/. Open your mouth a little. Move your tongue to the back of your mouth. Put the tip of your tongue close to, but not touching, the top of your mouth. Use your voice, and let air move over the top of your tongue. Say *run, rat, rip* and have children repeat. Stretch initial /r/.

Phonics

Sound-Spelling Cards

Introduce /f/f and /r/r

1 Model Display the *Fire* **Sound-Spelling Card**. *This is the Fire card. The sound is /f/. The /f/ sound is spelled with the letter* f. *Say it with me: /f/. This is the sound at the beginning of* fire. *Listen: /fff/ire, fire. What is the name of this letter?* (f) *What sound does this letter stand for?* (/f/)

Display "Let's Build a Fire" (see **Teacher's Resource Book** online). Read or sing the song with children. Reread the title and point out that *fire* begins with the letter *f*. Model placing a self-stick note below the *f* in *fire*.

2 Guided Practice/Practice Read each line of the song. Stop after each line and ask children to place self-stick notes below words that begin with *F* or *f* and say the letter name.

Repeat Steps 1–2 with /r/r and the song "A Rose."

Let's Build a Fire

"Let's build a fire," Fiona said to Farley.
"Let's build a fire and invite all our friends.
You bring the hot dogs. I'll bring the buns.
Lets build a fire and we'll have a lot of fun."

A Rose

A rose is nice.
A rose is sweet.
It's the loveliest flower that you will meet.
But here is a warning and a word to the wise:
Be careful or you're in for a sharp surprise!

ENGLISH LANGUAGE LEARNERS

Phoneme Variation in Language
Speakers of Korean may have difficulty perceiving and pronouncing /f/. Emphasize the /f/ sound and demonstrate correct mouth position. Speakers of Cantonese, Vietnamese, and Haitian Creole may have difficulty perceiving and pronouncing /r/. Emphasize the /r/ sound and demonstrate correct mouth position.

Corrective Feedback

Sound Error Say /f/, then have children repeat the sound. *My turn. Fire. /fff/. Now it's your turn.* Have children say the words *food* and *fine* and isolate /f/. Repeat for /r/r with *rose, rabbit, run*.

YOUR TURN PRACTICE BOOK pp. 143–146

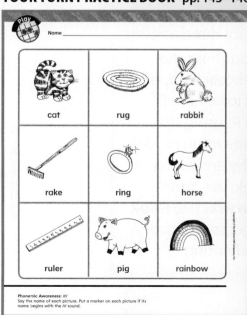

→ Word Work

MINILESSON
5 Mins

Handwriting: Write *Ff* and *Rr*

1 Model Say the handwriting cues below as you write and identify the uppercase and lowercase forms of *Ff*. Then trace the letters on the board and in the air as you say the sounds.

OBJECTIVES

 CCSS Write a letter or letters for most consonant and short-vowel sounds. **L.K.2c**

 CCSS Read common high-frequency words by sight. **RF.K.3c**

ACADEMIC LANGUAGE

uppercase, lowercase

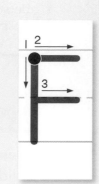

Straight down.
Straight across.
Straight across.

Circle back a little, then straight down. Go to the dotted line. Straight across.

2 Guided Practice/Practice

→ Say the cues together as children trace both forms of the letter with their index fingers. Have them identify the uppercase and lowercase forms.

→ Have children write *F* and *f* in the air as they say /f/ multiple times.

→ Distribute **Response Boards** or paper. Observe children's pencil grip and paper position, and correct as necessary. Have children say the appropriate sound every time they write the letter.

Daily Handwriting

Throughout the week teach upper- and lowercase *Ff* and *Rr* using the Handwriting models. At the end of the week, use **Your Turn Practice Book** p. 152 to practice handwriting.

Straight down.
Go back to the top. Around and in at the dotted line. Slant down.

Straight down. Curl forward.

Repeat Steps 1 and 2 with *Rr*.

T180 UNIT 5 WEEK 3

Go Digital

Handwriting

the	is
you	do

High-Frequency Words

High-Frequency Words

with, he

with

High-Frequency Word Cards

❶ **Model** Display page 4 of the **Big Book** *An Orange in January*. Read "In a land that glowed *with* spring light, an orange blossomed." Point to the high-frequency word *with*. Use the **Read/Spell/Write** routine to teach the word.

→ **Read** Point to the word *with* and say the word. *This is the word* with. *Say it with me:* with. *He came* with *me to pick oranges.*

→ **Spell** *The word* with *is spelled w-i-t-h. Spell it with me.*

→ **Write** *Write the word in the air as we say each letter: w-i-t-h.*

→ Point out to children that the letter *i* in *with* has the same /i/ sound as in *sit*.

→ Have partners create sentences using the word.

Repeat routine to introduce *he*. Use the sentence on page 28 of the Big Book. "That night, as ice gleamed on the branches, *he* dreamed of a land that shone in summer light." Point out that the /h/ sound in *he* is the same as in *hat*.

❷ **Guided Practice/Practice** Build sentences using the **High-Frequency Word Cards**, **Photo Cards**, and teacher-made punctuation cards. Have children point to the high-frequency words *with* and *he*. Use these sentences.

He *can jump* with *you.*

Can *he go* with *you?*

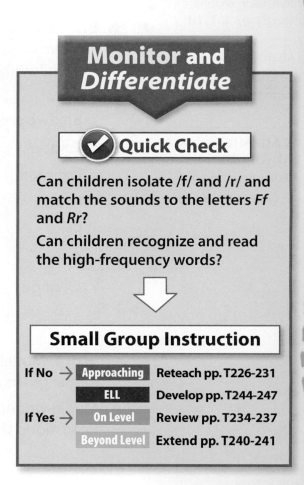

Monitor and *Differentiate*

✓ **Quick Check**

Can children isolate /f/ and /r/ and match the sounds to the letters *Ff* and *Rr*?

Can children recognize and read the high-frequency words?

Small Group Instruction

If No →	Approaching	Reteach pp. T226-231
	ELL	Develop pp. T244-247
If Yes →	On Level	Review pp. T234-237
	Beyond Level	Extend pp. T240-241

→ # Language Arts

 MINILESSON **10** Mins ## Shared Writing

OBJECTIVES

CCSS Use a combination of drawing, dictating, and writing to compose informative/ explanatory texts in which they name what they are writing about and supply some information about the topic. **W.K.2**

CCSS Use personal, possessive, and indefinite pronouns (e.g., *I, me, my; they, them, their; anyone, everything*). **L.1.1d**

• Identify sequence
• Learn about the pronoun *they*

ACADEMIC LANGUAGE

• *sequence, pronoun*
• Cognates: *secuencia*

Writing Trait: Organization

1 **Model** Tell children that some writers organize their ideas in the order in which they happen. They put them in sequence.

→ Write and read: *I take a shower. I dress. I eat breakfast. I brush my teeth. This is the order I do things in the morning.*

2 **Guided Practice/Practice** *What do you do before school in the morning?* Write some children's sentences on the board. Work together to put the sentences in order.

Write Story Sentences

Focus and Plan Tell children that this week they will learn how to write story sentences about food.

 Brainstorm Display the **Photo Cards** for *apple, peach, pear, pumpkin,* and *strawberry*. Have children identify each fruit. Make a list of fruits that children know. *Where are the fruits grown?*

> Strawberry
> Grape
> Pumpkin
> Peach
> Pear
> Apple
> Orange

Write Model writing about a fruit from the list. Write and read: *A farmer grows peach trees. He sells the peaches to stores. I buy a peach.*

Model writing an informative text. Use another example from the list. Read aloud the sentences with children.

Go Digital

Writing

I see a fish.
Grammar

MINILESSON 5 Mins

Grammar

Pronouns

1 Model Remind children that some of the pronouns they have learned include *he, she, it, we, you,* and *I*. Write *they* and explain that *they* is a pronoun, too.

→ Write and read aloud: *Joe and Tom play football. They play football*. Explain that *they* can be used in place of the names of two or more people.

2 Guided Practice/Practice *Nancy and Marina won the game.* Work together to identify which words can be replaced with *they*. (Nancy and Marina)

Mom and Dad have jobs. Mom and Dad work very hard. Explain that you want to change the second sentence so you don't repeat *Mom and Dad*. Ask children how to say the sentence using *They* in place of *Mom and Dad*. (They work very hard.)

Talk About It

COLLABORATE

Have children work with partners to orally generate sentences, using the pronoun *they*. Challenge children to tell who *they* refers to in their sentences.

ENGLISH LANGUAGE LEARNERS SCAFFOLD

Beginning

Review Write the pronouns *he, she, it, you, we, I,* and *they* on the board. Point to each pronoun and read it aloud. Have children echo-read each pronoun after you. Then use each in a sentence. Model correct pronunciation as needed.

Intermediate

Practice Write the pronouns *he, she, it, you, we, I,* and *they* on index cards. Give each child a pronoun and have children tell you a sentence using that pronoun correctly. Allow children ample time to respond.

Advanced/Advanced High

Practice Write and read a sentence that does not include a pronoun. Have children tell you a pronoun that can replace a noun or nouns in the sentence. Rewrite the sentence and choral-read it with children. Elicit more details to support children's answers.

Daily Wrap Up

- Review the Essential Question and encourage children to discuss it, using the new oral vocabulary words. *What kinds of things grow on a farm?*

- Prompt children to share the skills they learned. How might they use those skills?

Materials

Reading/Writing Workshop Big Book
UNIT 5

Literature Big Book
An Orange in January

Visual Vocabulary Cards
fresh
delicious

Response Board

Retelling Cards

Puppet

Word-Building Cards

Photo Cards
apple
berries
cheese
grapes
peach
pear
pumpkin
strawberry
yogurt

Sound-Spelling Cards
Fire

High-Frequency Word Cards
he
with

"Oats, Peas, Beans, and Barley Grow"

→ # Build the Concept

 MINILESSON 10 Mins

Oral Language

Go Digital

OBJECTIVES

 CCSS Use words and phrases acquired through conversations. **L.K.6**

CCSS Recognize rhyming words. **RF.K.2a**

CCSS Sort common objects into categories (e.g., shapes, foods) to gain a sense of the concepts the categories represent. **L.K.5a**

Develop oral vocabulary

ACADEMIC LANGUAGE
• *rhyme, sentence*
• Cognates: *rima*

ESSENTIAL QUESTION

What kinds of things grow on a farm?

Remind children that this week, they are learning about foods grown on farms. Ask them to name foods they have seen at the market or store that were grown on a farm.

Sing "Oats, Peas, Beans, and Barley Grow" with children.

Phonological Awareness
Recognize Rhyme
Tell children that these words from the song rhyme: *grow* and *know*. Remind them that words that rhyme have the same end sound. Have children repeat *grow, know* after you, stressing the end sounds. Then say each of the following sets of words and have children raise their hands if they hear words that rhyme: *cub, tub; wall, wish; lag, tag; rake, take; ball, bat; hot, tab.*

Review Oral Vocabulary

Use the **Define/Example/Ask** routine to review the oral vocabulary words **fresh** and **delicious**. Prompt children to use the words in sentences.

Vocab
Define:
Examp
Ask:

Visual Vocabulary Cards

Visual Glossary

Category Words

Category Words: Food Words

❶ Model Use the **Big Book** *An Orange in January* to discuss food words. Turn to the title page and point to each piece of fruit. *Let's name the food.* (banana, orange, apple, grapes, pear) All of these foods are called fruit. Explain that fruit is a type of food. Discuss other types of food.

Tell children that we can sort foods by groups. Use food realia or **Photo Cards** for *berries, grapes, cheese,* and *yogurt.* Display the *grapes* Photo Card. *These are grapes. Grapes are fruit. I will put them in the fruit group.* Display the *cheese* Photo Card. *This is cheese. Cheese is made from milk. I will put cheese in the milk, or dairy, group.* Continue to sort remaining Photo Cards or realia.

❷ Guided Practice/Practice Tell children that they will sort foods. Distribute food realia or Photo Cards to groups of children. Use two types of food with four examples of each type. If necessary use the suggested groups of Photo Cards: *zucchini, carrots, corn, celery; cherry, banana, apple, watermelon; soup, sandwich, pizza, egg; peach, pear, strawberry,* and *lemon.* Have children sort realia into groups. Then have them explain how they decided which foods belonged in a group. Guide practice as needed.

Vocabulary Strategy: Context Clues/ Sentence Clues

❶ Model Tell children that they can ask questions about words that they do not know the meaning of. Explain that they can also use clues in a sentence to figure out the meaning of unknown words. Use *An Orange in January* to model sentence clues.

Think Aloud What does *nectar* mean in this sentence? "Bees feasted on *nectar,* sweet as honey, until the petals fell away and the orange began to grow." The sentence tells me that nectar is sweet. I know that bees like to eat sweet things. The sentence talks about flower petals, and I know that bees feed on flowers. The clues tell me that nectar is something sweet that bees drink from flowers.

❷ Guided Practice Have children figure out the meaning of *glowed* in the sentence below. Tell them that the word *light* is a clue. Guide practice as needed to figure out that glowed means "bright."

*In a land that **glowed** with spring **light**, an orange blossomed.*

ENGLISH LANGUAGE LEARNERS

Reinforce Meaning Draw pictures of several fruits and vegetables on the board, such as *apple, orange,* and *carrot.* Say the name of each food and label it. Have children choose one of the foods and draw a picture of it. Then have children repeat the food words with you.

LET'S MOVE!

Name different fruit and vegetable words. If you say a fruit word, children should sit down. If you say a vegetable word, they should stand up.

WHOLE GROUP
DAY 2

 Listening Comprehension CLOSE READING

Literature Big Book

Go Digital

An Orange in January

Retelling Cards

OBJECTIVES

 With prompting and support, ask and answer questions about key details in a text. **RI.K.1**

 Confirm understanding of a text read aloud or information presented orally or through other media by asking and answering questions about key details and requesting clarification if something is not understood. **SL.K.2**

- Strategy: Reread
- Skill: Main Topic and Key Details

ACADEMIC LANGUAGE

- *informational text, reread*
- Cognates: *texto informativo*

MINILESSON 15 Mins
Reread Literature Big Book

Genre: Informational Text

Display *An Orange in January*. Remind children that informational text gives facts about real things or events. *How do you know that An Orange in January is informational text?* Have children point to evidence in the text and in the illustrations to show that this is informational text. (Possible answers: Oranges grow on trees in real life. Oranges are taken from trees to the store in real life.)

Strategy: Reread

Remind children that good readers sometimes reread, or read something again, to help them understand what they are reading. *What can you do when you don't understand what you are reading?* (You can go back, reread, and find details that will help you understand.)

Skill: Main Topic and Key Details

Tell children that the main topic is what a selection is mostly about. Key details in the text and illustrations give more information about the main topic. Explain that knowing what the main topic of a selection is can help you understand it better. As you read, have children listen for evidence in the text to figure out the main topic.

Access Complex Text

Sentence Structure This book includes many ellipses. This structure can confuse young readers. Make sure the words flow smoothly as you read aloud. Point out that three dots mean that the sentence keeps going.

→ Point out the word *until* on page 7. Then read aloud pages 7–9, allowing your intonation to rise as you read *until*. Point out that the sentence continues on the next page.

→ Repeat the routine with pages 13–15 and 20–24, having children echo.

PAGES 4–5

MAIN TOPIC

Think Aloud I wonder what the main topic of this book will be. On this page I read about an orange blossoming. I know that the title of the book is *An Orange in January*. I think that the main topic is probably oranges. I will look for key details as I keep reading.

pp. 4–5

glowed with spring light: Explain that *spring light* is sunlight in the springtime. Remind children that spring is one of the four seasons. Point to the sun or illustrations of the sun to help explain.

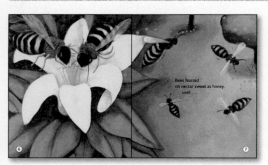

PAGES 6–7

PHONICS

Have children identify the word that begins with /f/. (feasted)

VOCABULARY

I hear the word "feast" in "feasted." To feast means to eat a large amount of food. Feast with /əd/ must mean that the bees ate a large amount of food.

pp. 6–7

feasted: Pantomime eating large quantities of food. If play food is available, use it. As you pretend to gobble food, say: *feasting.* Have children echo and mimic.

PAGES 8–9

KEY DETAILS

Think Aloud On this page I learn that the petals from the flower fall off, and the orange begins to grow. These details tell about the main topic of oranges.

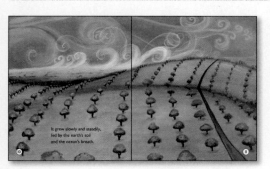

PAGES 10–11

MAIN TOPIC AND KEY DETAILS

What is the topic, or the big idea on these pages? (The orange grew.) *What are the details that tell about the big idea?* (The orange was fed by the earth's soil and the ocean's breath.) *What is the ocean's breath?* (water from the ocean)

pp. 10–11

fed by the earth's soil and the ocean's breath: Guide children in understanding that just as people need water and food, plants need water and food from the soil. Point to soil in the illustration and say: *soil.* Repeat with *water.* Have children point and repeat.

Listening Comprehension

CLOSE READING
ELL

PAGES 12–13

REREAD

Think Aloud I see different kinds of weather in the picture. I'll reread to find out why. Oh, I see. The orange grows when it gets rain and sunshine. It needs both kinds of weather.

pp. 12–13

plump: Explain that *plump* fruit is big and juicy. Say: *plump.* Have children echo and mimic.

PAGES 14–15

HIGH-FREQUENCY WORDS

Have children point to and read the high-frequency word *with.*

pp. 14–15

plucked: Pretend to pick the orange on page 14. Say: *I picked the orange. I plucked it.* Have children echo and mimic.

PAGES 16–17

KEY DETAILS

How does the illustration help you understand what "bag to basket" means? (I can see the worker pouring oranges out of a bag and into a huge basket. This shows me how the oranges go from the bag to the basket.)

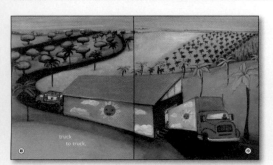

PAGES 18–19

REREAD

What has happened to the orange so far? How could we find out if we can't remember? (First, it grew on a tree. Next, it was plucked from the tree. Then it went from a bag to a basket. Now it's on a truck. We can reread to help us remember.)

PAGES 20–21

PHONICS

Reread page 20 aloud and invite a volunteer to point to the word that has the /f/ sound at the beginning. (followed) Read the word aloud and have children say it with you. *What letter makes the /f/ sound?* (f)

pp. 20–21

over; across: To guide children's understanding of these prepositions, walk your fingers over the mountains on page 20 as you say: *over.* Have children echo and mimic. Then slide a finger across the plains as you say: *across.*

PAGES 22–23

REREAD

Where is the orange now? Let's reread to find out. Reread page 22. *That's right, a grocery store.*

pp. 22–23

aglow with the goodness inside it: Tell children that the orange is not really glowing. This just means that the orange is delicious inside.

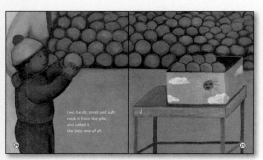

PAGES 24–25

ASK AND ANSWER QUESTIONS

Think Aloud I wonder what the boy will do with the orange next. I know that I like to eat oranges. Will he eat it next? Let's keep reading to find out.

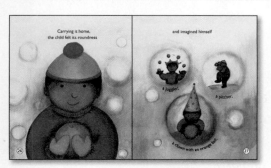

PAGES 26–27

REREAD

Think Aloud I'm not sure I understand all the things the boy imagined. I'll reread these pages to help me understand. Read aloud pages 26–27. Then say: Oh, I see now. The boy imagined ways he could use his orange. He could be a juggler. He could be a pitcher. He could be a clown.

pp. 26–27

roundness: Use your finger to track the shape of the orange as you say *roundness.* Have children echo and mimic. Repeat with other round objects in the classroom.

Listening Comprehension

PAGES 28–29

HIGH-FREQUENCY WORDS

Read aloud page 28. Then have a child point to and read aloud the high-frequency word *he*.

PAGES 30–31

CONCEPTS OF PRINT

Have a volunteer point to the last word in the sentence on page 30. (it) *How do you know this is the last word in the sentence?* (There is an end mark after the word. The end mark is a period.)

pp. 30–31

bursting with the seasons inside it: Make certain children understand that the orange had grown through spring and summer and now it was going to be very tasty.

PAGES 32–33

AUTHOR'S PURPOSE

Why do you think the author wrote this story? (Possible answer: She wanted to give information about how an orange grows and travels from a tree to a person.)

pp. 32–33

segments: A segment is a piece. If possible, show children the inside of an orange, pointing out the segments. Have them repeat *segments*. You might also use an object such as a math manipulative that contains segments.

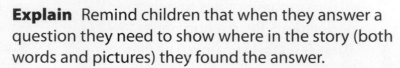

Text Evidence

Explain Remind children that when they answer a question they need to show where in the story (both words and pictures) they found the answer.

Discuss *What are some different ways the orange travelled? On which page did you see that part of the journey?*

Guided Retelling

Tell children that now they will use the **Retelling Cards** to retell the story.

→ Display Retelling Card 1. Based on children's needs, use either the Modeled, Guided or ELL retelling prompts. The ELL prompts contain support for English language learners based on levels of language acquisition. Repeat with the rest of the cards, using the prompts as a guide.

→ Have children choose a part of the orange's journey and give details about why it is important.

→ Invite children to choose a favorite part of the story and act it out.

Model Fluency

Model reading sentences with ellipses, making your voice rise with the final word—to show that something interesting is coming on the next page. Turn to pages 6–7. Read aloud: *Bees feasted on nectar sweet as honey,* (pause) *until* (voice rising with the word *until*). Have children echo. Repeat the routine with pages 13 and 20. Then read page 22, tracking the words as you say them, and invite children to say *until* with you.

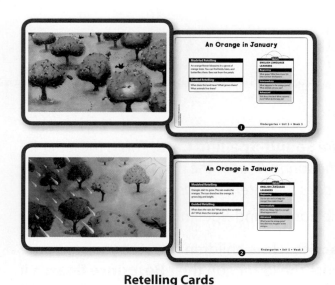

Retelling Cards

YOUR TURN PRACTICE BOOK p. 147

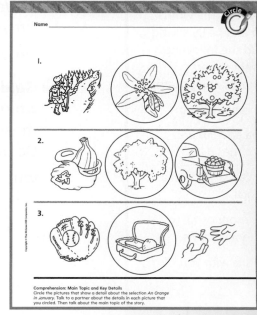

→ # Word Work

MINILESSON 5 Mins — Phonemic Awareness

Puppet

Phoneme Blending

OBJECTIVES

CCSS Demonstrate basic knowledge of one-to-one letter-sound correspondences by producing the primary or many of the most frequent sounds for each consonant. **RF.K.3a**

CCSS Read common high-frequency words by sight. **RF.K.3c**

Blend phonemes to make words.

❶ **Model** *The puppet is going to say sounds in a word, /f/ /a/ /n/. It can blend those sounds to make a word: /ffffaaannn/, fan. Listen as the puppet blends more sounds to make a word.* Model phoneme blending with the following words.

/f/ /i/ /t/ *fit*   /f/ /ī/ /n/ *fine*   /f/ /i/ /n/ *fin*   /i/ /f/ *if*

❷ **Guided Practice/Practice** Tell children to listen as the puppet says the sounds in words. Have them repeat the sounds, and then blend them to say the word.

/f/ /a/ /n/ *fan*   /f/ /u/ /n/ *fun*   /f/ /ē/ /t/ *feet*

Repeat Steps 1–2 with /r/ and the words *red, rug, ran* for Step 1 and *rat, ride, rise* for Step 2.

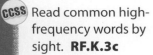 **ELL**

MINILESSON 5 Mins — Phonics

Review *f* and *r*

❶ **Model** Display the *Fire* **Sound-Spelling Card**. *This is the letter* f. *The letter* f *stands for the sound /f/ as in the word* fire. *What is the letter?* (f) *What sound does the letter* f *stands for?* (/f/)

Repeat for /r/r with the *Rose* Sound-Spelling Card.

❷ **Guided Practice/Practice** Have children listen as you say some words. Ask them to write the letter *f* on their **Response Boards** if the word begins with /f/ or the letter *r* if the word begins with /r/. Do the first two words with children.

four   rest   follow   five   rip   fun   red   ripe

Go Digital

Phonemic Awareness

Phonics

High-Frequency Word Routine

Handwriting

Blend Words with *f* and *r*

1 Model Place **Word-Building Cards** *r, e,* and *d* in a pocket chart. Point to *r. This is the letter* r. *The letter* r *stands for /r/. Say /r/. This is the letter* e. *The letter* e *stands for /e/. Say /e/. This is the letter* d. *The letter* d *stands for /d/. Say /d/. Listen as I blend the three sounds together: /rrreeed/ red. Let's blend the sounds to read the word.*

2 Guided Practice/Practice Change Word-Building Cards to *r, i, p.* Point to the letter *r* and have children say /r/. Point to the letter *i* and have children say /i/. Point to the letter *p* and have children say /p/. Then move your hand from left to right under the word and have children blend and read the word *rip.* Repeat with *rat.*

Repeat Steps 1–2 with *f* using the words *fat, fin, fit.*

High-Frequency Words

MINILESSON 5 Mins

with, he

High-Frequency Word Cards

1 Guided Practice Display the **High-Frequency Word Cards** *with* and *he.* Use the **Read/Spell/Write** routine to teach each word. Ask children to close their eyes, picture the spelling of each word in their minds, and then write both words the way they see it. Have children self-correct by checking the High-Frequency Word Cards.

2 Practice Add the words *he* and *with* to the word bank.

→ Have partners create sentences using the words.

→ Have children count the number of letters in each word and then write *with* and *he* again.

Cumulative Review Review *are, my, do, you, go.*

Repeat the **Read/Spell/Write** routine. Mix the words and have children chorally say each one.

Monitor and *Differentiate*

✓ **Quick Check**

Can children blend phonemes with /f/ and /r/ to make words and match /f/ to *Ff* and /r/ to *Rr*?

Can children recognize and read the high-frequency words?

Small Group Instruction

If No →	**Approaching**	Reteach pp. T226-231
	ELL	Develop pp. T244-247
If Yes →	**On Level**	Review pp. T234-237
	Beyond Level	Extend pp. T240-241

→ # Shared Read

Reading/Writing Workshop Big Book and Reading/Writing Workshop

---

OBJECTIVES

CCSS Read common high-frequency words by sight. **RF.K.3c**

CCSS Read emergent-reader texts with purpose and understanding. **RF.K.4**

ACADEMIC LANGUAGE
• *predict*
• Cognates: *predecir*

MINILESSON 10 Mins

Read "Ron With Red"

Model Skills and Strategies

Model Concepts About Print Turn to page 37 and read the sentence, tracking the print with your finger or a pointer to help children develop print to speech match. *Most of the words have three letters. Which word in the sentence has more letters?* Point to the word *with. The word* with *has more letters. Together let's count how many letters are in* with*: 1, 2, 3, 4. The word* with *has four letters. The words* Ron, Red, *and* pet *have three letters. With* is a longer word than Ron, Red, *and* pet.

Predict Read the title together. Invite children to look closely at the illustration on pages 36 and 37. Encourage them to describe what they see. Then have them predict what the story will be about.

Read Have children chorally read the story with you. Point to each word as you read it together. Help children sound out decodable words and say the sight words. If children have difficulty, provide corrective feedback and guide them page by page using the student **Reading/Writing Workshop**.

Ask the following:

→ *Look at page 37. Who is Red? Where are Ron and Red going?* (Possible answer: Red is a dog; It looks like Ron and Red are going to a place where oranges grow.)

→ *Look at page 38. What are Ron and Red doing?* (Ron is looking for a bird. Red sees a bird.)

→ *Look at page 41. What is Mom doing?* (Mom is putting ten tomatoes in a box.)

Go Digital

"Ron With Red"

"Ron With Red"

READING/WRITING WORKSHOP, pp. 36–43

Rereading

Have small groups use the **Reading/Writing Workshop** to reread "Ron With Red." Then review the skills and strategies using the *Phonics* and *Words to Know* pages that come before the selection.

→ Invite children to reread the story. Help children identify the main topic and key details in the story. If children don't remember a key detail, encourage them to reread a section of the story again.

→ Have children use page 35 to review the high-frequency words *he* and *with*.

→ Have children use page 34 to review the letters *f* and *r*, and their corresponding sounds. Guide them to blend the sounds to read the words.

ELL

ENGLISH LANGUAGE LEARNERS

Reinforce Vocabulary Display the **High-Frequency Word Cards** *with, he, are, my.* Point to pictures in the classroom and groups of children as you use the high-frequency word in sentences, such as the following: *I would like to play with the blocks. Would you like to play with the blocks?* (Yes, we would like to play with the blocks.) *Is he sitting in a chair?* (Yes, he is sitting in a chair.) *Are you ready for lunch?* (Yes, we are ready for lunch.) *Is my pencil in my hand?* (Yes, your pencil is in your hand.)

→ # Language Arts

 MINILESSON **10** Mins

Interactive Writing

OBJECTIVES

CCSS Use a combination of drawing, dictating, and writing to compose informative/explanatory texts in which they name what they are writing about and supply some information about the topic. **W.K.2**

CCSS Use personal, possessive, and indefinite pronouns (e.g., *I, me, my; they, them, their; anyone, everything*). **L.1.1d**

• Identify sequence
• Use pronouns

ACADEMIC LANGUAGE

• *sequence, pronoun*
• Cognates: *secuencia*

Writing Trait: Organization

Review Remind children that when they write events in the order they happen, they are writing those events in a sequence. Writing information in the proper sequence makes it easier to understand.

Write Story Sentences

Discuss Display the list of fruits from Day 1. Read the words on the list aloud, and point to a picture or **Photo Card** of each fruit. Discuss with children what they know about where each fruit grows.

Model/Apply Grammar Tell children that you will work together to write sentences that tell who grows pumpkins. Display the Photo Card for *pumpkin*.

Write and read aloud: *The farmer grows pumpkins. The farmer picks the pumpkins when they are big.*

Point to the words *The farmer* in the second sentence. *What pronoun can we use to replace the words* The farmer? *Yes, we can use either the pronoun* she *or* he. Rewrite the sentence and read it aloud: *She (he) picks the pumpkins when they are big.*

Write Have children help you write more informative story sentences with more information about what happens after the pumpkins are picked. Make sure the sentences are written in the proper sequence. Write the sentences as children suggest them. Share the pen with children and have them write the letters they know.

Go Digital

Writing

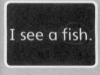

I see a fish.

Grammar

Grammar

Pronouns

1 Review Write and read aloud: *Jimmy went for a bike ride. Which pronoun can replace* Jimmy? (He) *Jimmy is a boy, so the pronoun* he *is used in its place.*

→ Write the following pronouns on index cards: *he, she, it, they, we, you,* and *I.* Read each word aloud. Point out that *I* is always written with a capital letter.

→ Write the following sentence frames and read them aloud:

_____ plays football. (he or she)

_____ is a square shape. (it)

_____ sit down. (we, you, I, or they)

_____ sing songs. (we, you, I, or they)

Have children tape an appropriate pronoun in the blank of each sentence frame. Discuss why different pronouns will work for each of the sentence frames.

2 Guided Practice Write and read aloud: *Dana, Olivia, and Anna are friends.* _____ *play together all the time.* Ask children to think of a pronoun that would complete the second sentence. (They) They *is the best pronoun for the sentence because* they *can be used in place of the names of two or more people in a sentence.* Write *They* in the blank to complete the sentence.

3 Practice Write and read aloud: _____ *like to eat peaches.* Have children work with a partner to find a pronoun that will complete the sentence. Give each pair a sentence strip and have them write the completed sentence on the sentence strip.

Talk About It

Have children work with partners to think of sentences, using the pronouns *I, you,* and *we.* Have partners share their sentences with the class.

ENGLISH LANGUAGE LEARNERS

Use Visuals Have children find a **Photo Card** showing a food they like to eat. Have children complete the sentence frame: *I like to eat* _____. Help children write the word as necessary. Have children read the completed sentence aloud and point to the pronoun.

Daily Wrap Up

- Review the Essential Question and encourage children to use the oral vocabulary words. *What kinds of fruit grow on farms?*

- Prompt children to review and discuss the skills they used today. How do those skills help them?

Materials

Reading/Writing Workshop Big Book
UNIT 5

Visual Vocabulary Cards
beneath
raise
special

Interactive Read-Aloud Cards

Word-Building Cards

Puppet

Photo Cards
fan   rake
feather   ring
feet   rock
five   rope
fork   rose
fox   ruby
mix   tree
rabbit

High-Frequency Word Cards
are
he
with

Think Aloud Cloud

→ Build the Concept

MINILESSON
10 Mins
Oral Language

OBJECTIVES

CCSS With prompting and support, identify basic similarities in and differences between two texts on the same topic (e.g., in illustrations, descriptions, or procedures). **RI.K.9**

CCSS Identify real-life connections between words and their use. **L.K.5c**

Develop oral vocabulary

ESSENTIAL QUESTION

COLLABORATE

Remind children that this week they are talking and learning about the kinds of things that grow on a farm. Guide children to discuss the Essential Question using information from the **Big Book** and the weekly song. Remind children about the foods that grow in "Oats, Peas, Beans, and Barley Grow." Sing the song and have children join in.

Oral Vocabulary

Review last week's oral vocabulary words, as well as *fresh* and *delicious* from Day 1. Then use the **Define/Example/Ask** routine to introduce *beneath, raise,* and *special.*

Oral Vocabulary Routine

Define: If you are **beneath** something, you are under it.

Example: The sidewalk is beneath our feet as we walk.

Ask: What is beneath a desk or table in the classroom?

Visual Vocabulary Cards

Define: When you **raise** something or someone, you take care of it to make sure it grows.

Example: People who raise horses give them plenty of exercise.

Ask: How can you care for a puppy as you raise it?

Define: When something is **special**, it is different in a good way.

Example: The coconut is a special food because every part of it can be used in some way.

Ask: Do you have a special food you like to eat? What is it? Why do you think it is special?

Go Digital

Visual Glossary

"Farms Around the World"

Think Aloud Cloud

Listening Comprehension

Read the Interactive Read Aloud

MINILESSON
10 Mins

Genre: Informational Text

Tell children you will be reading an informational text. Guide them in recalling that *informational text* gives facts, or true information, about a topic. Display the **Interactive Read-Aloud Cards**.

Read the title, "Farms Around the World." *This selection is going to tell facts about different kinds of farms.* Point out that different kinds of plants grow in different parts of the world.

Interactive Read-Aloud Cards

Strategy: Reread

Remind children that sometimes when they read, they might not understand something the first time. Good readers will go back and reread to help them understand. *When you reread you should pay close attention to details that will help you understand what is happening.* Model rereading using the **Think Aloud Cloud**.

Think Aloud I just read that potatoes can be used to make another product. I thought potatoes were just for eating. I'll reread to see if that helps me understand. I reread the last paragraph and now I understand. Potatoes can be made into fuel. *Fuel* is what people use to make cars and other machines work.

Read "Farms Around the World," pausing occasionally to model the strategy of rereading.

Make Connections

Guide partners to connect "Farms Around the World" with *An Orange in January*. Discuss the ways both selections show the different kinds of foods that grow on farms. *How are the farms similar? How are they different?*

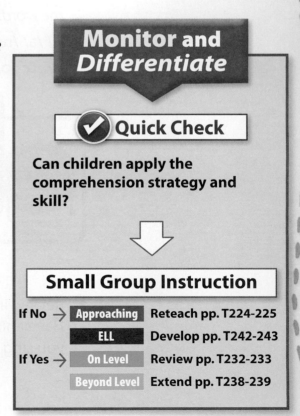

ENGLISH LANGUAGE LEARNERS

Reinforce Meaning As you read "Farms Around the World," make meaning clear by pointing to specific people, places, or objects in the photographs, demonstrating word meanings, paraphrasing text, and asking children questions. For example, on Card 2, point to a potato in the photo and say: *This is a potato.*

Monitor and *Differentiate*

✓ **Quick Check**

Can children apply the comprehension strategy and skill?

⬇

Small Group Instruction

If No → Approaching Reteach pp. T224-225
ELL Develop pp. T242-243
If Yes → On Level Review pp. T232-233
Beyond Level Extend pp. T238-239

→ # Word Work

Quick Review

Build Fluency: Sound-Spellings:
Display **Word-Building Cards:** *a, c, d, e, f, h, i, m, n, o, p, r, s, t.* Have children chorally say each sound. Repeat and vary the pace.

MINILESSON 10 Mins

Phonemic Awareness

Puppet

Phoneme Blending

OBJECTIVES

CCSS Isolate and pronounce the initial, medial vowel, and final sounds (phonemes) in three-phoneme words. **RF.K.2d**

CCSS Demonstrate basic knowledge of one-to-one letter-sound correspondences by producing the primary or many of the most frequent sounds for each consonant. **RF.K.3a**

Read and blend words with *f, r*

❶ **Model** *The puppet is going to say sounds in a word: /r/ /i/ /p/. It can blend those sounds to make a word: /rrriiip/,* rip. *When the puppet blends the sounds together, it makes the word* rip. Continue modeling blending with the following:

/r/ /a/ /p/ rap   /f/ /e/ /d/ fed   /f/ /i/ /sh/ fish

/r/ /e/ /d/ red   /f/ /i/ /t/ fit   /i/ /f/ if

❷ **Guided Practice/Practice** *Listen to the puppet as it says each sound: /f/ /i/ /g/. The puppet can blend these sounds together: /fffiiig/.* Fig. *Say the sounds with the puppet: /f/ /i/ /g/, /fffiiig/,* fig. *Now let's say the word with the puppet:* fig.

Place the following **Photo Cards** face down: *fan, fox, five, rose, rake, rock.* Choose a card but do not display it. Tell children that the puppet will say the sounds in the word. *Listen to the puppet as it says each sound. You will repeat the sounds, then blend them to say the word.* After children have said the word, show the Photo Card.

/f/ /a/ /n/ fan   /f/ /o/ /ks/ fox   /f/ /ī/ /v/ five

/r/ /ō/ /p/ rope   /r/ /ā/ /k/ rake   /r/ /o/ /k/ rock

Photo Cards

♪ Review initial /f/, /r/. Play and sing "Let's Build a Fire" and "A Rose." Have children clap when they hear initial /f/ or /r/. Demonstrate as you sing with them.

Go Digital

Phonemic Awareness

Phonics

Handwriting

Phonics

5 Mins
MINILESSON

Word-Building Cards

Review *f, r*

❶ Model Display **Word-Building Card** *r. This is the letter* r. *The letter* r *stands for /r/, the sound you hear in the beginning of* rose. *Say the sound with me: /r/. I will write the letter* r *because* rose *has /r/ at the beginning.* Repeat the routine for /f/f using the word *fire*.

❷ Guided Practice/Practice Tell children that you will say words that begin with /f/ or /r/. Have them say /f/ and write the letter *f* on their **Response Boards** when they hear words beginning with /f/. Tell them to say /r/ and write the letter *r* when they hear words beginning with /r/. Guide practice with the first word.

ride	fact	rope	run	fine
fun	rip	face	find	rat

Blend Words with Short *i, a, e* and *f, r, t, n, d, p*

❶ Model Display Word-Building Cards *i, f. This is the letter* i. *It stands for /i/. This is the letter* f. *It stands for /f/. Let's blend the two sounds together: /iiiffff/, /if/. The word is* if. Continue with the following words: *fed, ran, red*.

❷ Guided Practice/Practice Write the following words and sentences. Have children read each word, blending the sounds. Guide practice with the first word.

fat   rip   fit   red   fan   rat   if

Prompt children to read the connected text, sounding out the decodable words: *We fed the pet. The red hat fit. He ran with you.*

YOUR TURN PRACTICE BOOK p. 148

Name _____

fan red rip →

1.
fan | fan →

2.
red | red

3.
rip | rip →

Phonics: Blending /f/f, /r/r
Blend the sounds and say the word. Write the word. Repeat the word.

Corrective Feedback

Sound Error Model the sound that children missed, then have them repeat. For example, say: *My turn*. Tap under the letter *f* in the word *fan* and ask: *Sound?* (/f/) *What's the sound?* (/f/) Return to the beginning of the word. Say: *Let's start over*. Blend the word again.

→ # Word Work

 ## MINILESSON 5 Mins

Phonics

Photo Cards

OBJECTIVES

CCSS Read common high-frequency words by sight **RF.K.3c**

Sort words using initial consonants

ACADEMIC LANGUAGE
sort

Picture Sort

1 Model Remind children that the letter *f* stands for /f/ and the letter *r* stands for /r/. Place **Word-Building Card** *f* on the left side of the pocket chart. *What is this letter?* (f) *What sound does this letter stand for?* (/f/) Continue the routine for letter *r* placing the letter on the right side of the pocket chart.

Hold up the **Photo Card** for *fan*. *Here is the picture for* fan. *Fan has the /f/ sound at the beginning. I will place fan under the letter* f *because the letter* f *stands for /f/.* Continue the same routine for *rose*.

2 Guided Practice/Practice Have children sort the Photo Cards *feather, feet, fork, rabbit, ring, ruby*. Have them say the sound at the beginning of the word and tell which letter the Photo Card should be placed under.

Phonics

High-Frequency Word Routine

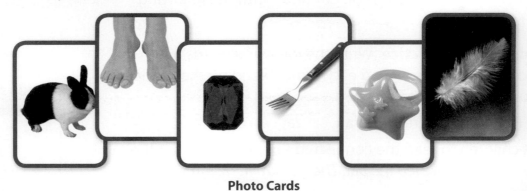

Photo Cards

High-Frequency Words

with, he

❶ Guided Practice Display the **High-Frequency Word Cards** *with* and *he*. Review the words using the **Read/Spell/Write** routine.

❷ Practice Point to the High-Frequency Word Card *with* and have children read it. Repeat with *he* and last week's word *are*.

Build Fluency

Word Automaticity Write the following sentences and have children chorally read aloud as you track the print. Repeat several times.

> Sam and Tim are *with* him.
> *He* ran *with* you.
> Pat ran *with* him.
> *He* and I are *with* Pam.

Read for Fluency Distribute pages 149–150 **Your Turn Practice Book** and help children assemble their Take-Home Books. Chorally read the Take-Home Books with children. Then have children reread the books to review high-frequency words and build fluency.

YOUR TURN PRACTICE BOOK pp. 149–150

He sat with mom.

Mom fed him!

High Frequency Words: he, with
Read the book aloud to a partner. Reread for fluency.

4 Unit 5: Wonders of Nature • Week 3

Tim

He fed the hen.
He sat with the cat.

1

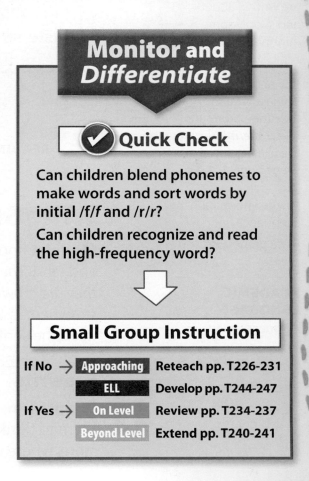

Monitor and *Differentiate*

✔ Quick Check

Can children blend phonemes to make words and sort words by initial /f/f and /r/r?

Can children recognize and read the high-frequency word?

⬇

Small Group Instruction

If No →	**Approaching**	Reteach pp. T226–231
	ELL	Develop pp. T244–247
If Yes →	**On Level**	Review pp. T234–237
	Beyond Level	Extend pp. T240–241

→ # Language Arts

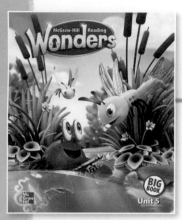

Reading/Writing Workshop Big Book

OBJECTIVES

 Use a combination of drawing, dictating, and writing to compose informative/ explanatory texts in which they name what they are writing about and supply some information about the topic. **W.K.2**

CCSS Use personal, possessive, and indefinite pronouns (e.g., *I, me, my; they, them, their; anyone, everything*). **L.1.1d**

• Write information in sequence

• Use pronouns

ACADEMIC LANGUAGE

• *sequence, pronoun*

• Cognates: *secuencia*

MINILESSON
10 Mins

Independent Writing

Writing Trait: Organization

1 Practice Tell children that today they will write an informative story to tell about where fruits grow.

2 Guided Practice Share the Readers to Writers page in the **Reading/Writing Workshop**. Read the model sentences aloud.

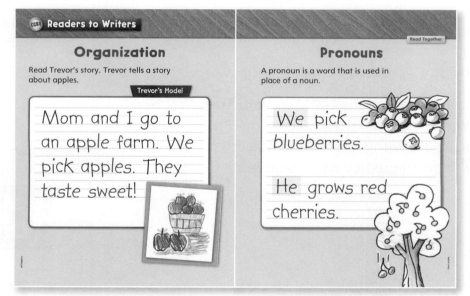

READING/WRITING WORKSHOP BIG BOOK, pp. 46–47

Write Story Sentences

Model Choose a fruit from the list on Day 1 to write about. Write and read: *The farmer grows strawberries. He picks the strawberries when they are grown. He drives the strawberries to a store. The store sells the strawberries. We eat the strawberries.* Draw pictures for your sentences. Read the sentences aloud, tracking the print.

Prewrite

 Brainstorm Have children work with a partner to choose a fruit. Ask them to think about where the fruit is grown and how it gets to the store, where they can buy the fruit.

Go Digital

Present the Lesson

Writing

I see a fish.

Grammar

Draft

Give each child a blank sheet of writing paper. Have children draw a picture, near the top of the paper, of the fruit they chose. Have children write sentences to tell where that fruit is grown. Help children write their sentences as needed. Encourage children who can generate more writing to do so.

Apply Writing Trait As children write their informative story sentences, remind them to organize the sentences so that events are in the correct sequence.

Apply Grammar Remind children that pronouns are used to replace nouns in sentences. Children can use pronouns in some sentences so they don't have to write the name of the fruit over and over again.

ENGLISH LANGUAGE LEARNERS

Demonstrate Understanding
Show pictures from the **Big Book** *An Orange in January*. Have children identify the things in the picture by using the pronoun *it* in a complete sentence. For example: *It is an orange.*

Grammar
MINILESSON 5 Mins

Pronouns

❶ **Review** Display the **Photo Card** for *tree*. Write and read: *The tree is tall. It is green. One of these sentences has a pronoun. What is the pronoun?* (It) *What noun does it replace?* (The tree)

❷ **Guided Practice/Practice** Display the Photo Card for *mix*. Have children tell you what the boy is doing. Write their sentences on sentence strips. Read each sentence strip aloud. For example: *The boy puts in flour. The boy puts in water. The boy mixes it up.*

Cut each sentence strip into two parts, dividing after *The boy*. Provide three short sentence strips with the word *He*. Have children take out *The boy* and replace it with *He*. Chorally read the new sentences, and have children point to the pronoun *He* in each sentence.

Talk About It

Have children work with partners to choose a game they like to play at school. Have them tell how to play the game. Remind children to use pronouns in their descriptions.

Daily Wrap Up

- Review the Essential Question and encourage children to discuss it, using the oral vocabulary words *fresh* and *delicious. How do you think fresh grown fruit tastes?*

- Prompt children to review and discuss the skills they used today. Guide them to give examples of how they used each skill.

Materials

Reading/Writing Workshop Big Book
UNIT 5

Literature Big Book
An Orange in January

Interactive Read-Aloud Cards

Word-Building Cards

Visual Vocabulary Cards
with
he

High-Frequency Word Cards
he
with

Photo Cards
banana   pitcher
bowl   vegetables
fork   yogurt
nut
olive
pea
pie

→ # Extend the Concept

MINILESSON
10 Mins

Oral Language

OBJECTIVES

CCSS Sort common objects into categories to gain a sense of the concepts the categories represent. **L.K.5a**

CCSS Use words and phrases acquired through conversations, reading and being read to, and responding to texts. **L.K.6**

CCSS Recognize and produce rhyming words. **RF.K.2a**

CCSS With prompting and support, ask and answer questions about unknown words in a text. **RI.K.4**

Develop oral vocabulary

ESSENTIAL QUESTION

Remind children that this week they have been talking and reading about things that grow on a farm. Have them sing "Oats, Peas, Beans, and Barley Grow" and discuss the kinds of food that grow on farms. Then ask them to tell what was growing in *An Orange in January*.

Phonological Awareness
Recognize Rhyme

Point out the words *grow* and *know* from the weekly rhyme. Remind children: *Words that rhyme have the same end sound. Listen:* grow, know. *I can say more words with this end sound:* snow, blow, low, show. Say the following word pairs and have children clap if the words rhyme: *bone/lone; take/tell; eat/even; sit/bit; race/face; go/toe.*

Review Oral Vocabulary

Reread the Interactive Read Aloud Use the **Define/Example/Ask** routine to review the oral vocabulary words *fresh, delicious, beneath, raise,* and *special*. Then have children listen as you reread "Farms Around the World."

→ *What do farmers do after they plant rice seeds beneath the dirt?* (They cover the field with water.)

→ *What kinds of things do people raise on farms?* (plants and animals)

Go Digital

Visual Glossary

"Farms Around the World"

Category Words

Category Words: Food Words

❶ Explain/Model Recite the following rhyme. Have children listen for which foods are fruits and which are vegetables. Then review which foods are fruits or vegetables.

Apples grow on trees, and grapes come from a vine.
Carrots grow underground, and peas form in a line.

Turn to pages 30-31 of the **Big Book** *An Orange in January*. Point to the plate and cup on the counter and explain that these are things we use to serve food. Tell children that we will sort food from the things we use to serve food. Use realia or **Photo Cards** for *bowl, fork, nut,* and *olive*. Demonstrate how to sort the food from the utensils.

❷ Guided Practice Tell children that they will sort foods from the things that are used to serve them. Distribute food and utensil realia or Photo Cards to groups. If necessary, use the suggested Photo Cards: *bowl, fork, plate, pitcher; pie, vegetables, pea, yogurt.* Have groups sort utensils from food. Guide practice as needed.

Vocabulary Strategy: Context Clues/ Sentence Clues

❶ Model Remind children that they can ask questions about words in a text that they do not know the meaning of. They can also use clues from the sentences and pictures in the book to make sense of words they do not know.

Think Aloud What does the word *segments* mean in this sentence? "And two hands, pink with cold, shared its *segments*, so that everyone could taste the sweetness of an orange in January. " I have eaten an orange, and I know that the fruit can be separated into small pieces. The sentence talks about sharing, and I see the boy hand a girl a small piece of orange in the picture. A *segment* must be "one small part of the orange."

❷ Guided Practice/Practice Read the following sentence from pages 16-22 of *An Orange in January*.

*From bag to basket, truck to truck, it followed the **skyway** over mountains, across deserts and **plains** until the orange arrived at a grocery store.*

Have children use sentence and picture clues to figure out the meaning of *skyway* and *plains*. Guide children as needed.

ENGLISH LANGUAGE LEARNERS

Describe Point to the Photo Cards for *banana, pea,* and *zucchini*. Say the fruit or vegetable word for each. Then ask children questions about each food. For example: *What color is the banana? Where do bananas grow? How do you eat a banana?*

LET'S MOVE!

Give simple directions that include food words for fruits and vegetables. For example: *Peel a banana. Pull a carrot from the ground. Pick an apple from a tree. Bite into a piece of celery.*

YOUR TURN PRACTICE BOOK p. 151

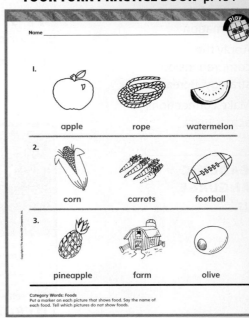

→ # Listening Comprehension

CLOSE READING

Literature Big Book

MINILESSON
10 Mins

Read "Farmers' Market"

Genre: Informational Text

Display "Farmers' Market" on pages 34–40 of the **Big Book** and read aloud the title. Remind children that informational text gives information about things from real life.

Set a Purpose for Reading

Read aloud the first two sentences on page 34. Tell children to listen as you continue reading to learn about how food is grown and sold.

Strategy: Reread

Remind children that good readers reread part of a text if there is something they do not understand. Reread the second sentence on page 34. *The word* they *is referring to the farmers' stands. Sometimes we may have to reread other sentences to better understand the text.*

Text Feature: Lists

Explain Point to the list on page 40. Explain that sometimes authors include extra information in a list. *This list shows what a shopper needs to buy at the market.*

Apply Read aloud the list on page 40. *Which fruit or vegetable would you want to add to the list?* (Answers will vary.) *Where would you add it?* (at the end of the list)

**Go
Digital**

"Farmers' Market"

OBJECTIVES

 CCSS With prompting and support, identify the main topic and retell key details of a text. **RI.K.2**

CCSS With prompting and support, identify basic similarities in and differences between two texts on the same topic (e.g., in illustrations, descriptions, or procedures). **RI.K.9**

• Use the text feature lists to gather information
• Apply the comprehension strategy: Reread
• Make connections across texts

ACADEMIC LANGUAGE
lists

Farmers' Market

Look at the farmers' stands. They are filled with fresh foods. Who grows the vegetables and fruits? How did they get here?

Farmers grow fruits and vegetables. Some farmers grow squash in the fall. Others grow peas in the spring.

LITERATURE BIG BOOK   **PAGES 34–35**

MAIN TOPIC AND KEY DETAILS

What is the main topic of these pages? (the farmers who grow food for farmers' markets)

LITERATURE BIG BOOK   PAGES 36–37

MAIN TOPIC AND KEY DETAILS

What is the main topic of these pages? (Vegetables and fruits grow in different ways.) *What are two details?* (Possible answers: Peas grow on vines; oranges grow on trees.)

LITERATURE BIG BOOK   PAGES 38–39

REREAD

Reread the pages aloud. Point out the words *Some farmers* on page 38 and *Other farmers* on page 39. *How are these farmers different?* (Some farmers sell their food nearby, and other farmers sell their food far away.)

LITERATURE BIG BOOK   PAGE 40

TEXT FEATURE

Why are there marks next to some of the things on the list? (to keep track of the things they have collected so far)

ENGLISH LANGUAGE LEARNERS

Reinforce Meaning As you read aloud the text, make the meaning clear by pointing to details in the photographs. Ask children questions and elicit language.

Retell and Respond

Have children discuss the selection by asking the following questions:

→ *Where do carrots grow?* (under ground)

→ *How do farmers get food to faraway places?* (boats, trains, airplanes)

Make Connections

COLLABORATE

Have children recall the selections they read this week.

→ *How are the selections alike?* (They are about food grown on farms.)

Write About It Write about how the selections are different.

SCIENCE **CONNECT TO CONTENT**

Fruits and Vegetables Review with children the vegetables that grow above ground (corn, peas) and the ones that grow below ground (carrots). Have children discuss the fruits and vegetables that grow on vines. Ask them to tell how they are alike and different.

STEM

Word Work

Quick Review
Build Fluency: Sound-Spellings: Display **Word-Building Cards:** *a, c, d, e, f, h, i, m, n, o, p, r, s, t*. Have children chorally say each sound. Repeat and vary the pace.

Phonemic Awareness

Phoneme Addition

OBJECTIVES

CCSS Add or substitute individual sounds (phonemes) in simple, one-syllable words to make new words. **RF.K.2e**

CCSS Distinguish between similarly spelled words by identifying the sounds of the letters that differ. **RF.K.3d**

CCSS Read common high-frequency words by sight. **RF.K.3c**

❶ **Model** Have children make different words by adding an initial phoneme to an existing word. *We can add sounds to the beginning of words to make new words. Listen as I say a word: an. Say it with me: an. What word do we have when we add /f/ to the beginning of an. When we add /f/ to an, we make the word fan.* Repeat substituting /r/ to make *ran.*

❷ **Guided Practice/Practice** *Listen carefully to these questions about words. Answer the questions by adding the beginning sound to make a new word.* Allow children ample time to respond. Guide practice with the first question.

What word do you have if you add /f/ to the beginning of *it*? (fit)
What word do you have if you add /r/ to the beginning of *Ed*? (red)
What word do you have if you add /f/ to the beginning of *in*? (fin)
What word do you have if you add /r/ to the beginning of *at*? (rat)

Phonics

Blend Words with Short *e, i, a* and *f, r, d, p, n*

❶ **Guided Practice** Display **Word-Building Cards** *r, e, d*. Point to the letter *r*. *This is the letter* r. *The letter* r *stands for /r/. Say /r/. This is the letter* e. *The letter* e *stands for /e/. Listen as I blend the two sounds together /rrreee/. This is the letter* d. *The letter* d *stands for /d/. Listen as I blend the three sounds /rrreeed/,* red. *Now you say it. Let's change the* r *to* f. Use the same routine to blend the word *fed.*

❷ **Practice** Write *rip, rap* and *fin, fan*. Have children blend the sounds to read the words. Have children point out the letters that are the same in each pair. (r, p; f, n) Ask children to tell which letters are different. (i, a) Discuss the sound each letter stands for and how it changes the word.

Go Digital

Phonemic Awareness

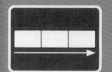

Phonics

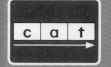

Handwriting

Visual Glossary

High-Frequency Word Routine

Dictation

Review Dictate these sounds for children to spell. Have them repeat the sound and then write the appropriate letter. Repeat several times.

/r/ /f/ /a/ /e/ /i/ /n/ /t/ /d/

Dictate the following words for children to spell: *ran, rat, red, fan, fed, fit.* Model for children how to segment each word to scaffold the spelling. *When I say the word* ran *I hear three sounds: /r/ /a/ /n/. I know the letter* r *stands for /r/, the letter* a *stands for /a/, and the letter* n *stands for /n/. I will write the letters* r, a, n *to spell the word* ran.

When children finish, write the letters and words for them to self-correct.

MINILESSON 5 Mins

High-Frequency Words

Visual Vocabulary Cards

Practice Say the words *with* and *he* and have children write them. Then display the **Visual Vocabulary Cards** *with* and *he*. Follow the Teacher Talk routine on the back.

Build Fluency Build sentences in the pocket chart using the **High-Frequency Word Cards**, **Photo Cards** and teacher-made punctuation cards. Have children chorally read the sentences as you track the print. Ask them to identify the words *with* and *he*.

He can go **with** you.
He can see the map **with** you.
He and I like to write.
I can go to the zoo **with** you.

Also online

High-Frequency Words Practice

COLLABORATE Have partners create sentences using the words *with* and *he*.

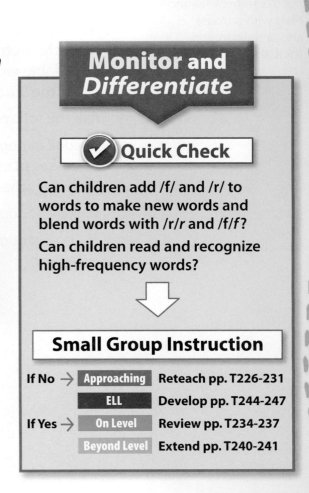

Monitor and Differentiate

Quick Check

Can children add /f/ and /r/ to words to make new words and blend words with /r/*r* and /f/*f*?

Can children read and recognize high-frequency words?

Small Group Instruction

If No →	Approaching	Reteach pp. T226-231
	ELL	Develop pp. T244-247
If Yes →	On Level	Review pp. T234-237
	Beyond Level	Extend pp. T240-241

→ # Shared Read

OBJECTIVES

CCSS Read common high-frequency words by sight. **RF.K.3c**

CCSS Read emergent-reader texts with purpose and understanding. **RF.K.4**

MINILESSON
10 Mins

Read "Ron With Red"

Model Skills and Strategies

Model Book Handling Demonstrate book handling. Point to the front cover of the book. *This is the front cover of the book.* Then display the back cover. *This is the back cover of the book.* Model turning the pages of the book.

Model Concepts About Print Read the story and model how to read from left to right and top to bottom. Then develop print-to-speech match. *As I read this sentence, I will point to each word I say as I move from left to right and from top to bottom, like this.* Read a sentence from the story and point to the last word. *This is the last word in the sentence. I will pause for a moment before I read the next sentence.* Finally, have volunteers point to words that are shorter in length and words that are longer in length in the story.

Reread Review each rebus and discuss what it stands for. Then have children chorally read the story. Children should sound out the decodable words and say the sight words. Offer support as needed using the student **Reading/Writing Workshop**.

Ask the following:

→ *Look at page 39. What is Dad holding?* (Possible answers: oranges; a basket of oranges; an orange in one hand and a basket of oranges in the other)

→ *Look at page 41. How many tomatoes does Mom have in all?* (ten)

→ *Look at page 43. What does Red see on top of the car that Ron doesn't?* (a bird)

Go Digital

"Ron With Red"

"Ron With Red"

Ron is **with** Red.
Red is a pet.

Red can see a bird.
Can Ron see it on top?

Dad can see ten oranges.
He can fit ten in a basket.

Red can see a bird.
Can Ron see it on top?

Mom can see ten tomatoes.
Mom can fit ten on top.

Ron can sit and sip.
Red can see a bird.

Ron did not see a bird.
Red can see it on top!

READING/WRITING WORKSHOP, pp. 36–43

Fluency: Expression

1 Explain Tell children that as you read the story, you will read with expression, or feeling. Mention that you will stress different words and change your voice when reading sentences that end with a period, a question mark, or an exclamation point. You will also pause after groups of words for effect.

2 Model Model reading "Ron With Red" with expression. *When I read the story, I change my tone when I read sentences with different kinds of punctuation. I also pause after sentences or groups of words for effect, like this.* Read each sentence with appropriate emotion, or feeling.

3 Guided Practice Invite children to choral read the story with appropriate expression. If necessary, have them listen to you first and then echo each sentence. Encourage them to match your intonation and expression.

→ # Language Arts

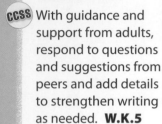
MINILESSON
10 Mins

Independent Writing

Write Story Sentences

Revise

Distribute children's draft sentences from Day 3.

Apply Writing Trait: Organization Explain that as writers revise, they make sure their writing is organized in a way that makes the most sense. *When you are writing to explain how something happens from start to finish, you want to organize the ideas in the proper sequence, or order.*

Write and read: *I go to school. I eat breakfast. I wake up.* Guide children in placing the sentences in the correct order. Then have children look at the story sentences they created on Day 3 and check for the following:

→ Did I write about one kind of fruit?

→ Did I draw a picture of the fruit?

→ Did I write my ideas in the correct order?

→ Did I use pronouns?

Apply Grammar Explain that writers use pronouns to avoid repeating some nouns over and over again. Have children look at their story sentences and underline the pronouns they used. Have children share some of the pronouns they used with the class.

COLLABORATE

Peer Edit Have children work in pairs to do a peer edit, in which they read their partner's draft. Ask partners to check that sentences begin with a capital letter and that *I* is always capitalized. Have children make sure all ideas are written in the proper sequence. Provide time for children to make revisions to their story sentences.

Final Draft

After children have edited their own story sentences and finished their peer edits, have them prepare a final draft of their sentences. Conference with children to provide guidance as they work.

OBJECTIVES

CCSS With guidance and support from adults, respond to questions and suggestions from peers and add details to strengthen writing as needed. **W.K.5**

CCSS Use personal, possessive, and indefinite pronouns (e.g., *I, me, my; they, them, their; anyone, everything*). **L.1.1d**

• Revise sentences
• Use pronouns in sentences

ACADEMIC LANGUAGE
• *revise, sequence, pronoun*
• Cognates: *revisar, secuencia*

Go Digital

Writing

I see a fish.

Grammar

Grammar

Pronouns

① Review Remind children that a pronoun is a word that takes the place of a noun or nouns. Say: *Mr. Smith is my neighbor. He is nice.* Ask: *Who are these sentences about?* (Mr. Smith) *What pronoun is used in place of Mr. Smith in the second sentence?* (He)

② Guided Practice Have a girl and a boy stand at the front of the classroom. Ask children to tell something about what each person is wearing. For example: *Jamal is wearing a blue shirt. Maria is wearing pink shoes.* Have children work together to say the same thing again using pronouns.

What pronoun can we use in place of Jamal? (He) *How do you know?* (Jamal is a boy, and *he* is the pronoun used to replace a boy's name.) *What pronoun can we use in place of Maria?* (She) *How do you know?* (Maria is a girl, and *she* is the pronoun used to replace a girl's name.)

Continue by asking children to say something that is true of both children. For example: *Jamal and Maria are both five years old.* Guide them to say the same thing using a pronoun. (They are both five years old.)

Now have children say things that are true for everyone in the classroom, using the word *we*. For example: *We are going to lunch soon.* Ask which word is the pronoun. (We)

③ Practice Have children work in pairs. Have one child say a sentence, telling about something the other child is wearing, using the pronoun *he* or *she*. Then have children switch roles. Ask children to share some of their sentences with the class.

Talk About It

Have children work with partners to use the pronoun *we* to tell about things they do as a class.

ENGLISH LANGUAGE LEARNERS

Photo Cards and Sentences
Provide sentences that go with images on the **Photo Cards**. As you read a sentence aloud, hold up a Photo Card as you say the pronoun or noun, such as *The pear tastes sweet. It is juicy.*

Daily Wrap Up

- Review the Essential Question and encourage children to discuss it, using the oral vocabulary words.

- Prompt children to discuss the skills they practiced and learned today. Guide them to share examples of each skill.

Go Digital

www.connected.mcgraw-hill.com
RESOURCES
Research and Inquiry

→ **Wrap Up the Week**
Integrate Ideas

RESEARCH AND INQUIRY

Fresh from the Farm

OBJECTIVES

CCSS Participate in shared research and writing projects (e.g., explore a number of books by a favorite author and express opinions about them). **W.K.7**

CCSS With guidance and support from adults, recall information from experiences or gather information from provided sources to answer a question. **W.K.8**

ACADEMIC LANGUAGE
resources

Make a Fruit Basket

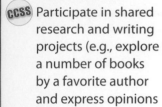

Tell children that today they will do a research project with a partner to make a display of fruits and vegetables. Review the steps in the research process below.

STEP 1 Choose a Topic

Guide children to think of fruits and vegetables that they like to eat. Point out which food is grown on farms. Have children brainstorm a list of different fruits and vegetables. Have partners select a fruit or vegetable from the list to research.

STEP 2 Find Resources

Review how to locate and use resources. Direct children to use selections from the week. Provide magazines and help children look for books in the library or online sites to find out more about fruits and vegetables. Have children use the Research Process Checklist online.

STEP 3 Keep Track of Information

Help children interpret and keep track of the information they find by writing words and marking pages in books with sticky notes.

Collaborative Conversations

Be Open to All Ideas As children engage in partner, small-group, and whole-class discussions, tell them to:

→ listen carefully because all ideas, questions, or comments are important.

→ ask a question if something is unclear.

→ respect the opinions of others.

→ give their opinions, even if they are different from those of other people.

STEM

This is a pumpkin.
Pumpkins grow on vines.

STEP 4 Create the Project: Fruit Basket

Explain the characteristics of the project:

→ **Information** The fruit basket will give information about different foods.

→ **Text** Each fruit or vegetable will have sentences that tell about it. Provide these sentence frames:

This is a _____. _____ grow _____.

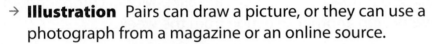

→ **Illustration** Pairs can draw a picture, or they can use a photograph from a magazine or an online source.

Have pairs choose one food that is grown on a farm. Explain that they will write and illustrate a page for the fruit basket.

→ Guide children to write more sentences with describing words that tells about their food.

→ Prompt children to include details in their illustration.

→ When children finish the fruit basket bulletin board have them compare and contrast the fruits and vegetables that are displayed.

ELL ENGLISH LANGUAGE LEARNERS SCAFFOLD

Beginning	Intermediate	Advanced/Advanced High
Use Sentence Frames Pair children with more fluent speakers. Provide sentence frames to help children talk about their chosen foods. For example: *This is a ____. It tastes ____.*	**Describe** Tell partners to include details in their pictures that show where and how the food grows. When children share their story page with the class, direct them to point to and name details in their illustration.	**Demonstrate Understanding** Encourage children to tell as much about their foods as they can. Prompt them with questions such as these: *How does this food grow? How do you like to eat this food?* Have children point to parts of their illustrations as they answer.

Materials

Reading/Writing Workshop Big Book
UNIT 5

Literature Big Book

Interactive Read-Aloud Cards

Word-Building Cards

Response Board

High-Frequency Word Cards
are
do
he
I
like
my
with
you

Visual Vocabulary Cards
with
he

→ Integrate Ideas

TEXT CONNECTIONS

Connect to Essential Question

OBJECTIVES

 With prompting and support, identify basic similarities in and differences between two texts on the same topic (e.g., in illustrations, descriptions, or procedures). **RI.K.9**

 Participate in collaborative conversations with diverse partners about *kindergarten topics and texts* with peers and adults in small and larger groups. **SL.K.1**

- Make connections among texts
- Make connections to the world

Text to Text

Remind children that all week they have been reading selections about food grown on farms. Tell them that now they will connect the texts, or think about how the selections are alike. Model comparing *An Orange in January* with another selection from the week.

 Think Aloud In *An Orange in January,* I learned how an orange grew, how it was picked, and how it ended up in a grocery store. In "Farmers' Markets," I learned how different fruits and vegetables grow. They ended up at a market. Both selections showed me how food grows and how it gets to a place where you or I could buy it.

Guide children to compare how the orange grows in *An Orange in January* with how the crops grow in "Farms Around the World."

Text to Self

Ask children to name a fruit or vegetable that they like to eat. Have them tell where their family gets that fruit or vegetable.

Text to World

Challenge children to name as many different fruits and vegetables as they can. Have children speculate where they come from. Help children understand that many workers and farmers work all year long to make sure that markets and grocery stores are full of food for us.

TALK ABOUT READING

OBJECTIVES

 CCSS Confirm understanding of a text read aloud or information presented orally or through other media by asking and answering questions about key details and requesting clarification if something is not understood. **SL.K.2**

Becoming Readers

Talk with children about the genres, strategy, and skill they have learned about this week. Prompt them to discuss how this knowledge helps them to read and understand selections.

→ Remind children that one genre they learned about is informational text. Review with them some characteristics of informational text.

→ Talk with children about the strategy of rereading. *How did rereading a page in "Farmers' Markets" help you to understand the text?*

→ Discuss with children how they identified the main topic and key details in *An Orange in January*. Talk about how knowing the main idea helped them to understand the text.

RESEARCH AND INQUIRY

OBJECTIVES

CCSS Participate in shared research and writing projects (e.g. explore a number of books by a favorite author and express opinions about them). **W.K.7**

Wrap Up the Project

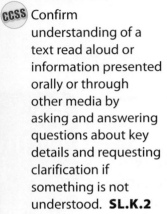

Guide partners to share their pages from the fruit basket and to point out details in their illustrations. Encourage children to use words and phrases they learned this week. Have children use the Presenting and Listening checklists online.

Word Work

Phonemic Awareness

OBJECTIVES

CCSS Add or substitute individual sounds in simple, one-syllable words to make new words. **RF.K.2e**

CCSS Spell simple words phonetically, drawing on knowledge of sound-letter relationships. **L.K.2d**

CCSS Read common high-frequency words by sight. **RF.K.3c**

Phoneme Addition

❶ **Model** *Listen to this word:* at. *Say it with me:* at. *What word do we make if we add /f/ to the beginning of* at? Allow children ample time to respond. *When we add /f/ to* at *we make the word* fat. Repeat substituting /r/ to make the word *rat*.

❷ **Guided Practice/Practice** *Answer these questions by adding the sound to make a new word.* Guide practice with the first question.

What word do you have if you add /f/ to the beginning of *an*? (fan)
What word do you have if you add /r/ to the beginning *an*? (ran)
What word do you have if you add /f/ to the beginning of *it*? (fit)
What word do you have if you add /r/ to the beginning of *am*? (ram)

Phonics

Read Words with Short *a, e, i, o* and *f, r, n, d, t, p*

❶ **Guided Practice** Display **Word-Building Cards** *f, a, n*. Point to *f*. *The letter* f *stands for /f/. Say /f/. The letter* a *stands for /a/. Say /a/. The letter* n *stands for /n/. Say /n/. Let's blend the sounds to make the word: /fffaaannn/* fan. *Now let's change the* f *to an* r *at the beginning of the word.* Blend and read *ran* with children.

❷ **Practice** Write these words and sentences for children to read:

rid   red   fit   fat   rod   rip   fad   fin   if

I like the red fan.   I fit in the hat.
We ran to the den.   He fed the pet rat.

Remove words from view before dictation.

♪ Review /f/f and /r/r. Have children write the letter *f* on their **Response Boards**. Play and sing "Let's Build a Fire." Have children hold up and show the letter *f* when they hear initial /f/. Demonstrate for children as you sing. Repeat with /r/r and the song "A Rose."

Go Digital

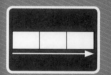

Phonemic Awareness

Phonics

High-Frequency Word Cards

Handwriting

Dictation

Review Dictate the following sounds for children to spell. As you say each sound, have children repeat it and then write the letter on their **Response Boards** that stands for the sound.

/r/   /f/   /e/   /h/   /d/   /o/   /k/   /n/   /i/

Dictate the following words for children to spell. Model for children how to segment words to scaffold the spelling. *I will say a word. You will repeat the word, then think about how many sounds are in the word. Use your sound boxes to count the sounds. Then write one letter for each sound you hear.*

fan   fit   ran   red   fin   rod   rid

Then write the letters and word for children to self-correct.

MINILESSON
5 Mins

High-Frequency Words

with, he

❶ **Review** Display **Visual Vocabulary Cards** *with* and *he*. Have children **Read/Spell/Write** each word. Then choose a Partner Talk activity.

Visual Vocabulary Cards

Distribute one of the following **High-Frequency Word Cards** to children: *he, with, are, my, do, you.* Tell children that you will say some sentences. *When you hear the word that is on your card, stand and hold up the word card.*

He likes fresh peaches.
Can *he* go *with you*?
Do you want to go to *my* house?
Apples *are* delicious.
Ron likes yogurt *with* strawberries.

❷ **Build Fluency: Word Automaticity** Display High-Frequency Word Cards *he, I, like, my, with,* and *are.* Point to each card, at random, and have children read the word as quickly as they can.

Monitor and *Differentiate*

✓ **Quick Check**

Can children add phonemes to words to make new words and read words with /f/f and /r/r?

Can children read and recognize high-frequency words?

Small Group Instruction

If No →	**Approaching**	Reteach pp. T226–231
	ELL	Develop pp. T244–247
If Yes →	**On Level**	Review pp. T234–237
	Beyond Level	Extend pp. T240–241

WHOLE GROUP DAY 5

→ # Language Arts

MINILESSON 10 Mins — Independent Writing

Write Story Sentences

Prepare

Tell children that they will present their finished informative story sentences from Day 4 to the class. Hold up an example from Day 4 and read it aloud, tracking the print as you read. *I read loudly so that everyone could hear me. I spoke loudly, but did not yell. I spoke slowly to make sure everyone could understand what I was saying.*

Present

Have children take turns standing up and presenting their story sentences. Children should read each sentence in the order they were written. Remind children to speak clearly. Prompt them to read at a consistent pace. Remind the other children to listen quietly until it is their turn.

Evaluate

Have children discuss their own presentations and evaluate their performances, using the presentation rubric. Use the teacher's rubric to evaluate children's writing.

Publish

After children have finished presenting, collect the story sentences. Put all of them together in a class book called *Fruits We Eat*. Encourage children to read the book with a partner during free time or as a center activity.

OBJECTIVES

 Speak audibly and express thoughts, feelings, and ideas clearly. **SL.K.6**

 Use personal, possessive, and indefinite pronouns (e.g., *I, me, my; they, them, their; anyone, everything*). **L.1.1d**

Present sentences

ACADEMIC LANGUAGE
• *present, publish*
• Cognates: *presente*

Go Digital

Writing

I see a fish.

Grammar

Grammar

Pronouns

1 Review Write and read aloud: *Max picks up the ball. He plays with it. Which words are naming words?* (Max, ball) *What pronoun replaces* Max? (He) *That's right. Max is a boy, and* he *is used in place of a boy's name. What pronoun replaces* ball? (it) *That's right. A ball is a thing, and* it *is used in place of a thing.*

2 Review Practice *Where do you go after school?* Have children tell you where they go directly after school every day. Make a list of those places on the board. Some children go home, some to a babysitter, some to a day-care center, some to a grandparent's house, etc. Read each item in the list aloud.

Have children work with a partner and tell the partner where he or she goes after school. For example: *I go to a babysitter after school.* The other child should then say, *You go to a babysitter after school.* Partners should switch roles.

Write on sentence strips some of the sentences that children shared. Have volunteers circle the pronouns in each sentence. Store the sentence strips for future review of the pronouns *I* and *you.*

Wrap Up the Week

- Review blending words with initial /f/*f* and /r/*r*. Remind children that a pronoun is a word that takes the place of a noun or nouns.

- Use the **High-Frequency Word Cards** to review the Words to Know.

- Remind children that they can write story sentences to explain how something happens.

→ Approaching Level

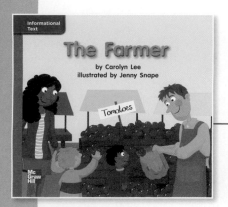

Leveled Reader

 OBJECTIVES

CCSS With prompting and support, identify the main topic and key details of a text. **RI.K.2**

CCSS With prompting and support, ask and answer questions about unknown words in a text. **RI.K.4**

CCSS Name the author and illustrator of a text and define the role of each in presenting the ideas or information in a text. **RI.K.6**

CCSS Read emergent-reader texts with purpose and understanding. **RF.K.4**

Leveled Reader:
The Farmer

Go Digital

Leveled Reader

Before Reading

Preview and Predict

Point to the cover and read the title and the names of the author and illustrator, as children follow along in their books. Ask: *What does the author do? What does the illustrator do?* Preview the illustrations and identify the rebus pictures in the book with children. Ask: *What do you think the story will be about?*

Review Genre: Informational Text

Remind children that informational text gives details and information about a topic. Ask children: *What kind of information do you think we might learn from this book?* (The things a farmer sells from his farm.)

Model Concepts of Print

Model reading a sentence as children follow along with their books. Say: *I begin reading at the left and move to the right. The sentence begins with a capital letter and ends with a period.*

Review High-Frequency Words

Point out the word *he* on page 2, and read it with children. Have them find the word on pages 3 and 4. Ask: *Who is "he"?* (the farmer)

Essential Question

Set a purpose for reading: *Let's find out what kinds of foods are grown on farms that a farmer might sell.* Remind children to use the illustrations as they read.

During Reading

Guided Comprehension

As children read *The Farmer,* monitor and provide guidance by correcting blending and modeling the strategy and skill.

Strategy: Reread

Remind children that if they find a part of the book confusing, they can reread the text to help them better understand what is happening.

Skill: Main Topic and Key Details

Review with children that reading the text and looking at the illustrations will help them learn about the key details and main topic in a story.

Think Aloud The words on page 2 don't tell me who the man is or where he is. The title of the book is *The Farmer*, and the picture shows a man selling red apples to a woman at a market. I can confirm that detail by reading the words on page 2: *He sells red apples.* The title and these details tell me that the main topic is about a farmer selling things at a farmer's market.

Guide children to identify key details on pages 4 and 5 that support the main topic. Ask: *Do these things grow on a farm?*

After Reading

Respond to Reading

→ *Where does this selection take place?* (at a farmer's market)

→ *How do you know?* (from the title and the pictures)

→ *What kinds of things does the farmer sell?* (apples, peppers, flowers)

→ *What color is everything the farmer sells?* (red)

Retell

Have children take turns retelling the story while another child acts it out. Help them make a personal connection. Ask: *What would you like to buy at a farmer's market?*

Model Fluency

Reread the story aloud, pausing after each page to have children chorally repeat.

Apply Have children practice reading with partners.

LITERACY ACTIVITIES

Have children complete the activities on the inside back cover of the reader.

Level Up

IF Children read *The Farmer* **Approaching Level** with fluency and correctly answer the Respond to Reading questions,

THEN Tell children that they will read another story about food that's grown on a farm.

• Have children page through *Let's Make a Salad!* **On Level** as you introduce the topic of a farmer growing food.

• Have children read the book, monitoring their comprehension and providing assistance as necessary.

→ Approaching Level
Phonological Awareness

TIER 2

RECOGNIZE RHYME

OBJECTIVES

CCSS Recognize and produce rhyming words. **RF.K.2a**

I Do Remind children that rhyming words have the same ending sounds. Tell them that the words *grow* and *know* rhyme with each other.

We Do Have children repeat *grow, know* after you, emphasizing the ending sounds. Then say *cub, tub* and have children repeat. *Do these words rhyme:* cub, tub? *Yes, because they have the same ending sounds*: /ub/.

You Do Say the following word pairs and have children touch their noses if the words rhyme: *feed, need; far, car; fan, fit; roof, room; land, hand.*

TIER 2

PHONEME ISOLATION

OBJECTIVES

CCSS Isolate and pronounce the initial, medial vowel, and final sounds (phonemes) in three-phoneme words. **RF.K.2d**

I Do Display the *Fan* **Photo Card**. *This is a* fan. *The first sound in* fan *is* /fff/. Have children repeat the word with you, emphasizing the initial sound. Then have children say the first sound with you: /fff/.

We Do Display the *Farm* Photo Card. Name the photo and have children say the name. *What is the first sound in* farm? (/f/) Say the sound together. Repeat with the *Feather* Photo Card.

You Do Show the *Feet* Photo Card. Have children name it and say the initial sound of the picture name. Repeat with the *Fire* Photo Card.

Repeat the routine for /r/ using the *Rock* Photo Card in *I Do* and the *Rabbit, Rake, Ring,* and *Rose* Photo Cards in the rest of the lesson.

You may wish to review Phonological Awareness and Phonemic Awareness with **ELL** using this section.

PHONEME BLENDING

OBJECTIVES

CCSS Isolate and pronounce the initial, medial vowel, and final sounds (phonemes) in three-phoneme words. **RF.K.2d**

The puppet is going to say the sounds in a word. Listen: /f/ /i/ /t/. The puppet can blend these sounds together: /fffiiit/, fit. Repeat with foot.

Now the puppet is going to say the sounds in another word. Say the sounds with the puppet: /f/ /a/ /n/. Let's blend the sounds together: /fffaaannn/, fan. Repeat with fox and fun.

Have children blend sounds to form words. Practice together: /f/ /ē/ /t/ /fffēēēt/, feet. Then have children blend sounds to say the words.

/f/ /i/ /l/ fill　　　/f/ /a/ /t/ fat　　　/f/ /ō/ /n/ phone　　　/f/ /e/ /d/ fed

Repeat the routine for /r/ and the sounds in the words *red, ripe, rat,* and *rip.*

PHONEME ADDITION

OBJECTIVES

CCSS Add or substitute individual sounds (phonemes) in simple, one-syllable words to make new words. **RF.K.2e**

Listen as the puppet says a word: in. Have children repeat the word. *The puppet will add /f/ to the beginning of* in. Have the puppet say *fin. By adding /f/ to in, the puppet made a new word:* fin. *Say the new word with the puppet:* fin. Repeat the routine using *an* and /f/.

Use the puppet. *Say* at. *Now add /f/ to the beginning of* at. *What is the new word?* (fat) Then have the puppet add /f/ to *it* to make the new word *fit.* Have children repeat the new word after you.

Have the puppet say *all* and the sound /f/. Ask children to add the /f/ sound to *all* to make *fall.* Repeat, having them add the /f/ sound to *ed.*

Repeat for /r/. Have children add /r/ to *an* (ran), *am* (ram), and *at* (rat).

ELL　ENGLISH LANGUAGE LEARNERS

For the **ELLs** who need **phonics, decoding,** and **fluency** practice, use scaffolding methods as necessary to ensure children understand the meaning of the words. Refer to the Language Transfer Handbook for phonics elements that may not transfer in children's native languages.

Approaching Level

Phonics

SOUND-SPELLING REVIEW

 TIER 2

OBJECTIVES
CCSS Demonstrate basic knowledge of one-to-one letter-sound correspondences by producing the primary sound for each consonant. **RF.K.3a**

I Do Display **Word-Building Card** *e*. Say the letter name and the sound it stands for: *e*, /e/. Repeat for *h, d, o, c, n, i*.

We Do Display Word-Building Cards one at a time and together say the letter name and the sound that each letter stands for.

You Do Display Word-Building Cards one at a time and have children say the letter name and the sound that each letter stands for.

CONNECT *f* TO /f/ AND *r* TO /r/

TIER 2

OBJECTIVES
CCSS Demonstrate basic knowledge of one-to-one letter-sound correspondences by producing the primary sound for each consonant. **RF.K.3a**

I Do Display the *Fire* **Sound-Spelling Card**. *The letter* f *stands for /f/ at the beginning of* fire. *What is this letter?* (f) *What sound does it stand for?* (/f/) *I will write* f *when I hear* /f/ *in these words:* fit, feet, neck, fin, peel, food.

We Do *The word* fair *begins with* /f/. *Let's write* f. Guide children to write *f* when they hear a word that begins with /f/. Say: *find, meet, den, fan, mop, fast.*

You Do Have children write *f* if a word begins with /f/: *face, orange, fish, far, fork.*

Repeat routine for /r/r using the *Rose* Sound-Spelling Card and the words *red, run, melt, arm, reach, come, duck, real,* and *rabbit.*

RETEACH

OBJECTIVES
CCSS Know and apply grade-level phonics and word analysis skills in decoding words. **RF.K.3**

I Do Display **Reading/Writing Workshop**, p. 34. *The letter* f *stands for the* /f/ *sound you hear at the beginning of* fire. Say *fire*, emphasizing /f/. Repeat with the letter *r* and *rose*.

We Do Have children name each picture in row 1. Repeat the names, emphasizing /f/. Repeat for row 2, emphasizing /r/.

You Do Have children read the words in rows 3 and 4 offering assistance as needed.

BLEND WORDS WITH /f/f AND /r/r

OBJECTIVES

CCSS Isolate and pronounce the initial, medial vowel, and final sounds (phonemes) in three-phoneme words. **RF.K.2d**

 I Do Display **Word-Building Cards** *f, e,* and *d. This is the letter* f. *It stands for /f/. This is the letter* e. *It stands for /e/. This is the letter* d. *It stands for /d/. Listen as I blend all three sounds: /fffeeed/,* fed. *The word is* fed. Repeat for *fit.*

 We Do *Now let's blend more sounds to make words.* Display the word *fan. Let's blend: /fffaaannn/,* fan. Have children blend to read the word. Repeat with the word *fin. Let's blend: /fffiiinnn/,* fin.

 You Do Distribute sets of Word-Building Cards with *f, a, d, e, i, n,* and *t.* Write: *fit, fan, fin,* and *fed.* Have children form the words and then blend and read the words.

Repeat the routine for /r/r using the words *red, rod, rot, rip, rid, rim,* and *ram.*

REREAD FOR FLUENCY

OBJECTIVES

CCSS Read emergent-reader texts with purpose and understanding. **RF.K.4**

 I Do Turn to p. 36 of **Reading/Writing Workshop** and read aloud the title. *Let's read the title together.* Page through the book. Ask children what they see in each picture. Ask children to find the words *with* on p. 37 and *he* on p. 39.

 We Do Then have children open their books and chorally read the story. Have children point to each word as they read. Provide corrective feedback as needed. After reading, ask children to recall what Ron and Red see in the apple orchard.

 You Do Have children reread "Ron with Red" with a partner for fluency.

BUILD FLUENCY WITH PHONICS

Sound/Spelling Fluency

Display the following Word-Building Cards: *e, h, d, o, c, n, i, f,* and *r.* Have children chorally say each sound. Repeat and vary the pace.

Fluency in Connected Text

Write the sentences. *The fat cat ran to me. My fan is red. Fit the pen in the top.* Have children read the sentences and identify the words with /f/f and /r/r.

→ Approaching Level

High-Frequency Words

 TIER 2

RETEACH WORDS

OBJECTIVES
 Read common high-frequency words by sight. **RF.K.3c**

 I Do Display **High-Frequency Word Card** *he* and use the **Read/Spell/Write** routine to reteach the word. Repeat for the high-frequency word *with*.

 We Do Have children turn to p. 35 of **Reading/Writing Workshop** and discuss the first photo. Then read aloud the first sentence. Reread the sentence with children. Have children point to the word *he* in the sentence. Use the same routine for *with* and the other sentence on the page.

 You Do Write the sentence frame *He can go with you to the _____.* Have children copy the sentence frame on their **Response Boards**. Then have partners work together to read and orally complete the frame by talking about a place that one boy in the class could visit.

CUMULATIVE REVIEW

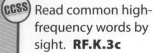

OBJECTIVES
Read common high-frequency words by sight. **RF.K.3c**

 I Do Display the **High-Frequency Word Cards** *I, can, the, we, see, a, like, to, and, go, you, do, my, are, he,* and *with*. Use the **Read/Spell/Write** routine to review words.

 We Do Use the High-Frequency Word Cards and **Word-Building Cards** to create sentences, such as *We like to go with you. Can the man see the cat?* Have children identify the high-frequency words that are used in each sentence.

 You Do Have partners use the High-Frequency Word Cards and Word-Building Cards to create short sentences.

Oral Vocabulary

REVIEW WORDS

OBJECTIVES

 Identify real-life connections between words and their use. **L.K.5c**

Develop oral vocabulary: *fresh, delicious, beneath, raise, special*

 Use the **Define/Example/Ask** routine to review words. Use the following definitions and provide examples:

fresh — Food that is **fresh** has just been grown or made.

delicious — If a food is **delicious**, it tastes very good.

beneath — If you are **beneath** something, you are under it.

raise — When you **raise** something or someone, you take care of it to make sure it grows.

special — When something is **special**, it is different in some way.

 Ask questions to build understanding. *Which is a fresh food: a can of corn or an ear of corn? Why? What is the most delicious food you have ever tried? What is beneath a boat on a lake? How can you help raise a pet? What is a special activity you do at school?*

You Do — Have children complete these sentences: *The market sells fresh _____. The lunchroom serves delicious _____. Beneath a flower in a garden is _____. It would be easy to raise a _____. To make a day special, I like to _____.*

Comprehension

SELF-SELECTED READING

OBJECTIVES

 With prompting and support, ask and answer questions about key details in a text. **RL.K.1**

Apply the strategy and skill to reread the text.

Read Independently

Help children select an illustrated informational text for sustained silent reading. Remind children that they can better understand what they read when they figure out the big idea. Remind children that they might not always know the big idea as they read the story for the first time, but that reading again can help them figure it out.

Read Purposefully

Before reading, tell children to take a picture walk through the book. Remind them that if they don't understand parts of the text at first, they can read again. After reading, ask children to tell the big idea. Then ask: *How did reading parts of the book again help you figure out the big idea?*

On Level

Leveled Reader

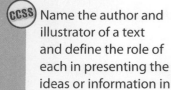

OBJECTIVES

With prompting and support, identify the main topic and retell key details of a text. **RI.K.2**

Name the author and illustrator of a text and define the role of each in presenting the ideas or information in a text. **RI.K.6**

Read emergent-reader texts with purpose and understanding. **RF.K.4**

Leveled Reader:
Let's Make a Salad!

Before Reading

Preview and Predict

Show children the cover of the book. Read aloud the title with children. Ask them to point to the names of the author and illustrator on their copies of the book. Ask: *What does the author do? What does the illustrator do?* Preview the illustrations in the book. Ask: *What is happening in the pictures? What do you think this book is about?*

Review Genre: Informational Text

Remind children that informational text presents ideas and information about a topic. Ask: *What do you think we will learn from this book?*

Model Concepts of Print

Have children follow along in their own books as you model reading from left to right and turning the pages. Say: *When I reach the end of a sentence, I pause before I begin a new sentence.*

Review High-Frequency Words

Point to the word *he* on page 2, and read it aloud with children. Have them find the word on pages 3 and 4.

Essential Question

Remind children of the Essential Question: *What kinds of things grow on a farm?* Set a purpose for reading: *Let's read the book to find out how the farmer will use foods that come from his farm.*

During Reading

Guided Comprehension

As children read, monitor and provide guidance by correcting blending and modeling the strategy and skill.

Go Digital

Leveled Reader

Strategy: Reread

Remind children that if they do not understand one part of the text, they can reread it to help them better understand what is happening.

Skill: Main Topic and Key Details

Tell children that reading the words and looking at the pictures will help them learn about the key details in a text. Explain that finding the key details will help them figure out the main topic of the selection.

Think Aloud On page 2 when I read the text and look at the illustration, I learn that the farmer gets the lettuce. I can see lettuce growing in the field behind him. On page 3, I read that he gets the carrots. Each of these items is in the picture, placed on the table near a salad bowl. These details help me understand that this book is about a farmer getting food that he grows on his farm to make a salad.

Have children use the pictures and words on pages 7 and 8 to find details about what else the farmer gets to make his salad.

After Reading

Respond to Reading

→ *What does the farmer get first?* (lettuce)

→ *What does he get next?* (carrots)

→ *What does the farmer get last?* (the family)

→ *What is the main topic of this book?* (A farmer making a salad with the vegetables he grows on his farm.)

Retell

Invite children to make pictures of each vegetable in the book. Have them use their pictures to retell the story. Help them make personal connections by asking: *What do you like to put in a salad?*

Model Fluency

Model reading a sentence in a flat tone of voice and one in an expressive voice. Ask: *What is the difference between these two readings?*

Apply Have children practice reading with expression with partners.

LITERACY ACTIVITIES

Have children complete the activities on the inside back cover of the reader.

Level Up

Level-up lessons available online.

IF Children read *Let's Make a Salad!* **On Level** with fluency and correctly answer the Respond to Reading questions,

THEN Tell children that they will read another story about a farm and how vegetables grow.

• Have children page through *Farm Fresh Finn* **Beyond Level** as you introduce the characters and the premise for the book. Say: *Finn is a boy who lives in the city and doesn't like eating vegetables. This changes, though, when he goes to visit his grandfather's farm.*

• Have children read the story, monitoring their comprehension and providing assistance as necessary.

On Level

Phonemic Awareness

PHONEME ISOLATION

 OBJECTIVES
CCSS Isolate and pronounce the initial, medial vowel, and final sounds (phonemes) in three-phoneme words. **RF.K.2d**

I Do Display the *Fox* **Photo Card**. *This is a* fox. *The first sound is* /f/. *Say it with me.* Repeat with /r/ and the *Rose* Photo Card.

We Do Say *fan* and have children repeat it. *What is the first sound in* fan? *Say the sound together.* Repeat with *face, fun, rat,* and *rope.*

You Do Say *feet, find, felt, fool, ramp, road, rest, rice* and have children tell the initial sound in each word.

PHONEME BLENDING

 OBJECTIVES
CCSS Isolate and pronounce the initial, medial vowel, and final sounds (phonemes) in three-phoneme words. **RF.K.2d**

I Do Place the *Fish, Five, Fox, Rake, Rock, Rope* Photo Cards facedown. Choose a card. Do not show the card. *These are the sounds in the word:* /f/ /i/ /sh/. *I will blend the sounds:* /fffiiish/, fish. *The word is* fish. Show the picture.

We Do Choose another picture and say the sounds in the word. Together say and blend the sounds to say the word. Then show the picture.

You Do Continue choosing Photo Cards. Say the sounds and have children blend the sounds and say the words.

PHONEME ADDITION

 OBJECTIVES
CCSS Add or substitute individual sounds (phonemes) in simple, one-syllable words to make new words. **RF.K.2e**

I Do *Listen as the puppet adds a sound to the beginning of a word to make a new word. Listen to this word:* an. *When the puppet adds* /f/ *to the beginning of* an, *the puppet makes the new word* fan. Repeat with adding /r/ to *an.*

We Do *Listen to this word:* in. *Say the word. Let's add* /f/ *to* in: fin. *Say the new word with the puppet:* fin. Repeat with *at* and /r/.

You Do Say *all. What word do you have when you add* /f/ *to the beginning of* all? (fall) Repeat, having them add /m/ to *ask* and /r/ and /k/ to *an* to make the words *mask, ran,* and *can.*

Phonics

REVIEW PHONICS

OBJECTIVES

Demonstrate basic knowledge of one-to-one letter-sound correspondences by producing the primary or many of the most frequent sounds for each consonant. **RF.K.3a**

 I Do Display **Reading/Writing Workshop**, p. 34. Point to the *Fire* **Sound-Spelling Card**. *What letter stands for the /f/ sound you hear at the beginning of* fire? *The letter is* f. Repeat the routine with the *Rose* Sound-Spelling Card.

 We Do Have children say the name of each picture in row 1. Then ask them to identify the words with /f/ at the beginning. Repeat with row 2 by having children identify words with /r/ at the beginning.

 You Do Have children read each word in rows 3 and 4. Repeat, asking them to raise their hands if they hear /f/ at the beginning of the word or touch their heads if they hear /r/ at the beginning of the word.

PICTURE SORT

OBJECTIVES

Isolate and pronounce the initial, medial vowel, and final sounds (phonemes) in three-phoneme words. **RF.K.2d**

 I Do Display **Word-Building Cards** *f* and *p* in a pocket chart. Then show the *Fan* **Photo Card**. Say: /f/ /a/ /n/, *fan*. Tell children that the beginning sound is /f/. *The letter* f *stands for* /f/. *I will put the fan under the letter* f. Show the *Pig* Photo Card. Say: /p/ /i/ /g/, *pig*. Tell children that the beginning sound is /p/. *The letter* p *stands for* /p/. *I will put the Photo Card for* pig *under the* p.

 We Do Show the Photo Card for *Fork* and say *fork*. Have children repeat. Then have them tell the sound they hear at the beginning of *fork*. Ask them if they should place the photo under the *f* or the *p*.

 You Do Continue the activity using Photo Cards *Five, Fire, Feet, Fox, Football, Pea, Pear, Pen, Pie,* and *Pillow*. Have children say the picture name and the initial sound. Then have them place the card under the *f* or *p*.

Repeat the routine for initial /r/r and /m/m with the Photo Cards *Rabbit, Rake, Rock, Rose, Ruby, Man, Mix, Moon, Moth,* and *Mouse*.

→ On Level

Phonics

BLEND WORDS WITH *f* AND *r*

OBJECTIVES

 Isolate and pronounce the initial, medial vowel, and final sounds (phonemes) in three-phoneme words. **RF.K.2d**

 I Do Use **Word-Building Cards** or write *f, i, t. This is the letter* f. *It stands for* /f/. *Say it with me:* /fff/. *This is the letter* i. *It stands for* /i/. *Say it with me:* /iii/. *This is the letter* t. *It stands for* /t/. *Say it with me:* /t/. *I'll blend the sounds together to read the word*: /fffiiit/, fit. *Repeat the routine with* /r/ *and the word* ran.

 We Do Use the words *fan* and *rip*. Guide children to blend the words sound by sound to read each word.

 You Do Use the following words and have children blend the words sound by sound to read each word.

| fat | if | rat | ram | rim | red | Ron | fed |

REREAD FOR FLUENCY

OBJECTIVES

 Read emergent-reader texts with purpose and understanding. **RF.K.4**

I Do Point to the title "Ron with Red" on p. 36 of **Reading/Writing Workshop**. Work with children to read for accuracy and expression. Model reading page 41: *When I read, "Mom can fit ten on top," I read all the way to the end of the sentence before pausing. This makes my reading sound natural, as if I were talking.* Tell children that when they see a period, they should pause because they have reached the end of a sentence.

 We Do Reread p. 41. Then have children chorally read the page with you. Continue choral reading the remainder of the pages.

 You Do Have children read "Ron with Red." Provide time to listen as children read the pages. Comment on their accuracy and expression and provide corrective feedback by modeling proper fluency.

High-Frequency Words

OBJECTIVES

CCSS Read common high-frequency words by sight. **RF.K.3c**

 Use the **High-Frequency Word Card** *he* with the **Read/Spell/Write** routine to review the word. Repeat for the high-frequency word *with*.

Have children turn to p. 35 of **Reading/Writing Workshop**. Discuss the photographs and read aloud the first sentence. Point to the word *he* and have children read it. Then chorally read the sentence. Have children frame the word *he* in the sentence and read the word. Repeat the routine with the word *with*.

 Say the word *he*. Ask children to close their eyes, picture the word, and write it as they see it. Have children self-correct. Repeat the routine with the word *with*.

Reteach previously introduced high-frequency words using the **Read/Spell/Write** routine.

Fluency Point to the High-Frequency Word Cards *I, can, the, we, see, a, like, to, and, go, you, do, my, are, he,* and *with* in random order. Have children chorally read. Repeat at a faster pace.

Comprehension

OBJECTIVES

CCSS With prompting and support, ask and answer questions about key details in a text. **RL.K.1**

Apply the strategy and skill to reread the text

Read Independently

Have children select an illustrated informational text for sustained silent reading. Remind them that knowing what a text is mainly about and looking for key details will help them better understand and enjoy what they are reading. Tell children that if they have difficulty figuring out what the story is mainly about, they can read parts of it again to help them understand.

Read Purposefully

Before reading, have children take a picture walk through the book and then write a sentence about what they think the book is mainly about. Remind children to stop and reread parts of the book to help them figure out the main idea. After reading, ask children to tell the main idea. Then ask them to explain how reading again helped them determine the main idea of the text.

→ Beyond Level

Leveled Reader

OBJECTIVES

CCSS With prompting and support, ask and answer questions about key details in a text. **RL.K.1**

CCSS With prompting and support, name the author and illustrator of a story and define the role of each in telling the story. **RL.K.6**

CCSS With prompting and support, describe the relationship between illustrations and the story in which they appear (e.g., what moment in a story an illustration depicts). **RL.K.7**

CCSS Read emergent-reader texts with purpose and understanding. **RF.K.4**

Leveled Reader:
Farm Fresh Finn

Before Reading

Preview and Predict

Point to the cover and read aloud the title and the author's and illustrator's names with children. Have them use the picture on the cover to predict what the book is about. Have children page through the book and look at the illustrations. Have children confirm or revise their predictions.

Review Genre: Fiction

Remind children that they have been reading informational text this week. Explain that they will now read a fiction story. Ask: *How is fiction different from informational text?* (Fiction stories are made up. Informational text gives facts and information about a topic.)

Essential Question

Remind children of the Essential Question: *What kinds of things grow on a farm?* Have children set a purpose for reading. Say: *Let's find out how people use the food they grow on farms.*

During Reading

Guided Comprehension

As children whisper-read *Farm Fresh Finn,* monitor and provide guidance by correcting blending and modeling the strategy and skill.

Stop periodically to ask open-ended questions, such as *What is happening now? How does Finn feel?* Build on children's responses to help them understand the text.

Strategy: Reread

Remind children that as they read, they can reread sentences to help them better understand what is going on in the story.

Leveled Reader

Skill: Key Details

Remind children that key details in the text and illustrations will help them figure out what the story is mainly about. Explain that they can find key details by looking at the illustrations and reading the sentences.

Think Aloud After reading page 2, I learned that Finn does not like carrots or corn. From the illustration, I learn that Finn lives in the city because I can see tall buildings in the background. On page 3, Finn's mother is asking him to please try his vegetables. This detail tells me that Finn probably does not eat most vegetables. I'll keep reading and looking at the pictures to find out what happens next.

Guide children to read the rest of the story. Have them use the text and the illustrations to find the key details in the story. Ask them to pay attention to how Finn changes when he is at his grandfather's farm.

After Reading

Respond to Reading

→ *Where does Finn live?* (in the city) *How can you tell?* (The picture shows the city skyline through the window.)

→ *Where did Finn and his mom go?* (To his grandpa's farm.)

→ *What does Grandpa grow on his farm*? (vegetables)

→ *How does Grandpa help Finn like vegetables?* (He invites Finn to help pick and prepare them for dinner.)

→ *How does Finn change from the beginning of the story to the end?* (He goes from not liking vegetables to liking them.)

Retell

Have children work in groups of three to retell the story by acting it out. Help them make a personal connection. Ask: *If you were Grandpa, what kinds of food would you grow on your farm?*

Gifted and Talented

EVALUATING Have children recall the different vegetables Grandpa grows at his farm and how he and Finn used those foods. Challenge children to think about the foods they eat. Ask: *How do you and your family use foods that are grown on a farm?*

HAVE children draw a picture of a vegetable plot and the vegetables and fruits they would grow there. Have them explain why they chose the foods they did.

LITERACY ACTIVITIES

Have children complete the activities on the inside back cover of the reader.

Beyond Level

Phonics

OBJECTIVES

(CCSS) Demonstrate basic knowledge of one-to-one letter-sound correspondences by producing the primary or many of the most frequent sounds for each consonant. **RF.K.3a**

 I Do Display **Reading/Writing Workshop**, p. 34. Point to the *Fire* **Sound-Spelling Card**. *What is the sound at the beginning of* fire? *What letter can stand for* /f/? *The letter is* f. Repeat the routine with the *Rose* Sound-Spelling Card and /r/.

 We Do Have children say the name of each picture in rows 1 and 2. Then ask children to share other words they know that begin with /f/ and /r/.

You Do Have partners read each word in rows 3 and 4. Ask them to write the words on their **Response Boards** and underline the letter in each word that stands for /f/ in row 3 and /r/ in row 4.

Fluency Have children reread the story "Ron with Red" for fluency.

Innovate Have children create a new page for "Ron with Red" by writing about another fruit Ron and Red might see at the orchard.

High-Frequency Words

OBJECTIVES

(CCSS) Read common high-frequency words by sight. **RF.K.3c**

 I Do Create **High-Frequency Word Cards** for *listen* and *all*. Introduce the words using the **Read/Spell/Write** routine.

 We Do Display the High-Frequency Word Cards for *I, can, the, we, see, a, like, to, and, go, you, do, my, are, he,* and *with*. Have children help you complete the following sentence frames using the High-Frequency Word Cards: *He can listen to _____. We all can see the _____.*

 You Do Have partners write sentences using the High-Frequency Words *listen* and *all* on their Response Boards. Have them read their sentences.

Vocabulary

ORAL VOCABULARY: SYNONYMS

OBJECTIVES

(CCSS) With guidance and support from adults, explore word relationships and nuances in word meaning. **L.K.5**

Develop oral vocabulary: Synonyms

 I Do Review the meanings of the oral vocabulary words *delicious* and *beneath*. Explain that a synonym is a word that means almost the same thing as another word. *A synonym for* delicious *is* tasty. *Something that is tasty has a good flavor.* I enjoyed eating the tasty yogurt. *A synonym for* beneath *is* below. *When one object is below another, it is lower.* The bottom shelf is below the top shelf.

 We Do Create sentences together using the new words *tasty* and *below*. Read the sentences aloud.

 You Do Have partners draw a picture and think of two or three sentences about an apple tree. Tell them to use the words *tasty* and *below* in their sentences. Ask them to share their pictures and sentences with the class.

 Gifted and Talented **Extend** Challenge children to list two or three opposite words for *tasty* and *below*. Then have them say a sentence using the opposite words.

Comprehension

SELF-SELECTED READING

OBJECTIVES

 (CCSS) With prompting and support, ask and answer questions about key details in a text. **RL.K.1**

Apply the strategy and skill to reread the text.

Read Independently

Have children select an informational text for sustained silent reading. Ask them to take a picture walk through the book and write a sentence to predict the main topic of the book. Have them also write two details they predict they will find as they read. Remind children to reread as needed.

Read Purposefully

Before reading, remind children to look for the main topic and details as they read and reread. Then, after reading, have children compare their predictions with the actual main topic and details.

 Gifted and Talented **Independent Study** Have children draw pictures of farms. Then ask them to create a short book by writing a sentence or two about each picture, and creating a title for their book. Challenge partners to predict what each other's book will be about by reading its title and looking at the photographs. Trade books and read to check predictions.

English Language Learners

Leveled Reader

OBJECTIVES

CCSS With prompting and support, ask and answer questions about key details in a text. **RI.K.1**

CCSS With prompting and support, identify the main topic and retell key details of a text. **RI.K.2**

CCSS Read emergent-reader texts with purpose and understanding. **RF.K.4**

Shared Read:
Let's Make a Salad!

Go Digital

Before Reading

Preview and Predict

Read the title and then ask children to read it with you. Point to the cover illustration and say: *This is lettuce. That is a bowl for salad.* Have children describe what they see on the cover. Walk children through the book, looking at the illustrations, labels, and rebus pictures to identify each item. Use simple language to describe each picture. Ask questions, such as: *What is this? What is he doing?*

Essential Question

Remind children of the Essential Question: *What kinds of things grow on a farm?* Set a purpose for reading: *Let's find out what kinds of food are grown on this farm.* Encourage children to seek clarification when they encounter a word or phrase that doesn't make sense. Model asking for help: *I'm not sure what he gets. Can you show me?* Remind children to look at the labels and the illustrations for support as they read.

Leveled Reader

During Reading

Interactive Question Response

Pages 2–3 Point to the illustration and label on page 2. Say: *I see a table. I see a salad bowl. What else do you see?* (lettuce, a field) *What is the farmer doing?* (putting the lettuce on the table) *Let's read the sentence that tells what he's doing.* Point to the illustration and label on page 3. Say: *I see carrots. What is he doing?* (putting carrots on the table)

Pages 4–5 Point to the illustration and the label on page 4. Ask: *What do you see?* (tomatoes) *Let's read the sentence that tells what he gets.* Point to the picture and the text on page 5. Say: *Let's read to find out what the farmer gets next. Where is he putting the peppers?* (on the table)

Pages 6–7 Point to the illustration and label on page 6. Ask: *What does he get now?* (He gets the peas.) Let's read the sentence that tells us that. Point to the illustration on page 7. Say: *The farmer is holding something. Can you tell me what it is?* (cheese) *Point to the label for cheese and read it aloud.*

Page 8 Say: *There are no sentences on this page. What do you see?* (The farmer's family helps make the salad.) Point to each member of the family and ask: *Who is this?* When children name the person, point to the label that corresponds with the illustration and say the word aloud: *mom, dad, sister, brother,* and *grandmother.*

After Reading

Respond to Reading

→ What is this selection about? (getting vegetables and making a salad)

→ What vegetable does the farmer get for the salad first? (the lettuce)

→ What does he get next? (the carrots)

→ What happens at the end of the selection? (The family helps make the salad.)

Retell

Have children draw pictures of each vegetable in the salad. Ask children to hold up their pictures and say the word out loud to fill in the missing word when you pause. Say: *Let's retell the story together. He gets the _____.*

Model Fluency

Read the sentences one at a time as you track the print with your finger. Have children chorally repeat. Model reading with expression.

Apply Have children practice reading with expression with partners.

Level Up

IF Children read *Let's Make a Salad!* **ELL Level** with fluency and correctly answer the Respond to Reading questions,

THEN Tell children that they will read a more detailed version of the story.

• Have children page through *Let's Make a Salad!* **On Level** and describe each picture in simple language.

• Have children read the story, monitoring their comprehension and providing assistance as necessary.

LITERACY ACTIVITIES

Have children complete the activities on the inside back cover of the reader.

→ English Language Learners
Vocabulary

PRETEACH ORAL VOCABULARY

OBJECTIVES

CCSS Speak audibly and express thoughts, feelings, and ideas clearly. **SL.K.6**

LANGUAGE OBJECTIVE

Preview vocabulary

 I Do Display the images from the **Visual Vocabulary Cards** and follow the routine to preteach the oral vocabulary words.

 We Do Display each image again and explain how it illustrates or demonstrates the word. Model using sentences to describe the image.

 You Do Display the word *delicious* again and have children talk to a partner about foods they think are delicious. Ask them to work together to form a complete sentence that describes what they think is delicious.

Beginning	Intermediate	Advanced/High
Use the words *fresh* and *delicious* in the same sentence and have children repeat it after you.	Ask pairs of children to work together to list foods that are *delicious*.	Ask pairs of children to ask each other questions using the words. Have them answer in complete sentences.

PRETEACH ELL VOCABULARY

OBJECTIVES

 CCSS Speak audibly and express thoughts, feelings, and ideas clearly. **SL.K.6**

LANGUAGE OBJECTIVE

Preview ELL vocabulary

 I Do Display images from the **Visual Vocabulary Cards** one at a time to preteach the ELL vocabulary words *teamwork* and *healthy*. Follow the routine. Say each word and have children repeat it. Define each word in English.

 We Do Display each image again and incorporate the words in a short discussion about the images. Model using sentences to describe the image.

 You Do Display *healthy* again. Have children say the word. Have them use the word in a sentence by using the sentence frame: *It is healthy to _____.*

Beginning	Intermediate	Advanced/High
Use each word in a sentence and have children chorally repeat the sentences after you.	Guide partners to talk about ways to stay healthy before completing the sentence frame.	Ask children to use each of the words in a sentence of their own. Provide guidance if necessary.

High-Frequency Words

REVIEW WORDS

OBJECTIVES

Read common high-frequency words by sight (e.g., *the, of, to, you, she, my, is, are, do, does*). **RF.K.3c**

LANGUAGE OBJECTIVE

Review high-frequency words

 I Do Display the **High-Frequency Word Cards** for *he* and *with*. Read the words. Use the **Read/Spell/Write** routine to teach the words. Have children write the words on their **Response Boards**.

 We Do Write a sentence frame that uses the week's high-frequency words: *He is with _____*. Track the print as children read and complete the sentence. Explain to children that the word *with* shows what things are together.

 You Do Display a sentence that uses the high-frequency words *he* and *with*. Ask children to point to the words and say them aloud. Then work with children to read and say the entire sentence aloud.

Beginning	Intermediate	Advanced/High
Have children draw a picture of a boy with another person. Ask: *Who is he? Who is he with?*	Ask partners to find the words *he* and *with* in any book. Then have them say sentences with the words.	Ask children to use the words *he* and *with* in sentences of their own.

REVIEW CATEGORY WORDS

OBJECTIVES

Identify real-life connections between words and their use (e.g., note places at school that are colorful). **L.K.5c**

LANGUAGE OBJECTIVE

Use category words

 I Do Display the **Visual Vocabulary Card** and say the words aloud. Define the words in English and then in Spanish, if appropriate, identifying any cognates.

 We Do Write and say words such as *banana, orange, apple, grapes,* and *pear* that are related to this week's category words about food. Ask children to repeat the words after you. Use pictures to identify and name each word.

 You Do Ask children to tell a partner the kinds of fruits they like. Then have them complete the following sentence frame with one of the category words: *A fruit I like is _____*.

Beginning	Intermediate	Advanced/High
Prompt children by asking if they like any of the fruit pictured on the card.	Ask children to use one of the category words in a complete sentence.	Have partners ask and answer questions using the category words.

→ English Language Learners
Writing

SHARED WRITING

OBJECTIVES

CCSS Use a combination of drawing, dictating, and writing to narrate a single event or several loosely linked events, tell about the events in the order in which they occurred, and provide a reaction to what happened. **W.K.3**

LANGUAGE OBJECTIVE

Contribute to a shared writing project

 I Do Review the list of foods from the Whole Group Shared Writing project. Then model writing story sentences in sequence: *First, Jen buys a pear. Then, she eats it.*

 We Do As a group, choose a food to write about. Have children help you write sentences that show a sequence of events: *First, he plants a pumpkin seed. Then, the seed grows into a pumpkin.*

 You Do Help partners choose a food and write two or more story sentences that show a sequence of events. Provide them with a sentence frame such as: *First, we _____. Then, we _____.*

Beginning	Intermediate	Advanced/High
Before writing, review order words with children, such as *first* and *next*. Ask: *What is the first thing you did today?*	Guide partners to complete the sentence frames.	Have children write sentences about their day.

WRITING TRAIT: ORGANIZATION

OBJECTIVES

CCSS With guidance and support from adults, respond to questions and suggestions from peers and add details to strengthen writing as needed. **W.K.5**

LANGUAGE OBJECTIVE

Organize ideas for writing

 I Do Explain to children that writers put their ideas in order. Show pictures of a plant growing and reinforce the use of the words *first, next,* and *last.*

Display the **Big Book** *An Orange in January.* Tell children the book explains how an orange grows from a blossom to when it is eaten. Ask children what they want to describe in order. Use the selection to help children get ideas.

 You Do Have children write at least two sentences to show something happening in order. Provide them with the sentence frame: *First, _____. Then, _____.*

Beginning	Intermediate	Advanced/High
Assist children as they use other selections from the week to help them come up with ideas to explain events in an order.	Ask children to talk in small groups and try to complete the sentence frames together.	After children complete the sentence frames, ask them why the events have to happen in a special order.

Grammar

PRONOUNS

OBJECTIVES

CCSS Produce and expand complete sentences in shared language activities. **L.K.1f**

LANGUAGE OBJECTIVE

Learn to use pronouns correctly

Language Transfers Handbook

The languages of Cantonese and Korean do not require number agreement with pronouns. You may find children using the wrong number agreement for pronouns, such as *I saw many red birds. It was pretty.* Guide children to choose the correct pronouns based on number and gender.

Review that a pronoun is a word that replaces the name of a person, an animal, or a thing. Say this sentence: *The boys play. They are friends.* Say: *The word* they *is a pronoun. It takes the place of* the boys.

Say the following sentence pairs. Guide children to identify the pronoun in the second sentence. Have them tell who or what the pronoun replaces.

Our parents helped with the school garden. They *watered* it *during the summer.*

The tree grew very tall. Soon it *will have fruit.*

My brother and I grew watermelons. We *will eat the fruit when it is ripe.*

Use the following sentences:

Pears are fruits. _____ *are* _____.

Pair children and have them orally complete the sentence frames by providing descriptive words and the correct pronoun. Circulate, listen in, and take note of each child's language use and proficiency.

Beginning	Intermediate	Advanced/High
Guide children to use illustrations from this week's readings to help them choose words to complete the sentence frame.	Have partners talk about pears. Then have them complete the sentence frame.	Have children complete the sentence frame. Then have them use the correct pronoun to write or say a sentence that describes what a partner likes to eat.

PROGRESS MONITORING

Weekly Assessment

Use your Quick Check observations and the assessment opportunities identified below to evaluate children's progress in key skill areas.

✔ TESTED SKILLS (CCSS)		Quick Check Observations	Pencil and Paper Assessment
PHONEMIC AWARENESS/ PHONICS /f/, /r/ (initial) **RF.K.3a**	f	Can children isolate /f/ and /r/ and match the sounds to the letters *Ff* and *Rr*?	Practice Book, pp. 143–144, 145–146, 148
HIGH-FREQUENCY WORDS *he, with* **RF.K.3c**	he	Can children recognize and read the high-frequency words?	Practice Book, pp. 149–150
COMPREHENSION Main Topic and Key Details **RI.K.2**		As you read *An Orange in January* with children, can they identify and discuss the main topic and key details in the text?	Practice Book, p. 147

Quick Check Rubric

Skills	1	2	3
PHONEMIC AWARENESS/ PHONICS	Does not connect the sounds /f/ and /r/ with the letters *Ff and Rr*.	Usually connects the sounds /f/ and /r/ with the letters *Ff and Rr*.	Consistently connects the sounds /f/ and /r/ with the letters *Ff and Rr*.
HIGH-FREQUENCY WORDS	Does not identify the high-frequency words.	Usually recognizes the high-frequency words with accuracy, but not speed.	Consistently recognizes the high-frequency words with speed and accuracy.
COMPREHENSION	Does not identify the main topic and key details in the text.	Usually identifies the main topic and key details in the text.	Consistently identifies the main topic and key details in the text.

 **Go Digital!** www.connected.mcgraw-hill.com

Using Assessment Results

✓ TESTED SKILLS	If ...	Then ...
PHONEMIC AWARENESS/ PHONICS	**Quick Check Rubric:** Children consistently score 1 or **Pencil and Paper Assessment:** Children get 0–2 items correct	... reteach tested Phonemic Awareness and Phonics skills using Lessons 16–17 in the *Tier 2 Phonemic Awareness Intervention Online PDFs* and Lessons 25–26 in the *Tier 2 Phonics/ Word Study Intervention Online PDFs.*
HIGH-FREQUENCY WORDS	**Quick Check Rubric:** Children consistently score 1	... reteach tested skills by using the High-Frequency Word Cards and asking children to read and spell the word. Point out any irregularities in sound-spellings.
COMPREHENSION	**Quick Check Rubric:** Children consistently score 1 or **Pencil and Paper Assessment:** Children get 0–1 items correct	... reteach tested skill using Lessons 85–87 in the *Tier 2 Comprehension Intervention Online PDFs.*

Response to Intervention

Use the children's assessment results to assist you in identifying children who will benefit from focused intervention.

Use the appropriate sections of the **Placement and Diagnostic Assessment** to designate children requiring:

TIER 2 **Tier 2 Intervention Online PDFs**

TIER 3 **WonderWorks Intervention Program**

→ Phonemic Awareness

→ Phonics

→ Vocabulary

→ Comprehension

→ Fluency

SUMMATIVE ASSESSMENT

Unit Assessment

✔ COMPREHENSION:	✔ HIGH-FREQUENCY WORDS:	✔ PHONEMIC AWARENESS:	✔ PHONICS:	✔ CATEGORY WORDS:
• Character, Setting, Events **RL.K.3** • Main Topic and Key Details **RI.K.2**	• *my, are, he, with* **RF.K.3c**	• Phoneme Isolation (initial) **RF.K.2d** • Phoneme Blending (medial) **RF.K.2d** • Phoneme Categorization **RF.K.2d** • Phoneme Segmentation **RF.K.2d** • Phoneme Addition **RF.K.2e**	• h (initial) **RF.K.3a** • e (initial/medial) **RF.K.3b** • f (initial) **RF.K.3a** • r (initial) **RF.K.3a**	• Size **L.K.5c** • Foods **L.K.5a**

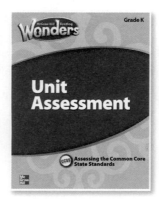

Use Multiple Assessments for Instructional Planning

To create instructional profiles for your children, look for patterns in the results from the following assessment.

Running Records

Use the instructional reading level determined by the Running Record calculations for regrouping decisions.

Using Assessment Results

TESTED SKILLS	If ...	Then ...
COMPREHENSION	Children answer 0–3 items correctly ...	... reteach tested skills using the *Tier 2 Comprehension Intervention Online PDFs*
HIGH-FREQUENCY WORDS	Children answer 0–1 items correctly ...	... reteach tested skills using Section 3 of the *Tier 2 Fluency Intervention Online PDFs*
PHONEMIC AWARENESS	Children answer 0–3 items correctly ...	... reteach tested skills using the *Tier 2 Phonemic Awareness Intervention Online PDFs*
PHONICS	Children answer 0–3 items correctly ...	... reteach tested skills using the *Tier 2 Phonics/Word Study Intervention Online PDFs* and Section 2 and 4 of the *Tier 2 Fluency Intervention Online PDFs*
CATEGORY WORDS	Children answer 0–1 items correctly ...	... reteach tested skills using the *Tier 2 Vocabulary Intervention Online PDFs*

Response to Intervention

Use the appropriate sections of the **Placement and Diagnostic Assessment** and children's assessment results to designate children requiring:

 Tier 2 Intervention Online PDFs

 WonderWorks Intervention Program

→ Phonological and Phonemic Awareness

→ Phonics

→ Vocabulary

→ Comprehension

→ Fluency

Program Information

Program Information

Go Digital For Additional Resources

Unit Bibliography

Word Lists

Literature and Informational Text Charts

Web Sites

Resources

www.connected.mcgraw-hill.com

SCOPE & SEQUENCE

	K	1	2	3	4	5	6
READING PROCESS							
Concepts About Print/Print Awareness							
Recognize own name							
Understand directionality (top to bottom; tracking print from left to right; return sweep, page by page)	✔						
Locate printed word on page	✔						
Develop print awareness (concept of letter, word, sentence)	✔						
Identify separate sounds in a spoken sentence	✔						
Understand that written words are represented in written language by a specific sequence of letters	✔						
Distinguish between letters, words, and sentences	✔						
Identify and distinguish paragraphs							
Match print to speech (one-to-one correspondence)	✔						
Name uppercase and lowercase letters	✔						
Understand book handling (holding a book right-side-up, turning its pages)	✔						
Identify parts of a book (front cover, back cover, title page, table of contents); recognize that parts of a book contain information	✔						
Phonological Awareness							
Recognize and understand alliteration							
Segment sentences into correct number of words							
Identify, blend, segment syllables in words		✔					
Recognize and generate rhyming words	✔	✔					
Identify, blend, segment onset and rime	✔	✔					
Phonemic Awareness							
Count phonemes	✔	✔					
Isolate initial, medial, and final sounds	✔	✔					
Blend spoken phonemes to form words	✔	✔					
Segment spoken words into phonemes	✔	✔					
Distinguish between long- and short-vowel sounds	✔	✔					
Manipulate phonemes (addition, deletion, substitution)	✔	✔					
Phonics and Decoding /Word Recognition							
Understand the alphabetic principle	✔	✔					
Sound/letter correspondence	✔	✔	✔	✔			
Blend sounds into words, including VC, CVC, CVCe, CVVC words	✔	✔	✔	✔			
Blend common word families	✔	✔	✔	✔			

KEY	✔ = Assessed Skill Tinted panels show skills, strategies, and other teaching opportunities.

	K	1	2	3	4	5	6
Initial consonant blends		✔	✔	✔			
Final consonant blends		✔	✔	✔			
Initial and medial short vowels	✔	✔	✔	✔	✔	✔	✔
Decode one-syllable words in isolation and in context	✔	✔	✔	✔			
Decode multisyllabic words in isolation and in context using common syllabication patterns		✔	✔	✔	✔	✔	✔
Distinguish between similarly spelled words	✔	✔	✔	✔	✔	✔	✔
Monitor accuracy of decoding							
Identify and read common high-frequency words, irregularly spelled words	✔	✔	✔	✔			
Identify and read compound words, contractions		✔	✔	✔	✔	✔	✔
Use knowledge of spelling patterns to identify syllables		✔	✔	✔	✔	✔	✔
Regular and irregular plurals	✔	✔	✔	✔	✔	✔	✔
Long vowels (silent *e*, vowel teams)	✔	✔	✔	✔	✔	✔	✔
Vowel digraphs (variant vowels)		✔	✔	✔	✔	✔	✔
r-Controlled vowels		✔	✔	✔	✔	✔	✔
Hard/soft consonants		✔	✔	✔	✔	✔	✔
Initial consonant digraphs		✔	✔	✔	✔	✔	
Medial and final consonant digraphs		✔	✔	✔	✔	✔	
Vowel diphthongs		✔	✔	✔	✔	✔	✔
Identify and distinguish letter-sounds (initial, medial, final)	✔	✔	✔				
Silent letters		✔	✔	✔	✔	✔	✔
Schwa words				✔	✔	✔	✔
Inflectional endings		✔	✔	✔	✔	✔	✔
Triple-consonant clusters		✔	✔	✔	✔	✔	
Unfamiliar and complex word families				✔	✔	✔	✔
Structural Analysis/Word Analysis							
Common spelling patterns (word families)		✔	✔	✔	✔	✔	✔
Common syllable patterns		✔	✔	✔	✔	✔	✔
Inflectional endings		✔	✔	✔	✔	✔	✔
Contractions		✔	✔	✔	✔	✔	✔
Compound words		✔	✔	✔	✔	✔	✔
Prefixes and suffixes		✔	✔	✔	✔	✔	✔
Root or base words			✔	✔	✔	✔	✔
Comparatives and superlatives			✔	✔	✔	✔	✔
Greek and Latin roots			✔	✔	✔	✔	✔
Fluency							
Apply letter/sound knowledge to decode phonetically regular words accurately	✔	✔	✔	✔	✔	✔	✔
Recognize high-frequency and familiar words	✔	✔	✔	✔	✔	✔	✔
Read regularly on independent and instructional levels							
Read orally with fluency from familiar texts (choral, echo, partner, Reader's Theater)							
Use appropriate rate, expression, intonation, and phrasing		✔	✔	✔	✔	✔	✔
Read with automaticity (accurately and effortlessly)		✔	✔	✔	✔	✔	✔
Use punctuation cues in reading		✔	✔	✔	✔	✔	✔

	K	1	2	3	4	5	6
Adjust reading rate to purpose, text difficulty, form, and style							
Repeated readings							
Timed readings		✔	✔	✔	✔	✔	✔
Read with purpose and understanding		✔	✔	✔	✔	✔	✔
Read orally with accuracy		✔	✔	✔	✔	✔	✔
Use context to confirm or self-correct word recognition		✔	✔	✔	✔	✔	✔

READING LITERATURE

Comprehension Strategies and Skills

	K	1	2	3	4	5	6
Read literature from a broad range of genres, cultures, and periods		✔	✔	✔	✔	✔	✔
Access complex text		✔	✔	✔	✔	✔	✔
Build background							
Preview and predict							
Establish and adjust purpose for reading							
Evaluate citing evidence from the text							
Ask and answer questions	✔	✔	✔	✔	✔	✔	✔
Inferences and conclusions, citing evidence from the text	✔	✔	✔	✔	✔	✔	✔
Monitor/adjust comprehension including reread, reading rate, paraphrase							
Recount/Retell	✔	✔					
Summarize			✔	✔	✔	✔	✔
Story structure (beginning, middle, end)	✔	✔	✔	✔	✔	✔	✔
Visualize							
Make connections between and across texts		✔	✔	✔	✔	✔	✔
Point of view		✔	✔	✔	✔	✔	✔
Author's purpose							
Cause and effect	✔	✔	✔	✔	✔	✔	✔
Compare and contrast (including character, setting, plot, topics)	✔	✔	✔	✔	✔	✔	✔
Classify and categorize		✔	✔				
Literature vs informational text	✔	✔	✔				
Illustrations, using	✔	✔	✔	✔			
Theme, central message, moral, lesson		✔	✔	✔	✔	✔	✔
Predictions, making/confirming	✔	✔	✔				
Problem and solution (problem/resolution)		✔	✔	✔	✔	✔	✔
Sequence of events	✔	✔	✔	✔	✔	✔	✔

Literary Elements

	K	1	2	3	4	5	6
Character	✔	✔	✔	✔	✔	✔	✔
Plot development/Events	✔	✔	✔	✔	✔	✔	✔
Setting	✔	✔	✔	✔	✔	✔	✔
Stanza				✔	✔	✔	✔
Alliteration						✔	✔
Assonance						✔	✔
Dialogue							
Foreshadowing						✔	✔

KEY
✔ = Assessed Skill
Tinted panels show skills, strategies, and other teaching opportunities.

	K	1	2	3	4	5	6
Flashback						✔	✔
Descriptive and figurative language		✔	✔	✔	✔	✔	✔
Imagery					✔	✔	✔
Meter					✔	✔	✔
Onomatopoeia							
Repetition		✔	✔	✔	✔	✔	✔
Rhyme/rhyme schemes		✔	✔	✔	✔	✔	✔
Rhythm		✔	✔				
Sensory language							
Symbolism							

Write About Reading/Literary Response Discussions

	K	1	2	3	4	5	6
Reflect and respond to text citing text evidence		✔	✔	✔	✔	✔	✔
Connect and compare text characters, events, ideas to self, to other texts, to world							
Connect literary texts to other curriculum areas							
Identify cultural and historical elements of text							
Evaluate author's techniques, craft							
Analytical writing							
Interpret text ideas through writing, discussion, media, research							
Book report or review							
Locate, use, explain information from text features		✔	✔	✔	✔	✔	✔
Organize information to show understanding of main idea through charts, mapping							
Cite text evidence	✔	✔	✔	✔	✔	✔	✔
Author's purpose/ Illustrator's purpose							

READING INFORMATIONAL TEXT
Comprehension Strategies and Skills

	K	1	2	3	4	5	6
Read informational text from a broad range of topics and cultures	✔	✔	✔	✔	✔	✔	✔
Access complex text		✔	✔	✔	✔	✔	✔
Build background							
Preview and predict	✔	✔	✔				
Establish and adjust purpose for reading							
Evaluate citing evidence from the text							
Ask and answer questions	✔	✔	✔	✔	✔	✔	✔
Inferences and conclusions, citing evidence from the text	✔	✔	✔	✔	✔	✔	✔
Monitor and adjust comprehension including reread, adjust reading rate, paraphrase							
Recount/Retell	✔	✔					
Summarize			✔	✔	✔	✔	✔
Text structure	✔	✔	✔	✔	✔	✔	✔
Identify text features		✔	✔	✔	✔	✔	✔
Make connections between and across texts	✔	✔	✔	✔	✔	✔	✔
Author's point of view				✔	✔	✔	✔
Author's purpose		✔	✔				

	K	1	2	3	4	5	6
Cause and effect	✔	✔	✔	✔	✔	✔	✔
Compare and contrast	✔	✔	✔	✔	✔	✔	✔
Classify and categorize		✔	✔				
Illustrations and photographs, using	✔	✔	✔	✔			
Instructions/directions (written and oral)		✔	✔	✔	✔	✔	✔
Main idea and key details	✔	✔	✔	✔	✔	✔	✔
Persuasion, reasons and evidence to support points/persuasive techniques						✔	✔
Predictions, making/confirming	✔	✔					
Problem and solution		✔	✔	✔	✔	✔	✔
Sequence, chronological order of events, time order, steps in a process	✔	✔	✔	✔	✔	✔	✔

Writing About Reading/Expository Critique Discussions

	K	1	2	3	4	5	6
Reflect and respond to text citing text evidence		✔	✔	✔	✔	✔	✔
Connect and compare text characters, events, ideas to self, to other texts, to world							
Connect texts to other curriculum areas							
Identify cultural and historical elements of text							
Evaluate author's techniques, craft							
Analytical writing							
Read to understand and perform tasks and activities							
Interpret text ideas through writing, discussion, media, research							
Locate, use, explain information from text features		✔	✔	✔	✔	✔	✔
Organize information to show understanding of main idea through charts, mapping							
Cite text evidence		✔	✔	✔	✔	✔	✔
Author's purpose/Illustrator's purpose							

Text Features

	K	1	2	3	4	5	6
Recognize and identify text and organizational features of nonfiction texts		✔	✔	✔	✔	✔	✔
Captions and labels, headings, subheadings, endnotes, key words, bold print	✔	✔	✔	✔	✔	✔	✔
Graphics, including photographs, illustrations, maps, charts, diagrams, graphs, time lines	✔	✔	✔	✔	✔	✔	✔

Self-Selected Reading/Independent Reading

	K	1	2	3	4	5	6
Use personal criteria to choose own reading including favorite authors, genres, recommendations from others; set up a reading log							
Read a range of literature and informational text for tasks as well as for enjoyment; participate in literature circles							
Produce evidence of reading by retelling, summarizing, or paraphrasing							

Media Literacy

	K	1	2	3	4	5	6
Summarize the message or content from media message, citing text evidence							
Use graphics, illustrations to analyze and interpret information	✔	✔	✔	✔	✔	✔	✔
Identify structural features of popular media and use the features to obtain information, including digital sources				✔	✔	✔	✔
Identify reasons and evidence in visuals and media message							
Analyze media source: recognize effects of media in one's mood and emotion							

KEY	✔ = Assessed Skill Tinted panels show skills, strategies, and other teaching opportunities.

	K	1	2	3	4	5	6
Make informed judgments about print and digital media							
Critique persuasive techniques							

WRITING

Writing Process

	K	1	2	3	4	5	6
Plan/prewrite							
Draft							
Revise							
Edit/proofread							
Publish and present including using technology							
Teacher and peer feedback							

Writing Traits

	K	1	2	3	4	5	6
Conventions		✔	✔	✔	✔	✔	✔
Ideas		✔	✔	✔	✔	✔	✔
Organization		✔	✔	✔	✔	✔	✔
Sentence fluency		✔	✔	✔	✔	✔	✔
Voice		✔	✔	✔	✔	✔	✔
Word choice		✔	✔	✔	✔	✔	✔

Writer's Craft

	K	1	2	3	4	5	6
Good topic, focus on and develop topic, topic sentence			✔	✔	✔	✔	✔
Paragraph(s); sentence structure				✔	✔	✔	✔
Main idea and supporting key details			✔	✔	✔	✔	✔
Unimportant details							
Relevant supporting evidence			✔	✔	✔	✔	✔
Strong opening, strong conclusion				✔	✔	✔	✔
Beginning, middle, end; sequence		✔	✔	✔	✔	✔	✔
Precise words, strong words, vary words			✔	✔	✔	✔	✔
Figurative and sensory language, descriptive details							
Informal/formal language							
Mood/style/tone							
Dialogue				✔	✔	✔	✔
Transition words, transitions to multiple paragraphs				✔	✔	✔	✔
Select focus and organization			✔	✔	✔	✔	✔
Points and counterpoints/Opposing claims and counterarguments							
Use reference materials (online and print dictionary, thesaurus, encyclopedia)							

Writing Applications

	K	1	2	3	4	5	6
Writing about text	✔	✔	✔	✔	✔	✔	✔
Personal and fictional narrative (also biographical and autobiographical)	✔	✔	✔	✔	✔	✔	✔
Variety of expressive forms including poetry	✔	✔	✔	✔	✔	✔	✔
Informative/explanatory texts	✔	✔	✔	✔	✔	✔	✔
Description	✔	✔	✔	✔			
Procedural texts		✔	✔	✔	✔	✔	✔
Opinion pieces or arguments	✔	✔	✔	✔	✔	✔	✔

	K	1	2	3	4	5	6
Communications including technical documents		✔	✔	✔	✔	✔	✔
Research report	✔	✔	✔	✔	✔	✔	✔
Responses to literature/reflection				✔	✔	✔	✔
Analytical writing							
Letters		✔	✔	✔	✔	✔	✔
Write daily and over short and extended time frames; set up writer's notebooks							
Penmanship/Handwriting							
Write legibly in manuscript using correct formation, directionality, and spacing							
Write legibly in cursive using correct formation, directionality, and spacing							

SPEAKING AND LISTENING

Speaking

	K	1	2	3	4	5	6
Use repetition, rhyme, and rhythm in oral texts							
Participate in classroom activities and discussions							
Collaborative conversation with peers and adults in small and large groups using formal English when appropriate							
Differentiate between formal and informal English							
Follow agreed upon rules for discussion							
Build on others' talk in conversation, adding new ideas							
Come to discussion prepared							
Describe familiar people, places, and things and add drawings as desired							
Paraphrase portions of text read alone or information presented							
Apply comprehension strategies and skills in speaking activities							
Use literal and nonliteral meanings							
Ask and answer questions about text read aloud and about media							
Stay on topic when speaking							
Use language appropriate to situation, purpose, and audience							
Use nonverbal communications such as eye contact, gestures, and props							
Use verbal communication in effective ways and improve expression in conventional language							
Retell a story, presentation, or spoken message by summarizing							
Oral presentations: focus, organizational structure, audience, purpose							
Give and follow directions							
Consider audience when speaking or preparing a presentation							
Recite poems, rhymes, songs							
Use complete, coherent sentences							
Organize presentations							
Deliver presentations (narrative, summaries, research, persuasive); add visuals							
Speak audibly (accuracy, expression, volume, pitch, rate, phrasing, modulation, enunciation)							
Create audio recordings of poems, stories, presentations							

Listening

	K	1	2	3	4	5	6
Identify musical elements in language							
Determine the purpose for listening							

KEY   ✔ = Assessed Skill
Tinted panels show skills, strategies, and other teaching opportunities.

	K	1	2	3	4	5	6
Understand, follow, restate, and give oral directions							
Develop oral language and concepts							
Listen openly, responsively, attentively, and critically							
Listen to identify the points a speaker makes							
Listen responsively to oral presentations (determine main idea and key details)							
Ask and answer relevant questions (for clarification to follow-up on ideas)							
Identify reasons and evidence presented by speaker							
Recall and interpret speakers' verbal/nonverbal messages, purposes, perspectives							
LANGUAGE							
Vocabulary Acquisition and Use							
Develop oral vocabulary and choose words for effect							
Use academic language		✔	✔	✔	✔	✔	✔
Identify persons, places, things, actions		✔	✔	✔			
Classify, sort, and categorize words	✔	✔	✔	✔	✔	✔	✔
Determine or clarify the meaning of unknown words; use word walls		✔	✔	✔	✔	✔	✔
Synonyms, antonyms, and opposites		✔	✔	✔	✔	✔	✔
Use context clues such as word, sentence, paragraph, definition, example, restatement, description, comparison, cause and effect		✔	✔	✔	✔	✔	✔
Use word identification strategies		✔	✔	✔	✔	✔	
Unfamiliar words		✔	✔	✔	✔	✔	✔
Multiple-meaning words		✔	✔	✔	✔	✔	✔
Use print and online dictionary to locate meanings, pronunciation, derivatives, parts of speech		✔	✔	✔	✔	✔	✔
Compound words		✔	✔	✔	✔	✔	
Words ending in -er and -est		✔	✔	✔	✔	✔	
Root words (base words)		✔	✔	✔	✔	✔	✔
Prefixes and suffixes		✔	✔	✔	✔	✔	✔
Greek and Latin affixes and roots			✔	✔	✔	✔	✔
Denotation and connotation					✔	✔	✔
Word families		✔	✔	✔	✔	✔	✔
Inflectional endings		✔	✔	✔	✔	✔	✔
Use a print and online thesaurus			✔	✔	✔	✔	✔
Use print and online reference sources for word meaning (dictionary, glossaries)	✔	✔	✔	✔	✔	✔	✔
Homographs				✔	✔	✔	✔
Homophones			✔	✔	✔	✔	✔
Contractions		✔	✔	✔			
Figurative language such as metaphors, similes, personification			✔	✔	✔	✔	✔
Idioms, adages, proverbs, literal and nonliteral language			✔	✔	✔	✔	✔
Analogies							
Listen to, read, discuss familiar and unfamiliar challenging text							
Identify real-life connections between words and their use							
Use acquired words and phrases to convey precise ideas							
Use vocabulary to express spatial and temporal relationships							

	K	1	2	3	4	5	6
Identify shades of meaning in related words	✔	✔	✔	✔	✔	✔	✔
Word origins				✔	✔	✔	✔
Morphology				✔	✔	✔	✔
Knowledge of Language							
Choose words, phrases, and sentences for effect							
Choose punctuation effectively							
Formal and informal language for style and tone including dialects							
Conventions of Standard English/Grammar, Mechanics, and Usage							
Sentence concepts: statements, questions, exclamations, commands		✔	✔	✔	✔	✔	✔
Complete and incomplete sentences; sentence fragments; word order		✔	✔	✔	✔	✔	✔
Compound sentences, complex sentences				✔	✔	✔	✔
Combining sentences		✔	✔	✔	✔	✔	✔
Nouns including common, proper, singular, plural, irregular plurals, possessives, abstract, concrete, collective		✔	✔	✔	✔	✔	✔
Verbs including action, helping, linking, irregular		✔	✔	✔	✔	✔	✔
Verb tenses including past, present, future, perfect, and progressive		✔	✔	✔	✔	✔	✔
Pronouns including possessive, subject and object, pronoun-verb agreement, indefinite, intensive, reciprocal; correct unclear pronouns		✔	✔	✔	✔	✔	✔
Adjectives including articles, demonstrative, proper adjectives that compare		✔	✔	✔	✔	✔	✔
Adverbs including telling how, when, where, comparative, superlative, irregular		✔	✔	✔	✔	✔	✔
Subject, predicate; subject-verb agreement		✔	✔	✔	✔	✔	✔
Contractions		✔	✔	✔	✔	✔	✔
Conjunctions				✔	✔	✔	✔
Commas			✔	✔	✔	✔	✔
Colons, semicolons, dashes, hyphens						✔	✔
Question words							
Quotation marks			✔	✔	✔	✔	✔
Prepositions and prepositional phrases, appositives		✔	✔	✔	✔	✔	✔
Independent and dependent clauses						✔	✔
Italics/underlining for emphasis and titles							
Negatives, correcting double negatives					✔	✔	✔
Abbreviations			✔	✔	✔	✔	✔
Use correct capitalization in sentences, proper nouns, titles, abbreviations		✔	✔	✔	✔	✔	✔
Use correct punctuation		✔	✔	✔	✔	✔	✔
Antecedents				✔	✔	✔	✔
Homophones and words often confused			✔	✔	✔	✔	✔
Apostrophes				✔	✔	✔	✔
Spelling							
Write irregular, high-frequency words	✔	✔	✔				
ABC order	✔	✔					
Write letters	✔	✔					
Words with short vowels	✔	✔	✔	✔	✔	✔	✔
Words with long vowels	✔	✔	✔	✔	✔	✔	✔

KEY	✔ = Assessed Skill Tinted panels show skills, strategies, and other teaching opportunities.

	K	1	2	3	4	5	6
Words with digraphs, blends, consonant clusters, double consonants		✔	✔	✔	✔	✔	✔
Words with vowel digraphs and ambiguous vowels		✔	✔	✔	✔	✔	✔
Words with diphthongs		✔	✔	✔	✔	✔	✔
Words with r-controlled vowels		✔	✔	✔	✔	✔	✔
Use conventional spelling		✔	✔	✔	✔	✔	✔
Schwa words				✔	✔	✔	✔
Words with silent letters			✔	✔	✔	✔	✔
Words with hard and soft letters			✔	✔	✔	✔	✔
Inflectional endings including plural, past tense, drop final e and double consonant when adding -ed and -ing, changing y to i		✔	✔	✔	✔	✔	✔
Compound words		✔	✔	✔	✔	✔	✔
Homonyms/homophones			✔	✔	✔	✔	✔
Prefixes and suffixes		✔	✔	✔	✔	✔	✔
Root and base words (also spell derivatives)				✔	✔	✔	✔
Syllables: patterns, rules, accented, stressed, closed, open				✔	✔	✔	✔
Words with Greek and Latin roots						✔	✔
Words from mythology						✔	✔
Words with spelling patterns, word families		✔	✔	✔	✔	✔	✔

RESEARCH AND INQUIRY

Study Skills

	K	1	2	3	4	5	6
Directions: read, write, give, follow (includes technical directions)			✔	✔	✔	✔	✔
Evaluate directions for sequence and completeness				✔	✔	✔	✔
Use library/media center							
Use parts of a book to locate information							
Interpret information from graphic aids		✔	✔	✔	✔	✔	✔
Use graphic organizers to organize information and comprehend text		✔	✔	✔	✔	✔	✔
Use functional, everyday documents				✔	✔	✔	✔
Apply study strategies: skimming and scanning, note-taking, outlining							

Research Process

	K	1	2	3	4	5	6
Generate and revise topics and questions for research				✔	✔	✔	✔
Narrow focus of research, set research goals				✔	✔	✔	✔
Find and locate information using print and digital resources		✔	✔	✔	✔	✔	✔
Record information systematically (note-taking, outlining, using technology)				✔	✔	✔	✔
Develop a systematic research plan				✔	✔	✔	✔
Evaluate reliability, credibility, usefulness of sources and information						✔	✔
Use primary sources to obtain information					✔	✔	✔
Organize, synthesize, evaluate, and draw conclusions from information							
Cite and list sources of information (record basic bibliographic data)					✔	✔	✔
Demonstrate basic keyboarding skills							
Participate in and present shared research							

Technology

	K	1	2	3	4	5	6
Use computer, Internet, and other technology resources to access information							
Use text and organizational features of electronic resources such as search engines, keywords, e-mail, hyperlinks, URLs, Web pages, databases, graphics							
Use digital tools to present and publish in a variety of media formats							

INDEX

A

ABC Big Book, read, **1**:S7

Animals in the Park, **1**:S31, S55

Academic language, **1**:S13, S18, S22, S24, S27, S28, S32, S37, S38, S42, S46, S48, S52, S56, S62, S66, S69, S70, S72, S75, S76, T12, T16, T18, T20, T30, T32, T34, T38, T40, T44, T50, T52, T58, T94, T98, T100, T102, T104, T112, T114, T116, T120, T122, T126, T132, T134, T140, T176, T180, T184, T194, T196, T204, T208, T214, T222, **2**:T12, T18, T20, T30, T32, T34, T38, T40, T44, T52, T58, T94, T100, T102, T104, T112, T114, T116, T120, T122, T126, T132, T140, T176, T182, T184, T194, T196, T198, T202, T204, T208, T214, T222, **3**:T12, T14, T16, T18, T20, T22, T30, T32, T34, T38, T40, T44, T50, T58, T94, T98, T100, T102, T104, T112, T114, T116, T120, T122, T126, T132, T134, T140, T176, T182, T184, T186, T194, T196, T198, T202, T204, T208, T214, T216, T222, **4**:T12, T16, T18, T20, T30, T32, T34, T38, T40, T44, T58, T94, T98, T100, T102, T104, T112, T114, T116, T120, T122, T126, T132, T134, T140, T176, T182, T184, T186, T192, T194, T196, T198, T202, T204, T208, T214, T222, **5**:T12, T16, T18, T20, T30, T32, T34, T38, T40, T44, T50, T94, T98, T100, T102, T104, T112, T114, T116, T120, T122, T126, T132, T134, T140, T176, T182, T184, T186, T194, T196, T202, T204, T208, T214, T222, **6**:T12, T16, T18, T20, T22, T30, T32, T34, T38, T40, T44, T50, T52, T58, T94, T98, T100, T102, T104, T112, T114, T116, T120, T122, T126, T132, T134, T140, T176, T180, T182, T184, T186, T194, T196, T198, T202, T204, T208, T214, T216, T222, T248, **7**:T12, T16, T18, T20, T22, T30, T32, T34, T38, T40, T44, T50, T52, T58, T94, T98, T100, T102, T104, T112, T114, T116, T120, T122, T126, T132, T134, T140, T176, T180, T182, T184, T186, T194, T196, T198, T202, T204, T208, T214, T216, T222, T248, **8**:T12, T18, T20, T22, T30, T32, T34, T38, T40, T44, T52, T58, T94, T100, T102, T104, T112, T114, T116, T120, T122, T126, T132, T140, T176, T182, T184, T186, T194, T196, T198, T202, T204, T208, T214, T216, T222, T248, **9**:T12, T18, T20, T22, T30, T32, T34, T38, T40, T44, T50, T52, T54, T94, T98, T100, T102, T104, T112, T114, T116, T120, T122, T126, T132, T134, T136, T140, T176, T180, T182, T184, T194, T196, T198, T204, T214, T222, T248, **10**:T12, T18, T20, T32, T34, T36, T40, T42, T46, T52, T54, T60, T96, T100, T102, T104, T114, T116, T118, T120, T122, T124, T134, T136, T142, T184, T196, T198, T204, T210, T216, T224

Access complex text

connection of ideas, **2**:T22, T104, **3**:T22, T104, **4**:T22, **10**:T22, T106, T188

genre, **8**:T104

organization, **1**:T22, T104, T186, **3**:T22, **5**:T104, **6**:T22, **7**:T104, **8**:T22, **9**:T22, T104

prior knowledge, **6**:T104, **7**:T22

purpose, **5**:T22, **7**:T186

sentence structure, **3**:T186, **4**:T104, **5**:T186, **6**:T186, **8**:T186

specific vocabulary, **2**:T186, **4**:T186, **9**:T186

Adjectives. *See* **Grammar**.

Alliteration, **2**:T20, T42, T62, **6**:T184, T206, T226, **7**:T44, **10**:T186, T208, T228

Alphabet

letter recognition, **1**:S8, S13, S18, S23, S28, S32, S37, S42, S47, S52, S56, S61, S66, S71, S76

uppercase/lowercase letter formation, **1**:T16, T98, T180, **2**:T16, T98, **3**:T16, T98, T180, **4**:T16, T98, **5**:T16, T98, **6**:T16, T98, **7**:T16, T98, **8**:T16, T98, **9**:T16

See also **Fluency: sound/spelling; Phonics/Word analysis: letter-sound association.**

Antonyms, **10**:T105, T127

Approaching Level Options

comprehension, **1**:T67, T149, T231, **2**:T67, T149, **3**:T67, T149, T231, **4**:T67, T149, T231, **5**:T67, T149, T231, **6**:T67, T149, T231, **7**:T67, T149, T231, **8**:T67, T149, T231, **9**:T67, T149, T231, **10**:T69, T151, T233

fluency, **1**:T65, T147, T148, T229, T230, **2**:T65, T66, T147, T148, T229, T230, **3**:T65, T66, T146, T147, T148, T229, T230, **4**:T65, T147, T229, **5**:T65, T147, T229, **6**:T65, T147, T229, **7**:T65, T147, T229, **8**:T65, T147, T229, **9**:T65, T147, T229

high-frequency words, **1**:T66, T148, T230, **2**:T66, T148, T230, **3**:T66, T148, T230, **4**:T66, T148, T230, **5**:T66, T148, T230, **6**:T66, T148, T230, **7**:T66, T148, T230, **8**:T66, T148, T230, **9**:T66, T148, T230, **10**:T68, T150, T232

Leveled Reader lessons, **1**:T60–T61, T142–T143, T224–T225, **2**:T60–T61, T142–T143, T224–T225, **3**:T60–T61, T142–T143, T224–T225, **4**:T60–T61, T142–T143, T224–T225, **5**:T60–T61, T142–T143, T224–T225, **6**:T60–T61, T142–T143, T224–T225, **7**:T60–T61, T142–T143, T224–T225, **8**:T60–T61, T142–T143, T224–T225, **9**:T60–T61, T142–T143, T224–T225, **10**:T62–T63, T144–T145, T226–T227

oral vocabulary, **1**:T67, T149, T231, **2**:T67, T149, T231, **3**:T67, T149, T231, **5**:T67, T149, T231, **6**:T67, T149, T231, **7**:T67, T149, T231, **8**:T67, T149, **9**:T67, T149, T231, **10**:T69, T151, T233

phonemic awareness, **1**:T62–T63, T144–T145, T226–T227, **2**:T62–T63, T144–T145, T226–T227, **3**:T62–T63, T144–T145, T226–T227, **4**:T62–T63, T144–T145, T226–T227, **5**:T62–T63, T144–T145, T226–T227, **6**:T62–T63, T144–T145, T226–T227, **7**:T62–T63, T144–T145, T226–T227, **8**:T62–T63, T144–T145, T226–T227, **9**: T62–T63, T144–T145, T226–T227, **10**:T64–T65, T146–T147, T228–T229

phonics, **1**:T64–T65, T146–T147, T228–T229, **2**:T64–T65, T146–T147, T227–T228, **3**:T64–T65, T146–T147, T228–T229, **4**:T64–T65, T146–T147, T228–T229, **5**:T64–T65, T146–T147, T228–T229, **6**:T64–T65, T146–T147, T228–T229, **7**:T64–T65, T146–T147, T228–T229, **8**:T64–T65, T146–T147, T227–T228, **9**:T64–T65, T146–T147, T228–T229, **10**:T66–T67, T148–T149, T229–T230

phonological awareness, **1**:T62, T144, T226, **2**:T62, T144, T226, **2**:T62, T144, T226, **3**:T62, T144, T226, **4**: T62, T144, T226, **5**:T62,

B

G

speaking activities, **1**:T33, T115,
T197, **2**:T33, T115, T197, **3**:T33,
T115, T197, **4**:T33, T115, T197,
5:T33, T115, T197, **6**:T33, T115,
T197, **7**:T33, T115, T197, **8**:T33,
T115, T197, **9**:T33, T115, T197,
10:T35, T117, T199

verbs (action words), **2**:T19, T32, T33,
T41, T50, T51, T59, T83, T101, T114,
T115, T123, T132, T133, T141, T165,
T183, T196, T197, T205, T214, T215,
T223, T247, **7**:T19, T33, T41, T51,
T59, T83, T101, T115, T123, T133,
T141, T165, T183, T197, T205, T215,
T223, T247

Graphic organizers

charts, **1**:S74, **2**:T18, T100, **3**:T100,
4:T32, **6**:T27, T191, **7**:T191, **8**:T27,
T109, T191, **9**:T109, **10**:T29

lists, **1**:T18, T100, **8**:T100, T182,
9:T182, **10**:T18, T184

Venn diagram, **7**:T27

webs, **1**:S16, S20, S26, S40, S44, S50,
S64, S68, T182, **2**:T182, **6**:T100,
7:T18, **8**:T18, **10**:T136

Guided retelling. *See* **Retell.**

H

Handwriting. *See* **Penmanship.**

High-frequency words

a, **2**:T17, T23, T26, T29, T39, T47, T57,
T60, T66, T68, T72, T81, T181, T193,
T203, T211, T221, T236, T245, **3**:T72,
4:T148, T230, T240, **5**:T148, T230,
7:T230, **8**:T66, T148, **9**:T66, **10**:T68

and, **3**:T99, T107, T111, T121, T129,
T139, T142, T148, T150, T154, T163,
4:T148, T181, T188, T193, T203,
T211, T221, T230, T237, T240, T245,
5:T148, T230, **7**:T230, **8**:T66, **9**:T66,
10:T68

are, **5**:T99, T108, T111, T121, T129,
T139, T142, T148, T150, T155, T163,
T230, **6**:T181, T193, T203, T211,
T221, T230, T237, T245, **7**:T230,
8:T66, T148, **9**:T66, **10**:T68

can, **1**:S33, S39, S43, S49, S53, S57,
S63, S67, S77, **2**:T236, **3**:T72,
4:T148, T230, T240, **5**:T148, T230,
7:T230, **8**:T66, **9**:T66, **10**:T68

do, **4**:T99, T105, T107, T111, T121,
T129, T139, T142, T148, T150, T155,
T163, T181, T193, T203, T209, T211,
T221, T230, T237, T240, T245,

5:T148, T230, **7**:T230, **8**:T66, **9**:T66,
10:T68

for, **7**:T17, T24, T29, T39, T47, T57, T66,
T73, T81, T230, **8**:T66, T148, T181,
T193, T203, T211, T221, T237, T245,
9:T66

go, **3**:T181, T193, T203, T209, T211,
T221, T224, T230, T236, T245,
4:T148, T181, T193, T203, T211,
T221, T230, T237, T245, **5**:T148,
T230, **7**:T230, **8**:T66, **9**:T66, **10**:T68

good, **10**:T17, T31, T41, T59, T68, T75,
T83

have, **7**:T17, T25, T29, T37, T39, T47,
T57, T60, T66, T68, T73, T81, T230,
8:T66, T148, T181, T187, T193,
T203, T211, T221, T237, T245, **9**:T66

he, **5**:T181, T190, T193, T203, T211,
T221, T224, T230, T232, T237, T245,
6:T181, T193, T203, T221, T230,
T237, T245, **7**:T230, **8**:T66, T148,
9:T66, **10**:T68

help, **9**:T17, T29, T39, T47, T57, T66,
T73, T81

here, **8**:T17, T29, T39, T47, T57, T66,
T73, T181, T193, T203, T211, T221,
T230, T237, T245

I, **1**:S9, S15, S19, S25, S29, S57, S62,
S67, S73, S77, **2**:T236, T245, **3**:T72,
4:T148, T230, T240, **5**:T148, T230,
7:T230, **8**:T66, T148, **9**:T66, **10**:T68

is, **6**:T17, T23, T29, T39, T47, T57, T60,
T66, T73, T81, T181, T193, T221,
T230, T237, T245, **7**:T230, **8**:T66,
T148, **9**:T66, **10**:T68

like, **2**:T99, T111, T121, T129, T139,
T142, T148, T150, T154, T163, T181,
T193, T203, T209, T211, T221, T236,
T245, **3**:T72, **4**:T148, T230, **5**:T148,
T230, **7**:T230, **9**:T66, **10**:T68

little, **6**:T17, T23, T29, T39, T47, T57,
T66, T68, T73, T81, T181, T193,
T203, T221, T230, T237, T245,
7:T230, **8**:T66, T148, **9**:T66, **10**:T68

me, **8**:T17, T29, T39, T47, T57, T66, T73,
T181, T193, T203, T211, T221, T230,
T237, T245

my, **5**:T17, T24, T29, T39, T47, T57,
T60, T66, T68, T73, T81, T148, T230,
6:T181, T193, T203, T221, T230,
T237, T245, **7**:T230, T237, T245,
8:T66, T148, **9**:T66, **10**:T68

of, **7**:T99, T111, T121, T129, T139,
T148, T155, T163, **8**:T81, T181,
T193, T203, T211, T221, T230, T237,
T245

said, **8**: T181, T193, T203, T211, T221,
T230, T237, T245

see, **1**:T181, T187, T190, T193, T203,
T211, T221, T224, T230, T232,
T236, T240, T245, **2**:T181, T193,
T203, T211, T221, T232, T236, T245,
3:T72, **4**:T148, T230, **5**:T148, T230,
7:T230, **8**:T66, T148, **9**:T66, **10**:T68

she, **6**:T99, T105, T111, T121, T129,
T139, T148, T155, T163, T181, T193,
T203, T221, T224, T230, T232, T237,
T245, **7**:T230, **8**:T66, T148, **9**:T66,
10:T68

the, **1**:T17, T29, T39, T45, T47, T57,
T60, T66, T72, T81, T163, **2**:T181,
T193, T203, T211, T221, T224, T236,
T245, **3**:T72, **4**:T148, T230, T240,
5:T148, T230, **7**:T230, **8**:T66, T148,
9:T29, T66, T76, **10**:T68

they, **7**:T99, T111, T121, T129, T139,
T148, T155, T163, **8**:T181, T193,
T203, T211, T221, T230, T237, T245

this, **8**:T99, T111, T121, T129, T139,
T148, T155, T181, T193, T203, T211,
T221, T230, T237, T245

to, **3**:T17, T23, T29, T39, T47, T57, T66,
T68, T72, T81, **4**:T148, T181, T188,
T193, T203, T209, T211, T221, T230,
T237, T240, T245, **5**:T148, T230,
7:T230, **8**:T66, T148, **9**:T66, **10**:T68

too, **9**:T17, T29, T39, T47, T57, T66,
T73, T81

want, **8**:T181, T193, T203, T221, T230,
T237, T245

was, **6**:T99, T108, T111, T121, T129,
T139, T142, T148, T150, T155, T163,
T181, T193, T203, T221, T230, T237,
T245, **7**:T230, **8**:T66, T148, **9**:T66,
10:T68

we, **1**:T99, T111, T121, T129, T139,
T148, T150, T154, T163, **2**:T181,
T193, T203, T211, T221, T245,
3:T72, **4**:T148, T230, **5**:T148, T230,
7:T230, **8**:T66, T148, **9**:T66, **10**:T68

what, **8**:T99, T111, T121, T129, T139,
T148, T155, T181, T193, T203, T211,
T221, T230, T237, T245

who, **10**:T17, T31, T41, T59, T68, T75,
T83

with, **5**:T181, T188, T193, T203, T211,
T221, T230, T237, T245, **6**:T181,
T190, T193, T203, T221, T230, T237,
T245, **7**:T230, **8**:T66, T148, **9**:T66,
10:T68

Key X = Unit X

M

N

O

alliteration, **7**:T44

repetition, **7**:T177, **9**:T177

rhyme/rhyme scheme, **6**:T44, **7**:T177, **9**:T177

rhythm, **7**:T177, **9**:T177

writing, **5**:T18, T32, T40, T50, T58

See also **Genre; Songs, rhymes, chants.**

Pre-Decodable Reader, 1:S14, S24, S38, S48, S62, S72

Predict, 1:S14, S24, S38, S48, S62, S72, T30, T48, T60, T68, T78, T112, T130, T194, T242, **2**:T60, T68, T78, T112, T142, T150, T156, T160, T224, T232, T238, T242, **3**:T30, T48, T60, T112, T130, T142, T150, T156, T160, T194, T212, T224, T232, T238, T242, **4**:T30, T60, T68, T74, T78, T112, T142, T150, T156, T160, T194, T224, T232, T238, T242, **5**:T60, T68, T74, T78, T112, T142, T150, T156, T160, T194, T224, T232, T238, T242, **6**:T30, T78, T112, T142, T150, T156, T160, T194, T224, T232, T238, T242, **7**:T30, T74, T78, T112, T142, T150, T156, T160, T194, T224, T232, T238, T242, **8**:T60, T68, T112, T142, T150, T156, T160, T194, T224, T232, T238, T242, **9**:T30, T60, T68, T74, T78, T112, T142, T150, T156, T194, T224, T238, T242, **10**:T32, T62, T70, T76, T114, T144, T152, T158, T162, T196, T226, T234, T240, T244

See also **Comprehension strategies: predictions, make, confirm, revise; Setting purposes for reading.**

Prefixes. *See* **Vocabulary strategies.**

Presentation, oral. *See* **Oral presentations.**

Previewing literature. *See* **Predict; Setting purposes for reading.**

Print awareness

book handling, opening, parts, **1**:S14, S24, S31, S38, S55, S62, S72, T12, T30, T48, T60, T94, T112, T130, T142, T176, T194, **2**:T12, T30, T48, T94, T112, T130, T176, T194, T212, **3**:T12, T30, T48, T60, T112, T130, T194, T212, **4**:T30, T48, T112, T130, T194, T212, **5**:T212, **9**:T194

book parts, **1**:T176, **2**:T212, T224, **3**:T48, **4**:T130, **5**:T12, T94

print type, **1**:T106

sentences, **6**:T12, T24, T30, T48, T68, T107, T130, T142, T150, T176, T194, T212, T224, **7**:T30, T48, T60, T130

uppercase and lowercase letters, **4**:T189, T194, T212, T232, **5**:T12, **6**:T224, **8**:T30

word boundaries, **2**:T176, T232, **5**:T94, **7**:T194, T212, **9**:T188, T194, T224, T232, **10**:T114, T178, T196, T214, T226

See also **Concepts of/about print.**

Procedural text. *See* **Genre: reading informational text.**

Punctuation. *See* **Grammar: punctuation of sentences.**

Q

Questions, asking. *See* **Comprehension strategies: ask and answer questions.**

R

Read alouds. *See* **Big Book, read the literature; Big Book, reread the literature; Interactive Read Aloud; Shared read.**

Reading across texts, 1:S27, S51, S75, T44–T45, T126–T127, T208–T209, **2**:T44–T45, T126–T127, **3**:T44–T45, T126–T127, T208–T209, **4**:T44–T45, T126–T127, T208–T209, **5**:T44–T45, T126–T127, T208–T209, **6**:T44–T45, T126–T127, T208–T209, **7**:T44–T45, T126–T127, T208–T209, **8**:T44–T45, T126–T127, T208–T209, **9**:T44–T45, T126–T127, T208–T209, **10**:T46–T47, T128–T129, T210–T211

See also **Text connections: text to text.**

Reading independently, 1:T67, T73, T77, T149, T155, T159, T231, T237, T241, **2**:T67, T73, T77, T149, T155, T159, T231, T237, T241, **3**:T67, T73, T77, T149, T155, T159, T231, T237, T241, **4**:T67, T73, T77, T149, T155, T159, T231, T237, T241, **5**:T67, T73, T77, T149, T155, T159, T231, T237, T241, **6**:T67, T73, T77, T149, T155, T159, T231, T237, T241, **7**:T67, T73, T77, T149, T155, T159, T231, T237, T241, **8**:T67, T73, T77, T149, T155, T159, T231, T237, T241, **9**:T67, T73, T77, T149, T155, T159, T231, T237, T241, **10**:T69, T75, T79, T151, T157, T161, T233, T239, T243

Reading purposefully, 1:T67, T73, T77, T149, T155, T159, T231, T237, T241, **2**:T67, T73, T77, T149, T155, T159, T231, T237, T241, **3**:T67, T73, T77, T149, T155, T159, T231, T237, T241, **4**:T67, T73, T77, T149, T155, T159, T231, T237, T241, **5**:T67, T73, T77, T149, T155, T159, T231, T237, T241, **6**:T67, T73, T77, T149, T155, T159, T231, T237, T241, **7**:T67, T73, T77, T149, T155, T159, T231, T237, T241, **8**:T67, T73, T77, T149, T155, T159, T231, T237, T241, **9**:T67, T73, T77, T149, T155, T159, T231, T237, T241, **10**:T69, T75, T79, T151, T157, T161, T233, T239, T243

Rereading, 1:S14, S17, S24, S38, S41, S48, S62, S65, S72, T31, T42, T49, T113, T124, T131, T195, T206, T213, **2**:T31, T49, T113, T131, T195, T213, **3**:T31, T49, T113, T131, T195, T213, **4**:T31, T48, T113, T130, T195, T212, **5**:T31, T42, T48, T113, T130, T195, T212, **6**:T31, T48, T113, T130, T195, T212, **7**:T31, T48, T113, T130, T195, T212, **8**:T31, T48, T113, T124, T131, T195, T212, **9**:T31, T48, T113, T130, T195, T206, T212, **10**:T33, T44, T50, T115, T126, T132, T197, T208, T214

See also **Big Book, reread the literature; Comprehension strategies: reread.**

Research and inquiry, 1:T52–T55, T134–T137, T216–T219, **2**:T52–T55, T134–T137, T216–T219, **3**:T52–T55, T134–T137, T216–T219, **4**:T52–T55, T134–T137, T216–T219, **5**:T52–T55, T134–T137, T216–T219, **6**:T52–T55, T134–T137, T216–T219, **7**:T52–T55, T134–T137, T216–T219, **8**:T52–T55, T134–T137, T216–T219, **9**:T52–T55, T134–T137, T216–T219, **10**:T54–T55, T136–T139, T218–T221

Research process, 1:T52–T53, T134–T135, T216–T217, **2**:T52–T53, T134–T135, T216–T217, **3**:T52–T53, T134–T135, T216–T217, **4**:T52–T53, T134–T135, T216–T217, **5**:T52–T53, T134–T135, T216–T217, **6**:T52–T53, T134–T135, T216–T217, T248–T249, **7**:T52–T55, T134–T135, T216–T217, T249, **8**:T52–T53, T134–T135, T216–T217, T249, **9**:T52–T53, T134–T135, T216–T217, **10**:T54–T55, T136–T137, T218–T219

Respond to reading

informational text, **1**:S31, S55, S60, T45, T127, T160–T161, T177, T225, T233, T239, T243, **2**:T13, T45, T61,

S

T

U

Uppercase/lowercase letters

   letter recognition, **1**:S8, S13, S18, S23, S28, S32, S37, S42, S47, S52, S56, S61, S66, S71, S76

   penmanship, **1**:T16, T98, T180, **2**:T16, T98, **3**:T16, T98, T180, **4**:T16, T98, **5**:T16, T98, **6**:T16, T98, **7**:T16, T98, **8**:T16, T98, **9**:T16

V

Visualize. *See* **Comprehension strategies**.

Visual Vocabulary Cards, **1**:T11, T20, T34, T80, T81, T93, T102, T116, T162, T184, T198, T244, **2**:T20, T34, T47, T80, T93, T102, T116, T129, T163, T175, T198, **3**:T11, T34, T124, T162, T184, T198, **4**:T11, T20, T34, T80, T93, T102, T116, T175, T184, T198, **5**:T11, T20, T34, T80, T93, T102, T116, T175, T184, T198, **6**:T11, T20, T34, T75, T93, T102, T116, T124, T162, T175, T184, T198, **7**:T11, T20, T34, T93, T102, T116, T124, T162, T175, T184, T198, T206, **8**:T20, T34, T47, T80, T102, T116, T124, T129, T163, T175, T184, T198, **9**:T20, T34, T80, T81, T93, T102, T116, T162, T175, T198, T244, **10**:T11, T20, T36, T49, T82, T95, T104, T164, T177, T186, T200, T246

Vocabulary acquisition

   category words

      action words, **3**:T21, T43, T81

      animal homes, **7**:T185, T207, T245

      animal parts, **7**:T21, T43, T81

      baby animals, **10**:T187, T209, T247

      colors, **2**:T21, T43, T81

      days of the week, **1**:S59, S69

      family words, **1**:T103, T125, T163

      farm animals, **9**:T103, T125, T163

      feeling words, **1**:T21, T43, T81

      food words, **4**:T103, T125, T163, **5**:T185, T207, T245, **9**:T185, T207, T245

      household furniture, **9**:T21, T43, T81

      job words, **4**:T21, T43, T81

      movement words, **2**:T185, T207, T245

      names, **1**:S11, S21

      numbers, **1**:S35, S45

      opposites, **8**:T185, T207, T245, **10**:T105, T127, T165

      ordinal numbers, **8**:T103, T125, T163

      pets, **7**:T103, T125, T163

      position words, **4**:T185, T207, T245

      question words, **6**:T185, T207, T245, **10**:T21, T45, T83

      seasons, **6**:T21, T43, T81

      sensory words, **1**:T185, T207, T245

      sequence words, **3**:T185, T207, T245

      shape words, **2**:T103, T125, T163

      size words, **5**:T21, T43, T81

      sound words, **3**:T103, T125, T163

      tree parts, **5**:T103, T125, T163

      vehicles, **8**:T21, T43, T81

      weather words, **6**:T103, T125, T163

   cognates, **1**:T81, T163, T245, **2**:T81, T163, T245, **3**:T81, T163, T245, **4**:T81, T163, T245, **5**:T81, T163, T245, **6**:T81, T163, T245, **7**:T81, T163, T245, **8**:T81, T163, T245, **9**:T81, T163, T245, **10**:T83, T165, T247

   computer-related, **6**:T248, **7**:T248, **8**:T248, **9**:T248, **10**:T248

   domain-specific, **1**:T103, T125, T163, **4**:T21, T43, T81, T103, T125, T163, **5**:T103, T125, T163, T185, T207, T245, **6**:T21, T43, T81, T103, T125, T163, **7**:T21, T43, T81, T103, T125, T163, T185, T207, T245, **8**:T21, T43, T81, **9**:T21, T43, T81, T103, T125, T163, T185, T207, T245, **10**:T187, T209, T247

   function words and phrases. *See* **English Language Learners: high-frequency words, vocabulary**.

   general academic, **1**:S14, S62, S69, T38, T52, T134, T176, T216, **2**:T52, T122, T126, T132, T134, T140

   oral vocabulary, **1**:S16, S20, S26, S40, S44, S50, S64, S68, S74, T10–T11, T20, T34, T42, T67, T77, T80, T92–T93, T102, T116, T124, T149, T159, T162, T174–T175, T184, T198, T206, T231, T241, T244, **2**:T10–T11, T20, T34, T42, T67, T77, T80, T92–T93, T116, T124, T149, T159, T162, T174–T175, T184, T198, T206, T231, T241, T244, **3**:T10–T11, T20, T34, T42, T67, T77, T80, T92–T93, T102, T116, T124, T149, T159, T162, T174–T175, T184, T198, T206, T231, T241, T244, **4**:T10–T11, T20, T34, T42, T77, T80, T92–T93, T102, T116, T124, T149, T159, T162, T174–T175, T184, T198, T206, T231, T241, T244, **5**:T10–T11, T20, T34, T42, T77, T80, T92–T93, T102, T116, T124, T149, T159, T162, T174–T175, T184, T198, T206, T231, T241, T244, **6**:T10–T11, T20, T34, T42, T67, T77, T80, T92–T93, T102, T116, T124, T149, T159, T162, T174–T175, T184, T198, T206, T231, T241, T244, **7**:T10–T11, T20, T34, T42–T43, T67, T77, T80, T92–T93, T102, T116, T124, T149, T159, T162, T174–T175, T184, T198, T206, T231, T241, T244, **8**:T10–T11, T20–T21, T34, T42, T67, T77, T80, T92–T93, T102, T116, T124, T149, T159, T162, T174–T175, T184, T198, T206, T231, T241, T244, **9**:T10–T11, T20, T34, T42, T67, T77, T80, T92–T93, T102, T116, T124, T149, T159, T162, T174–T175, T184, T198, T206, T231, T241, T244, **10**:T10–T11, T20, T36, T44, T69, T79, T82, T94–T95, T104, T118, T126, T151, T161, T164, T176–T177, T186, T200, T208, T233, T243, T246

   selection words, **2**:T12, T94, **4**:T12, T176, **7**:T12, **9**:T176, **10**:T178

   story words, **1**:T12, T94, T176, **2**:T176, **3**:T12, T94, T176, **4**:T94, **5**:T12, T94, T176, **6**:T12, T94, T176, **7**:T94, T176, **8**:T12, T94, T176, **9**:T12, **10**:T12, T96

   word walls, **1**:S33. *See also* **High-frequency words**.

   word webs, **1**:S16, S20, S26, S40, S44, S64, S68, T182, **2**:T182, **6**:T100, **7**:T18, **8**:T18, **10**:T136

   See also **Academic language; High-frequency words; Oral language**.

Vocabulary strategies

   ask and answer questions, **10**:T97

   compound words, **7**:T21, T43

   context clues, sentence clues, **5**:T207, **6**:T21, T43, **8**:T43, **9**:T185, T207, **10**:T21, T45

   figurative language, **6**:T103, T125, **7**:T185, T207

   inflectional endings, **5**:T103, T125

   plurals, **5**:T21, T43

   shades of meaning, **6**:T103, T125, **7**:T185, T207

Common Core State Standards Correlations

English Language Arts

College and Career Readiness Anchor Standards for READING

The K–5 standards on the following pages define what students should understand and be able to do by the end of each grade. They correspond to the College and Career Readiness (CCR) anchor standards below by number. The CCR and grade-specific standards are necessary complements—the former providing broad standards, the latter providing additional specificity—that together define the skills and understandings that all students must demonstrate.

Key Ideas and Details

1. Read closely to determine what the text says explicitly and to make logical inferences from it; cite specific textual evidence when writing or speaking to support conclusions drawn from the text.

2. Determine central ideas or themes of a text and analyze their development; summarize the key supporting details and ideas.

3. Analyze how and why individuals, events, and ideas develop and interact over the course of a text.

Craft and Structure

4. Interpret words and phrases as they are used in a text, including determining technical, connotative, and figurative meanings, and analyze how specific word choices shape meaning or tone.

5. Analyze the structure of texts, including how specific sentences, paragraphs, and larger portions of the text (e.g., a section, chapter, scene, or stanza) relate to each other and the whole.

6. Assess how point of view or purpose shapes the content and style of a text.

Integration of Knowledge and Ideas

7. Integrate and evaluate content presented in diverse media and formats, including visually and quantitatively, as well as in words.

8. Delineate and evaluate the argument and specific claims in a text, including the validity of the reasoning as well as the relevance and sufficiency of the evidence.

9. Analyze how two or more texts address similar themes or topics in order to build knowledge or to compare the approaches the authors take.

Range of Reading and Level of Text Complexity

10. Read and comprehend complex literary and informational texts independently and proficiently.

CCSS Common Core State Standards
English Language Arts

Grade K

Each standard is coded in the following manner:

Strand	Grade Level	Standard
RL	K	1

Reading Standards for Literature

Key Ideas and Details	*McGraw-Hill Reading Wonders*
RL.K.1	With prompting and support, ask and answer questions about key details in a text.	**READING WRITING WORKSHOP BIG BOOK:** Unit 1, Week 3: 44-49 **LEVELED READERS:** Unit 1, Week 2: *Hop!* (A), *We Hop!* (O), *We Can Move!* (B) **Unit 2, Week 3:** *We Like Bugs!* (A), *The Bugs Run* (O), *I See a Bug!* (B) **Unit 3, Week 1:** *We Run* (A), *Go, Nat!* (O) **Unit 3, Week 2:** *A Noisy Night* (B) **Unit 4, Week 2:** *My Neighbors* (A), *Neighborhood Party* (O), *Parade Day* (B) **Unit 5, Week 1:** *My Garden* (A), *My Garden Grows* (O) **Unit 6, Week 2:** *The Rain* (A), *Weather Is Fun* (O), *Kate and Tuck* (B) **Unit 7, Week 3:** *We Want Water* (A), *A New Home* (O), *Bird's New Home* (B) **Unit 8, Week 3:** *Going Up* (A), *In the Clouds* (O), *How Sun and Moon Found Home* (B) **Unit 9, Week 1:** *Let Me Help You* (A), *How Can Jane Help?* (O), *I Used to Help Too* (B) **Unit 10, Week 1:** *Animal Band* (A), *We Want Honey* (O), *A Good Idea* (B) **YOUR TURN PRACTICE BOOK:** 29, 37, 45, 234 **READING WORKSTATION ACTIVITY CARDS:** 1, 2 **TEACHER'S EDITION:** Unit 1: T23, T106, T189 **Unit 2:** T177, T186-191 **Unit 3:** T25, T104-109 **Unit 4:** T35, T104-108, T142-143, T150-151, T186-191, T224-225, T232-233, T238-239 **Unit 5:** T61, T69, T238-239 **Unit 6:** T23-26, T61, T69, T75, T105-108, T143, T151, T186-191 **Unit 7:** T45, T107 **Unit 8:** T61, T69, T75, T105-108, T186-191 **Unit 9:** T22-26, T61, T69, T75, T104-109 **Unit 10:** T106-110, T145, T153, T159 **LITERATURE BIG BOOKS:** Unit 1, Week 1: *What About Bear?* **Unit 2 Week 3:** *I Love Bugs!* **Unit 3, Week 1:** *How Do Dinosaurs Go to School?* **Unit 4, Week 2:** *What Can You Do With a Paleta?* **Unit 6, Week 1:** *Mama, Is It Summer Yet?* **Unit 6, Week 2:** *Rain* **Unit 7, Week 2:** *The Birthday Pet* **Unit 7, Week 3:** *Bear Snores On* **Unit 8, Week 1:** *When Daddy's Truck Picks Me Up* **Unit 9, Week 2:** *Hen Hears Gossip* **Unit 10, Week 2:** *All Kinds of Families* **INTERACTIVE READ-ALOUD CARDS:** SS: "The Ugly Duckling", "Tikki Tikki Tembo" **Unit 1, Week 1:** "The Lion and the Mouse" **Unit 1, Week 2:** "The Tortoise and the Hare" **Unit 2, Week 1:** "Timimoto" **Unit 4, Week 1:** "Little Juan and the Cooking Pot" **Unit 4, Week 3:** "A Bundle of Sticks"
RL.K.2	With prompting and support, retell familiar stories, including key details.	**LEVELED READERS:** Unit 1, Week 2: *Hop!* (A), *We Hop!* (O, ELL), *We Can Move!* (B) **Unit 2, Week 3:** *I See a Bug!* (B) **Unit 3, Week 1:** *We Run* (A), *Go, Nat!* (O, ELL), *The Birdhouse* (B) **Unit 3, Week 2:** *City Sounds* (A), *Farm Sounds* (O, ELL), *A Noisy Night* (B) **Unit 4, Week 3:** *We Clean!* (A), *Can You Fix It?* (O, ELL), *Helping Mom* (B) **Unit 5, Week 1:** *The Mystery Seeds* (B) **Unit 6, Week 1:** *It Is Hot!* (A), *Little Bear* (O, ELL), *Ant and Grasshopper* (B) **Unit 6, Week 2:** *The Rain* (A), *Weather Is Fun* (O, ELL), *Kate and Tuck* (B) **Unit 8, Week 1:** *I Go Places* (A), *Run, Quinn!* (O, ELL), *Going to Gran's House* (B) **Unit 10, Week 2:** *My Box* (A), *Let's Make a Band* (O, ELL), *Going Camping* (B) **READING WORKSTATION ACTIVITY CARDS:** 5 **YOUR TURN PRACTICE BOOK:** 157, 167 **TEACHER'S EDITION:** Unit 1: T27, T109, T191 **Unit 2:** T75, T109, T143, T151, T157, T161, T186-191 **Unit 3:** T27, T109, T191 **Unit 4:** T109, T143, T151, T157, T225, T233, T239 **Unit 5:** T61, T69, T75, T79, T109, T143, T151, T157, T191, T225, T233, T239 **Unit 6:** T27, T61, T109, T191, T225 **Unit 7:** T109, T143, T144, T151, T157, T158, T191, T225, T233, T239 **Unit 8:** T61, T69, T75, T143, T151, T157, T191, T225, T233, T239 **Unit 9:** T27, T61, T69, T75, T79, T109, T143, T151, T159, T225, T233, T239 **Unit 10:** T29, T63, T71, T77, T81, T111, T145, T153, T157, T191, T227, T235, T241 **LITERATURE BIG BOOKS:** Unit 1, Week 1: *What About Bear?* **Unit 1, Week 2:** *Pouch!* **Unit 3, Week 1:** *How Do Dinosaurs Go to School?* **Unit 3, Week 2:** *Clang! Clang! Beep! Beep! Listen to the City* **Unit 6, Week 1:** *Mama, Is It Summer Yet?* **Unit 7, Week 2:** *The Birthday Pet*

Reading Standards for Literature

Key Ideas and Details		McGraw-Hill Reading Wonders
RL.K.3	With prompting and support, identify characters, settings, and major events in a story.	**LEVELED READERS: Unit 1, Week 2:** *Hop!* (A), *We Hop!* (O), *We Can Move!* (B) **Unit 2, Week 3:** *The Bugs Run* (O) **Unit 3, Week 2:** *A Noisy Night* (B) **Unit 3, Week 3:** *We Can Go* (A), *Going by Cab* (O), *Cal's Busy Week* (B) **Unit 4, Week 2:** *My Neighbors* (A), *Neighborhood Party* (O) **Unit 5, Week 1:** *My Garden* (A), *My Garden Grows* (O), *The Mystery Seeds* (B) **Unit 7, Week 2:** *My Cats* (A), *Their Pets* (O), *Will's Pet* (B) **Unit 8, Week 1:** *I Go Places* (A), *Run, Quinn!* (O), *Going to Gran's House* (B) **Unit 9, Week 2:** *Mike Helps Out* (A), *Clive and His Friend* (O), *Farmer White's Best Friend* **YOUR TURN PRACTICE BOOK:** 129, 217, 234 **READING WORKSTATION ACTIVITY CARDS:** 3, 4, 6, 7, 10, 11 **TEACHER'S EDITION: Unit 1:** T75, T108 **Unit 3:** T156-157, T186-191, T224-225 **Unit 4:** T104-109, T142-143, T150-151 **Unit 5:** T22-27, T60-61, T68-69, T74-75 **Unit 7:** T104-109, T142-143, T150-151, T156-157, T186-191, T224-225, T232-233, T238-239 **Unit 8:** T22-27, T60-61, T68-69, T75, T186-191 **Unit 9:** T22-29, T60-61, T68-69, T74-75, T104-109, T117, T142-143, T150-151, T156-157 **Unit 10:** T22-29, T62-63, T70-71, T76-77 **LITERATURE BIG BOOKS: Unit 3, Week 3:** *Please Take Me for a Walk* **Unit 4, Week 2:** *What Can You Do with a Paleta?* **Unit 7, Week 3:** *Bear Snores On* **Unit 8, Week 3:** *Bringing Down the Moon* **Unit 9, Week 1:** *Peter's Chair* **Unit 9, Week 2:** *Hen Hears Gossip* **Unit 10, Week 1:** *What's the Big Idea, Molly?* **INTERACTIVE READ-ALOUD CARDS: SS:** "The Ugly Duckling", "Tikki Tikki Tembo" **Unit 1, Week 1:** "The Lion and the Mouse" **Unit 1, Week 2:** "The Tortoise and the Hare" **Unit 3, Week 1:** "The Boy Who Cried Wolf" **Unit 4, Week 1:** "Little Juan and the Cooking Pot" **Unit 7, Week 3:** "Anansi: An African Tale" **Unit 9, Week 2:** "The Little Red Hen"

Craft and Structure		McGraw-Hill Reading Wonders
RL.K.4	Ask and answer questions about unknown words in a text.	**READING/WRITING WORKSHOP BIG BOOK: Unit 1, Week 2:** 32-37 **Unit 2, Week 1:** 8-13 **LEVELED READERS: Unit 4, Week 3:** *We Clean!* (A), *Can You Fix It?* (O, ELL), *Helping Mom* (B) **TEACHER'S EDITION: Unit 1:** T74 **Unit 4:** T127, T225, T238 **Unit 6:** T23, T189 **Unit 7:** T45 **Unit 9:** T45 **Unit 10:** T47
RL.K.5	Recognize common types of texts (e.g., storybooks, poems).	**LEVELED READERS: Unit 6, Week 1:** *Ant and Grasshopper* (B) **TEACHER'S EDITION: Unit 1:** T25, T208, T218 **Unit 4:** T126-127 **Unit 5:** T44-45, T54-55 **Unit 6:** T44, T74-75, T186 **Unit 7:** T44-45 **Unit 9:** T44-45, T126 **Unit 10:** T46 **LITERATURE BIG BOOK: Unit 1, Week 3:** *I Smell Springtime* **Unit 5, Week 1:** *Tommy* **Unit 6, Week 1:** *Covers* **Unit 7, Week 1:** *Kitty Caught a Caterpillar* **INTERACTIVE READ-ALOUD CARDS: SS:** "The Ugly Duckling", "Tikki Tikki Tembo" **Unit 1, Week 1:** "The Lion and the Mouse" **Unit 1, Week 2:** "The Tortoise and the Hare" **Unit 2, Week 1:** "Timimoto" **Unit 3, Week 1:** "The Boy Who Cried Wolf" **Unit 4, Week 3:** "A Bundle of Sticks" **Unit 5, Week 2:** "The Pine Tree" **Unit 6, Week 2:** "The Frog and the Locust" **Unit 6, Week 3:** "Rainbow Crow" **Unit 7, Week 3:** "Anansi: An African Tale" **Unit 8, Week 1:** "The King of the Winds" **Unit 9, Week 2:** "The Little Red Hen" **Unit 9, Week 3:** "Spider Woman Teaches the Navajo" **Unit 10, Week 1:** "The Elves and the Shoemakers"
RL.K.6	With prompting and support, name the author and illustrator of a story and define the role of each in telling the story.	**LEVELED READERS: Unit 2, Week 3:** *I See a Bug!* (B) **Unit 4, Week 2:** *Parade Day* (B), *Helping Mom* (B) **Unit 10, Week 1:** *A Good Idea* (B) **TEACHER'S EDITION: Unit 1:** T68, T94, T142 **Unit 2:** T176, T238-239 **Unit 3:** T12, T94, T176 **Unit 4:** T94, T156, T238 **Unit 5:** T12 **Unit 6:** T12, T94, T176 **Unit 7:** T94, T176 **Unit 8:** T12, T176 **Unit 9:** T12, T94-95 **Unit 10:** T12, T76, T96 **LITERATURE BIG BOOKS: Unit 1, Week 1:** *What About Bear?* **Unit 1, Week 2:** *Pouch!* **Unit 2, Week 3:** *I Love Bugs!* **Unit 3, Week 1:** *How Do Dinosaurs Go to School?* **Unit 5, Week 1:** *My Garden* **Unit 6, Week 2:** *Rain* **Unit 7, Week 2:** *The Birthday Pet* **Unit 8, Week 1:** *When Daddy's Truck Picks Me Up* **Unit 9, Week 2:** *Hen Hears Gossip* **Unit 10, Week 1:** *What's the Big Idea, Molly?* **READING WORKSTATION ACTIVITY CARDS:** 6

Reading Standards for Literature

Integration of Knowledge and Ideas		*McGraw-Hill Reading Wonders*
RL.K.7	With prompting and support, describe the relationship between illustrations and the story in which they appear (e.g., what moment in a story an illustration depicts).	**LEVELED READERS:** Unit 5, Week 1: *My Garden Grows* (O, ELL) Unit 5, Week 3: *Farm Fresh Finn* (B) Unit 6, Week 1: *It Is Hot!* Unit 7, Week 3: *Bird's New Home* (B) **READING WORKSTATION ACTIVITY CARDS:** 1, 4, 11 **TEACHER'S EDITION:** Unit 1: T25, T60-61, T108 Unit 3: T24, T60-T61, T68-T69 Unit 5: T22-27, T68-69, T238-239 Unit 6: T25, T60-61, T105, T188 Unit 7: T238-239 Unit 8: T25 Unit 10: T46-47 **LITERATURE BIG BOOKS:** Unit 1, Week 1: *What About Bear?* Unit 2, Week 3: *I Love Bugs!* Unit 3, Week 1: *How Do Dinosaurs Go to School?* Unit 3, Week 2: *Clang! Clang! Beep! Beep! Listen to the City* Unit 5, Week 1: *My Garden* Unit 6, Week 3: *Waiting Out the Storm* Unit 8, Week 1: *When Daddy's Truck Picks Me Up* Unit 9, Week 1: *The Clean Up!* Unit 10, Week 1: *The Variety Show* Unit 10, Week 2: *All Kinds of Families!* **INTERACTIVE READ-ALOUD CARDS:** Unit 5, Week 2: "The Pine Tree" Unit 6, Week 2: "The Frog and the Locust" Unit 6, Week 3: "Rainbow Crow"
RL.K.8	(Not applicable to literature.)	
RL.K.9	With prompting and support, compare and contrast the adventures and experiences of characters in familiar stories.	**LEVELED READERS:** Unit 3, Week 1: *Go, Nat!* (O, ELL) **READING WORKSTATION ACTIVITY CARD:** 15 **TEACHER'S EDITION:** Unit 1: S27, S51, S75, T35, T117, T136 Unit 2: T218-219 Unit 3: T35, T136, T218-219 Unit 4: T136-137 Unit 6: T54, T117, T136, T199, T218 Unit 7: T136-137, T199, T218 Unit 8: T35, T54, T218 Unit 9: T54, T117, T136 Unit 10: T37, T56, T138 **LITERATURE BIG BOOKS:** Unit 1, Week 1: *What About Bear?* Unit 1, Week 2: *Pouch!, Baby Animals on the Move* **INTERACTIVE READ-ALOUD CARDS:** Unit 1, Week 1: "The Lion and the Mouse" Unit 1, Week 2: "The Tortoise and the Hare" Unit 2, Week 1: "Timimoto" Unit 7, Week 3: "Anansi: An African Tale" Unit 8, Week 1: "The King of the Winds" Unit 10, Week 1: "The Elves and the Shoemakers"

Range of Reading and Level of Text Complexity		*McGraw-Hill Reading Wonders*
RL.K.10	Actively engage in group reading activities with purpose and understanding.	**READING/WRITING WORKSHOP BIG BOOKS:** SS: 36-41 Unit 1: 34-39, 46-51 Unit 2: 10-15, 28-33, 34-39 Unit 3: 10-15, 28-33, 46-51 Unit 4: 24-31, 38-45 Unit 5: 10-17, 38-45 Unit 6: 24-31, 38-45 Unit 7: 24-31, 38-45 Unit 8: 10-17, 24-31 Unit 9: 10-17, 24-31 Unit 10: 10-17, 24-31 **LEVELED READERS:** Unit 5, Week 1: *My Garden Grows* (ELL) Unit 7, Week 2: *Their Pets* (ELL) Unit 7, Week 3: *A New Home* (ELL) **TEACHER'S EDITION:** Unit 1: S12, S14, S17, S22, S24, S31, S36, S38, S41, S46, S48, S55, S62, S65, S70, S72, T22-27, T126-127 Unit 2: T30-31, T112-113, T130-131 Unit 3: T34-35, T94-95, T212-213 Unit 4: T112-113, T126-127, T130-131, T194-195, T199 Unit 5: T12-13, T48-49, T78-79, T117, T194-195 Unit 6: T12-13, T22-26, T94-95, T104-108, T117, T130-131, T176-177, T186-190, T194-195, T199 Unit 7: T112-113, T130-131, T160-161, T176-177, T194-195, T199, T212-213, T242-243 Unit 8: T12-13, T30-31, T34-35, T48-49, T112-113, T176-177, T212-213 Unit 9: T12-13, T30-31, T48-49, T94-95, T112-113, T117, T199, T212-213 Unit 10: T12-13, T32-33, T50-51, T96-97, T132-133 **INTERACTIVE READ-ALOUD CARDS:** SS: "The Ugly Duckling", "Tikki Tikki Tembo" Unit 1, Week 1: "The Lion and the Mouse" Unit 1, Week 2: "The Tortoise and the Hare" Unit 3, Week 2: "The Turtle and the Flute" Unit 4, Week 1: "Little Juan and the Cooking Pot" Unit 4, Week 3: "A Bundle of Sticks" Unit 5, Week 2: "The Pine Tree" Unit 6, Week 2: "The Frog and the Locust" Unit 6, Week 3: "Rainbow Crow" Unit 7, Week 3: "Anansi: An African Tale" Unit 8, Week 1: "The King of the Winds" Unit 9, Week 2: "The Little Red Hen" Unit 9, Week 3: "Spider Woman Teaches the Navajo" Unit 10, Week 1: "The Elves and the Shoemakers"

Reading Standards for Informational Text

Key Ideas and Details		McGraw-Hill Reading Wonders
RI.K.1	With prompting and support, ask and answer questions about key details in a text.	**READING/WRITING WORKSHOP BIG BOOKS:** Unit 2: 14-19 **LEVELED READERS:** Unit 1, Week 3: *The Beach* (A), *At School* (O), *See It Grow!* (B) **Unit 2, Week 1:** *We Need Tools* (A), *A Trip* (O), *What Can You See?* (B) **Unit 2, Week 2:** *Shapes!* (A), *Play with Shapes!* (O), *Use a Shape!* (B) **Unit 4, Week 1:** *You Cook* (A), *On the Job* (O), *The Neighborhood* (B) **Unit 8, Week 2:** *See This!* (A), *Places to See* (O), *My Trip to Yellowstone* (B) **Unit 9, Week 3:** *Look Where It is From* (A), *What's for Breakfast?* (O), *Nature at the Craft Fair* (B) **Unit 10, Week 3:** *Help Clean Up* (A), *Let's Save Earth* (O), *Babysitters for Seals* (B) **YOUR TURN PRACTICE BOOK:** 53, 147 **READING WORKSTATION ACTIVITY CARDS:** 1 **TEACHER'S EDITION: Unit 1:** T126-127, T186-191, T225, **Unit 2:** T22-27, T44-45, T107 **Unit 4:** T22-27, T44-45, T61, T69, T75, T186-191, T208-209 **Unit 5:** T104-109, T151, T157, T186-191, T209 **Unit 6:** T23-26, T105-108, T187-188 **Unit 7:** T23, T25 **Unit 8:** T104-109, T126-127, T142-143, T151, T157, T209 **Unit 9:** T35, T127, T186-191 **Unit 10:** T188-193, T227, T241 **LITERATURE BIG BOOKS: Unit 1, Week 2:** *Baby Animals on the Move* **Unit 1, Week 3:** *Senses at the Seashore* **Unit 2, Week 1:** *The Handiest Things in the World, Discover with Tools* **Unit 4, Week 1:** *Whose Shoes?* "*A Shoe for Every Job*" **Unit 4, Week 3:** *Roadwork* **Unit 5, Week 2:** *A Grand Old Tree* **Unit 5, Week 3:** *An Orange in January* **Unit 7, Week 1:** *ZooBorns!* **Unit 9, Week 3:** *Bread Comes to Life* **Unit 10, Week 3:** *Panda Kindergarten* **INTERACTIVE READ-ALOUD CARDS: SS:** "Kindergarteners Can!" **Unit 1, Week 3:** "A Feast of the Senses" **Unit 2, Week 3:** "From Caterpillar to Butterfly" **Unit 4, Week 2:** "Cultural Festivals" **Unit 9, Week 1:** "Helping Out at Home" **Unit 10, Week 2:** "The Perfect Color"
RI.K.2	With prompting and support, identify the main topic and retell key details of a text.	**LEVELED READERS: Unit 1, Week 3:** *The Beach* (A), *At School* (O, ELL), *See It Grow!* (B) **Unit 2, Week 1:** *We Need Tools* (A), *A Trip* (O, ELL), *What Can You See?* (B) **Unit 5, Week 2:** *The Tree* (A), *Many Trees* (O, ELL), *Our Apple Tree* (B) **Unit 5, Week 3:** *The Farmers' Market* (A), *Let's Make a Salad!* (O, ELL) **Unit 9, Week 3:** *Look Where It Is From* (A) **READING WORKSTATION ACTIVITY CARDS:** 5 **TEACHER'S EDITION: Unit 4:** T191 **Unit 5:** T104-109, T126-127, T142-143, T150-151, T156-157, T186-T190, T208-209, T224-225 **Unit 8:** T104-109, T127, T160-161, T248-249 **Unit 9:** T127, T186-191, T224-225, T232-233, T248-249 **Unit 10:** T188-193, T211, T226-227, T240-241, T250-251 **LITERATURE BIG BOOKS: Unit 1, Week 3:** *Senses on the Seashore* **Unit 5, Week 2:** *A Grand Old Tree,* "From a Seed to a Tree" **Unit 5, Week 3:** *An Orange in January* **Unit 8, Week 2:** *Ana Goes to Washington, D.C.* **Unit 9, Week 3:** *Bread Comes to Life* **Unit 10, Week 3:** *Panda Kindergarten* **INTERACTIVE READ-ALOUD CARDS: Unit 1, Week 3:** "A Feast of the Senses" **Unit 2, Week 3:** "From Caterpillar to Butterfly" **Unit 4, Week 2:** "Cultural Festivals" **Unit 9, Week 1:** "Helping Out at Home" **Unit 10, Week 2:** "The Perfect Color"
RI.K.3	With prompting and support, describe the connection between two individuals, events, ideas, or pieces of information in a text.	**LEVELED READERS: Unit 7:** *Two Cubs* (A), *Animal Bodies* (O, ELL), *Two Kinds of Bears* (B); **Unit 9:** *Look Where it is From* (A), *What's for Breakfast?* (O, ELL) **READING WORKSTATION ACTIVITY CARDS:** 8, 9 **TEACHER'S EDITION: Unit 6:** T24, T25, T106 **Unit 7:** T22-26, T60-61, T68-69, T74-75, T208-209 **Unit 8:** T44-45, T95 **LITERATURE BIG BOOKS: Unit 2, Week 2:** *Shapes All Around* **Unit 7, Week 1:** *ZooBorns!* **Unit 7, Week 3:** "Animal Homes" **Unit 8, Week 1:** *Getting from Here to There* **Unit 8, Week 2:** *Ana Goes to Washington, D.C.* **Unit 9, Week 3:** *Bread Comes to Life* **INTERACTIVE READ-ALOUD CARDS: Unit 2, Week 3:** "From Caterpillar to Butterfly" **Unit 6, Week 1:** "A Tour of the Seasons" **Unit 8, Week 2:** "The Best of the West" **Unit 9, Week 1:** "Helping Out at Home" **Unit 10, Week 3:** "Protect the Environment"

Craft and Structure		McGraw-Hill Reading Wonders
RI.K.4	With prompting and support, ask and answer questions about unknown words in a text.	**LEVELED READERS: Unit 1, Week 3:** *At School* (O, ELL), *See It Grow!* (B) **Unit 2, Week 1:** *A Trip* (O, ELL) **Unit 4, Week 1:** *You Cook* (A), *On the Job* (O, ELL) **Unit 5, Week 2:** *The Tree* (A) **Unit 5, Week 3:** *The Farmers' Market* (A) **Unit 7, Week 1:** *Animal Bodies* (O, ELL) **Unit 9, Week 3:** *Nature at the Craft Fair* (B) **Unit 10, Week 3:** *Let's Save Earth* (O, ELL), *Babysitters for Seals* (B) **TEACHER'S EDITION: Unit 4:** T127 **Unit 5:** T107 **Unit 7:** T209 **Unit 8:** T127, T209 **Unit 10:** T234
RI.K.5	Identify the front cover, back cover, and title page of a book.	**READING/WRITING WORKSHOP: Unit 1:** 8-13, 26-31, 44-49 **Unit 2:** 8-13, 26-31, 44-49 **Unit 3:** 8-13, 26-31, 44-49 **Unit 4:** 8-15, 22-29, 36-43 **LEVELED READERS: Unit 10, Week 3:** *Help Clean Up* (A) **TEACHER'S EDITION: Unit 1:** T30-31, T176 **Unit 4:** T12 **Unit 5:** T94, T176, T232 **Unit 7:** T12, T60, T68, T74, T94 **Unit 8:** T87, T94 **Unit 9:** T176 **Unit 10:** T178, T226 **LITERATURE BIG BOOKS: Unit 1, Week 3:** *Senses at the Seashore* **Unit 2, Week 1:** *The Handiest Things in the World* **Unit 4, Week 1:** *Whose Shoes? A Shoe for Every Job*

Reading Standards for Informational Text

Craft and Structure		McGraw-Hill Reading Wonders
RI.K.6	Name the author and illustrator of a text and define the role of each in presenting the ideas or information in a text.	**LEVELED READERS:** Unit 5, Week 3: *Let's Make a Salad!* (O, ELL), Unit 7, Week 1: *Two Cubs* (A), *Animal Bodies* (O, ELL), *Two Kinds of Bears* (B) **READING WORKSTATION ACTIVITY CARDS:** 12 **TEACHER'S EDITION:** Unit 1: T176 Unit 2: T12 Unit 4: T12 Unit 5: T94, T176, T232 Unit 6: T12, T94, T176 Unit 7: T12, T60, T68, T74, T94 Unit 8: T94 Unit 9: T176 Unit 10: T178 **LITERATURE BIG BOOKS:** Unit 1, Week 3: *Senses at the Seashore* Unit 2, Week 1: *The Handiest Things in the World* Unit 2, Week 2: *Shapes All Around* Unit 8, Week 2: *Ana Goes to Washington, D.C.* Unit 9, Week 3: *Bread Comes to Life*

Integration of Knowledge and Ideas		McGraw-Hill Reading Wonders
RI.K.7	With prompting and support, describe the relationship between illustrations and the text in which they appear (e.g., what person, place, thing, or idea in the text an illustration depicts).	**READING/WRITING WORKSHOP BIG BOOK:** Unit 2, Week 1: 14-19 **LEVELED READERS:** Unit 1, Week 3: *The Beach* (A) Unit 2, Week 1: *We Need Tools* (A) Unit 2, Week 2: *Shapes!* (A), *Play with Shapes!* (O, ELL), *Use a Shape!* (B) Unit 9, Week 3: *What's for Breakfast?* (O, ELL) **READING WORKSTATION ACTIVITY CARDS:** 1 **TEACHER'S EDITION:** Unit 1: T126-T127, T186-191, T224-225 Unit 2: T24, T60-61, T124-T127, 143 Unit 3: T45, 127, T208-209 Unit 4: T22-27 Unit 6: T126-127, T209 Unit 9: T208-209, T232-233 Unit 10: T190, T244-245 **LITERATURE BIG BOOKS:** Unit 1, Week 3: *Senses at the Seashore*, pp. 4-34 Unit 2, Week 1: *The Handiest Things in the World* Unit 2, Week 2: *Shapes All Around* Unit 3, Week 2: *Sounds Are Everywhere* Unit 3, Week 3: *A Neighborhood* Unit 4, Week 1: *Whose Shoes? A Shoe for Every Job* Unit 6, Week 2: *Cloud Watch* Unit 9, Week 3: *Nature's Artists* **INTERACTIVE READ-ALOUD CARDS:** Unit 3, Week 3: "Field Trips" Unit 6, Week 1: "A Tour of the Seasons" Unit 9, Week 1: "Helping Out at Home"
RI.K.8	With prompting and support, identify the reasons an author gives to support points in a text.	**READING WORKSTATION ACTIVITY CARDS:** 12 **TEACHER'S EDITION:** Unit 2: T26, T108 Unit 4: T26, T190 Unit 5: T108, T190 Unit 8: T108 Unit 9: T190 Unit 10: T210-211 **LITERATURE BIG BOOKS:** Unit 1, Week 3: *Senses at the Seashore* Unit 2, Week 1: *The Handiest Things in the World* Unit 2, Week 2: *Shapes All Around* Unit 4, Week 1: *Whose Shoes? A Shoe for Every Job* Unit 4, Week 3: *Roadwork* Unit 5, Week 2: *A Grand Old Tree* Unit 5, Week 3: *An Orange in January* Unit 8, Week 2: *Ana Goes to Washington, D.C.* Unit 9, Week 3: *Bread Comes to Life* Unit 10, Week 3: *Save Big Blue!*
RI.K.9	With prompting and support, identify basic similarities in and differences between two texts on the same topic (e.g., in illustrations, descriptions, or procedures).	**READING/WRITING WORKSHOP BIG BOOK:** Unit 1, Week 3: *A Feast of the Senses* **READING WORKSTATION ACTIVITY CARDS:** 16 **TEACHERS EDITION:** Unit 1: T199 Unit 2: T54-55, T117, T126-127 Unit 4: T116-117, T218-219 Unit 5: T136-137, T198-199, T208-209, T218-219 Unit 7: T35, T54, T117 Unit 8: T136 Unit 9: T218 Unit 10: T128-129, T201, T220 **LITERATURE BIG BOOKS:** Unit 1, Week 3: *Senses at the Seashore* Unit 2, Week 1: *The Handiest Things in the World* Unit 2, Week 2: *Shapes All Around*, "Find the Shapes" Unit 5, Week 3: *An Orange in January*, "Farmers' Market" Unit 10, Week 2: *Good For You* **INTERACTIVE READ-ALOUD CARDS:** Unit 1, Week 3: "A Feast of the Senses" Unit 2, Week 2: "Kites in Flight" Unit 5, Week 3: "Farms Around the World" Unit 7, Week 1: "Baby Farm Animals" Unit 7, Week 2: "The Family Pet" Unit 10, Week 3: "Protect the Environment!"

Range of Reading and Level of Text Complexity		McGraw-Hill Reading Wonders
RI.K.10	Actively engage in group reading activities with purpose and understanding.	**READING/WRITING WORKSHOP BIG BOOKS:** Start Smart: 18-23, 53-58 Unit 1: 10-15, 28-33, 52-57 Unit 2: 16-21, 52-57 Unit 3: 34-39, 52-57 Unit 4: 10-17 Unit 5: 24-31 Unit 6: 10-17 Unit 7: 10-17 Unit 8: 38-45 Unit 9: 38-45 Unit 10: 38-45 **LEVELED READERS:** Unit 5, Week 2: *Many Trees* (ELL) **TEACHER'S EDITION:** Unit 1: S60, T112-113, T126-127, T199 Unit 2: T22-27, T44-45, T74-75, T186-191 Unit 3: T126-127, T198-199, T212-213 Unit 4: T12-13, T30-31, T116-117, T176-177 Unit 5: T34-35, T92-95, T160-161, T174-177, T198-199 Unit 6: T35, T126-127, T208-209 Unit 7: T12-13, T22-27, T30-31, T34-35, T48-49, T116-117 Unit 8: T94-95, T116-117 Unit 9: T34-35, T176-177, T194-195, T208-209 Unit 10: T118-119, T178-179, T201 **INTERACTIVE READ-ALOUD CARDS:** SS: "Kindergarteners Can!" Unit 1, Week 3: "A Feast of the Senses" Unit 2, Week 3: "From Caterpillar to Butterfly" Unit 3, Week 3: "Field Trips" Unit 4, Week 2: "Cultural Festivals" Unit 5, Week 1: "Growing Plants" Unit 5, Week 3: "Farms Around the World" Unit 6, Week 1: "A Tour of the Seasons" Unit 7, Week 1: "Baby Farm Animals" Unit 7, Week 2: "The Family Pet" Unit 8, Week 2: "The Best of the West" Unit 8, Week 3: "A View from the Moon" Unit 9, Week 1: "Helping Out at Home" Unit 10, Week 2: "The Perfect Color" Unit 10, Week 3: "Protect the Environment"

Reading Standards for Foundational Skills

These standards are directed toward fostering students' understanding and working knowledge of concepts of print, the alphabetic principle, and other basic conventions of the English writing system. These foundational skills are not an end in and of themselves; rather, they are necessary and important components of an effective, comprehensive reading program designed to develop proficient readers with the capacity to comprehend texts across a range of types and disciplines. Instruction should be differentiated: good readers will need much less practice with these concepts than struggling readers will. The point is to teach students what they need to learn and not what they already know—to discern when particular children or activities warrant more or less attention.
Note: In Kidergarten, children are expected to demonstrate increasing awareness and competence in the areas that follow.

Print Concepts		McGraw-Hill Reading Wonders
RF.K.1	Demonstrate understanding of the organization and basic features of print.	**TEACHER'S EDITION:** Unit 1: S10, S18, S23, S28, S29, S32, S37, S39, S42, S43, S47, S52, S53, S56, S61, S62, S63, S66, S71, S77, T12, T15, T16, T60, T97, T98, T180, T189, T192 **Unit 2:** T12, T15, T30, T97, T112, T179, T180, T212, T224 **Unit 3:** T15, T26, T94, T97, T106, T112, T130, T142, T176, T179, T211, T232 **Unit 4:** T12, T15, T23, T30, T47, T48, T60, T68, T94, T97, T105, T108, T112, T129, T130, T142, T150, T179, T187, T194, T211, T212, T224 **Unit 5:** T12, T15, T30, T47, T48, T60, T68, T94, T97, T112, T129, T130, T142, T150, T176, T179, T211, T212, T224, T232 **Unit 6:** T12, T15, T29, T37, T47, T97, T129, T179, T211 **Unit 7:** T15, T16, T47, T94, T97, T98, T129, T150, T176, T179, T180, T211, T212, T232 **Unit 8:** T12, T15, T47, T48, T68, T94, T97, T129, T142, T179 **Unit 9:** T12, T15, T25, T47, T60, T94, T97, T129, T142, T176, T179, T211 **Unit 10:** T12, T15, T49, T62, T96, T97, T13, T144, T178, T179, T213
RF.K.1a	Follow words from left to right, top to bottom, and page by page.	**READING/WRITING WORKSHOP:** Start Smart: 4-5, 22-23, 40-41 **LITERATURE BIG BOOK:** Start Smart, Week 3: *ABC Big Book* Unit 4, Week 2: *What Can You Do With a Paleta?* **TEACHER'S EDITION:** Unit 1: S10, S62, T12, T60, T189 **Unit 2:** T30, T112, T224 **Unit 3:** T26, T94, T176 **Unit 4:** T12, T23, T30, T48, T60, T68, T94, T105, T108, T112, T130, T142, T150, T187, T194, T212, T224 **Unit 5:** T68, T94, T112, T130, T142, T150, T176, T212, T224, T232 **Unit 6:** T12 **Unit 7:** T94, T150 **Unit 8:** T12, T68, T94, T142 **Unit 9:** T12, T25, T60, T94, T142 **Unit 10:** T12, T62, T96, T144, T178
RF.K.1b	Recognize that spoken words are represented in written language by specific sequences of letters.	**TEACHER'S EDITION:** Unit 1: S39, S63 **Unit 2:** T212 **Unit 3:** T47-129, T211 **Unit 4:** T47, T129, T211 **Unit 5:** T47, T129, T211 **Unit 6:** T29, T37, T47, T129, T211 **Unit 7:** T47, T129, T176, T211, T212 **Unit 8:** T47, T48, T129, T211 **Unit 9:** T47, T129, T176, T211 **Unit 10:** T49, T131, T213
RF.K.1c	Understand that words are separated by spaces in print.	**TEACHER'S EDITION:** Unit 1: S29, S39, S43, S53, S63, S77 **Unit 2:** T12, T180 **Unit 3:** T94, T106, T112, T130, T142, T232 **Unit 5:** T12, T30, T48, T60, T94 **Unit 7:** T232
RF.K.1d	Recognize and name all upper- and lowercase letters of the alphabet.	**YOUR TURN PRACTICE BOOK:** 3, 7, 8, 11, 15, 16, 20, 24, 34, 42, 50, 58, 66, 84, 92, 100, 108, 116, 134, 142, 143-144, 162, 172, 192, 202, 212, 222, 232 **TEACHER'S EDITION:** Unit 1: S23, S18, S23, S28, S32, S37, S42, S47, S52, S56, S61, S66, S71, T15, T16, T97, T98, T180, T192 **Unit 2:** T15, T97, T179 **Unit 3:** T15, T97, T179 **Unit 4:** T15, T97, T179 **Unit 5:** T15, T97, T179 **Unit 6:** T15, T97, T179 **Unit 7:** T15, T16, T97, T98, T179, T180 **Unit 8:** T15, T97, T179 **Unit 9:** T15, T97, T179 **Unit 10:** T15, T97, T179

Phonological Awareness		McGraw-Hill Reading Wonders
RF.K.2	Demonstrate understanding of spoken words, syllables, and sounds (phonemes).	**TEACHER'S EDITION:** Unit 1: S13, S18, S23, S42, S47, S52, S56, S61, S66, S71, T14, T36, T102, T118, T124, T184, T206 **Unit 2:** T14, T20, T42, T70, T96, T102, T124, T144, T178, T184, T206, T210, T226 **Unit 3:** T20, T36, T42, T62, T96, T102, T118, T124, T144, T184, T206, T226 **Unit 4:** T20, T28, T42, T56, T62, T70, T102, T118, T128, T138, T145, T152, T184, T192, T200, T206, T210, T220, T226 **Unit 5:** T14, T20, T28, T36, T42, T62, T63, T72, T102, T110, T118, T124, T138, T144, T145, T152, T184, T192, T206, T210, T226, T227, T234 **Unit 6:** T20, T28, T36, T42, T46, T56, T62, T63, T70, T102, T124, T138, T144, T152, T154, T184, T192, T206, T210, T220, T227, T234 **Unit 7:** T20, T28, T36, T42, T46, T62, T102, T110, T118, T124, T128, T138, T144, T145, T178, T184, T206, T210, T220, T226, T234 **Unit 8:** T20, T28, T42, T46, T56, T62, T63, T102, T110, T118, T124, T128, T138, T144, T145, T152, T184, T200, T206, T226, T227, T234 **Unit 9:** T14, T20, T42, T62, T102, T124, T144, T184, T206, T210, T220, T226, T227, T234 **Unit 10:** T20, T44, T48, T58, T64, T72, T104, T126, T130, T140, T146, T147, T154, T212, T222, T229, T236
RF.K.2a	Recognize and produce rhyming words.	**LITERATURE BIG BOOKS:** Start Smart, Weeks 1-3: *Big Book of Rhymes* **TEACHER'S EDITION:** Unit 1: S23, S42, S47, S52, T102, T124 **Unit 2:** T210 **Unit 3:** T20, T42, T62 **Unit 4:** T184, T206, T226 **Unit 5:** T184, T206, T226 **Unit 6:** T102, T124, T144 **Unit 7:** T102, T124, T144 **Unit 8:** T102, T124, T144 **Unit 9:** T102, T124, T144
RF.K.2b	Count, pronounce, blend, and segment syllables in spoken words.	**LITERATURE BIG BOOK:** Smart Start, Week 3: *Big Book of Rhymes* **TEACHER'S EDITION:** Unit 1: S56, S61, S66, S71 **Unit 2:** T184, T206, T226 **Unit 3:** T184, T206, T226 **Unit 5:** T20, T42, T62 **Unit 9:** T20, T42, T62, T184, T206, T226 **Unit 10:** T20, T44, T64

Reading Standards for Foundational Skills

Phonological Awareness		McGraw-Hill Reading Wonders
RF.K.2c	Blend and segment onsets and rimes of single-syllable spoken words.	**YOUR TURN PRACTICE BOOK:** 88, 96, 104, 112, 124, 130, 138, 148, 158, 168, 182, 183, 188, 198, 208, 228, 242, 243, 248, 256, 264, 272, 280, 293 **TEACHER'S EDITION:** Unit 1: T184, T206 **Unit 2:** T102, T124, T144 **Unit 3:** T102, T124, T144 **Unit 4:** T20, T42, T62 **Unit 5:** T102, T124, T144 **Unit 6:** T20, T42, T62 **Unit 7:** T20, T42, T62, T184, T206, T226 **Unit 8:** T20, T42, T62, T184, T206, T226 **Unit 10:** T104, T126, T146
RF.K.2d	Isolate and pronounce the initial, medial vowel, and final sounds (phonemes) in in three-phoneme (consonant-vowel-consonant, or CVC) words. (This does not include CVCs ending with /l/, /r/, or /x/.)	**YOUR TURN PRACTICE BOOK:** 80, 193 **TEACHER'S EDITION:** Unit 1: T14, T36, T118 **Unit 2:** T14, T70, T96, T178 **Unit 3:** T36, T96, T118 **Unit 4:** T28, T70, T110, T118, T128, T138, T145, T152, T192, T200, T210, T220 **Unit 5:** T14, T28, T36, T63, T72, T110, T118, T138, T145, T152, T192 **Unit 6:** T28, T36, T46, T56, T62, T63, T70, T138, T152, T154, T184, T192, T206 **Unit 7:** T28, T36, T110, T118, T178 **Unit 8:** T28, T46, T56, T63, T110, T118, T145, T152
RF.K.2e	Add or substitute individual sounds (phonemes) in simple, one-syllable words to make new words.	**TEACHER'S EDITION:** Unit 5: T210, T220, T227, T234 **Unit 6:** T210, T220, T227, T234 **Unit 7:** T128, T138, T145, T152, T210, T220, T227, T234 **Unit 8:** T128, T138, T145, T152, T200, T227, T234 **Unit 9:** T210, T220, T227, T234 **Unit 10:** T48, T58, T72, T130, T140, T147, T154, T212, T222, T229, T236
Phonics and Word Recognition		**McGraw-Hill Reading Wonders**
RF.K.3	Know and apply grade-level phonics and word analysis skills in decoding words.	**TEACHER'S EDITION:** Unit 1: S19, S43, S67, T28, T29, T97, T105, T121, T179, T181, T210, T211, T220, T245 **Unit 2:** T15, T39, T46, T97, T128-129, T179, T203, T221 **Unit 3:** T15, T38, T39, T46, T56, T97, T110, T111, T128, T179, T181, T210 **Unit 4:** T15, T17, T28-29, T30-31, T37, T39, T46, T47, T48-49, T57, T66, T73, T76, T81, T97, T99, T110, T111, T112-113, T121, T128, T129, T130-131, T139, T148, T155, T158, T163, T179, T181, T193, T194-195, T203, T210, T211, T212-213, T221, T230, T237, T240, T245 **Unit 5:** T14, T17, T28, T29, T30-31, T36, T39, T47, T48-49, T56, T57, T66, T73, T76, T81, T99, T110-111, T112-113, T118, T119, T121, T128, T129, T130-131, T138, T139, T146, T148, T153, T155, T158, T163, T181, T192, T193, T194-195, T200, T203, T210, T211, T212-213, T220, T221, T228, T230, T237, T240, T245 **Unit 6:** T15, T17, T29, T30-31, T39, T46, T47, T48-49, T57, T66, T73, T81, T97, T99, T111, T112-113, T121, T128, T129, T130-131, T139, T148, T155, T158, T163, T178, T179, T181, T193, T194-195, T201, T203, T210, T212-213, T221, T230, T237, T240, T245 **Unit 7:** T15, T17, T28-29, T30-31, T37, T46, T47, T48-49, T56, T57, T64, T65, T66, T73, T76, T81, T96, T97, T99, T110, T112-113, T119, T121, T128, T129, T130-131, T139, T146, T148, T155, T158, T163, T178, T179, T181, T192, T193, T194-195, T201, T203, T210, T211, T212-213, T220, T221, T230, T237, T240, T245 **Unit 8:** T15, T17, T29, T30-31, T39, T46, T47, T48-49, T57, T66, T73, T76, T81, T97, T99, T111, T112-113, T121, T128, T129, T130-131, T139, T148, T155, T158, T163, T179, T181, T193, T194-195, T201, T203, T210, T211, T212-213, T220, T221, T230, T237, T240, T245 **Unit 9:** T15, T17, T29, T30-31, T37, T39, T46, T47, T48-49, T56, T57, T64, T65, T66, T71, 72, T73, T76, T81, T97, T99, T110-111, T112-113, T119, T120, T121, T128, T129, T130-131, T138, T139, T146, T147, T148, T153, T154, T155, T158, T163, T179, T181, T192-193, T194-195, T201, T202, T203, T210, T211, T212-213, T220, T221, T228, T229, T230, T235, T236, T237, T240, T245 **Unit 10:** T15, T17, T30-31, T32-33, T39, T40, T41, T48, T49, T50-51, T58, T59, T66, T67, T68, T74, T75, T83, T97, T99, T101, T110, T112-113, T114-115, T121, T123, T130, T131, T140, T141, T148, T149, T150, T156, T157, T160, T165, T179, T181, T182, T183, T191, T194-195, T196-197, T203, T204, T205, T212-213, T222, T223, T230, T231, T232, T238, T239, T242, T247
RF.K.3a	Demonstrate basic knowledge of one-to-one letter-sound correspondences by producing the primary or many of the most frequent sounds for each consonant.	**PHONICS/WORD STUDY WORKSTATION ACTIVITY CARDS:** 1, 2, 3, 4, 5, 6, 7, 8, 9, 10, 11, 12, 13, 14, 15, 16, 17, 18, 19, 20, 21, 22, 23, 24 **TEACHER'S EDITION:** Unit 1: T28, T179, T210, T220 **Unit 2:** T15, T97, T179 **Unit 3:** T97, T110, T179 **Unit 4:** T97, T110, T179 **Unit 5:** T14, T28, T36, T56, T118, T138, T192, T200, T220, T228 **Unit 6:** T15, T97, T179 **Unit 7:** T56, T96, T97, T110, T146, T178, T179, T192, T220 **Unit 8:** T15, T97, T179 **Unit 10:** T97, T110, T179

Reading Standards for Foundational Skills

Phonics and Word Recognition		*McGraw-Hill Reading Wonders*
RF.K.3b	Associate the long and short sounds with the common spellings (graphemes) for the five major vowels.	**YOUR TURN PRACTICE BOOK:** 36, 62, 101-102, 135-136, 138, 246, 248, 254, 256, 262, 264, 270, 278 **PHONICS/WORD STUDY WORKSTATION ACTIVITY CARDS:** 2, 7, 10, 14, 19, 25, 26, 27, 28, 29, 30 **TEACHER'S EDITION:** Unit 1: T97, T105 Unit 2: T46, T128–T129, T221 Unit 3: T15, T38, T56 Unit 4: T15, T28-29, T37 Unit 5: T110-111, T119, T146, T153 Unit 6: T193, T201, T211 Unit 7: T15, T28-29, T37, T46, T64, T65, T119, T201 Unit 8: T201, T220 Unit 9: T15, T29, T37, T56, T64, T65, T71, 72, T76, T97, T110-111, T119, T120, T138, T146, T147, T153, T154, T179, T192-193, T201, T202, T220, T228, T229, T235, T236 Unit 10: T15, T30-31, T39, T40, T58, T66, T67, T74, T99, T112-113, T121, T140, T148, T149, T156, T181, T182, T191, T194-195, T203, T204, T222, T230, T231, T238

Phonological Awareness		*McGraw-Hill Reading Wonders*
RF.K.3c	Read common high-frequency words by sight (e.g., *the, of, to, you, she, my, is, are, do, does*).	**READING/WRITING WORKSHOP:** Start Smart: 9, 16-22, 27 Unit 1: 7-13, 14-19, 25-31 Unit 2: 7-13, 14-19, 25-31 Unit 3: 7-13, 25-31, 32-37 Unit 4: 7-15, 21-29, 35-43 Unit 5: 7-15, 21-29, 35-43 Unit 6: 7-15, 21-29, 35-43 Unit 7: 7-15, 21-29, 35-43 Unit 8: 7-15, 21-29, 35-43 Unit 9: 7-15, 21-29, 35-43 Unit 10: 7-15, 21-29, 35-43 **YOUR TURN PRACTICE BOOK:** 4, 9-10, 12, 17-18, 21, 25-26], 31-32, 39-40, 47-48, 55-56, 63-64, 71-72, 89-90, 97-98, 105-106, 113-114,121-122, 131-132, 139-140, 149-150, 159-160, 169-170, 179-180, 189-190, 199-200, 209-210, 219-220, 229-230, 239-240, 249-250, 257-258, 265-266, 273-274, 281-282, 291-292 **TEACHER'S EDITION:** Unit 1: S19, S43, S67, T29, T121, T181, T211, T245 Unit 2: T39, T129, T203 Unit 3: T39, T111, T181 Unit 4: T17, T29, T30-31, T39, T47, T48-49, T57, T66, T73, T76, T81, T99, T111, T112-113, T121, T129, T130-131, T139, T148, T155, T158, T163, T181, T193, T194-195, T203, T211, T212-213, T221, T230, T237, T240, T245 Unit 5: T17, T29, T30-31, T39, T47, T48-49, T57, T66, T73, T76, T81, T99, T111, T112-113, T121, T129, T130-131, T139, T148, T155, T158, T163, T181, T193, T194-195, T203, T211, T212-213, T221, T230, T237, T240, T245 Unit 6: T17, T29, T30-31, T39, T47, T48-49, T57, T66, T73, T81, T99, T111, T112-113, T121, T129, T130-131, T139, T148, T155, T158, T163, T181, T193, T194-195, T203, T211, T212-213, T221, T230, T237, T240, T245 Unit 7: T17, T29, T30-31, T39, T47, T48-49, T57, T66, T73, T76, T81, T99, T111, T112-113, T121, T129, T130-131, T139, T148, T155, T158, T163, T181, T193, T194-195, T203, T211, T212-213, T221, T230, T237, T240, T245 Unit 8: T17, T29, T30-31, T39, T47, T48-49, T57, T66, T73, T76, T81, T99, T111, T112-113, T121, T129, T130-131, T139, T148, T155, T158, T163, T181, T193, T194-195, T203, T211, T212-213, T221, T230, T237, T240, T245 Unit 9: T17, T29, T30-31, T39, T47, T48-49, T57, T66, T73, T76, T81, T99, T111, T112-113, T121, T129, T130-131, T139, T148, T155, T158, T163, T181, T193, T194-195, T203, T211, T212-213, T221, T230, T237, T240, T245 Unit 10: T17, T31, T32-33, T41, T49, T50-51, T59, T68, T75, T78, T83, T101, T113, T114-115, T123, T131, T141, T150, T157, T160, T165, T183, T195, T196-197, T205, T212-213, T223, T232, T239, T242, T247
RF.K.3d	Distinguish between similarly spelled words by identifying the sounds of the letters that differ.	**TEACHER'S EDITION:** Unit 2: T46, T128 Unit 3: T46, T128, T210 Unit 4: T46, T128, T210 Unit 5: T128, T210 Unit 6: T46, T128, T210 Unit 7: T46, T128, T210 Unit 8: T46, T128, T210 Unit 9: T46, T128, T210 Unit 10: T48, T130, T212

Reading Standards for Foundational Skills

Fluency		McGraw-Hill Reading Wonders
RF.K.4	Read emergent-reader texts with purpose and understanding.	**READING/WRITING WORKSHOP:** Unit 1: 32-37, 44-49, 50-55 Unit 2: 32-37, 44-49, 50-55 Unit 3: 8-13, 32-37, 50-55 Unit 4: 8-15, 22-29, 36-43 Unit 5: 8-15, 22-29, 36-43 Unit 6: 8-15, 22-29, 36-43 Unit 7: 8-15, 22-29, 36-43 Unit 8: 8-15, 22-29, 36-43 Unit 9: 8-15, 22-29, 36-43 Unit 10: 8-15, 22-29, 36-43 **LEVELED READERS:** Unit 1, Week 1: *Soup!* (A), *Mouse and Monkey* (O, ELL), *Come and Play!* (B) **Unit 1 Week 2:** *Hop!* (A), *We Hop!* (O, ELL) *We Can Move!* (B) **Unit 1, Week 3:** *The Beach* (A), *At School* (O, ELL), *See It Grow!* (B) **Unit 2, Week 1:** *We Need Tools* (A), *A Trip* (O, ELL), *What Can You See?* (B) **Unit 2, Week 2:** *Shapes!* (A), *Play with Shapes!* (O, ELL), *Use a Shape!* (B) **Unit 2, Week 3:** *We Like Bugs!* (A), *The Bugs Run* (O, ELL), *I See a Bug!* (B) **Unit 3, Week 1:** *We Run* (A), *Go, Nat!* (O, ELL), *The Birdhouse* (B) **Unit 3, Week 2:** *City Sounds* (A), *Farm Sounds* (O, ELL), *A Noisy Night* (B) **Unit 3, Week 3:** *We Can Go* (A), *Going by Cab* (O, ELL), *Cal's Busy Week* (B) **Unit 4, Week 1:** *You Cook* (A), *On the Job* (O, ELL), *The Neighborhood* (B) **Unit 4, Week 2:** *My Neighbors* (A), *Neighborhood Party* (O, ELL), *Parade Day* (B) **Unit 4, Week 3:** *We Clean!* (A) *Can You Fix It?* (O, ELL), *Helping Mom* (B) **Unit 5, Week 1:** *My Garden* (A), *My Garden Grows* (O, ELL), *The Mystery Seeds* (B) **Unit 5, Week 2:** *The Tree* (A), *Many Trees* (O, ELL), *Our Apple Tree* (B) **Unit 5, Week 3:** *The Farmer* (A), *Let's Make a Salad!* (O, ELL), *Farm Fresh Finn* (B) **Unit 6, Week 1:** *It Is Hot!* (A), *Little Bear* (O, ELL), *Ant and Grasshopper* (B) **Unit 6, Week 2:** *The Rain* (A), *Weather Is Fun* (O, ELL), *Kate and Tuck* (B) **Unit 6 Week 3:** *Bad Weather* (A), *Getting Ready* (O, ELL), *The Storm* (B) **Unit 7, Week 1:** *Two Cubs* (A), *Animal Bodies* (O, ELL), *Two Kinds of Bears* (B) **Unit 7, Week 2:** *My Cats* (A), *Their Pets* (O, ELL), *Will's Pet* (B) **Unit 7, Week 3:** *We Want Water* (A) *A New Home* (O, ELL), *Bird's New Home* (B) **Unit 8, Week 1:** *I Go Places* (A), *Run, Quinn!* (O, ELL), *Going to Gran's House* (B) **Unit 8, Week 2:** *See This!* (A), *Places to See* (O, ELL), *My Trip to Yellowstone* (B) **Unit 8, Week 3:** *Going Up* (A), *In the Clouds* (O, ELL), *How Sun and Moon Found Home* (B) **Unit 9, Week 1:** *Let Me Help You* (A), *How Can Jane Help?* (O, ELL), *I Used to Help, Too* (B) **Unit 9, Week 2:** *Mike Helps Out* (A), *Clive and His Friend* (O, ELL), *Farmer White's Best Friend* (B) **Unit 9, Week 3:** *Look Where It Is From* (A), *What's for Breakfast?* (O, ELL), *Nature at the Craft Fair* (B) **Unit 10, Week 1:** *Animal Band* (A), *We Want Honey* (O, ELL), *A Good Idea* (B) **Unit 10, Week 2:** *My Box* (A), *Let's Make a Band* (O, ELL), *Going Camping* (B) **Unit 10, Week 3:** *Help Clean Up* (A), *Let's Save Earth* (O, ELL), *Babysitters for Seals* (B) **TEACHER'S EDITION:** Unit 1: S14, S48, T48-49, T112-113, T150-151, T232-233 Unit 2: T48-49, T130-131, T224-225 Unit 3: T60-61, T130-131, T212-213 Unit 4: T30-31, T48-49, T60-61, T65, T68-69, T72, T74-75, T78-79, T112-113, T130-131, T142-143, T147, T150-151, T156-157, T160-161, T194-195, T212-213, T224-225, T229, T232-233, T236, T238-239, T242-243 Unit 5: T30-31, T48-49, T60-61, T65, T68-69, T72, T74-75, T78-79, T112-113, T130-131, T142-143, T147, T150-151, T156-157, T160-161, T194-195, T212-213, T224-225, T229, T232-233, T236, T238-239, T242-243 Unit 6: T30-31, T48-49, T60-61, T65, T68-69, T72, T74-75, T78-79, T112-113, T130-131, T142-143, T147, T150-151, T194-195, T212-213, T224-225, T229, T232-233, T236 Unit 7: T30-31, T48-49, T60-61, T65, T68-69, T72, T74-75, T78-79, T112-113, T130-131, T142-143, T147, T150-151, T156-157, T160-161, T194-195, T212-213, T224-225, T229, T232-233, T236, T238-239, T242-243 Unit 8: T30-31, T48-49, T60-61, T65, T68-69, T72, T74-75, T78-79, T112-113, T10-131, T142-143, T147, T150-151, T156-157, T160-161, T194-195, T212-213, T224-225, T229, T232-233, T236, T238-239, T242-243 Unit 9: T30-31, T48-49, T60-61, T65, T68-69, T72, T74-75, T78-79, T112-113, T130-131, T142-143, T147, T150-151, T156-157, T160-161, T194-195, T212-213, T224-225, T229, T232-233, T236, T238-239, T242-243 Unit 10: T32-33, T50-51, T62-63, T67, T70-71, T74, T76-77, T80-81, T114-115, T132-133, T144-145, T149, T152-153, T156, T158-159, T162-163, T196-197, T214-215, T226-227, T231, T234-235, T238, T240-241, T244-245

College and Career Readiness Anchor Standards for WRITING

The K–5 standards on the following pages define what students should understand and be able to do by the end of each grade. They correspond to the College and Career Readiness (CCR) anchor standards below by number. The CCR and grade-specific standards are necessary complements—the former providing broad standards, the latter providing additional specificity—that together define the skills and understandings that all students must demonstrate.

Text Types and Purposes

1. Write arguments to support claims in an analysis of substantive topics or texts, using valid reasoning and relevant and sufficient evidence.

2. Write informative/explanatory texts to examine and convey complex ideas and information clearly and accurately through the effective selection, organization, and analysis of content.

3. Write narratives to develop real or imagined experiences or events using effective technique, well-chosen details, and well-structured event sequences.

Production and Distribution of Writing

4. Produce clear and coherent writing in which the development, organization, and style are appropriate to task, purpose, and audience.

5. Develop and strengthen writing as needed by planning, revising, editing, rewriting, or trying a new approach.

6. Use technology, including the Internet, to produce and publish writing and to interact and collaborate with others.

Research to Build and Present Knowledge

7. Conduct short as well as more sustained research projects based on focused questions, demonstrating understanding of the subject under investigation.

8. Gather relevant information from multiple print and digital sources, assess the credibility and accuracy of each source, and integrate the information while avoiding plagiarism.

9. Draw evidence from literary or informational texts to support analysis, reflection, and research.

Range of Writing

10. Write routinely over extended time frames (time for research, reflection, and revision) and shorter time frames (a single sitting or a day or two) for a range of tasks, purposes, and audiences.

CCSS Common Core State Standards
English Language Arts

Grade K

Writing Standards

Text Types and Purposes		McGraw-Hill Reading Wonders
W.K.1	Use a combination of drawing, dictating, and writing to compose opinion pieces in which they tell a reader the topic or the name of the book they are writing about and state an opinion or preference about the topic or book (e.g., My favorite book is…).	**READING/WRITING WORKSHOP:** Unit 1: 38-39 Unit 3: 58 Unit 5: 32-33 Unit 6: 18-19 Unit 9: 18-19 Unit 10: 46-47 **TEACHER'S EDITION:** Unit 1: T87, T100, T114, T122 Unit 3: T196, T204, T214 Unit 5: T100, T114, T122-123, T132, T144 Unit 6: T32, T40, T41 Unit 9: T5, T18, T32, T40-41, T50 Unit 10: T17, T184, T198, T206, T216 **WRITING WORKSTATION ACTIVITY CARDS:** 5, 20
W.K.2	Use a combination of drawing, dictating, and writing to compose informative/explanatory texts in which they name what they are writing about and supply some information about the topic.	**READING/WRITING WORKSHOP:** Unit 2: 20-21 Unit 4: 44 Unit 5: 44-45 Unit 6: 44 Unit 7: 16-17, 44 Unit 8: 30-31 Unit 9: 44 **TEACHER'S EDITION:** Unit 1: S15, S33, S53, S67, S77, T182, T196, T204 Unit 2: T100, T122, T164 Unit 3: T18, T32, T40 Unit 4: T18, T32, T40, T114, T122, T196, T204 Unit 5: T182, T196, T204 Unit 6: T52-53, T135 Unit 7: T18, T32, T40, T100, T114, T122 Unit 8: T53, T100, T114, T122, T135 Unit 9: T182, T196, T204, T214 Unit 10: T18, T34, T42-43, T52 **WRITING WORKSTATION ACTIVITY CARDS:** 18, 23
W.K.3	Use a combination of drawing, dictating and writing to narrate a single event or several loosely linked events, tell about the events in the order in which they occurred, and provide a reaction to what happened.	**READING/WRITING WORKSHOP:** Unit 3: 38-39, 56 Unit 5: 44 Unit 6: 30 Unit 8: 16, 46-47 Unit 9: 30 Unit 10: 16 **TEACHER'S EDITION:** Unit 2: T196, T204, T246 Unit 3: T114, T122, T164 Unit 5: T32, T40, T82, T164, T246 Unit 6: T114, T123, T164, T246 Unit 8: T32, T40, T82, T196, T204 Unit 9: T82, T100, T114, T122-123, T132 Unit 10: T18, T34, T42, T43, T52, T84, T116, T166, T248 **WRITING WORKSTATION ACTIVITY CARDS:** 1, 4, 5, 7, 15

Writing Standards

Production and Distribution of Writing		McGraw-Hill Reading Wonders
W.K.4	(Begins in grade 3.)	
W.K.5	With guidance and support from adults, respond to questions and suggestions from peers and add details to strengthen writing as needed.	**TEACHER'S EDITION: Unit 1:** T32, T40 (Go Digital: Writing), T50, T58 (Go Digital: Writing), T122 (Go Digital: Writing), T132, T140 (Go Digital: Writing), T204 (Go Digital: Writing), T214, T222 (Go Digital: Writing) **Unit 2:** T40 (Go Digital: Writing), T50, T58 (Go Digital: Writing), T122 (Go Digital: Writing), T132, T140 (Go Digital: Writing), T204 (Go Digital: Writing), T214, T222 (Go Digital: Writing) **Unit 3:** T40 (Go Digital: Writing), T50, T58 (Go Digital: Writing), T122 (Go Digital: Writing), T132, T140 (Go Digital: Writing), T204 (Go Digital: Writing), T222 (Go Digital: Writing) **Unit 4:** T40 (Go Digital: Writing), T50, T58 (Go Digital: Writing), T122 (Go Digital: Writing), T132, T140 (Go Digital: Writing), T204 (Go Digital: Writing), T214, T222 (Go Digital: Writing) **Unit 5:** T40 (Go Digital: Writing), T50, T58 (Go Digital: Writing), T122 (Go Digital: Writing), T132, T140 (Go Digital: Writing), T204 (Go Digital: Writing), T214, T222 (Go Digital: Writing) **Unit 6:** T40 (Go Digital: Writing), T50, T58 (Go Digital: Writing), T122 (Go Digital: Writing), T132, T140 (Go Digital: Writing), T204 (Go Digital: Writing), T214, T222 (Go Digital: Writing) **Unit 7:** T40 (Go Digital: Writing), T58 (Go Digital: Writing), T122 (Go Digital: Writing), T140 (Go Digital: Writing), T164, T204 (Go Digital: Writing), T222 (Go Digital: Writing) T246 **Unit 8:** T40 (Go Digital: Writing), T50, T58 (Go Digital: Writing), T122 (Go Digital: Writing), T132, T140 (Go Digital: Writing), T164, T204 (Go Digital: Writing), T214, T222 (Go Digital: Writing), T246 **Unit 9:** T40 (Go Digital: Writing), T50, T58 (Go Digital: Writing), T122 (Go Digital: Writing), T132, T140 (Go Digital: Writing), T204 (Go Digital: Writing), T214, T222 (Go Digital: Writing) **Unit 10:** T42 (Go Digital: Writing), T52, T60 (Go Digital: Writing), T124 (Go Digital: Writing), T134, T142 (Go Digital: Writing), T166, T206 (Go Digital: Writing), T224 (Go Digital: Writing), T248 **WRITING WORKSTATION ACTIVITY CARDS:** 10, 11, 12, 13, 14, 16
W.K.6	With guidance and support from adults, explore a variety of digital tools to produce and publish writing, including in collaboration with peers.	**TEACHER'S EDITION: Unit 1:** T134 **Unit 2:** T216 **Unit 6:** T248-249 **Unit 7:** T52, T134, T216, T248-249 **Unit 8:** T52, T134, T216, T248-249 **Unit 9:** T216, T248-249 **Unit 10:** T218, T250-251 **ConnectED Digital Resources:** My Binder (My Work)
Research to Build and Present Knowledge		**McGraw-Hill Reading Wonders**
W.K.7	Participate in shared research and writing projects (e.g., explore a number of books by a favorite author and express opinions about them).	**TEACHER'S EDITION: Unit 1:** T52, T134, T216 **Unit 2:** T52, T134, T216 **Unit 3:** T52, T134, T216 **Unit 4:** T52, T134, T216 **Unit 5:** T52, T100, T114, T122-123 **Unit 6:** T52, T134, T216 **Unit 7:** T52, T134, T216, T248-249 **Unit 8:** T52, T134, T216 **Unit 9:** T52, T134, T216 **Unit 10:** T54, T136, T218 **WRITING WORKSTATION ACTIVITY CARDS:** 20, 23 **ConnectED Digital Resources:** Collaborate (Projects)
W.K.8	With guidance and support from adults, recall information from experiences or gather information from provided sources to answer a question.	**READING/WRITING WORKSHOP: Unit 7:** 44 **TEACHER'S EDITION: Unit 1:** T32, T40, T100 **Unit 2:** T52, T134, T216 **Unit 3:** T100, T214 **Unit 4:** T18, T52, T100, T134, T182, T216 **Unit 5:** T18, T52, T134, T216 **Unit 6:** T52, T100, T134, T216 **Unit 7:** T50, T52, T132, T134, T196, T204, T214, T216 **Unit 8:** T52, T134, T216 **Unit 9:** T52, T134, T216 **Unit 10:** T54, T102, T136, T218
W.K.9	(Begins in grade 4.)	
Range of Writing		**McGraw-Hill Reading Wonders**
W.K.10	(Begins in grade 3.)	

College and Career Readiness Anchor Standards for **SPEAKING** AND **LISTENING**

The K–5 standards on the following pages define what students should understand and be able to do by the end of each grade. They correspond to the College and Career Readiness (CCR) anchor standards below by number. The CCR and grade-specific standards are necessary complements—the former providing broad standards, the latter providing additional specificity—that together define the skills and understandings that all students must demonstrate.

Comprehension and Collaboration
1. Prepare for and participate effectively in a range of conversations and collaborations with diverse partners, building on others' ideas and expressing their own clearly and persuasively.
2. Integrate and evaluate information presented in diverse media and formats, including visually, quantitatively, and orally.
3. Evaluate a speaker's point of view, reasoning, and use of evidence and rhetoric.

Presentation of Knowledge and Ideas
4. Present information, findings, and supporting evidence such that listeners can follow the line of reasoning and the organization, development, and style are appropriate to task, purpose, and audience.
5. Make strategic use of digital media and visual displays of data to express information and enhance understanding of presentations.
6. Adapt speech to a variety of contexts and communicative tasks, demonstrating command of formal English when indicated or appropriate.

Common Core State Standards
English Language Arts
Grade K

Speaking and Listening Standards

Comprehension and Collaboration		McGraw-Hill Reading Wonders
SL.K.1	Participate in collaborative conversations with diverse partners about kindergarten topics and texts with peers and adults in small and larger groups.	**TEACHER'S EDITION:** Unit 1: S10-11, S44, S58, T11, T54-55, T117, T134, T136-137, T216 Unit 2: T34, T51, T52, T134, T222 Unit 3: T20, T33, T45, T175, T216 Unit 4: T11, T20, T52, T54, T58, T93, T134, T136, T140, T175, T216, T218 Unit 5: T11, T20, T52, T93, T120, T136, T174, T175, T216, T222 Unit 6: T11, T52, T54, T93, T136, T140, T216, T218 Unit 7: T10-11, T52, T54, T55, T93, T134, T136, T137, T175, T218, T219 Unit 8: T11, T54, T58, T80, T92, T93, T134, T136, T140, T175, T218, T222 Unit 9: T10-11, T52, T54, T93, T136, T140, T175, T218, T222 Unit 10: T11, T20, T56, T60, T95, T104, T136, T138, T142, T177, T186, T220, T224
SL.K.1a	Follow agreed-upon rules for discussions (e.g., listening to others and taking turns speaking about the topics and texts under discussion).	**READING/WRITING WORKSHOP:** Unit 1: 6-7, 24-25 Unit 2: 24-25 Unit 3: 6-7, 24-25, 42-43 Unit 4: 6-7, 20-21, 34-35 Unit 5: 6-7, 20-21, 34-35 Unit 6: 6-7, 20-21, 36-43 Unit 7: 6-7, 20-21, 34-35 Unit 8: 6-7, 20-21 Unit 9: 6-7, 8-15, 20-21, 34-35 Unit 10: 6-7, 20-21 **YOUR TURN PRACTICE BOOK:** 31-32, 45, 68, 70-71, 81-82, 93 **READING WORKSTATION ACTIVITY CARDS:** 1, 6, 18, 19 **WRITING WORKSTATION ACTIVITY CARDS:** 1, 11, 13, 21+D89 **TEACHER'S EDITION:** Unit 1: T11, T134, T216 Unit 2: T52, T134, T222 Unit 3: T175, T216 Unit 4: T11, T52, T58, T93, T134, T140, T216 Unit 5: T11, T52, T93, T175, T216 Unit 6: T11, T52, T93, T140, T216 Unit 7: T11, T52, T55, T93, T134, T137, T219 Unit 8: T11, T58, T93, T134, T140, T222 Unit 9: T11, T52, T93, T140, T175, T222 Unit 10: T11, T60, T95, T142, T224
SL.K.1b	Continue a conversation through multiple exchanges.	**READING/WRITING WORKSHOP:** Unit 1: SS4-SS5, SS22-SS23, SS40-SS41, 6-7, 24-25, 42-43 Unit 2: 6-7, 8, 14-19, 24, 25, 42-43, 46, 47, 48, 51, 54, 55, 58 Unit 3: 6-7, 14-19, 24-35, 42-43 Unit 4: 6-7, 20-21, 34-35 Unit 5: 6-7, 20-21, 34-35 Unit 6: 8-15 Unit 7: 6-7, 8-15, 20-21, 22-29, 34-35, 36-43 Unit 8: 6-7, 8-15, 20-21, 22-29, 34-35, 36-43 Unit 9: 6-7, 8-15, 20-21, 22-29, 34-35 Unit 10: 6-7, 8-15, 20-21, 22-29, 34-35, 36-43 **YOUR TURN PRACTICE BOOK:** 29, 45, 53, 61, 68 **READING WORKSTATION ACTIVITY CARDS:** 1, 6, 17, 18 **WRITING WORKSTATION ACTIVITY CARDS:** 1, 9, 11 **PHONICS/WORD STUDY WORKSTATION ACTIVITY CARDS:** W11, W12, R2, R3 **SCIENCE/SOCIAL STUDIES WORKSTATION ACTIVITY CARDS:** W4, W26, R10 **LITERATURE BIG BOOKS:** Smart Start: *Animals in the Park* Unit 2, Week 1: *The Handiest Things in the World* Unit 2, Week 2: *Shapes All Around* Unit 3, Week 2: *Clang! Clang! Beep! Beep! Listen to the City* Unit 4, Week 1: *Whose Shoes? A Shoe for Every Job* Unit 4, Week 2: *What Can You Do with a Paleta?* Unit 4, Week 3: *Roadwork* Unit 5, Week 3: *An Orange in January* Unit 6, Week 1: *Mama, Is It Summer Yet?* Unit 6, Week 2: *Rain* Unit 7, Week 1: *ZooBorns!* Unit 7, Week 2: *The Birthday Pet* Unit 8, Week 1: *When Daddy's Truck Picks Me Up* Unit 8, Week 2: *Ana Goes to Washington, D.C.* Unit 9, Week 3: *Bread Comes to Life* Unit 10, Week 3: *Panda Kindergarten* **TEACHER'S EDITION:** Unit 1: S10-S11, S21, S26-S27, S34-S35, S44-S45, S54, S58-S59, S64, S68-S69, S74-S75, T11, T34, T35, T52, T53, T54-55, T81, T84, T93, T101, T117, T123, T133, T134, T135, T136-137, T162, T175, T183, T197, T199, T215, T216, T217, T218 Unit 2: T11, T19, T33, T41, T51, T52, T64, T93, T134, T136, T137, T175, T204, T215, T216, T217, T218 Unit 3: T11, T19, T54-55, T58, T93, T117, T134, T135, T136-137, T175, T216, T217, T218 Unit 4: T11, T54, T93, T134, T136, T175, T216, T218 Unit 5: T11, T52, T54, T93, T136, T175, T216, T218 Unit 6: T11, T52, T54, T136, T218 Unit 7: T10-11, T52, T54, T93, T134, T136, T175, T218 Unit 8: T11, T54, T58, T80, T92, T93, T136, T140, T175, T218, T222 Unit 9: T10-11, T54, T93, T136, T140, T175, T218 Unit 10: T11, T56, T95, T136, T138, T177, T220 **INTERACTIVE READ-ALOUD CARDS:** Smart Start, Week 1: "The Ugly Duckling" Smart Start, Week 2: "Tikki Tikki Tembo" Smart Start, Week 3: "Kindergarteners Can!" Unit 1, Week 1: "The Lion and the Mouse" Unit 1, Week 2: "The Tortoise and the Hare" Unit 1, Week 3: "A Feast of the Senses" Unit 2, Week 1: "Timimoto" Unit 2, Week 2: "Kites in Flight" Unit 2, Week 3: "From Caterpillar to Butterfly" Unit 3, Week 1: "The Boy Who Cried Wolf" Unit 3, Week 2: "The Turtle and the Flute" Unit 3, Week 3: "Field Trips" Unit 4, Week 1: "Little Juan and the Cooking Pot" Unit 4, Week 2: "Cultural Festivals" Unit 4, Week 3: "The Bundle of Sticks" Unit 5, Week 1: "Growing Plants" Unit 5, Week 2: "The Pine Tree" Unit 5, Week 3: "Farmers Around the World" Unit 6, Week 1: "A Tour of the Seasons" Unit 6, Week 1: "The Frog and the Locust" Unit 6, Week 3: "Rainbow Crow" Unit 7, Week 1: "Baby Farm Animals" Unit 7, Week 2: "The Family Pet" Unit 7, Week 3: "Anansi, An African Tale" Unit 8, Week 1: "The King of the Winds" Unit 8, Week 2: "The Best of the West" Unit 8, Week 3: "A View From the Moon" Unit 9, Week 1: "Helping Out at Home" Unit 9, Week 2: "The Little Red Hen" Unit 9, Week 3: "Spider Woman Teaches the Navajo" Unit 10, Week 1: "The Elves and the Shoemakers" Unit 10, Week 1: "Good for You!" Unit 10, Week 1: "Help Save Big Blue!"

Speaking and Listening Standards

Comprehension and Collaboration	*McGraw-Hill Reading Wonders*
SL.K.2	Confirm understanding of a text read aloud or information presented orally or through other media by asking and answering questions about key details and requesting clarification if something is not understood.	**READING/WRITING WORKSHOP: Unit 1:** 6-7, 26-31, 33, 35, 37, 42-43, 45, 47, 49, 51, 53, 55 **Unit 2:** 6-7, 8, 9, 10, 13, 14-19, 24-25, 27, 28, 30, 33, 34, 35, 46, 47, 48, 51, 54, 55, 58 **Unit 3:** 6-7, 9, 12, 13, 16, 17, 19, 33, 34, 37, 42-43, 46, 47, 49, 51, 53, 55 **Unit 4:** 6-7, 9-15, 20-21, 23-25, 28-29, 34-43 **Unit 5:** 8-15, 23-28 **Unit 6:** 8-15, 22-29 **Unit 7:** 8-15, 18-19, 20-21, 22-29, 34-35, 36-43 **Unit 8:** 6-7, 8-15, 20-21, 22-29, 34-35, 36-43 **Unit 9:** 6-7, 8-15, 20-21, 22-29, 34-35, 36-43 **Unit 10:** 6-7, 8-15, 20-21, 22-29, 34-35, 36-43

LEVELED READERS: Unit 1, Week 3: *The Beach* (A), *See It Grow!* (O, ELL), *At School* (B) **Unit 2, Week 1:** *We Need Tools* (A), *A Trip* (O, ELL), *What Can You See?* (B) **Unit 3, Week 1:** *We Run* (A), *Go, Nat!* (O, ELL), *The Birdhouse* (B) **Unit 4, Week 2:** *My Neighbors* (A), *Neighborhood Party* (O, ELL), *Parade Day* (B) **Unit 5, Week 1:** *My Garden* (A), *My Garden Grows* (O, ELL), *The Mystery Seeds* (B) **Unit 5, Week 3:** *The Farmer* (A), *Let's Make a Salad!* (O, ELL), *Farm Fresh Finn* (B) **Unit 6, Week 1:** *It Is Hot!* (A), *Little Bear* (O, ELL), *Ant and Grasshopper* (B) **Unit 7, Week 2:** *My Cats* (A), *Their Pets* (O, ELL), *Will's Pet* (B) **Unit 7, Week 3:** *We Want Water* (A), *A New Home* (O, ELL), *Bird's New Home* (B) **Unit 8, Week 2:** *See This!* (A), *Places to See* (O, ELL), *My Trip to Yellowstone* (B) **Unit 8, Week 3:** *Going Up* (A), *In the Clouds* (O, ELL) *How Sun and Moon Found Home* (B) **Unit 9, Week 2:** *Mike Helps Out* (A), *Clive and His Friend* (O, ELL), *Farmer White's Best Friend* (B) **Unit 9, Week 3:** *Look Where It Is From* (A), *What's for Breakfast?* (O, ELL), *Nature at the Craft Fair* (B) **Unit 10, Week 2:** *My Box* (A), *Let's Make a Band* (O, ELL), *Going Camping* (B) **Unit 10, Week 3:** *Help Clean Up* (A), *Let's Save Earth* (O, ELL) *Babysitters for Seals* (B)

YOUR TURN PRACTICE BOOK: 29-30, 35-38, 45-46, 53, 59-61, 68, 79-80, 85-86, 93-94, 99, 101-103, 107, 109-111, 115, 118, 123, 127-128, 129, 137, 141, 143-144, 147, 153-154, 164-165, 174, 187, 207, 217, 221, 227, 231, 234

READING WORKSTATION ACTIVITY CARDS: 7, 8, 16, 20

WRITING WORKSTATION ACTIVITY CARDS: 4, 6, 9

TEACHER'S EDITION: Unit 1: T11, T22-26, T186-191 **Unit 2:** T35, T186-191, T244 **Unit 3:** T104-108, T137, T175 **Unit 4:** T11, T55, T92, T137, T175, T219, T244 **Unit 5:** T11, T52, T93, T175, T186 **Unit 6:** T11, T20, T26, T93, T175 **Unit 7:** T11, T52, T55, T93, T137, T175, T219, T242 **Unit 8:** T11, T55, T78, T92-93 **Unit 9:** T11, T52, T55, T80, T93, T137, T162, T175, T219, T242 **Unit 10:** T11, T57, T80, T95, T139, T221, T244

LITERATURE BIG BOOKS: Unit 1, Week 1: *What About Bear?* **Unit 1, Week 2:** *Pouch!* **Unit 1, Week 3:** *Senses at the Seashore* **Unit 2, Week 1:** *The Handiest Things in the World* **Unit 2, Week 2:** *Shapes All Around* **Unit 3, Week 1:** *How Do Dinosaurs Go to School?* **Unit 3, Week 2:** *Clang! Clang! Beep! Beep! Listen to the City* **Unit 3, Week 3:** *Please Take Me for a Walk* **Unit 4, Week 1:** *Whose Shoes? A Shoe for Every Job* **Unit 4, Week 2:** *What Can You Do with a Paleta?* **Unit 4, Week 3:** *Roadwork* **Unit 5, Week 1:** *My Garden* **Unit 5, Week 2:** *A Grand Old Tree* **Unit 6, Week 3:** *Waiting Out the Storm* **Unit 7, Week 3:** *Bear Snores On* **Unit 8, Week 3:** *Bringing Down the Moon* **Unit 9, Week 1:** *Peter's Chair* **Unit 9, Week 2:** *Hen Hears Gossip* **Unit 10, Week 1:** *What's the Big Idea, Molly?* **Unit 10, Week 2:** *All Kinds of Families*

INTERACTIVE READ-ALOUD CARDS: Smart Start, Week 1: "The Ugly Duckling" **Smart Start, Week 2:** "Tikki Tikki Tembo" **Smart Start, Week 3:** "Kindergarteners Can!" **Unit 1, Week 1:** "The Lion and the Mouse" **Unit 1, Week 2:** "The Tortoise and the Hare" **Unit 1, Week 3:** "A Feast of the Senses" **Unit 2, Week 1:** "Timimoto" **Unit 2, Week 2:** "Kites in Flight" **Unit 2, Week 3:** "From Caterpillar to Butterfly" **Unit 4, Week 1:** "Little Juan and the Cooking Pot" **Unit 4, Week 2:** "Cultural Festivals" **Unit 4, Week 3:** "The Bundle of Sticks" **Unit 5, Week 1:** "Growing Plants" **Unit 5, Week 2:** "The Pine Tree" **Unit 6, Week 1:** "A Tour of the Seasons" **Unit 6, Week 2:** "The Frog and the Locust" **Unit 6, Week 3:** "Rainbow Crow" **Unit 8, Week 1:** "The King of the Winds" **Unit 8, Week 2:** "The Best of the West" **Unit 8, Week 3:** "A View From the Moon" **Unit 9, Week 1:** "Helping Out at Home" **Unit 9, Week 2:** "The Little Red Hen" **Unit 9, Week 3:** "Spider Woman Teaches the Navajo" **Unit 10, Week 1:** "Help Save Big Blue!" |

Speaking and Listening Standards

Comprehension and Collaboration		McGraw-Hill Reading Wonders
SL.K.3	Ask and answer questions in order to seek help, get information, or clarify something that is not understood.	**READING/WRITING WORKSHOP:** Unit 1: 6-7, 26-31, 33, 36, 37, 42-43, 45, 47, 49, 51, 53, 55 **Unit 2:** 6, 7, 14-19 **Unit 3:** 8-13, 14-19, 42-43 **Unit 4:** 6-7, 9, 11, 14, 20-29, 34-43 **Unit 5:** 6-7, 9, 11, 14, 20-29, 34-43 **Unit 6:** 6-7, 9, 11, 14, 20-29, 34-43 **Unit 7:** 6-7, 20-21 **Unit 8:** 6-7, 20-21 **Unit 9:** 6-7, 20-21 **Unit 10:** 6-7 **LEVELED READERS:** Unit 2, Week 1: *We Need Tools* (A), *What Can You See?* (O, ELL), *A Trip* (B) **Unit 4, Week 1:** *You Cook* (A), *On the Job* (O, ELL), *The Neighborhood* (B) **Unit 4, Week 3:** *We Clean!* (A), *Can You Fix It?* (O, ELL), *Helping Mom* (B) **Unit 5, Week 1:** *My Garden* (A), *My Garden Grows* (O, ELL), *The Mystery Seeds* (B) **Unit 5, Week 3:** *The Farmer* (A), *Let's Make a Salad!* (O, ELL), *Farm Fresh Finn* (B) **Unit 6, Week 1:** *It Is Hot!* (A), *Little Bear* (O, ELL), *Ant and Grasshopper* (B) **Unit 6, Week 3:** *Bad Weather* (A), *Getting Ready* (O, ELL), *The Storm* (B) **Unit 7, Week 1:** *Two Cubs* (A), *Animal Bodies* (O, ELL), *Two Kinds of Bears* (B) **Unit 8, Week 2:** *See This!* (A), *Places to See* (O, ELL), *My Trip to Yellowstone* (B) **Unit 9, Week 1:** *Let Me Help You* (A) *How Can Jane Help?* (O, ELL), *I Used to Help Too* (B) **Unit 10, Week 1:** *Animal Band* (A), *We Want Honey* (O, ELL), *A Good Idea* (B) **Unit 10, Week 3:** *Help Clean Up* (A), *Let's Save Earth* (O, ELL) *Babysitters for Seals* (B) **READING WORKSTATION ACTIVITY CARDS:** 7, 16, 20 **WRITING WORKSTATION ACTIVITY CARDS:** 4, 6, 9 **TEACHER'S EDITION:** Unit 1: T13, T216, T233 **Unit 2:** T95, T131, T137 **Unit 3:** T31, T49 **Unit 4:** T11, T55, T93, T137, T216, T219 **Unit 5:** T11, T52, T134, T216 **Unit 6:** T11, T93 **Unit 7:** T52, T93, T134, T182, T196, T205 **Unit 8:** T11, T93, T175 **Unit 9:** T13, T22, T52, T55 **Unit 10:** T11, T95, T97 **LITERATURE BIG BOOKS:** Unit 1, Week 1: *What About Bear?* **Unit 1, Week 2:** *Pouch!* **Unit 1, Week 3:** *Senses at the Seashore* **Unit 2, Week 1:** *The Handiest Things in the World* **Unit 2, Week 2:** *Shapes All Around* **Unit 3, Week 1:** *How Do Dinosaurs Go to School?* **Unit 3, Week 2:** *Clang! Clang! Beep! Beep! Listen to the City* **Unit 3, Week 3:** *Please Take Me for a Walk* **Unit 4, Week 1:** *Whose Shoes? A Shoe for Every Job* **Unit 4, Week 2:** *What Can You Do with a Paleta?* **Unit 4, Week 3:** *Roadwork* **Unit 9, Week 1:** *Peter's Chair* **Unit 9, Week 2:** *Hen Hears Gossip* **Unit 10, Week 2:** *All Kinds of Families!* **Unit 10, Week 3:** *Panda Kindergarten* **INTERACTIVE READ-ALOUD CARDS:** Unit 1, Week 1: "The Lion and the Mouse" **Unit 1, Week 2:** "The Tortoise and the Hare" **Unit 1, Week 3:** "A Feast of the Senses" **Unit 2, Week 1:** "Timimoto" **Unit 2, Week 2:** "Kites in Flight" **Unit 2, Week 3:** "From Caterpillar to Butterfly" **Unit 3, Week 1:** "The Boy Who Cried Wolf" **Unit 3, Week 2:** "The Turtle and the Flute" **Unit 4, Week 1:** "Little Juan and the Cooking Pot" **Unit 4, Week 2:** "Cultural Festivals" **Unit 9, Week 2:** "The Little Red Hen"

Presentation of Knowledge and Ideas		McGraw-Hill Reading Wonders
SL.K.4	Describe familiar people, places, things, and events and, with prompting and support, provide additional detail.	**READING/WRITING WORKSHOP BIG BOOK:** Unit 1: 6-7, 42-43 **Unit 2:** 6-7, 24-25, 42-43 **Unit 3:** 6-7, 24-25, 42-43 **Unit 4:** 6-7, 20-21, 34-35 **Unit 5:** 6-7, 20-21, 34-35 **Unit 6:** 6-7, 20-21, 34-35 **Unit 7:** 6-7, 20-21, 34-35 **Unit 8:** 6-7, 20-21, 34-35 **Unit 9:** 6-7, 20-21, 34-35 **Unit 10:** 6-7, 20-21, 34-35 **YOUR TURN PRACTICE BOOK:** 27-28, 35-38, 51-52, 61, 67, 68, 83, 85-86, 93-94, 103, 107, 109-110, 115, 117, 118, 141, 157, 167, 174, 193, 221, 231 **READING WORKSTATION ACTIVITY CARDS:** 10, 12, 14, 16 **WRITING WORKSTATION ACTIVITY CARDS:** 1, 2, 8, 16, 19, 22 **TEACHER'S EDITION:** Unit 1: S58, S74-75, T19, T33, T134, T183, T197, T205 **Unit 2:** T175, T182 **Unit 3:** T11, T93, T175, T177 **Unit 4:** T10-11, T18-19, T92, T114-115, T132-133, T135, T175, T182-183, T197, T214-215 **Unit 5:** T54, T136, T175, T218 **Unit 6:** T11, T13, T52, T54, T136, T175, T218 **Unit 7:** T54, T136, T163, T175, T218 **Unit 8:** T54, T175, T216 **Unit 9:** T11, T93, T136, T175, T183 **Unit 10:** T102, T116, T136, T177 **LITERATURE BIG BOOKS:** Smart Start: *Animals in the Park* **Unit 1, Week 1:** *What About Bear?* **Unit 1, Week 2:** *Pouch!* **Unit 1, Week 3:** *Senses at the Seashore* **Unit 2, Week 3:** *I Love Bugs!* **Unit 4, Week 1:** *Whose Shoes? A Shoe for Every Job* **Unit 4, Week 2:** *What Can You Do with a Paleta?* **Unit 4, Week 3:** *Roadwork* **Unit 5, Week 1:** *My Garden* **Unit 5, Week 2:** *A Grand Old Tree* **Unit 5, Week 3:** *An Orange in January* **Unit 6, Week 1:** *Mama, Is It Summer Yet?* **Unit 6, Week 2:** *Rain* **Unit 7, Week 1:** *ZooBorns!* **Unit 7, Week 2:** *The Family Pet* **Unit 7, Week 3:** *Bear Snores On* **Unit 8, Week 1:** *When Daddy's Truck Picks Me Up* **Unit 8, Week 2:** *Ana Goes to Washington, D.C.* **Unit 9, Week 1:** *Peter's Chair* **Unit 9, Week 2:** *Hen Hears Gossip* **Unit 9, Week 3:** *Bread Comes to Life* **Unit 10, Week 1:** *What's the Big Idea, Molly?* **Unit 10, Week 2:** *All Kinds of Families!* **INTERACTIVE READ-ALOUD CARDS:** Smart Start, Week 2: "Tikki Tikki Tembo" **Smart Start, Week 3:** "Kindergarteners Can!" **Unit 1, Week 1:** "The Lion and the Mouse" **Unit 1, Week 2:** "The Tortoise and the Hare" **Unit 1, Week 3:** "A Feast of the Senses" **Unit 2, Week 1:** "Timimoto" **Unit 2, Week 2:** "Kites in Flight" **Unit 2, Week 3:** "From Caterpillar to Butterfly" **Unit 3, Week 1:** "The Boy Who Cried Wolf" **Unit 3, Week 2:** "The Turtle and the Flute" **Unit 4, Week 3:** "The Bundle of Sticks" **Unit 5, Week 3:** "Farms Around the World" **Unit 6, Week 3:** "Rainbow Crow" **Unit 7, Week 3:** "Anansi: An African Tale" **Unit 8, Week 3:** "A View From the Moon" **Unit 9, Week 3:** "Spider Woman Teaches the Navajo" **Unit 10, Week 1:** "The Elves and the Shoemakers" **Unit 10, Week 1:** "Good for You!"

Speaking and Listening Standards

Presentation of Knowledge and Ideas		McGraw-Hill Reading Wonders
SL.K.5	Add drawings or other visual displays to descriptions as desired to provide additional detail.	**YOUR TURN PRACTICE BOOK:** 27-28, 30-32, 35-38, 43-46, 51-53, 59-60, 61, 62, 67-70, 77-80, 83, 85-86, 88, 93-94, 99, 101-102, 103-104, 107, 109-112, 115, 117-118, 123, 127-128, 129, 130, 133, 135-136, 137, 138, 141, 143-144, 147, 148, 151, 153-154, 157, 158, 164-165, 167, 168, 174, 187, 193, 207, 217, 221, 227, 231, 234 **READINGWORK STATION ACTIVITY CARDS:** 1, 6, 12, 15, 16, 20 **WRITING WORKSTATION ACTIVITY CARDS:** 1, 2, 4, 9, 17, 20, 23 **TEACHER'S EDITION: Unit 1:** T32, T41, T123, T214 **Unit 2:** T40-41, T123, T132 **Unit 3:** T41, T134, T217 **Unit 4:** T32, T41, T52, T123, T134, T205 **Unit 5:** T53, T134, T217 **Unit 6:** T53, T122-123, T135, T140, T163, T197, T205, T222 **Unit 7:** T33, T41, T114, T123 **Unit 8:** T53, T132, T134, T216 **Unit 9:** T41, T53, T123, T205, T214, T241 **Unit 10:** T43, T137, T216
SL.K.6	Speak audibly and express thoughts, feelings, and ideas clearly.	**READING/WRITING WORKSHOP: Unit 1:** 6-7, 8-13, 14-19, 24-25, 26-31, 42-43 **Unit 2:** 6-7, 8, 9, 10, 13, 14-19, 24-25, 33, 34, 35, 42-43, 46, 47, 48, 51, 54, 55, 58 **Unit 3:** 6-7, 13, 26, 27, 30, 31, 42-43, 44-49 **Unit 4:** 6-8, 22-29, 34-35 **Unit 5:** 6-7 **Unit 6:** 6-7 8-15, 22-29 **Unit 7:** 6-7 **Unit 8:** 20-21, 34-35 **LEVELED READERS: Unit 1, Week 2:** *Hop!* (A), *We Hop!* (O, ELL), *We Can Move!* (B) **Unit 2, Week 3:** *We Like Bugs!* (A), *The Bugs Run* (O, ELL), *I See a Bug* (B) **Unit 3, Week 1:** *We Run* (A), *Go, Nat!* (O, ELL), *The Birdhouse* (B) **Unit 5, Week 3:** *The Farmer* (A), *Let's Make a Salad!* (O, ELL), *Farm Fresh Finn* (B) **Unit 6, Week 1:** *It Is Hot!* (A), *Little Bear* (O, ELL), *Ant and Grasshopper* (B) **Unit 6, Week 2:** *The Rain* (A), *Weather Is Fun* (O, ELL), *Kate and Tuck* (B) **YOUR TURN PRACTICE BOOK:** 29, 37, 39-40, 43-44, 45, 47-48, 53, 61, 68, 71-72, 81-82, 83, 89-90, 97-98, 103, 105-106, 107, 113-114, 115, 121-122, 129, 131-132, 137, 141, 147, 149-150, 151, 187, 221, 227, 231 **READING WORKSTATION ACTIVITY CARDS:** 1, 3, 12, 17 **WRITING WORKSTATION ACTIVITY CARDS:** 1, 2, 6, 20, 25 **TEACHER'S EDITION: Unit 1:** T134, T175, T222 **Unit 2:** T58, T175, T222 **Unit 3:** T58, T140, T222 **Unit 4:** T58, T140, T175, T222 **Unit 5:** T11, T58, T140, T222 **Unit 6:** T11, T58, T140, T175, T222 **Unit 7:** T52, T58, T140, T175, T222 **Unit 8:** T11, T58, T93, T40, T175, T222 **Unit 9:** T11, T52, T58, T140, T222, T245 **Unit 10:** T11, T95, T142, T177, T224 **LITERATURE BIG BOOKS: Unit 1, Week 1:** *What About Bear?* **Unit 1, Week 2:** *Pouch!* **Unit 1, Week 3:** *Senses at the Seashore* **Unit 2, Week 1:** *The Handiest Things in the World* **Unit 2, Week 2:** *Shapes All Around* **Unit 2, Week 3:** *I Love Bugs!* **Unit 3, Week 2:** *A Grand Old Tree* **Unit 3, Week 3:** *An Orange in January* **Unit 5, Week 1:** *My Garden* **Unit 6, Week 1:** *Mama, Is It Summer Yet?* **Unit 8, Week 2:** *Ana Goes to Washington, D.C.* **INTERACTIVE READ-ALOUD CARDS: Unit 1, Week 1:** "The Lion and the Mouse" **Unit 1, Week 2:** "The Tortoise and the Hare" **Unit 1, Week 3:** "A Feast of the Senses" **Unit 2, Week 1:** "Timimoto" **Unit 2, Week 2:** "Kites in Flight" **Unit 2, Week 3:** "From Caterpillar to Butterfly" **Unit 3, Week 1:** "The Boy Who Cried Wolf" **Unit 3, Week 2:** "The Turtle and the Flute" **Unit 3, Week 3:** "Field Trips" **Unit 4, Week 1:** "Little Juan and the Cooking Pot" **Unit 4, Week 2:** "Cultural Festivals" **Unit 4, Week 3:** "The Bundle of Sticks" **Unit 5, Week 1:** "Growing Plants" **Unit 7, Week 2:** "The Family Pet"

College and Career Readiness Anchor Standards for LANGUAGE

The K–5 standards on the following pages define what students should understand and be able to do by the end of each grade. They correspond to the College and Career Readiness (CCR) anchor standards below by number. The CCR and grade-specific standards are necessary complements—the former providing broad standards, the latter providing additional specificity—that together define the skills and understandings that all students must demonstrate.

Conventions of Standard English

1. Demonstrate command of the conventions of standard English grammar and usage when writing or speaking.

2. Demonstrate command of the conventions of standard English capitalization, punctuation, and spelling when writing.

Knowledge of Language

3. Apply knowledge of language to understand how language functions in different contexts, to make effective choices for meaning or style, and to comprehend more fully when reading or listening.

Vocabulary Acquisition and Use

4. Determine or clarify the meaning of unknown and multiple-meaning words and phrases by using context clues, analyzing meaningful word parts, and consulting general and specialized reference materials, as appropriate.

5. Demonstrate understanding of figurative language, word relationships, and nuances in word meanings.

6. Acquire and use accurately a range of general academic and domain-specific words and phrases sufficient for reading, writing, speaking, and listening at the college and career readiness level; demonstrate independence in gathering vocabulary knowledge when encountering an unknown term important to comprehension or expression.

CCSS Common Core State Standards
English Language Arts
Grade K

Language Standards

Conventions of Standard English		McGraw-Hill Reading Wonders
L.K.1	Demonstrate command of the conventions of standard English grammar and usage when writing or speaking.	**TEACHER'S EDITION:** Unit 1: T16, T19, T32-33, T41, T36, T98, T101, T114-115, T122-123, T125, T133, T141, T165, T180, T183, T197, T205, T214-215, T223, T247 Unit 2: T16, T18-19, T32-33, T40-41, T50-51, T59, T83, T98, T101, T115, T123, T133, T141, T165, T180, T183, T185, T197, T205, T215, T223 Unit 3: T16, T98, T180, T183, T197, T215 Unit 4: T16, T18-19, T32-33, T40-41, T47, T51, T59, T98, T101, T114-115, T122-123, T129, T133, T139, T141, T180, T182-183, T196-197, T204-205, T211, T215, T221, T223 Unit 5: T16, T21, T43, T83, T98, T103, T180, T196, T247 Unit 6: T16, T19, T33, T41, T44, T47, T51, T53, T59, T83, T98, T101, T114, T115, T123, T129, T133, T141, T180, T183, T185, T197, T205, T207, T211, T215, T223, T247 Unit 7: T16, T19, T33, T41, T47, T51, T83, T98, T114-115, T123, T129, T133, T139, T141, T165, T180, T182, T183, T196, T197, T204-205, T211, T215, T223, T247 Unit 8: T16, T19, T21, T33, T41, T47, T50-51, T83, T98, T101, T115, T123, T129, T133, T141, T180, T182-183, T196-197, T205, T211, T215, T223 Unit 9: T16, T19, T21, T32-33, T41, T47, T51, T59, T83, T98, T101, T103, T114-115, T123, T133, T141, T165, T129, T180, T183, T185, T197, T205, T211, T215, T223, T247 Unit 10: T16, T21, T34, T42, T49, T85, T100, T131, T182, T187, T198, T213, T249
L.K.1a	Print many upper- and lowercase letters.	**TEACHER'S EDITION:** Unit 1: T16, T98, T180 Unit 2: T16, T98, T180 Unit 3: T16, T98, T180 Unit 4: T16, T47, T98, T129, T139, T180, T211, T221 Unit 5: T16, T98, T180 Unit 6: T16, T47, T98, T129, T180, T211 Unit 7: T16, T47, T98, T129, T139, T180, T211 Unit 8: T16, T47, T98, T129, T180, T211 Unit 9: T16, T47, T98, T129, T180, T211 Unit 10: T16, T49, T100, T131, T182, T213 **YOUR TURN PRACTICE BOOK:** 34, 42, 50, 58, 66, 76, 84, 92, 100, 108, 116, 126, 134, 142, 152, 162, 172, 184, 192, 202, 212, 222, 232, 244, 252, 260, 268, 276, 284
L.K.1b	Use frequently occurring nouns and verbs.	**TEACHER'S EDITION:** Unit 1: T19, T32-33, T41, T36, T101, T114-115, T122-123, T125, T133, T141, T165, T183, T197, T205, T214-215, T223, T247 Unit 2: T18-19, T32-33, T40-41, T50-51, T59, T83, T101, T115, T123, T133, T141, T165, T183, T185, T197, T205, T215, T223 Unit 5: T103 Unit 6: T19, T33, T44, T51, T53, T83, T114, T223, T247 Unit 7: T19, T33, T41, T51, T83, T114-115, T123, T133, T141, T165, T183, T197, T205, T215, T223, T247 Unit 8: T10, T18, T114, T115 Unit 9: T21, T103, T185 Unit 10: T187 **YOUR TURN PRACTICE BOOK:** 23, 41, 65, 73, 83, 107, 115, 141, 151, 161, 191, 201, 211, 221, 241, 251, 259, 267, 295
L.K.1c	Form regular plural nouns orally by adding /s/ or /es/ (e.g., *dog, dogs; wish, wishes*).	**TEACHER'S EDITION:** Unit 5: T21, T43 Unit 6: T33, T41, T51, T59, T101, T115, T123, T133, T141, T183, T197, T205, T215
L.K.1d	Understand and use question words (interrogatives) (e.g., *who, what, where, when, why, how*).	**TEACHER'S EDITION:** Unit 3: T183, T197, T215 Unit 6: T185, T207 Unit 7: T182, T196, T204-205 Unit 9: T103, T125 Unit 10: T21
L.K.1e	Use the most frequently occurring prepositions (e.g., *to, from, in, out, on, off, for, of, by, with*).	**TEACHER'S EDITION:** Unit 3: T29, T47 Unit 5: T193, T211 Unit 7: T29, T47 Unit 8: T19, T33, T41, T50-51, T83, T101, T115, T123, T133, T141, T183, T197, T205, T223
L.K.1f	Produce and expand complete sentences in shared language activities.	**TEACHER'S EDITION:** Unit 4: T18-19, T32-33, T40-41, T51, T59, T101, T114-115, T122-123, T133, T141, T182-183, T196-197, T204-205, T215, T223 Unit 5: T83, T196, T247 Unit 8: T182-183, T196-197, T215, T223; Unit 9: T19, T32-33, T41, T51, T59, T83, T101, T114-115, T123, T133, T141, T165, T183, T197, T205, T215, T223, T247 Unit 10: T34, T42, T85, T198, T249

Language Standards

Conventions of Standard English		McGraw-Hill Reading Wonders
L.K.2	Demonstrate command of the conventions of standard English capitalization, punctuation, and spelling when writing.	**TEACHER'S EDITION: Unit 1:** T16, T72, T129, T211, T221 **Unit 2:** T47, T57, T129, T139, T211, T221 **Unit 3:** T19, T47, T50-51, T53, T57, T59, T83, T101, T115, T120, T123, T132-133, T139, T141, T183, T196-197, T205, T211, T214-215, T221, T223, T247 **Unit 4:** T16, T47, T57, T98, T129, T139, T211, T221 **Unit 5:** T16, T47, T57, T98, T101, T115, T123, T139, T180, T211, T221 **Unit 6:** T12, T16, T47, T57, T98, T129, T139, T176, T211, T221 **Unit 7:** T16, T47, T57, T98, T129, T139, T180, T211, T214, T221 **Unit 8:** T16, T32, T47, T98, T101, T114, T129, T132, T164, T211, T221 **Unit 9:** T47, T129, T211 **Unit 10:** T49, T53, T103, T116, T131, T213, T216
L.K.2a	Capitalize the first word in a sentence and the pronoun *I*.	**TEACHER'S EDITION: Unit 3:** T19, T50-51, T53, T59, T83, T115, T123, T132-133, T197, T223 **Unit 5:** T101, T115, T123 **Unit 8:** T32, T101, T114, T132 **Unit 10:** T53, T103, T116, T216
L.K.2b	Recognize and name end punctuation.	**TEACHER'S EDITION: Unit 3:** T101, T115, T123, T132-133, T141, T183, T196-197, T205, T214-215, T223, T247 **Unit 6:** T12, T176 **Unit 7:** T214 **Unit 8:** T32, T101, T114, T132, T164
L.K.2c	Write a letter or letters for most consonant and short-vowel sounds (phonemes).	**TEACHER'S EDITION: Unit 1:** T16, T72, T129, T211 **Unit 2:** T47, T129, T211 **Unit 3:** T47, T120, T211 **Unit 4:** T16, T47, T98, T129, T139, T211, T221 **Unit 5:** T16, T47, T98, T180, T211 **Unit 6:** T16, T47, T98, T129, T211 **Unit 7:** T16, T47, T57, T98, T129, T139, T180, T211 **Unit 8:** T16, T47, T98, T129, T211 **Unit 9:** T47, T129, T211 **Unit 10:** T49, T131, T213 **YOUR TURN PRACTICE BOOK:** 34, 42, 50, 58, 51-52, 62, 66, 76, 84, 85, 86, 88, 92, 100, 104, 108, 116, 126, 130, 134, 138, 142, 148, 158, 162, 164-165, 168, 172, 192, 202, 212, 222, 232 **PHONICS AND WORD STUDY WORKSTATION ACTIVITY CARDS:** 1, 2, 3, 4, 5, 6, 7, 8, 9, 10, 11, 12, 13, 14, 15, 16, 17, 18, 19, 20, 21, 22, 23, 24
L.K.2d	Spell simple words phonetically, drawing on knowledge of sound-letter relationships.	**TEACHER'S EDITION: Unit 1:** T221 **Unit 2:** T57, T139, T221 **Unit 3:** T57, T139, T221 **Unit 4:** T47, T57, T129, T139, T211, T221 **Unit 5:** T57, T139, T221 **Unit 6:** T57, T139, T221 **Unit 7:** T47, T57, T129, T139, T211, T221 **Unit 8:** T47, T129, T139, T211, T221 **YOUR TURN PRACTICE BOOK:** 30, 38, 46, 54, 62, 74, 75, 80, 88, 96, 104, 112, 124, 125, 130, 138, 148, 158, 168, 182, 183, 188, 198, 208, 228, 242, 243, 256, 264, 272, 280, 293, 294

Knowledge of Language		McGraw-Hill Reading Wonders
L.K.3	(Begins in grade 2.)	

Vocabulary Acquisition and Use		McGraw-Hill Reading Wonders
L.K.4	Determine or clarify the meaning of unknown and multiple-meaning words and phrases based on *kindergarten reading and content*.	**TEACHER'S EDITION: Unit 4:** T127 **Unit 5:** T45, T46, T108, T187 **Unit 6:** T21, T23, T33, T41 **Unit 7:** T24, T45, T189, T209 **Unit 9:** T21, T24, T25, T43, T185, T189, T207 **Unit 10:** T25, T187, T209
L.K.4a	Identify new meanings for familiar words and apply them accurately (e.g., knowing *duck* is a bird and learning the verb to *duck*).	**TEACHER'S EDITION: Unit 5:** T108, T185, T187 T207 **Unit 6:** T21, T189 **Unit 7:** T24, T45, T189 **Unit 8:** T21 **Unit 9:** T25, T45, T185, T207 **Unit 10:** T25, T47
L.K.4b	Use the most frequently occurring inflections and affixes (e.g., *-ed, -s, re-, un-, pre-, -ful, -less*) as a clue to the meaning of an unknown word.	**TEACHER'S EDITION: Unit 5:** T45, T46, T187 **Unit 6:** T23, T33, T41 **Unit 9:** T21, T24, T43, T189 **Unit 10:** T187, T209

Language Standards

Vocabulary Acquisition and Use		McGraw-Hill Reading Wonders
L.K.5	With guidance and support from adults, explore word relationships and nuances in word meanings.	**TEACHER'S EDITION: Unit 1:** T10-11, T34, T43 **Unit 2:** T10, T43, T103, T116, T125, T135, T175, T185, T207, T245 **Unit 3:** T10, T116, T175 **Unit 4:** T10-11, T12-13, T21, T34, T43, T44-45, T54, T67, T80, T81, T83, T92-93, T94-95, T103, T116, T125, T126-127, T133, T136, T141, T149, T165, T174-175, T176-177, T183, T185, T188, T198, T207, T208-209, T218, T231, T245, T247 **Unit 5:** T10-11, T12-13, T21, T34, T43, T54, T67, T80, T81, T92-93, T94-95, T116, T149, T174-175, T185, T195, T207, T218, T245 **Unit 6:** T10-11, T20, T34, T35, T42, T43, T44, T67, T81, T92-93, T103, T108, T116, T125, T126-127, T136, T149, T163, T174-175, T176-177, T185, T198, T208-209, T218, T231, T245 **Unit 7:** T10-11, T12-13, T21, T25, T34, T43, T54, T67, T81, T92-93, T94-95, T103, T116, T126-127, T136, T149, T163, T174-175, T185, T190, T207, T208-209, T218, T231, T245 **Unit 8:** T10-11, T12-13, T21, T23, T34, T43, T44-45, T54, T67, T81, T92-93, T94-95, T103, T116, T125, T126-127, T136, T149, T163, T174-175, T185, T198, T207, T208-209, T218, T231, T245 **Unit 9:** T10-11, T12-13, T34, T44-45, T54, T67, T81, T92-93, T103, T116, T126-127, T136, T149, T163, T174-175, T176-177, T185, T198, T207, T208-209, T218, T231, T245 **Unit 10:** T10-11, T25, T36, T46-47, T56, T69, T83,T94-95, T96-97, T105,T106-111, T118, T127, T128-129, T136-137, T138, T151, T165, T176-177, T178-179, T187, T189, T190, T200, T209, T210-211, T220, T233, T247
L.K.5a	Sort common objects into categories (e.g., shapes, foods) to gain a sense of the concepts the categories represent.	**TEACHER'S EDITION: Unit 2:** T43, T103, T125, T135 **Unit 4:** T103, T183 **Unit 5:** T21, T185, T207 **Unit 6:** T43 **Unit 8:** T43 **Unit 10:** T127, T129, T136-137
L.K.5b	Demonstrate understanding of frequently occurring verbs and adjectives by relating them to their opposites (antonyms).	**YOUR TURN PRACTICE BOOK:** 241, 283 **TEACHER'S EDITION: Unit 6:** T44 **Unit 7:** T25 **Unit 8:** T23, T185, T207 **Unit 9:** T189 **Unit 10:** T25, T105, T127, T189, T190
L.K.5c	Identify real-life connections between words and their use (e.g., note places at school that are colorful).	**READING/WRITING WORKSHOP: Unit 1:** Smart Start: 4-5, 22-23, 40-41; 6-7, 24-25, 42-43 **Unit 2:** 6-7, 24-25, 42-43 **Unit 3:** 6-7, 24-25, 42-43 **Unit 4:** 6-7, 20-21, 34-35 **Unit 5:** 6-7, 20-21, 34-35 **Unit 6:** 6-7, 20-21, 34-35 **Unit 7:** 6-7, 20-21, 34-35 **Unit 8:** 6-7, 20-21, 34-35 **Unit 9:** 6-7, 20-21, 34-35 **Unit 10:** 6-7, 20-21, 34-35 **YOUR TURN PRACTICE BOOK:** 23, 33, 41, 49, 57, 65, 73, 83, 107, 115, 133, 141, 151, 161, 171, 191, 201, 211, 221, 241, 251, 259, 267, 275, 283, 295 **TEACHER'S EDITION: Unit 1:** T10-11, T34, T43 **Unit 2:** T10, T116, T175 **Unit 3:** T10, T116, T175 **Unit 4:** T10-11, T12-13, T21, T34, T43, T44-45, T54, T67, T80, T81, T83, T92-93, T94-95, T103, T116, T125, T126-127, T133, T136, T141, T149, T165, T174-175, T176-177, T183, T185, T198, T207, T208-209, T218, T231, T245, T247 **Unit 5:** T10-11, T12-13, T21, T34, T43, T54, T67, T80, T81, T92-93, T94-95, T116, T149, T174-175, T185, T198, T218, T245 **Unit 6:** T10-11, T20, T34, T35, T42, T67, T81, T92-93, T103, T116, T125, T126-127, T136, T149, T163, T174-175, T176-177, T185, T198, T208-209, T218, T231, T245 **Unit 7:** T10-11, T12-13, T21, T25, T34, T43, T54, T67, T81, T92-93, T94-95, T103, T116, T126-127, T136, T149, T163, T174-175, T185, T207, T208-209, T218, T231, T245 **Unit 8:** T10-11, T34, T81, T92-93, T102, T116, T124, T136, T149, T163, T174-175, T185, T198, T207, T208-209, T218, T231, T245 **Unit 9:** T10-11, T12-13, T20, T34, T42-43, T54, T67, T92-93, T103, T116-117, T124-125, T136, T149, T174-175, T176-177, T185, T198, T206-207, T218, T231 **Unit 10:** T10-11, T25, T36, T46-47, T56, T69, T83, T94-95, T96-97, T106-111, T118, T128-129, T138, T151, T165, T176-177, T178-179, T187, T190, T200, T209, T210-211, T220, T233, T247 **INTERACTIVE READ-ALOUD CARDS: SS:** "The Ugly Duckling", "Kindergarteners Can!", "Tikki Tikki Tembo" **Unit 1, Week 1:** "The Lion and the Mouse" **Unit 1, Week 2:** "The Tortoise and the Hare" **Unit 2, Week 3:** "From Caterpillar to Butterfly" **Unit 3, Week 2:** "The Turtle and the Flute" **Unit 4, Week 1:** "Little Juan and the Cooking Pot" **Unit 4, Week 2:** "Cultural Festivals" **Unit 4, Week 3:** "A Bundle of Sticks" **Unit 6, Week 3:** "Rainbow Crow" **Unit 7, Week 3:** "Anansi: An African Tale" **Unit 9, Week 2:** "The Little Red Hen" **Unit 9, Week 3:** "Spider Woman Teaches the Navajo" **Unit 10, Week 1:** "The Elves and the Shoemakers" **ConnectED Digital Resources:** Visual Glossary

Language Standards

Vocabulary Acquisition and Use		McGraw-Hill Reading Wonders
L.K.5d	Distinguish shades of meaning among verbs describing the same general action (e.g., *walk, march, strut, prance*) by acting out the meanings.	**TEACHER'S EDITION:** Unit 2: T185, T207, T245 Unit 4: T188 Unit 6: T35, T108 Unit 7: T185, T190, T207
L.K.6	Use words and phrases acquired through conversations, reading and being read to, and responding to texts.	**READING/WRITING WORKSHOP:** Smart Start: 4-5, 22-23, 40-41 Unit 1: 6-7, 24-25, 42-43 Unit 2: 6-7, 24-25, 42-43 Unit 3: 6-7, 24-25, 42-43 Unit 4: 6-7, 20-21, 34-35 Unit 5: 6-7, 20-21, 34-35 Unit 6: 6-7, 20-21, 34-35 Unit 7: 6-7, 20-21, 34-35 Unit 8: 6-7, 20-21, 34-35 Unit 9: 6-7, 20-21, 34-35 Unit 10: 6-7, 20-21, 34-35 **TEACHER'S EDITION:** Unit 1: S26, S34, S44 Unit 2: T20-21, T93, T198 Unit 3: T20, T93, T198 Unit 4: T10-11, T12-13, T20-21, T22-27, T34, T42-43, T44-45, T54-55, T67, T80, T81, T92-93, T94-95, T176-177, T184-185, T186-191, T198, T205, T206-207, T208-209, T215, T218-219, T223, T218-219, T231, T244, T245 Unit 5: T10-11, T12-13, T20-21, T22-27, T34, T42-43, T44-45, T54-55 , T117, T162-163, T174-175, T176-177, T184-185, T186-191, T198, T199, T206-207, T208-209, T218-219, T231, T244-245 Unit 6: T10-11, T20-21, T34-35, T42-43, T44-45, T54-55, T67, T80, T81, T92-93, T94-95, T102-103, T104-109, T116, T124-125, T126-127, T136-137, T149, T231, T244 Unit 7: T10-11, T12-13, T20-21, T22-27, T34-35, T42-43, T44-45, T54-55, T67, T80, T81, T92-93, T94-95, T102-103, T104-109, T116, T124-125, T126-127, T136-137, T149, T231, T244, T245 Unit 8: T10-11, T12-13, T20-21, T22-27, T34-35, T42-43, T44-45, T54-55, T67, T80, T81, T92-93, T94-95, T102-103, T104-109, T116, T124-125, T126-127, T136-137, T149, T231, T244, T245 Unit 9: T10-11, T12-13, T20-21, T22-27, T34-35, T42-43, T44-45, T54-55, T162, T163, T174-175, T176-177, T184-185, T186-191, T198, T199, T206-207, T208-209, T218-219, T231, T244, T245 Unit 10: T10-11, T12-13, T20-21, T22-29, T36, T44-45, T46-47, T56-57, T69, T82, T83, T94-95, T96-97, T104-105, T106-111, T118, T126-127, T128-129, T138-139, T151, T179, T233, T246, T247 **LITERATURE BIG BOOKS:** Unit 1, Week 2: *Pouch!* Unit 2, Week 2: *Shapes All Around* Unit 2, Week 3: *I Love Bugs!* Unit 3, Week 1: *How Do Dinosaurs Go to School?* Unit 4, Week 1: *Whose Shoes? A Shoe for Every Job* Unit 4, Week 2: *What Can You Do with a Paleta?* Unit 5, Week 2: *A Grand Old Tree* Unit 5, Week 3: *An Orange in January* Unit 6, Week 1: *Mama, Is It Summer Yet?* Unit 7, Week 1: *ZooBorns!* Unit 7, Week 2: *The Birthday Pet* Unit 8, Week 2: *Ana Goes to Washington, D.C.* Unit 8, Week 3: *Bringing Down the Moon* Unit 9, Week 3: *Bread Comes to Life* Unit 10, Week 1: *What's the Big Idea, Molly?* Unit 10, Week 2: *All Kinds of Families!* **INTERACTIVE READ-ALOUD CARDS:** SS: "The Ugly Duckling", "Kindergarteners Can!", "Tikki Tikki Tembo" Unit 1, Week 1: "The Lion and the Mouse" Unit 1, Week 2: "The Tortoise and the Hare" Unit 2, Week 3: "From Caterpillar to Butterfly" Unit 3, Week 2: "The Turtle and the Flute" Unit 4, Week 1: "Little Juan and the Cooking Pot" Unit 4, Week 2: "Cultural Festivals" Unit 4, Week 3: "A Bundle of Sticks" Unit 6, Week 3: "Rainbow Crow" Unit 7, Week 3: "Anansi: An African Tale" Unit 9, Week 2: "The Little Red Hen" Unit 9, Week 3: "Spider Woman Teaches the Navajo" Unit 10, Week 1: "The Elves and the Shoemakers"